The Information Age and Diplomacy:
An Emerging Strategic Vision in World Affairs

by

Amir Dhia

DISSERTATION.COM

Boca Raton

The Information Age and Diplomacy: An Emerging Strategic Vision in World Affairs

Dissertation.com
Boca Raton, Florida
USA • 2006

ISBN: 1-58112- 336-1

THE INFORMATION AGE AND DIPLOMACY:

AN EMERGING STRATEGIC VISION IN WORLD AFFAIRS

BY

AMIR DHIA, (B.A., M.A.)

UNDER THE SUPERVISION OF DR. THIERRY GARCIN

A DISSERTATION SUBMITTED TO
LE CENTRE D'ETUDES DIPLOMATIQUES ET STRATEGIQUES, PARIS,
IN PARTIAL FULFILLMENT OF THE REQUIREMENTS FOR

THE DEGREE OF

DOCTOR OF PHILOSOPHY
IN
INTERNATIONAL RELATIONS AND DIPLOMACY

SEPTEMBER 2005

To my leader in life, my dear Father;
to my loving Mother;
to my three supportive brothers Yasir, Thaar, Hadir;
and to my generous sister Rana…
all with utmost admiration and gratefulness.

TABLE OF CONTENTS

LIST OF FIGURES

LIST OF TABLES

LIST OF ILLUSTRATIONS

ACKNOWLEDGEMENTS

My highest consideration, sincere gratitude and utmost appreciation is foremost due to Dr. Pascal CHAIGNEAU, Director General of the Center of Diplomatic and Strategic Studies (C.E.D.S.) in Paris, for entitling me this unique occasion to achieve my ambitions of pursuing my post-graduate studies in the beautiful country of France.

My honest words of esteem are forwarded to my supervisor, Dr. Thierry GARCIN, for his enriching thoughts, sharp observations, valuable time and constant interest throughout this work.

The impressive, academic staff at C.E.D.S. offered indispensable intellectual guidance and professional insights, all meriting recognition.

All along my years of studies, a number of people have contributed, in one way or another, to this achievement. My thankfulness is addressed to, among others, Dr. Abdul Ghafour Ibrahim, Mr. Me'ad Ismaeil, Dr. Saleh Ali, Dr. Jalal Safa Al Din, and to Dr. Daoud Suleiman. Furthermore, I appreciate with consideration the support of His Royal Highness Prince Faisal Al Saud and his generous family.

I thank as well Mr. Michel VAN STEENBRUGGHE, his wife Marie-Claude, and Benôit, for their unforgettable, generous hospitality and assistance ever since my early days in Paris. A word of thanks is also presented to Dr. Marc HENRY and his wife Nadine, for their kind hospitality; recalling here the numerous conversations with Dr. HENRY that helped me draw a better understanding of French cultural matters. For their help, I also thank Mr. Eric RAVELSON and Mr. Jean-Pierre FANTIN.

This work would have been harder to realize without the continuous encouragement, enduring understanding and intellectual interest of Ms. Cécile VIALLE, Director of the International Training Center in Languages and Communication (C.F.I.L.C.). Through Ms. VIALLE, I would like to thank the entire C.F.I.L.C. staff for their support.

And not to forget to acknowledge, last but not least, the moral support and enthusiasm of my close relatives and friends at home despite their hardships.

INTRODUCTION

More than ever before, advances in the fields of information and communication technologies (ICTs) have substantially affected most segments of our individual life in today's world. Manifested in various aspects and to varying extents, the changes and evolution are often collectively referred to as the "Information Age," or the "Information Revolution."

It is this Information Age that has been posing a direct or indirect influence–whether positive or negative–on the way we think, behave, communicate, work, and even on how we earn our living. 'Information' has become a principal 'commodity' by which one measures levels of not only education, skills and knowledge, but also levels of well-being, prosperity, wealth, and development on a personal, local, national, and international scale.

The ability to acquire and efficiently employ knowledge and information is a critical consideration for success in an information-based society, with "knowledge workers" and "information workers" becoming an ever-increasing fraction of the work force in all countries. Appropriately developing 'human capital' is a key priority for both individuals and nations as they cope with the Information Age. Over time, numerous businesses in "knowledge industries" relocate to new areas more suitable for information work than for "manufacturing work," affecting in turn where people live. As a consequence, the rise in information work has an implication on the education people are required to have, both initially and throughout their career. This, in turn, has a long-term impact on educational establishments and systems all over the world.

As the worldwide information landscape becomes more and more interconnected and interdependent, it is argued that the existing gap between the "haves" and "have-nots" will diminish. Interdependencies growing in all aspects of our lives should, after all, lead to real possibilities for achieving economic prosperity and attaining global peace. Nevertheless, they also produce powerful forces of social fragmentation, open critical vulnerabilities, and breed violence and conflict. Crises now bypass traditional state borders. The expanding global economic interactions, the spread of knowledge, the dispersion of advanced technologies, and the movements of people are just some of the threats, which are global in scope.

It is, hence, not surprising that concerns over the ever-widening gulf between knowledge and ignorance, the development gap between the rich and poor nations, and the distancing margins within societies of a given country, all pushed the United Nations to adopt the World Summit on the Information Society (WSIS) in its agenda in its first and second phases, in Geneva in 2003, and in Tunisia in 2005.

Scholars differ in defining and marking the early signs and stages of the Information Age. Nevertheless, the evolving era of the Information Age in the contemporary world may be credited for four distinctive global developments. First, the end of the Cold War–as celebrating Germans swarmed over the graffiti-covered Berlin Wall in November 1989–instantly rendered superfluous the Western world's highly expensive political-military infrastructure. During the Cold War, the United States of America had one principal target in terms of information and intelligence gathering, namely the Soviet Union. Its narrow set of intelligence 'customers' was mainly composed of political-military officials in the U.S. government, and it drew its limited information from limited sources, namely surveillance satellites and spies. Information analysis and gathering was designated to a central (although not monopolized) agency. Now, the wide-scale dissemination of information on open-network systems, minute by minute, no longer characterizes the feature as "secret business."

Second, a seismic shift has been acknowledged in the tremendous proliferation of non-governmental organizations (NGOs), international governmental organizations (IGOs), private voluntary organizations (PVOs), and other non-state actors. Thousands of organizations in the global arena (ranging in activity from humanitarian relief to landmines to HIV/AIDS to environment protection to anti-war campaigns) often set the agenda for defining priority issue policies. Thanks to their intellectual members and elites, theses organizations are enjoying more compelling concerted global action. More of a frequent trend, street barricades and tear gas have become standard expectations at world summit gatherings of political and economic leaders.

Even more so, the global reach and influence of transnational corporations (TNCs) have ended any remaining illusions that states will continue to hold a quasi-exclusive monopoly over the conduct of foreign affairs. Seldom is the case now of a state leader traveling to another state without being accompanied by a number of businessmen and company chiefs. In other words, governments of sovereign states will continue to play the major role in world politics, but will have to share the stage with actors who can make better use of information to enhance their "soft power" and mobilize their publics and potentials.

Third, an expansion and redefinition of a state's foreign policy agenda has occurred, which covers both traditional and non-traditional issues. The conventional diplomatic practice of establishing and promoting bilateral and multilateral relations among countries is still in place. However, much attention is increasingly being devoted to issues such as climate warming, global health matters and standards, the mobility and trafficking of people (whether illegal, refugees, or immigrants), and more recently global terrorism threats. The diplomatic world is fully aware of the heat of competition, especially from non-state actors, which are being enforced by the Information Age. The conditions for classic diplomacy, currently based on "hard power," are gradually being undermined to favor the emergence of a more adaptable diplomacy based on the concept of "soft power."

Even at the local government level, certain traditional mechanisms of governance, such as taxation, regulation, and licensing are turning out to be problematic, since the Information Age allows for action beyond the reach or control of national governments. While governments attempt to meet those challenges, new mechanisms are being introduced, usually making use of Information Technology (IT) and under the concept of "electronic governance" (e-governance), to upgrade and improve interaction with and provide public services to their citizens.

The fourth development that has significantly speeded the evolution of the Information Age is the constant and rapid advancements in ICT (along with a variety of other technologies). Some further 'technology' developments may be foreseen for at least the new few decades or so such as continued exponential growth in computing power, continued convergence in voice and data communications as well as in available bandwidth, improvements in machine translation for useful and practical applications, and strong synergies emerging between info-, bio-, nano-, and material technologies.

Future developments in 'products' will enable information devices to be ever-present, wearable, and in constant link to one another. Among the expectations are a multitude of powerful, inexpensive sensors and devices permitting wireless communication; increasing convergence of wireless telephones, personal digital assistants (PDAs), radio, voice and electronic mail messaging; and smart home appliances. Last but not least, developments in 'services' are predicted to greatly extend access to, and the usefulness of, information services. Kiosks are to provide easy access to some services, with entertainment taking the leading edge of novel information services. This prospective will also play a growing role in health care and telemedicine. Online education will increase but with specialized, tailored effects; and micro payment schemes will emerge to handle essential online financial and payment matters.[1]

This work seeks to cover the emerging trends of diplomatic practice in the rapidly expanding Information Age. It focuses on both its opportunities and threats, with the overall objective of forecasting current and future implications. Chapter One traces the evolution of the Information Age, and highlights its main features. Chapter Two examines the course of classic diplomacy, and how it needs to cope with the era–leading in one way or another to a transformation in the manner diplomatic affairs are conducted. Also outlined are the characteristic qualifications of diplomats required at the present and coming stages of professionalism.

---

[1] The foreseen developments are summarized from: Richard O. Hundley et al., *The Global Course of the Information Revolution: Recurring Themes and Regional Variations*, RAND Corporation, Santa Monica, CA, 2003, pp. xxiii-xxiv.

Chapter Three deals with the cultural and social implications directly associated with the Information Age, namely rising cultural and identity awareness and the evolution of languages. This work concludes with a set of observations in the aftermath of the September 11, 2001 attacks on the United States of America. The observations concern particular notions and events that have a certain influence, in one way or another, on the global practices of diplomacy and on our common way of life.

Stemming from the fact that the Information Age is currently evolving at unprecedented speed, it is deemed necessary to note that both effort and attention have been devoted to provide, whenever available, up-dated details and data to the possible extent. Also, where appropriate as well as illuminating, a number of illustrations have been documented, with the mere objective of reflecting global perceptions on the issues concerned. Finally, it is to be acknowledged that the vast scope of the Information Age and the diplomatic practices implied remain infinite in volume to be all covered in this work.

I. CHAPTER ONE:

THE INFORMATION AGE

I.I. **The Evolution of the Knowledge Society**

Humanity is in the midst of a social, economic, and political transformation, just as far-reaching as the Agricultural Revolution was thousands of years ago. As that revolution utterly changed the way we live and relate to one another, so too has the Information Revolution.

The early signs of this transformation go back some five hundred years to the Renaissance in Western Europe.[2] Yet deeper in history, traces of the evolution root even back to the Sumerians who were the first to introduce and use clay balls and tokens to treat information (transactions, memory, management and control).[3] Individual initiatives and scientific exploration flourished and gave birth a few centuries later to the Industrial Revolution. New forms of energy, such as steam, coal and oil were discovered and used to power new forms of production and transportation such as the assembly line and the railroad. These inventions in turn, brought the world to the present Information Age, symbolized by technologies such as radio and television, telephones and fax machines, and above all, computers.

Accordingly, a shift is taking place in the basic resource of human society-from land to knowledge. Today, almost everything people use to live, from clothing to food and from houses to means of transportation and communications, is produced by scientific knowledge. Whereas land is a fixed pie lending itself to destructive fights over its division, the new basic resource is, as in hunter-gathered times, an expandable pie. And while there are limits to land and material resources, there are no known limits to knowledge since everyone can make use of it and contribute to it.

Land, however, is not the only major source of destructive conflict. People and groups also fight fiercely about power. Like land, power over others is a fixed

---

[2] William Ury, *Getting to Peace: Transforming Conflict at Home, at Work, and in the World*, New York: Viking, 1999, pp. 83-84.

[3] See: «Histoire de l'informatique: Traitement de l'information et automatisation», ('History of Computer Science: Treatment of information and automation'), at: http://www.histoire-informatique.org/grandes_dates/1_2.html.

pie. Here knowledge represents a different kind of power, one that can be used to satisfy needs and desires. This new kind of power–power to do things–is not a fixed pie, but an expandable one as well. This knowledge power should not be applied to subdue others but rather be employed to liberate and empower them. Thanks to it, billions of ordinary citizens all over the world with virtually no power over others possess the force to live longer, travel faster and further, and interact globally–both virtually and physically.

While it may make sense to go to war to acquire territory, there is little logic to go to war to acquire the new reward of knowledge. For knowledge cannot easily be conquered. It is best acquired through learning and cooperation. In contrast to land, which is typically improved through the act of possession, knowledge is improved through the act of sharing. The core entity of knowledge, science, relies on the exchange of theories and information. Scientists compete with one another but the decisive factor in the competition, past and present, is mostly in the timing. Through effective cooperation and sharing, knowledge as a resource eventually grows more and more abundant for everyone.

With knowledge emerging as a key resource of our present society, "knowledge workers" constitute the dominant group in its work force. Drucker qualifies it to three essential features:

- borderlessness, because knowledge travels even more effortlessly than money;
- upward mobility, available to everyone through easily acquired formal education; and,
- the potential for failure as well as for success. Anyone can acquire the "means of production," but not everyone can win. [4]

These three features together make the knowledge society a highly competitive one, for individuals and organizations alike. Information Technology (IT), for example and although only one of many new aspects of the current development in

---

[4] Peter Drunker, "The Next Society," *The Economist,* online edition at*: www.economist.com*, November 1, 2001.

knowledge, is already having a huge impact by allowing information and knowledge to spread near-instantly, and even more importantly, making it accessible to everyone. Given the ease and speed at which information travels, every institution in the knowledge society–not only businesses, yet also schools, universities, hospitals, and increasingly, government agencies–has to be globally competitive, even though most organizations and structures will remain local in their activities and in their respective sectors.

Respectively, job skill requirements have been shifting across all sectors thanks to new technologies. Machines with microprocessors, for instance, can now be programmed to do the sort of routine activities that less-skilled workers used to do. Meanwhile, business computer systems generate demand for highly skilled labor in the form of technical staff that operate (and repair the equipment), develop (and install) the software, and build (as well as monitor) the networks. Furthermore, computer systems normally generate more data that may be profitably analyzed, and thus increasing the demand for analytical, problem-solving competence, such as communication skills of workers, managers, and other professionals. The term *knowledge workers* applies more and more to the workers who go beyond just proving information to these new being responsible for generating and conveying knowledge needed for decision making.

As the recent technological advances may favor either skilled or unskilled workers (depending on the application), the overwhelming evidence is that on balance, recent technological advances favor more skilled workers and the same can be expected for future advances. Those demand differentials have, obviously, been driving up the salary premium paid to workers with higher education levels. Between 1973 and 2001, for example, the wage premium for a college degree compared with a high school diploma increased by 30%, from 46% to 76%.[5] (See Figure 1.1.)

---

[5] Lynn A. Karoly and Constantijn W.A. Panis, *The 21st Century at Work: Forces Shaping the Future Workforce and Workplace in the United States*, RAND Corporation, Santa Monica, CA, 2004.

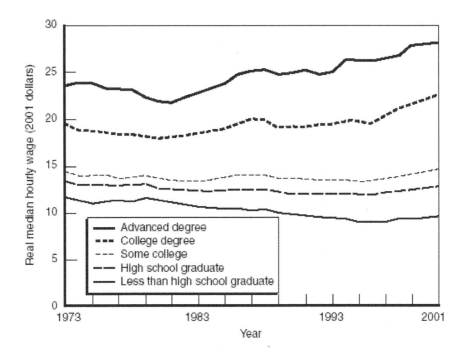

Figure 1. 1. Real Median Hourly Wage by Education Level, 1973-2001 (Source: cited in Karoly and Panis, p. xxiv)

To give an example, the same study by Karoly and Panis (p. xiv) concludes that in the next 10 to 15 years demographic trends, technological advances, and economic globalization will shape work in the United States. Among other findings, it states:

> Rapid technological change and increased international competition place the spotlight on the skills and preparation of the workforce, particularly the ability to adapt to changing technology and shifting product demand. Shifts in the nature of business organizations and the growing importance of knowledge-based work also favor strong non routine cognitive skills, such as abstract reasoning, problem-solving, communication, and collaboration. Within this context, education and training become a continuous process throughout the life course involving training and retraining that continues well past initial entry into the labor market. Technology mediated learning offers the potential to support lifelong learning both on the job and through traditional public and private education and training institutions.

However, a thorough review of the Information Age would be incomplete without recalling current illiteracy trends. Much has been learned about the issue of illiteracy ever since the United Nations declared it to be a basic human right along with the right to adequate food, health care and housing. While these last three provisions may be thought to be more pressing needs than literacy education, literacy is now considered as a vital tool to help address these other necessities. Fortunately, there is overwhelming agreement among countries that illiteracy poses a major problem in today's world, as literacy (and education) nearly tops the policy agenda of most industrialized and developing countries.

After World War II, educational development efforts stressed expanding formal schooling, based on the assumption that higher school attendance would help to end the scourge of illiteracy. Yet, both research and experience have proved that schooling does not necessarily lead to literacy or the kinds of literacy that students do need. In other words, formal schooling programs might not be the best way of investing scarce literacy resources, while there may be more effective means of teaching literacy skills in certain regions which are more tailored to the demands of the community.

It is important to note that the situations and statistics of literacy when compared among countries and/or regions need to be examined with caution. This is because different countries have different social and cultural contexts, different definitions and standards of literacy, different methodologies for collecting and compiling literacy data, in addition to the various qualities of the data collected. Data from some countries may represent the entire country, whereas some may represent only part of the country.

Another divergence may arise from the lack of a common, formal definition of literacy–at least for reporting data to international agencies. Existing definitions or criteria of literacy already vary in several ways. Some imply that literacy is static and absolute. In this case, a person is considered "literate" if, for instance, he/she is: able to sign his/her name, able to read/write a simple sentence describing his/her daily activities, able to pass a written test of reading comprehension at a level comparable to that achieved by an average Grade 4 student, and is able to engage in all those activities in which literacy is required for effective functioning in his/her community.

Now adopted by most educators and organizations, other definitions view literacy as dynamic or relative. Here, they assume that literacy should be defined only with a certain context of functioning, which may change from one country/culture to another, or over time. Lastly, some definitions may also include as part of literacy other mental skills, such as numeracy and problem solving.

Nevertheless, more and more countries are nowadays interested in starting to collect data on different levels of literacy skills based on their own national, cultural, linguistic and educational contexts. This trend seems to stem from the growing awareness that literacy is of central importance to development, and that it is increasingly correlated with higher income and job opportunity. Not excluded here is the notion that some countries may even highlight such data and figures as they seek development funds in the educational sector.

Recent estimates by the UNESCO Institute for Statistics reveal a steady drop in the number of illiterate adults (aged 15 and over) from 22.4% of the world's population in 1995 to 20.3% in 2000 (see Figure 1.2.).[6] This represents a progress from an estimated 872 million illiterates in 1995 to 862 million in 2000. Based on such a trend, there should be a drop to 824 million, or 16.5%, by the year of 2010.

Africa and Asia demonstrated the best performances, with their overall percentage of illiterate populations shrinking by 5.4% and 2.8% respectively. Although women still constitute two thirds of the world's adult illiterates, they are gaining access to education and literacy in all regions, and at a faster rate than men. The proportion of illiterate adult women fell from 28.5% to 25.8%.

---

[6] "Statistics show slow progress towards universal literacy," UNESCO Institute for Statistics (UIS), Paris, September 1, 2002.

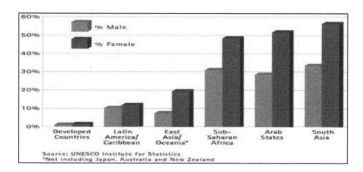

Figure 1. 2. Estimated world illiteracy rates, by region and by gender, 2000

The above figures clearly illustrate an increasingly literate world, but also demonstrate a slow progress. One adult out of five remains illiterate, and nearly two to three times that number who would be considered technologically illiterate. Without extraordinary efforts, the percentage of illiterate adults will fall by only another 5% by the year 2015.

Nevertheless, a more realistic view indicates three non-negligible factors. First, data on world literacy are again misleading, and underestimate the nature and scope of literacy problems. In the United States, for example, it was assumed for many years that over 90% of the citizens are literate. Yet in 1993, a wide scale survey examined literacy skills using functional tasks, and it was revealed that up to 50% of the population were identified as having trouble with several essential literacy tasks.[7] Second, neither increases in primary schooling nor adult literacy programs have been that quite effective at reducing illiteracy, partly due to mere population growth.

Finally, general views of literary rates mask large inequities, with higher illiteracy in rural communities, among girls and women, and probably more importantly for the future, among marginalized, minority and indigenous peoples

---

[7] International Literacy Explorer, Statistics, "Introduction: The Limitations of Literacy Statistics," University of Pennsylvania, Graduate School of Education, at: http://literacy.org/explorer/stats_critical.html, retrieved January 6, 2005.

(see Figure 1.3.).[8] In an aim to address those marginalized, it is thus not surprising that the United Nations General Assembly proclaimed the UN Literacy Decade for the period 2003-2012, under the banner *Literacy for all: voice for all, learning for all*. Severe educational inefficiencies still prevail in most developing (and in many industrialized) countries. In brief, universal primary schooling and increased adult literacy appear much harder to attain than previously believed.

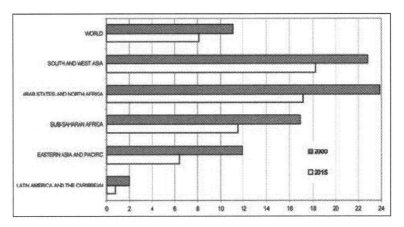

Figure 1. 3. Difference in male and female literacy rates: percentage point (Source: UIS, 2002)

I.I.I. Features of the Information Age

The leading characteristic of the Information Revolution is not only the *speed of* communications between the wealthy and powerful. For over a hundred years, virtually instantaneous communications have been possible between Europe and North America. The fundamental change also implies the enormous reduction in the *cost* of transmitting information. For all practical purposes, the actual transmission costs have become negligible, and thus, the amount of information that can be transmitted worldwide is effectively infinite. The result is an explosion of information.

---

[8] International Literacy Explorer, "Literacy Overview: Using Literacy Statistics," at: http://literacy.org/explorer/overview.html, retrieved January 6, 2005.

One may, then, ask for the volume of information created each year. Newly created information is stored in four *physical media*: print, film, magnetic and optical; and seen or heard in four *information flows through electronic channels*: telephone, radio and TV, and the Internet. One study of information storage and flows analyzed the year 2002 in order to estimate the annual size of the stock of new information flows.[9] According to reliable and available data, the findings of the year 2002 were compared to those of the year 2000 (based on 1999 data) in an attempt to describe a few trends in the growth rate of information. Among the findings:

- Print, film, magnetic, and optical storage media produced around five exabytes of new information in 2002. Some 92% of the new information was stored on magnetic media, mostly in hard disks. Film represents 7% of the total, paper 0.01%, and optical media 0.002%.

  The United States produces about 40% of the world's new stored information, including 33% of the world's new printed information, some 30% of the world's new film titles, around 40% of the world's information stored on optical media, and something like 50% of the information stored on magnetic media.

  To illustrate this in simple terms, with a current world population of 6.3 million, almost 800 megabytes (MB) of recorded information is produced per person each year.[10] It would take some 30 feet (9 meters) of books to store the equivalent of 800 MB of information on paper. Estimations show that new stored information grew by about 30% a year between 1999 and 2002. Although the amount of information printed on paper is still increasing, the vast majority of original information on paper is produced by individuals in office documents and postal mail, not in formally published titles such as books, newspapers and journals.

---

[9] "How Much Information? 2003,"
available at: http://www.sims.berkeley.edu/research/projects/how-much-info-2003.

[10] 1 MB is the equivalent of 20 static pages downloaded from the Internet, or the equivalent of a standard text document (.txt) of 250 pages filled with the letter *a*. See Appendix I for an illustration chart of measurement units used here.

With the amount of new original information stored on paper increasing 36% between 1999 and 2002, it is important to recall here the increase in simultaneous publication of printed information in digital format, such as online newspapers and journals.

Since a tree can produce around 80,500 sheets of **paper**, it would thus, require some 786 million trees to produce the world's annual paper supply. According to the UNESCO Statistical Handbook for 1999, paper production provides an estimated 1,510 sheets of paper per inhabitant of the world on average. However, paper consumption is not equal. Each of the inhabitants of North America consumes 11,916 sheets of paper (24 reams) annually, while inhabitants of the European Union consume 7,280 sheets of paper (15 reams). And at least half of this paper is used in printers and copiers to produce office documents.

Film is a storage medium for analog images that is increasingly evolving towards digital images stored on magnetic and optical media (because of lower editing costs). A growth has been observed in the production of new movies and in TV, particularly in developing countries. Approximately 370,000 motion pictures were produced all over the world from 1890 to 2002. And if the entire universe of original film and video titles were played continuously, the show would last for 2,108 years.

Global production of new information recorded on **magnetic storage media** has also grown by 80% since 1999. Analog-based magnetic tape (audio and videotape) is witnessing a decrease as digital storage is growing. Note that the decreasing cost and increasing variety of form factors has made hard disk technologies the fastest growing segment of all storage media for information.

Finally, **optical storage media** are the medium of choice for the distribution of software, data, cinema and music. A decline in the production and sale of retail audio CD title has occurred due to the growing popularity of writeable CDs (CD-R and CD-RW). And DVDs have achieved the fastest market penetration of any recent technology innovation–though mostly in the developed economies.

- Information flows through electronic channels represented by the telephone, radio, TV and the Internet contained nearly 17.7 exabytes of new information in 2002, three and a half times more than what is recorded in storage media. Some 98% of this volume covers the information sent and received in telephone calls, including voice and data on both fixed lines and wireless.

Telephone calls worldwide (on both landlines and mobile phones) included 17.3 exabytes of new information if stored in digital form, representing around 98% of the total of all information transmitted in electronic information flows, mostly person to person. As of the year 2002, there were reported to be 1.1 billion main telephone lines in the world.

Most **radio and TV broadcast** content is not new information. Around 70 million hours (3,500 terabytes) of the overall 320 million hours of radio broadcasting is original programming (70,000 terabytes) out of 123 million total hours of broadcasting. In the United States, there are 13,261 radio stations producing 19.7 million hours of original programming, or some 987 terabytes of original programming. And as of 2002, there were 1,686 broadcast TV stations in the United States producing around 14.5 million hours of content a year; some 3.6 million hours are original information, equivalent to between 4,700 and 8,200 terabytes (depending on the compression standard employed).

The **Internet**, although it is the newest medium for information flows, is the fastest growing new medium of all time–becoming the information medium of first resort for its users. To precise beforehand, the Web consists of the surface Web (fixed web pages) and the deep Web (the database driven Web sites that create Web pages on demand).

An average Internet user spends 11 hours and 24 minutes online per month, noting that the average user in the United States spends more than twice that amount of time online: 25 hours and 25 minutes at home and another 743 hours and 26 minutes at work. Internet access, in the United States for instance, is used to send e-mail (52%), get news (32%), use a search engine to find information (29%), surf the Web (23%), do research for work (19%), check the weather (17%), or to send an instant message (14%).

The estimated volume of information on the public Web, in 2000, was at 20 to 50 terabytes (with a rate of growth of 7.3 million new pages per day); where in 2003 the measured volume of information on the Web reached 167 terabytes,[11] at least triple the amount of information. With the surface Web somewhere around 167 terabytes as of summer 2003, the deep Web is estimated to be 400 to 450 times larger (and hence, between 66,800 and 91,850 terabytes). There are, as well, about 20 million "live" registered domains on the Internet,[12] embodying Web sites of over six billion pages.[13]

Ranking second behind the telephone as the largest information flow, e-mails sent *daily* mount to about 31 billion. This figure is expected to double by 2006. Instant messaging generates five million messages a day (750 gigabytes), or simply 274 terabytes a year. Lastly to note, only two-thirds of e-mail traffic is personal, since spam (known as unsolicited e-mail) totals to one-third of today's e-mail traffic. This proportion is projected to increase to 50% over the next four years.

---

[11] In volume, this is 17 times the size of the U.S. Library of Congress print collections.

[12] "Cyveillanec Study Reveals Strong eBusiness Activity Beyond .com, .net, .org, .info and .biz Domains," *www.cyveillance.com*, March 25, 2003, retrieved November 6, 2004.

[13] "Quick Stats," *www.cyveillance.com*, retrieved November 6, 2004.

To better understand the association of information to power in world politics (as well as in commerce), Nye distinguishes three dimensions of information that are sometimes lumped together: [14]

- The first is the flow of data such as news or statistics. There has been an enormous and measurable increase in the amount of information flowing across international borders. The average cost of such information has been declining, and a large portion of it is virtually free. Declining costs and added points of access help small states and non-state actors. On the other hand, however, the vast scale of free flows puts a premium on the capacities of editors and systems integrators, which is a benefit to the large and powerful.

- The second is information that is used to gain advantage in competitive situations. What comes first here matters most, and that usually favors the more powerful. While much competitive information is associated with commerce, the effect of information on military power can also be thought of as a subset of competitive information.

- The third dimension of information is strategic information, that is, "knowledge of your competitor's game plan." Strategic information, virtually priceless, is as old as espionage. While information "hunters" may still be hired, and to the extent that commercial technologies and market research provide technical capabilities that were previously available only at the cost of vast investment, there is an equalizing effect. Since it is also true that fewer of the interesting intelligence questions in a post-Cold War era are secrets (which can be stolen) than mysteries (to which no one knows the answers), immense intelligence collection capabilities still provide important strategic advantages.

---

[14] Joseph S. Nye Jr., *The Paradox of American Power: Why the World's Only Superpower Can't Go It Alone*, New York: Oxford University Press, Inc., 2002, p. 66.

One of the most interesting aspects of power in relation to increasing flows of information is the "paradox of plenty." Nye (2002, p. 67) points out that a plenitude of information leads to a poverty of attention. Being overwhelmed with the volume of information, it is hard to know what to focus on. *Attention* rather than information then becomes the scarce resource, and those who can distinguish and pick out valuable signals gain power.

As editors, filters and cue givers become more in demand, credibility turns into a crucial resource and an important facet of power. Reputation becomes even more important than in the past, and political struggle occur over the creation and destruction of credibility. In this respect, Garcin outlines that the treatment of international news is subject to a number of powers (or influences), namely, *le pouvoir d'amplification, le pouvoir de distorsion, le pouvoir d'apitoiement* and *le pouvoir d'euphorie.*[15] With people now tending to cluster around credible cue givers, perceived credibility, in turn tends to reinforce communities. Internet users, for instance, seem to frequent Web sites that provide information they find both interesting and reliable.[16] Furthermore, governments are competing for that facet–

---

[15] That is, 'the power of amplification, the power of distortion, the power of compassion, and the power of euphoria.' Thierry GARCIN, «Les risques liés à la globalisation de l'information», in *Gestion des risques internationaux,* ('The Risks Linked to the Globalization of Information', in *'Management of International Risks'*), sous la direction de Pascal CHAIGNEAU, Paris: Economica, 2001, pp. 147-48.

[16] Thinking counterfactually, Iraq might have found it easier to have won acceptance for its view of the invasion of Kuwait as a post colonial vindication, analogous to India's 1975 capture of the Goa, if Cable News Network (CNN) had framed the issues from Baghdad rather than from Atlanta. At that time, the Emir of Kuwait in exile hired the services of U.S.-based public relations firm Hill & Knowlton at a cost of some $10.8 million. Hill & Knowlton's duty was to massage the image of the Al Sabah family, persuading Americans that Kuwait was a state worthy of their sacrifices. However, initial attempts to work on 'positive' themes that Kuwaiti women could drive (even if they could not vote), that the regime was amongst the freest in the Gulf region all fell on unreceptive ears, as Hill & Knowlton's polling subcontractors found in their telephone surveys and focus groups.
While many Americans were not moved to sympathy for Kuwait, what inspired them more rather was dislike of Saddam Hussein and an acquired eagerness to punish the 'butcher' of Baghdad. The firm then concentrated efforts on demonizing the Iraqi leader, while portraying the Kuwaiti regime as passive victims. It sought to publicize Iraqi atrocities in occupied Kuwait–recalling World War I atrocity propaganda. The best-known story of this kind–that plundering Iraqi troops had thrown Kuwaiti babies out of their hospital incubators–was tearfully repeated to the U.S. Congressional Caucus on Human Rights (on Oct. 10, 1990) by a 15 year-old Kuwaiti girl, known only as Nayirah. The credibility of her account was enhanced by the respected Amnesty International, which repeated allegations that over 300 babies had died in this way in its own report on Iraqi violations of Human rights in Kuwait (published on Dec. 19, 1990). And as then president Bush was able to cite Amnesty, an almost unimpeachable source, rather than an unknown Kuwaiti girl,

not only with other governments but also with a broad range of alternatives including news media, corporations, non-governmental organizations (NGOs), intergovernmental organizations, as well as with networks of scientific communities.

Because of the pouring flood of free information and the "paradox of plenty" in the Information Age, politics has become a contest of competitive credibility. Each side tries to enhance its own credibility, while trying to weaken that of its opponents.

I.I.II. Power in the Information Age

Power in the Information Age, as described by Nye (2002, p. 39), is distributed among countries in a pattern that resembles a complex three-layer chess game. On the top chessboard, military power is largely uni-polar. The United States of America is the only country with both intercontinental nuclear weapons and large, state-of-the-art air, naval, and ground forces capable of global deployment. It, furthermore, leads in the information-based "Revolution in Military Affairs" (RMA). Yet, on the middle chessboard, economic power is multi-polar, with the United States, Europe, and Japan representing two-thirds of world product–along with China's dramatic growth likely to make it a major player early in the century. On this economic board, the United States is not hegemony and often must bargain as an equal with Europe.

Then there is the bottom chessboard, which embodies a realm of transnational relations that cross borders outside of government control. This realm includes non-state actors as diverse as bankers electronically transferring sums larger than

---

the incubator story become tremendously resonant, turning into one of the key facts to support the 'Saddam-as-Hitler' analogy.
After the war, Amnesty International distanced itself from this story. But by then, and by the time it was revealed that Nayirah was in fact the daughter of the Kuwaiti ambassador to the U.S., and that her tearful testimony was not that of a traumatized witness, but of a well-coached accessory to Hill & Knowlton, the repudiation was too late (source: Susan L. Carruthers, *The Media At War*, London: Macmillan Press Ltd., 2000, pp. 42-43).

most national budgets, at one extreme, and others carrying out attacks and hackers disrupting Internet operations, at the other. Power, on this bottom board is widely dispersed, and it makes no sense to speak of uni-polarity, multi-polarity, or hegemony. In other words, in a three dimensional composition failure results when focus is only on the interstate military board–while neglecting the other two boards and the vertical connections among them. See Illustration 1.1.

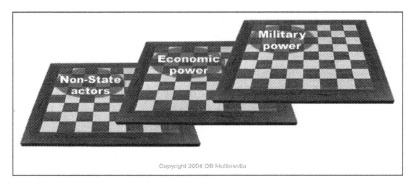

Illustration 1. 1. The distribution of power in the Information Age (according to Nye, 2002)

As a consequence, the Information Revolution is making world politics more complex by enabling transnational actors and reducing control by central governments, but it is also affecting power among states. While some poorer countries such as China, India and Malaysia have achieved significant progress in entering the information economy, Norris states that 87% of people online live in post industries societies.[17] In other words, the world in the Information Age remains a mixture of agricultural, industrial and service-dominated economies. The post-industrial societies and governments most heavily affected by the current era now coexist and interact with countries thus far little affected by the information revolution.

---

[17] Pippa Norris, *The Digital Divide: Civic Engagement, Information Poverty, and the Internet Worldwide*, New York: Cambridge University Press, 2001, p. 8.

A commonly asked question in this respect is whether or not such a digital divide will reign for a long time. Decreasing costs, illustrates Nye (2002, p. 62), may allow poor countries to *leapfrog* or *skip* over certain stages of development. For example, wireless communications are already replacing costly landlines, and voice recognition technologies can give illiterates access to computer communications. Also, the Internet may enable poor farmers to better understand weather and market condition before they plant crops. Distance learning and Internet connections may even more assist isolated doctors and scientists in poor remote areas. Yet, what poor countries need most urgently is basic education and infrastructure.

Logically, the overall decentralizing and leveling effect of the Information Revolution should equalize power among nations. As it reduces costs and barriers, it should also reduce the power of large states and enhance the power of small states and non-state actors. But in practice, international relations are more complex than such technological determinism implies. While some aspects of the information revolution help the small, others help the already large and powerful, according to Nye (2002, p. 63). And for that, he points to several reasons:

- First: size still matters. What economists call barriers to entry and economies of scale remain in some of the aspects of power that are related to information. For example, *soft power* is strongly affected by the cultural content of what is broadcast or appears in movies and television programs.

- Second: even where it is now cheap to disseminate existing information, the collection and production of new information often requires major investment. Information, in some dimensions, is a nonrivalrous public good: one person's consumption does not diminish that of another. However, in a competitive situation, it may make a great difference to whoever takes hold of it first.

A good example here is intelligence gathering. The United States, Russia, Britain and France have collection and production capabilities that overshadow those of other nations. Published accounts (Nye: 2002, p. 64) suggest that the United States spends some $30 billion a year on intelligence. In some commercial situations, a fast follower can do better than a first mover, but in terms of power among states, it is usually better to be a first mover than a fast follower.

- Third: first movers are often the creators of the standards and architecture of information systems. Where sometimes crude, low-cost technologies open shortcuts that make it possible to overtake the first mover, in many instances the path-dependent development of information systems reflects the advantage of the first mover. Partly because of the transformation of the American economy in the 1980s, and partly because of huge investments driven by Cold War military competition, the United States was usually the first mover and still leads in the application of a wide variety of information technology.

- Fourth: military power remains important in some critical domains of international relations. Indeed, information technology has effects on the use of force that benefit the small and some that favor the already powerful. The commercial availability of formerly costly military technologies benefits small states and non-governmental actors while it increases the vulnerability of large states.

Today, for example, anyone can order inexpensive satellite images, or simply go to the Internet and get access to satellite photographs that were until just recently, top-secret and cost governments a fortune. Global positioning devices, once the property of the military alone, are now available at local electronics stores. Freelance cyber attacks are more and more of a prospect to consider. Tens of thousands of U.S. military and government computers containing sensitive information are easily accessible over the Internet. Military encryption techniques, correspondences between generals, recruits' Social Security and credit cards numbers and other personal information is often stored on Internet-connected computers that use easily guessed passwords–or even in some cases no passwords at all.[18]

For instance, see how after the collision between the American surveillance plane and the Chinese fighter in April 2001, both Chinese and American hackers[19] entered a series of "virtual attacks" on both government and private Web sites of each other.

Consider also how supporters of Israel and the Palestine moved their conflict battlefield to the Internet over the outcome of a little-known photo contest that included the picture of the 12-year-old Palestinian boy Mohammed Durrah huddled by his father moments before the boy was killed in September 2000. For the first three weeks of the "Year in Picture 2000" contest, in which visitors of the *www.msnbc.com* Web site vote for their favorite news photo of that year, the photo of the boy was the clear leader–just until supporters of Israel waged a widespread e-mail campaign and besieged msnbc.com with votes for pictures mostly featuring dogs, cats and other animals.

While the Palestinians saw the photo, which was taken from a video frame by "France 2" television channel, as probably bringing sympathy to their cause, the Israelis wanted to make sure that it did not win most votes and attract even more attention around the world.[20] This example illustrates how the escalated tension spread well beyond the boundaries of the Middle East to the computer networks of foreign companies and groups

---

[18] See: Thom Shanker, ".Mil Sites Can Create Unintended Buzz," *International Herald Tribune* (IHT), August 22, 2001, 11; and "Experts: U.S. Military Computers Easily Cracked," *USA Today*, online edition at: *www.usatoday.com*, August 16, 2002.

[19] It is interesting to note that back in the 1960s, "hacker" was a positive term that described a person with a mastery of computers who could push programs beyond what they were designed to do (source: Brock N. Meeks, "Hackers Hit 155 Government Sites," *www.msnbc.com*, April 5, 2001).

[20] Dean E. Murphy, "Mideast Cyber Strife Over a Photo," *IHT*, March 3-4, 2001, 1.

seen as partisan to the conflict.

However, other trends strengthen the already powerful. With the rise of RMA, space-based sensors, direct broadcasting, high-speed mobile computers, and complex software provide the ability to gather, sort, process, transfer and disseminate information–anywhere and at anytime, instantly. With this puissant advantage, and as the Iraq-Kuwait conflict (1991) and the U.S. invasion in Iraq (2003) have proved, traditional assessment of balance-of-weapons platforms (such as tanks and planes) become obviously irrelevant unless they include the ability to integrate information with those weapons.

Many of the relevant technologies are commercially available to weaker states. Yet, the key, as Nye (2002, p. 66) concludes, will not be possession of hi-tech hardware or advanced systems but certainly the ability to integrate a "system of systems." And in information warfare, a small edge makes a great difference.

I.I.III. The Failure of Some Countries to Cope with the Information Age and Science

Around the turn of the 19th century, referred by some as the first industrial revolution, the application of steam to mills and transportation had a powerful effect on the economy, society, and government. Patterns of production, work, living conditions, social class and political power were being transformed. Even public education arose to satisfy the need for literate, trained workers to perform in increasingly complex and potentially dangerous factories.

Then the turn of the 20th century, illustrates Nye (2002, pp. 43-47), brought along the second industrial revolution and introduced electricity, synthetics, and the internal combustion engine–leading to similar economic and social changes. The United States gradually moved from a predominantly agrarian nation to a primarily industrial one. Social class and political cleavages were altered as urban labor and trade unions became more important, and once again, leading to a change in the role of government.

In the Soviet Union, the state perfected by Josef Stalin represented the height of 20th century centralization. Stalin's economic model was based on central planning, where quantity rather than profits were the main criterion of a manager's success. With prices being set by planners rather than by markets, consumers as customers played a minor role. Indeed, the Stalinist economy was successful in mastering relatively unsophisticated technologies and producing basic goods such as steel and electricity on a massive scale. It was, evermore, effective in extracting capital from the agricultural sector in the 1930s, in using it to build a heavy industry and post-war reconstruction when labor was plentiful. Yet, with a diminishing birth rate and scarce capital, Nye (2002, pp. 43-47) emphasizes that Stalin's model of central planning simply "ran out of steam."

Soviet central planners, furthermore, lacked the flexibility to keep up with the rapid pace of technological change in the emerging, increasingly information-based global economy; and therefore, they were not able to adapt to the requirements of the third industrial revolution (i.e., the Information Age).

Politically, an information-based society required (and still does) broadly shared and freely flowing information. Horizontal communication among computers become more important and urgent than top-to-bottom vertical communication, although that would imply political risks in that computers could become the equivalent of printing presses. Also, telephones have multiplied such risks by providing instant communication among computers. These reasons, necessarily, made the Soviet leaders reluctant to foster the widespread and free use of computers. Nye (2002, p. 47) presents two simple statistics to demonstrate the Soviet disadvantage in the expanding information economy of the 1980s.

First, by the middle of the decade, there were only fifty thousand personal computers in the Soviet Union (compared to thirty million in the United States).[21] And second, at the end of the decade Soviet officials admitted that their computer technology lagged seven to ten years behind that of the West.[22] Although this central control made political control easier, it did have its counter effects on the economy.

The countries in the Middle East, with their rich resources, created a society that in the Middle Ages was the scientific center of the world. As Arabic language became synonymous with learning and science for five hundred years–particularly in astrology, mathematics, physics and medicine–the infusion of knowledge into Western Europe during that golden age, claim historians,[23] was what fueled the Renaissance and the Industrial Revolution.

In 9th century Baghdad, the "Dar Al-Hikma" (House of Wisdom) was set up as an institute to translate manuscripts. The 10th and 11th centuries saw the flourishing of science pioneers, notably, Abu Ali Al-Hassan Ibn Al-Haytham (also known as Al-Hazen, laying the foundation for modern optics), Abu Royham Muhammed Al-Biruni (a mathematician, astronomer and geographer), and Abu Ali Al-Hussein Ibn Sina (known as Avicenna, a physician). Meanwhile, the Europeans from the 10th to the 13th century were translating Arabic works into other languages–giving rebirth to learning that ultimately transformed the West.

As an eventual consequence of the religious wars between the East and West, the Arab and Islamic centers of learning began to lose touch with one another and with the West. This led to gradual erosion in two of the main pillars of science: communication and financial support. So while science in the West was able to pay for itself in new technology (like the steam engine) and was able to attract

---

[21] "Life Beyond the Kremlin," *The New York Times*, online edition at: *www.nytimes.com*, May 30, 1988.

[22] "Soviets Launch Computers Literacy Drive," *Science*, January 10, 1986, 109-10.

[23] See: Dennis Overbye, "How Islam Won, and Lost, the Lead in Science," *The New York Times*, online edition, October 30, 2001.

financing from industry, science in the East remained to be dependent on "the patronage and curiosity of sultans and caliphs" (Overbye, 2001).

Furthermore, after science had drifted to the West, it became ever more difficult to introduce it back to the East–where the latter would only be reclaiming their own, since the West inherited science from them to begin with. These add to other contributing causes, such as sociological and economic factors (such as the lack of a middle class) and to the effort at that time to "Islamicize" science by portraying the Holy Koran as the sole source of scientific knowledge.

I.I.IV. Global Trends of Science and Technology in the Information Age

As the Information Age moves on quicker than ever, efforts to define and envision its orientation remain limited in scope. Numerous intellectuals, scientists as well as institutions present several predictions of the near and far future to come–all basing their assumptions on the previous rapid evolution, necessities and ambitions. Yet, they all do agree on the mounting, progressive pace of the Information Age. For instance:

> The integration–or fusion–of continuing revolutions in information technology, biotechnology, materials science, and nanotechnology will generate a dramatic increase in investment in technology, which will further stimulate innovation within the more advanced countries.[24]

More precisely, the growing effects of multidisciplinary technology will revolutionize life in 2015 across all dimensions of life: social, economic, political and personal. Biotechnology will enable us to identify, understand, manipulate, improve and control living organisms (not excluding human beings). The evolving nature of information, its availability and utility will continue to profoundly affect the world in all these dimensions.

---

[24] *Global Trends 2015: A Dialogue About the Future With Nongovernment Experts*, Washington, DC: U.S. National Intelligence Council (NIC), December 2000, p. 9.

Hence, the results could be astonishing and mixed in prospective. Consider, for example, significant improvements in human quality of life and life span, high rates of industrial turnover, lifetime worker training, continued globalization, and reshuffling of wealth. But also consider the tracing potential for increased tension and conflict as well as shifts in power from nations states to non-state actors and individuals, where disaffected states, proliferators, narcotraffickers, and organized criminals can take advantage of the new high-speed information environment along with other advances in technology to integrate their illegal activities–pressuring their threat anti-clockwise.

The actual realization of these possibilities, signals *The Global Technology Revolution,*[25] will depend on a number of factors, including local acceptance of technological change, levels of technology and infrastructure investments, market drivers and limitations, in addition to technology breakthroughs and advancements. Since these factors vary across the globe, as mentioned earlier, the implementation and effects of technology will also respectively vary, particularly in developing countries. Yet, once again, the fast pace of technological development and breakthroughs make foresight difficult, though the technology revolution seems globally significant and quite likely.

For instance, the *MIT Technology Review*[26] draws attention to ten emerging areas of technology that are expected to have a profound impact on the economy and on how we live and work in the decade to come. The areas are:

- Brain-Machine Interface
- Flexible Transistors
- Data Mining
- Digital Rights Management
- Biometrics
- Natural Language Processing

---

[25] Philip S. Anton, Richard Silberglitt and James Schneider, *The Global Technology Revolution: Bio/Nano/Materials Trends and Their Synergies with Information Technology by 2015,* RAND, 2001, Summary, p. 1.

[26] "MIT Technology Review," at: *www.technologyreview.com*, January/February 2001.

- Microphotonics
- Untangling Code
- Robot Design
- Microfluidics.

Back to biotechnology, some advances might be viewed as accelerations of human-engineered evolution of plants, animals, and in some ways even humans with accompanying changes in the ecosystem. On how biotechnology will begin to revolutionize life by 2015, *The Global Technology Revolution* points to major significant effects and issues.[27]

One is increased quantity and quality of human life. Better disease control, custom drugs, gene therapy, age mitigation and reversal, memory drugs, prosthetics, bionic implants, animal transplants, all may continue to increase human lifespan and the quality of life. Some of these advances, among others, may even improve human performances beyond current levels (e.g., through artificial sensors).

A second is the approaching capability to use genetic engineering techniques to "improve" the human species and to clone humans. Eugenics and cloning are indeed controversial developments–among the most controversial in the entire history of mankind. Despite so, we are already observing some narrow attempts such as gene therapy for genetic diseases and cloning by rogue experimenters.

The revolution in biology, therefore, will not come without issue and unforeseen redirections. Significant ethical, moral, religion, privacy, and environment debates and protests are already being raised in such areas as genetically modified foods, cloning and genomic profiling. And while these issues are not halting the progressing developments for the meantime, they might straighten out its course over the next fifteen years as the population comes to grips with the new powers enabled by biotechnology. Also the pace of this revolution will rely heavily on technological trends not only in the biological

---

[27] *The Global Technology Revolution*, Summary, 2001, pp. 1-2.

sciences and technology but as well in "micro electromechanical systems, imaging, sensor, and information technology," concludes the summary.

Another remarkable progress is also taking place in physics. Here, researchers have slowed *light* to a 'dead stop,' stored it and then released it as if it were an ordinary material article. The achievement, illustrates Cornell,[28] is a landmark feat that, by reining in nature's swiftest and most ethereal form of energy for the first time, could help realize what are now theoretical concepts for vastly increasing the speed of computers and the security of communications.

The biggest impact of this work comes in futuristic technologies called "quantum computing" and "quantum communication." Both concepts, according to Cornell,[29] depend heavily on the ability of light to carry so-called "quantum information," involving particles that can exist in many places or states at once. Quantum computers are able to crank out certain operations vastly faster than existing machines, noting that quantum communications are supposedly *never* to be eavesdropped upon.

Higher in altitude, consider as well commercial satellite photography which began gaining momentum in 1994 when the U.S. Federal Government started allowing companies to make and sell images precise enough to show features just a few centimeters in diameter on the ground.

The industry's biggest customer, points out Feder,[30] is in fact the American government itself, which uses the commercial companies' services for activities like map-making, monitoring beach erosion or air pollution, and reporting on crops. The largest government demand comes from the military and intelligence agencies, which rely heavily on the industry to supplement data from satellites owned by the U.S. and other governments.

---

[28] Eric A. Cornell, "Stopping Light in its Tracks," *Nature*, London: Nature Publishing Group, Vol. 409, Issue no. 6819, January 25, 2001, 461-62.

[29] *Ibid.*

[30] Barnaby J. Feder, "Bird's Eye Views, Made to Order," *The New York Times*, online edition, October 11, 2001.

Commercial satellites, yet, cannot gather data as precise as what the newest government satellites glean about the dimensions, position and physical nature of objects in a photograph. While commercial satellites can distinguish between different crops planted in adjacent fields, the latest military satellites can recognize different varieties of the same crop–a comparison offered by military officials.

There is also anxiety about the quality of education because of an increasing sense of comparative failure in equipping students with the necessary intellectual tools of survival in the contemporary world. This has led to an almost unpleasant fascination with education statistics expressed in terms of global comparison. This is mainly because the degree of technological education present in a society has now become part of its ability to attract its share of the loose capital erasing global markets. The result is a tension between the increasing poverty and debts of governments whose tax base has been eroding and their certainty that more resources need to be put into education at each and every level. According to Langhorne,[31] the responsibilities here have increased because of two major changes.

First, the provision of education used to be based on the notion that there was a finite quantity required for individuals to function effectively in particular life roles. High school and college education give or take some relatively small special skill–an extra language for example–that would enable the newly minted adult to perform in almost any employment. Education was over and life began. This notion is no longer the case and impossible now in a world where the progress of knowledge is already rapid and gaining speed. The rate of obsolescence in the high tech information technology, to state an example, requires a continuous progress of re-education. And meeting this need requires major transformations in attitudes, to some degree already under way, and major expenditures.

Second, the educational systems of the developed world naturally reflect the practices and expectations of the past, when education was seen to be part of a cultural training. It existed within a particular cultural tradition; French education

---

[31] Richard Langhorne, *The Coming of Globalization: Its Evolution and Contemporary Consequences*, New York: Palgrave, 2001, pp. 59-61.

was different from British, which was different from Russian and different again from the American. The process acknowledged a local cultural past and contributed to a particular way of thinking about the present. Like states themselves, it was organized within and not above the society. To an important degree it taught you who you were in an individual cultural environment; and as scientific education steadily increased in importance during the 20th century, serious effects were put into making sure that scientists did not entirely miss out on this part of their education.

But now, the global economic system requires knowledge and expertise above and beyond the acquisition of intellectual skills and admission into the traditions and modes of thought of a single culture. Like communications, employment, banking and commerce, education has as well become de-territorialized. The specific skills required to create the kind of global economic asset that it represents have no basis in any one traditional culture, and may be actually damaging to some of them. Those traveling around or dealing with the rest of the world on a routine basis cannot escape understanding how far this development has gone or to what extent that it will become ever more pervasive in the future.

Education and learning approaches are, thus already adapting to cope with the information/knowledge society. In *A Vision for Life Long Learning – Year 2020,* Microsoft envisions children, from the first few months of life, playing with toys that teach them various concepts:[32]

> In 2020, toys begin capturing children's learning experiences by using embedded technology that records information about the child's habits, preferences and projects to provide parents with a better understanding of their child's development. Toys provide parents with the child's learning profile, sending private information to the parent's information appliance so they can use the information in the selection and purchase of additional toys that will enhance the child's motivation and experience....
>
> Over the course of the preschool years, children increase their play in learning 2020 by engaging in supportive virtual reality games...The games

---

[32] Randy Hinrichs, "A Vision for Life Long Learning – Year 2020," (Introduction by Bill Gates), p. 2, in *Vision 2020: Transforming Education and Training Through Advanced Technologies*, U.S. Department of Commerce, September 2002.

> build critical thinking skills using simulated, situational environments that engage other members of the family and community to play along.
>
> The technology objective is to construct a safe environment for the child while engage in technology drive learning experiences. For real world interactions, video playbacks of children engage in learning activities are frequent and reviewed by student, teacher and parent.

Indeed, some Japanese teachers at high schools and universities have already encouraged a remote-learning environment in class. They ask their students to bring with them their Internet-enabled cellphones to respond to questions posed via an interactive computer system that displays the results on the phone's screen. With oversize classes in Japanese universities, students tend to be more attentive and less sleepy while interactively using their cellphones.[33]

An important aspect of education and learning is the movement of students and scholars across national boundaries to exchange knowledge, a cornerstone of cultural diplomacy that has been going on for centuries and is deeply rooted in the traditions of the university as an institution. As the Information Age moves forward, it is quite essential to anticipate the future of international education exchange in an era of instantaneous, global communication.

Obviously, the development of modern communication technologies is having a profound impact on all aspects of human life and society, and international education and cultural relations are certainly no exception. Distance education technologies, for instance, offer the assurance of taking learning to learners, no matter where and when. Pedagogically, they break the time and space connection between the teacher and the learner. However, does this mean that CD-ROM and Web-based education applications are now replacing (or will replace) the need for learners to travel across the globe to link with their teachers or with their learning environment?

That does not seem to be so obvious to Olsen and Peterson, who believe that "technology will *not* replace the global movement of people for educational purposes but that it *will* have a profound impact on how such programs are

---

[33] Miki Tanikawa, "Wireless: In Japan, classroom bane becomes teachers' pet," *IHT*, February 14, 2005, 14.

conducted."[34] Modern communication technologies cannot and will not, in most cases, replace traditional international exchange activities, but instead, with sound planning and understanding, new technologies may offer enormous potential to complement and strengthen exchange programs. It is necessary, therefore, to encourage those engaged in international educational and cultural programs to focus their efforts on finding ways to effectively blend traditional and technological elements and, working with those in communication technologies, enhance the effectiveness of international education and cultural communication thanks to this technology.

To illustrate the argument with a crude analogy, Olsen and Peterson refer to the significant development of the erotic dimension of the Internet. Although it is sometimes argued that sex today represents the largest commercial use of the World Wide Web, no one suggests for the moment that virtual sex will usurp real exercise. In other words, while the Internet can transmit erotic material and is certainly capable of arousing desires, it cannot by its very nature provide the immediacy of communication between human beings that is essential to sexual fulfillment. And so the very same limitations prevent 'virtual' communications across cultures from fulfilling the traditional role of 'actual' exchanges involving people moving to live, study and work in other cultures.

Since technology-based international communication cannot, as assumed above, take the place of actual experiences in other cultures, the way in which these technologies may be best used is then by complementing and enhancing direct experiences in living, studying and working in other cultures.

For instance, the National Security Educational Program (NSEP)[35] uses distance education technologies combined with study abroad to provide access to Arabic language to students at institutions which do not have Arabic language faculty to offer traditional instruction in the increasingly important world language.

---

[34] Jody K. Olsen and Norman J. Peterson, "International Education Exchange in the Information Age," in *iMP: The Magazine on Information Impacts*, McLean, Virginia: Center for Information Strategy and Policy, July 23, 2001.

[35] The NSEP, a U.S. federal program that begun in 1993, funds innovative programs to increase knowledge of other languages and cultures critical to American security interests.

The program is currently focused on 80 countries and 45 languages, and has grown in size even as information technology has made communication and information more accessible to U.S. students and scholars.

As for the media and press, one may wonder if there will still be a need for government international broadcasting in the years to come. On this, Roberts responds with a resounding "yes" for two reasons: one, international broadcasting is an important element in the conduct of public diplomacy, which will have an ever increasing role in international affairs, and two, radio will continue to play an eminent part in the communications sphere–where millions of people will tune into radio broadcasts despite the development of other media, such as television and the Internet.[36]

The further advancement of the Information Age, by 2015, will have had a major impact upon the conduct of foreign policy. Traditional diplomacy (government-to-government) will increasingly need to be supplemented by public diplomacy (government-to-people). Fostering understanding and influencing audiences (i.e., publics) will play an ever more important role in the pursuit of foreign policy objectives. Radio broadcasting, both direct and relatively inexpensive, will continue to play a major role.

By 2015, radio audience, as Roberts views (2001), will continue to exist. The history of radio listening in modern societies, for instance in the United States and Western Europe, proves that despite all other advances in technology, radio continues to play an important role in the transmission and reception of information. And because radio has since ever become an important element in the pursuit of foreign policy objectives, a short review of international broadcasting may point to a framework to the year 2015.

When the United Stated entered World War II in December 1941, after Pearl Harbor, a decision was made at the highest level of the government that the country should immediately start international broadcasting. The impetus for the decision

---

[36] Walter R. Roberts, "Government Broadcasting," *iMP Magazine*, July 23, 2001.

was not only the undoubted success of German radio propaganda at that time but also the high reputation that the British Broadcasting Corporation (BBC) had earned.[37] Thus, an international broadcasting operation was set up as government-run, and within two months and a half (February 25, 1942) after Pearl Harbor, the first broadcast to Germany went on air.[38]

The international broadcasting picture, reveals Roberts, changed in 1950 when the United States added a new radio service: Radio Free Europe (RFE). While the Cold War was raging along with the information battle, a plan was prepared under which the American people–outraged by Soviet policy in eastern Europe–would through advertising campaigns come up with funds that would run a radio operation targeting Poland, Hungary and other Eastern European countries under Soviet domain. Here, the broadcasts would deal mostly with their problems rather than with American news and policies; and they would be funded by the Central Intelligence Agency (CIA). The cover was eventually uncovered at the U.S. Senate in 1971.

Since the 1950s, accordingly, the United States has operated two international radio operations, namely the *government-run* Voice of America (VOA) and the *privately-run* RFE along with several other ones modeled after RFE, such as "Radio Liberty" (addressed to the Soviet Union and its successor states), "Radio Marti" (to Cuba) and "Radio Free Asia" (essentially to China, Vietnam, Laos, Cambodia).[39]

---

[37] Speaking of propaganda, during World War II, a young Japanese American woman (born Ikuko Toguri) became famously known as "Tokyo Rose" for her broadcasts over Radio Tokyo of a program called 'Zero Hour' which had became part of Japanese psychological warfare designed to lower the morale of the United States armed forces in the South Pacific. See: *http://www.fbi.gov/libref/historic/famcases/rose/rose.htm.*

[38] The British Broadcasting Company, as the BBC was originally named, was formed on October 18, 1922. It sought to become an independent British broadcaster able to "educate, inform and entertain the whole nation, free from political interference and commercial pressure." Its first foreign-language service was Arabic, introduced in 1938. And on the eve of the Second World War, the BBC launched services to Europe in French, German, Italian, Portuguese, Spanish and in English. (See: "History of the BBC," at: *www.bbc.co.uk*). Meanwhile, Radio France International (rfi) was established as *Le Poste Colonial* on May 6, 1931, and had its first foreign-language broadcast in 17 languages in 1973. (See: «RFI: principales dates», 'RFI: Principal dates', at: *http://rfi.fr/Fichiers/RFI/Historie/histoire.asp*).

[39] The United States also established "Liberty TV," a satellite television program broadcasting from London. Funded by the American Congress and administered by the State Department, the

While the years went by, VOA and RFE programs inevitably resembled each other more and more. VOA programs to Eastern Europe, in order to stay competitive, began to deal with internal developments in the target area, while RFE programs, to stay competitive as well, had to deal with American news and policies. Analyses made over the years showed that VOA and RFE programs, though different in objectives, were hardly distinguishable in their *raison d'être* and content. Whether or not the United States will, in the coming years, continue to fund several broadcasting programs–bearing their costs and duplicative versions–is still to be observed.[40]

The relationship between technology and propaganda reflects how wartime information has become a weapon every bit as powerful as the most sophisticated missile. Propaganda, in recent conflicts, has been more diffused than in the past, in part because of the rise of user-friendly technologies such as the Internet and mobile phones–rendering it more difficult for governments to monopolize the message reaching their citizens, allies and enemies.

Until World War II, the printing press remained the prime source of propaganda technology. American revolutionaries used the press to make their case for independence at the end of the 18th century. And the U.S. government printed

television channel aimed to topple Saddam Hussein. See: "Opponents of Baghdad to Beam in Satellite TV," Thom Shanker, *IHT*, August 29, 2001, 4. A few months after the invasion in 2003, the Pentagon then funded the TV channel "Al-Iraqiya"–perceived 'as a pawn' of the U.S.–led occupation authorities. ("U.S. funds Iraqi television network," *www.msnbc.com*, November 29, 2003).

[40] In its latest developments, VOA intended to broadcast round the clock through the Arab World, targeting much of its programming to the under-30 audience that most likely blame the United States for the region's ills. In a region with vast cultural differences and wide variations in vocabulary and pronunciation, the service beamed the same programs across the entire region, using a formal dialect that many Arabs considered laughable. If VOA can neutralize some of that anti-Americanism, it will move U.S. international broadcasting closer to its World War II and Cold War roots. The key broadcast network was to split into five geographical segments to focus on local interest and regional accents: Israel, the West Bank and Jordan; Iraq; Egypt; the Gulf region; and Sudan and Yemen. Meanwhile, VOA planned to curtail broadcasts in the following languages: Bulgarian, Romanian, Slovak, Uzbek, Portuguese (to Brazil), Thai, Turkish, Armenian, Azerbaijani, and Georgian. (Source: Norman Kempster, "Voice of America Seeks New Accent," *IHT*, April 4, 2001, 2.)

In a similar approach, Israel Broadcasting Authority began on June 25, 2002 a nightly English news broadcast to the Middle East and Europe, with the intention of having impact on Israel's relations with the Arab World. The channel is called "Channel 3 Arabic IBA TV," and works on the same satellite that broadcasts the powerful Arabic Al-Jazeera network. (Source: Gil Hoffman, "IBA English News goes international," *The Jerusalem Post*, online edition at: *www.jpost.com*, June 26, 2002.)

thousands of posters during World War I. Then came the radio, which was embraced by all sides during World War II. Unlike printing, radio or even television, modern communications technology does not require a press or a studio. With a satellite phone and a laptop, *anyone anywhere* can deliver anything.

The Internet, for example, creates a system in which power over information is much more widely distributed. Compared with radio, television, and newspapers, all controlled by editors and broadcasters, the Internet creates unlimited communication one-to-one (e.g., via e-mail), one-to-many (e.g., via a personal home page or electronic conference), many-to-one (e.g., via electronic broadcast), and perhaps most important, many-to-many (e.g., an online chat room). Internet messages have the *power* to flow farther, faster, and with fewer intermediaries.

And even with these developments in technology, central surveillance still remains possible. Yet, governments that aspire to control information flows face high costs and ultimate frustration. Rather than reinforcing centralization and bureaucracy, the new information technologies have tended to foster network organizations, new types of community, and demands for different roles of government.

Belgrade's editor and chief of "Radio B92" and chairman of the Association of Independent Electronic Media (ANEM) reveals how his organization's early adoption of the Internet during the 1996 opposition movement began the long, inevitable rally to Slobodan Milosevic's fall:

> We started to develop our Internet program before the regime because we were afraid that the regime might also try to control that area of communication. Thus, we became the first internet provider in Yugoslavia which understood the Internet as a new medium, and which use the Internet as an alternative means of disseminating information throughout Yugoslavia, as well as to the outside world. However, in a society as closed as ours, the impact of the Internet was not truly visible until after the radio was banned at the height of 1996-1997 mass civic protest. It was then that we started to broadcast our program via the Internet using Real Audio. In addition to reaching citizens outside of Belgrade for the first time, B92, via the transmitters of the Voice of America, Radio Free Europe, the BBC, etc., was able to broadcast to the world. The radio's swift move to harness its knowledge of the Internet to the immediate need to break the government-imposed silence thus made the ban pointless.

During B92's two-day ban and the new Internet broadcast, the students began to use the Internet intensively to distribute information about the student protest, its activities and its aims. In this way, the student movement too was able to attract the attention of the world public, who in turn began to help the students by redistributing their information, sending help and money.[41]

In the Information Age, thanks to uncountable sources and channels, most people tend to focus on those that closely match their own beliefs. Despite the promise of the Internet in expanding the diversity of voices, studies have shown that after an initial period, the user tends–over time–to habitually go to the same sites for information.[42] Similar to television channels, bigger Web sites get bigger and the smaller ones seem to get smaller in audience.

---

[41] Veran Matic, "Between an Electronic Gulag and the Global Village," presentation at 'The Information Revolution and its Impact on the Foundations of National Power' conference, September 23-25, 1997, at:
http://wwwz.opennet.org/b92/radio/info/people/veran_matic/vmatic-tx2.html.

[42] Christine Frey and David Colker, "Wartime Propaganda is a Powerful Weapon," *Los Angeles Times,* online edition at: *www.latimes.com*, October 11, 2001.

I.II. <u>The Rise of Globalization</u>

Globalization, with particular reference to its role as a generator of capitalism and markets, has emerged as a frequently voiced expression all over the world. Politicians, economists and individuals refer to it as they express both opportunities or tensions and anxieties. They employ it as well to justify action or inaction of political or economic nature. This section reviews the understandings that underline the contemporary reality of globalization, while tracing its early phases of the evolution. It also reflects on the increasing significance of non-state actors on the global stage, and their role in framing foreign state policies.

I.II.I. <u>The Emergence and Implications of Globalization</u>

Globalization is the latest stage in a long accumulation of technological advances that has enabled human beings to conduct their affairs across the world without reference to nationality, government authority, time of day or any physical environment. These activities may be commercial, financial, religious, cultural, social and political; nothing is barred. The effects of these practices on the whole range of humanity's expectations, systems and structures have been and are a heady mixture: they have come and keep coming at different paces in different places; sometimes they create entirely new significant activities, sometimes they share them with older systems and structures; sometimes they induce adaptation, but sometimes they completely erode and destroy. In other words, these effects represent both opportunities and threats.

In an in-depth, thorough analysis, Langhorne attributes globalization to the technological advances that have broken down many physical barriers to worldwide communication that used to limit how much connected or cooperative activity of any kind could happen over long distances.[43] The result of these technological advances, he explains, has been a huge increase in human activities

---

[43] Richard Langhorne, *The Coming of Globalization: Its Evolution and Contemporary Consequences*, 2001, pp. 1-14.

carried on without hindrance across the world; and the consequences are also often described as "globalization," quite plainly when politicians wish to find a useful explanation for action or inaction at particular moments.

An examination of the process and evolution of globalization traces back to the progresses in communication that have accelerated steadily since the early 19th century. Three stages of development occurred. The first was the longest, flowing from the combined effects of applying the steam engine to land and sea transport and the invention and worldwide installation of the electric telegraph. The second, which began during the World War II, was also a combination. The perfection of rocket propulsion led to the ability to launch orbiting satellites. With the invention of the telephone, launching rockets and orbiting satellites, global and reliable communications coverage was assured. The third stage, following briskly in the 1970s, applied the computer, itself being transformed in speed, volume and efficiency by the evolution of the microchip, as both manager and transmitter of the system. The result gave birth to the Internet.

In global communications, the development of digital information transfers was probably the technological advance that mattered most. This advance emerged from the need to safeguard information and systems in the event of nuclear attack and followed from the realization that in order to send data, which is subject to distortion, it should be transmitted digitally if it is to be both quick and reliable. It also become clear that, not like in the early days of computer involvement when its principal use was a tool to keep increasingly complicated systems up and running, the future required the computer itself act as the actual transmitting device.

Following, in 1962 the first steps were taken to bring these developments together, and the idea of sending data digitally in packets was introduced. A few years later (in 1966), the U.S. Defense Advance Research Projects Agency designed the mechanism for putting this principle to work on computer networks. The first form of the contemporary Internet, ARPANET (Advanced Research Projects Agency Networks) was eventually planned and published in 1967.[44] The

---

[44] Richard Langhorne, *The Coming of Globalization*, 2001, p. 9.

outcome network was a combination of computer programs and devices–both hard and soft–used to compress messages into packets and send them over the telephone line. Further simplifications to make the system more broadly available had to be made, along with the World Wide Web and the emergence of search engines, up to the Internet (as we know it) became possible. It represented the completion of the junction between the telephone facilities offered by the orbiting satellite, as well as existing ground based networks, and the computer networked system developed by ARPANET.

These systems have produced a communications revolution at least the equal of that yielded by the train/telegraph combination and with equally momentous consequences. The first phase, playing out during the 19th century, altered the scope of human economic and political activity and created a global distribution of power among the states. In doing so, it significantly increased the power and security of the United States and Russia, and gradually reduced relatively the power of others. However, the scope of government of every size and description was increased and they maintained supervision or control over all communication instruments. This remained the case during the essentially military-driven second phase, serving the needs of the Cold War.

The third and most recent phase, dominated by modern computer technology, placed the instruments of communications above and beyond the control of governments. Such technology was, after all, designed to withstand a nuclear war which governments themselves were deemed unlikely to do, and created a network that serves individuals and their activities rather than specific societies and their authorities. More clearly, activities have been the beneficiaries, and not traditional governmental authorities. As a result, many previously important, even formerly vital, systems of administration–political, economic and social–have been rendered increasingly redundant. It may well also turn out, assumes Langhorne (2001, pp. 10-11), that future historians will attribute the end of the Cold War, at least in part, to the emergence of a self-propelling and universal communications systems.

Whether large or small, all governments have been to some extent bypassed by these events. The advantages the first phase gave to the great land mass states led to no successors, while the second phase has not transferred power and security to a different optimum size of state–so much as drift them away from existing states of any sort. This may lead to the complete reconstruction of the institutions of human society; and if it does so, then the likely patterns will be one of large-scale, global activities, generating their own styles of management and authority, accompanied by small-scale geographically described local mechanisms designed to accomplish the basic minimum of local government.

These circumstances help to explain both the collapse of the Soviet Union and the puzzling weaknesses that seem to affect the United States in its lonely role as only remaining superpower (for the moment). What had once propelled their rise to global dominance and then sustained them both no longer does so: the Soviet Union which was inherently more divided, internally split into pieces and may have further falling yet to do. The United States, which was essentially a unitary structure, survived but sits uncomfortably in such a changed environment, uncertain how to behave. This is chiefly because such predominance arrived suddenly and unexpectedly, after a period of considerable self-doubt, and, even more difficult to interpret, since predominance itself has lost a clear definition.

I.II.I.I. Dimensions of Globalization

Globalization–the worldwide network of interdependence–does not imply universality. In fact, globalization is accompanied by increasing gaps, and in many respects, among the rich and poor. It implies neither homogenization nor equity.

Globalization has a number of dimensions, although economists often write as if it and the world economy were one and the same. Other forms of globalization do have significant effects on our day-to-day lives. The oldest form of globalization, asserts Nye (2002, p. 82), is **environmental interdependence**. The first smallpox epidemic, for instance, is recorded in Egypt in 1350 B.C. The diseases reached China is A.D. 49, Europe after 700, the Americas in 1520, and then Australia in 1789.[45] The plague or Black Death originated in Asia, but its spread killed a quarter to a third of the population of Europe in the 14th century. Europeans carried diseases to the Americas in the 15th and 16th centuries that harmed up to 95% of the indigenous population.[46] And since 1973, thirty previously unknown infectious diseases have emerged, while other familiar diseases have spread geographically in new drug-resistant forms.[47] The spread of foreign species of flora and fauna to new areas has wiped out native species, with efforts to control them costing a fortune a year.[48]

Not all effects of environmental globalization, on the other hand, are adverse. For example, nutrition and cuisine in both Europe and Asia benefited from the importation of such new world crops as potatoes, corn and tomatoes. In addition, the green revolution agricultural technology of the past few decades has helped poor farmers all over the planet.[49]

Global climate change affects, as well, the lives of people everywhere. In early 2001, scientists from around the world reported new evidence that most of the warming observed over the last fifty years is attributable to human activities, and that average global temperatures in the 21st century are projected to increase. That signals to possible mounting sever variations in climate, with too much water in some regions, and not enough in others. Furthermore, the rate at which the sea level rose in the last century was ten times faster than the average rate over the last three millennia.[50]

---

[45] William J. Broad, "Smallpox: The Once and Future Scourge?" *The New York Times*, June 15, 1999, F1.

[46] Jared Diamond, *Guns, Germs and Steel: The Fates of Human Societies,* New York: W.W. Norton, 1998, pp. 202, 210.

[47] United Kingdom Ministry of Defense, *The Future Strategic Context for Defense,* London, 2001, p. 6.

[48] The foot and mouth disease that damaged Europe livestock in 2001 reflects an example where "a virus finding on natural defenses was able to propagate at an alarming rate." Barry James, "Mischievous Species Capitalize on Globalization," *IHT,* May 21, 2001, 1.

[49] Alfred Crosby, *The Columbian Exchange: Biological and Cultural Consequences of 1492,* Westport, CT: Greenwood Press, 1972.

[50] Craig Smith, "150 Nation's Start Groundwork for Global Warming Policies," *The New York Times*, January 18, 2001, A7.

Another form of globalization is **military globalization**. It implies networks of interdependence in which force, or the threat of force, is employed. The world wars of the 20th century are a case in point. The global strategic interdependence between the United States and the Soviet Union during the Cold War was acute and well recognized. Not only did it create alliances, but also either side could have used intercontinental missiles to destroy the other within minutes. Such interdependence, continues Nye (2002, p. 83), was distinctive not because it was totally new, but because the scale and speed of the potential conflict were so enormous. Today, networks involving "terrorists" or "freedom fighters" constitute a new form of military globalization.

With migration representing a concrete example, **social globalization** is the spread of people, cultures, images and ideas. In the 19th century, around eighty million people crossed oceans to new homes–far more than in the 20th century.[51] Four principal religions, namely, Buddhism, Christianity, Islam and Judaism have spread across great distances worldwide over the last two centuries, as have ideas and beliefs.

Political globalization is manifest in the spread of constitutional arrangements, and in the development of international rules and institutions. Consider for example the importance of the global spread of political ideas such as the anti-slavery movement in the 19th century, anti-colonialism after World War II, and the environmental and feminist movements today. Also of importance are the anti-globalization and anti-war movements and demonstrations that are growing in numbers day after day.

More recently is the **globalization of justice**, reflected in the International Criminal Law. The guidelines, titled the "Princeton Principles on Universal Jurisdiction,"[52] are arranged under fourteen provisions governing all aspects of international trials, from definitions of crime to disputes between governments

---

[51] David Held et al., *Global Transformations: Politics, Economics and Culture,* Stanford: Stanford University Press, 1999, pp. 295-96.

[52] See "Standardizing Human Rights Trials," by Barbara Crossette, *IHT*, July 24, 2001, 5. Also consult: http://www.wws.princeton.edu/wws_headlines.html.

over the accused. Principle One defines universal jurisdiction; Principle Two covers the crimes to be considered, covering privacy, slavery, war crimes, crimes against peace, crimes against humanity, genocide and torture; and Principle Three allows for the use of universal jurisdiction by a country even if its laws do not specifically provide for it.[53]

Once again, globalization is the result of both technological progress and government policies that have reduced barriers to international exchange. While the United States may have been a major launching engine and beneficiary of the current phase of globalization, it no longer enjoys solid grip or absolute control over it.

I.II.II. Globalization and the Role of National Governments

In an age when the communications revolution has enabled manufacturing to be located anywhere on the globe, the role of a government remains significant, though it is reduced in terms of its macroeconomic-decision making capacity. It is even rather enhanced in respect of the policies it adopts that endorse encouragement for global companies to locate part of their operation within its territory. The state does not, therefore, disappear, but is *downsized*. With workforces cheaper elsewhere and no less usable, vastly improved communications are making the use of precisely focused small-scale suppliers more efficient than in-house provision. As a result, the number of less skilled employment in the developed world falls, while advanced societies provide even more skills, knowledge and the products of higher technology.

Eventually, this situation raises problems and concerns of adjustment of global wage levels. At a conservative estimate, states Langhorne (2001, p. 24), "the move to market-oriented production in the newly industrializing work is going to

---

[53] In this respect, the Israeli Foreign Ministry in late July 2001 clearly warned government, army and security officials to be careful in choosing destinations when traveling abroad over concerns that certain countries (notably Belgium, Britain and Spain) might be prepared to charge ranking Israelis with violating Palestinians' human rights. See: Clyde Haberman, "Israel Warns Officials of Legal Risks Abroad," *IHT*, July 30, 2001, 1.

increase the labor force by 1.2 billion during the next generation." The vast majority of these workers at present earn less than three dollars a day–if not less. Consider how their interests are to be reconciled with those of 250 million North American and European workers who earn 30 times as much. According to Langhorne (2001, p. 24), some commentators foresee wage depression of up to 50% in some areas, and/or unemployment reaching 20% in developed economies.

With such circumstances, governments need to decide whether to resist or to accept the consequences of globalization. Resistance would mean either forcing down domestic wage levels in order to restore a competitive labor market and bring about the return of jobs, though at much lower rates of pay, or trying to isolate the domestic economy by means of protection. The first could not be achieved without serious social consequences and the probable breakdown of the political will to maintain the policies required in the face of massive public objections to the *wholesale* lowering of living standards. Protectionism, the second, bears a strong risk of being unsustainable in a globalized economic environment. In other words, both will be difficult to realize. The tit-for-tat penalties that protectionism induces would be economically unpleasant in themselves and futile,[54] given the fact that isolation of every kind in today's world is impossible to maintain.

This issue becomes of major concern whenever there is a public discussion of the dilemma all governments find themselves in as they try to determine policies and priorities in their national interest. Even more difficult is to reach consensus on what "national interest" actually is. The effects of globalization now mean that part of the national economic interests may be bound up in the fate of externally based

---

[54] Consider for example the decision and fruitless action of the Iraqi government in April 2002 to stop oil exportations in support of the Palestinian Case. Many of the world's main producers are overwhelmingly dependent on oil revenues, and have more to lose from an embargo than many of the customers. That is, an embargo is more likely to be felt within the oil-production country than it would abroad. The roughly 778,000 barrels per day of Iraqi oil imported by American companies, through third parties amounts to about 13% of all U.S. oil imports, which total about 5.8 million barrels a day. According to the U.S. Energy Information Agency, the top suppliers of oil to the United States during a typical year (2000) were: Canada at 1.18 million barrels/day; Saudi Arabia at 1.57 million barrels/day; Venezuela at 1.55 million barrels/day; and Mexico at 1.37 million barrels/day. In other words, Iraq's decision to cut oil exports for 30 days, 'or until Israel withdraws from Palestinian territories,' was in fact ineffective without Saudi Arabia and Kuwait (who had rejected Iraq's call to use oil as a weapon). Also, Iran and Libya (two other major oil producers) had backed Iraq's move only in words. See: "Iraq stops oil flow over Israeli action," at: *www.msnbc.com*, April 8, 2002.

companies partly operating within national territories. Take an example: how American or French is a Dell computer assembled in Paris? Or to what extent are foreign banks and their operations in a given country independent?

Policies that accept the potential advantages of globalization, on the other hand, will mean not attempting to stem the outward flow of manufacturing industry to cheaper labor markets, but concentrating on the development of ever more highly advanced technology and knowledge, both in educational and technological terms. "The intention has to be that the wealth thus generated will create inward-flowing resources sufficient to maintain a deliberately generous reconstructed system of social welfare at the expense of employment," explains Langhorne (2001, p. 25). The message of such a response for lifestyle expectations, most specifically the meaning of work, for educational practices and for the fabric of society generally is revolutionary, but it may be a less destructive revolution than that inherent in the possible results of policies of resistance.

Therefore, governments are entitled to an essential task in making the global economic system work both better and more acceptable. First and foremost in this is the uneasy responsibility of arranging socially just relief for those economically destroyed by the advance of globalization, thus preserving the basic fabric of society. This is part of the provision of social capital and common grounds. And while governments may not be the sole agencies for achieving this, they are the most important in their localities.

Similarly, governments are the initiators of policies and regulations promoting environmental protection and health and safety standards. They need to improve their information and statistical data-providing services. They need to set the rules governing the economic environment in an effort to restrain the excesses of the market and discourage corruption. They need, as well, to be the facilitators of efficient factor and product markets and the guardians of the legal and commercial institutions ruling these markets, in addition to the rules and standards that oversee market transactions. It is, even more, important for governments to follow the provision of constantly upgraded communications and other physical infrastructures so as to offer the best possible immobile assets to capital that might thus be encouraged to import its mobile assets and so boost employment.

Encouraging innovation, particularly among individuals and small to medium-size enterprises, is another essential and beneficial action of a similar kind. Governments have the essential means of protecting national economic interests at international forums such as the World Trade Organization (WTO) and the International Monetary Fund (IMF), even if their roles are becoming more problematic. Generally speaking, what is lost in terms of economic sovereignty and the ability to pursue macroeconomic policies is balanced by new responsibilities created by the outbreak of global capitalism.

The need for governments is therefore not disappearing, but being reconfigured. Populations, as far as they are concerned, may look at the resulting changes as signs of serious loss of authority. And it is this sense of losing a role, concludes Langhorne (2001, p. 27), which raises the problem of decaying political legitimacy and at the same time makes it more difficult for governments to accommodate themselves to their contemporary responsibilities.

Setting local rules, relieving distress, doing everything possible to stimulate inward investment, even creating the general moral and political atmosphere in which global capitalism operates locally, is simply not traditional sovereignty. It is, yet, another contradiction of globalization that national governments are both losers and gainers. The losses have led to political weakness, quite sufficient to make their current and coming responsibilities difficult to fulfill. The following section examines certain cases to help us better comprehend the political consequences of globalization.

I.II.II.I. Russia

The presence of political legitimacy in any state is and has always been the product of a domestic coalition of interests based on the belief that the abandonment of some particular desires, traditions and loyalties by each local interest was worth it for the sake of the advantages conferred by belonging to the larger group. It was the collapse of this kind of coalition rather than the failure of a given ideology that ended the Soviet Union.

Former president Mikhail Gorbachev plainly recognized the domestic system of the Soviet Union had ceased to deliver the social, economic and security benefits that justified its existence in the face of a multitude of particular issues–cultural, ethnic and religious–divided all across the land from Eastern Europe to Eastern Asia. He attempted to reform it in an aim to deliver those benefits before their absence brought on disaster, yet failed to do so due to a system inflexible and too corrupt at the time. What followed has partly been the result of particular conditions and traditions within the Russian Federation, which in the face of faltering rule has had a historic tendency to go into a state of suspended political and administrative animation, until heard out of it by some over-whelming event or ruler.

Interestingly as well, however, is that it has seemed natural to an important group within Russia to replace the communist structure with economic and political versions of what had served the capitalist world as a result of so many years of development. It may be at least as remarkable in accounting for the fragility of democratic machinery in Russia and even more the utter collapse of any incipient free mark economy–each made more or less conditions of outside assistance–which both notions arise from highly traditional ideas about what a state structure ought to be like. But if those notions are themselves now quite unreliable guides, they may currently be of minor significance. The mixture of some unhelpful Russian traditions, which elevate the role of corruption and degrade the rule of law, with the effective imposition of structurally inappropriate compositions, has had devastating impacts on both Russians and their creditors as well.

Russia is now expected to demonstrate how to adjust the state institutions in order to suit contemporary circumstances, when to do so could easily involve the fatal dissolution of the national government, as it exists, leading to the evolution of an entirely new form of entity. Otherwise, by resisting the flow, it will itself court public disorder and violent responses.

I.II.II.II. The United States of America

Unlike the Soviet Union, the United States is not an existing entity that bears the consequences of having been an empire in the past. In other words, it is not an agglomeration of historically distinguishable ethnicities and societies, presided over or forcibly held together by a master. Though it does have clear social and ethnic divisions, they were not created in the same way as those within the Russian Empire, nor has its profound geographical variations–so far–stimulated serious regional focuses of loyalty to match those of Europe or India. It is politically a genuine federation, capable of devolution at any level required, determinable by constitutional practice. This aspect is already in use, where recent years have seen a reduction of federal power and a resumption of formerly yielded powers by individual state governments. Also noteworthy is the hostility to big government–a feature easy to accommodate in the United States.

That stated, the constant pressure to be economically successful in the global environment is felt no less. In common with other societies, there is anxiety about the quality of education because of an increasing sense of comparative failure in equipping students with the necessary intellectual tools of survival in the contemporary world. This stems from the fact that the degree of technological education present in a society has become part of its ability to attract its share of the loose capital around global markets. The result is a tension between the increasing poverty of government whose tax base has been eroding and their certainty that more resources need to be placed on education at every level.

The United States is certainly not immune from the deeply difficult problems inherent in the falling prices of labor worldwide. In fact, its internally high wage levels make it a potentially serious victim; and a protectionist tax and duty system would do no more than postpone the inevitable lowering of the American average wage. The "traditionally autarkic structure of the USA economy has been superseded by events and is beyond recovery," emphasizes Langhorne (2001, p. 61), where "its global trading imbalance makes it crucial that the USA remains an irresistible object of inward investment." This means that the United States has also lost independent control of its economy. Bilateral and multilateral agreements concluded by the United States, like the North American Free Trade Agreement (NAFTA), arise more of consequences of such a change. Yet, and because of its great size and traditional wealth, the United States needs to consider more seriously the essential political task of raising public understanding and acceptance of what is really happening along with the growing limitations on what the government, like any government, can actually do.

I.II.II.III. The European Union

The case of the European Union is interesting to consider. Here we have an increasing potential of economic activity within the world's markets–thanks to its mounting technological inventions, its sound cultural systems, and the high living standards of its people, in general. This does not imply that it has not suffered from severe structural unemployment, endured extreme pressure on the future of its social welfare systems from decreasing population numbers, nor went through an easy period finding remedies to the political, security and economic problems resulting from the collapse of the Soviet Union. As a matter of fact, it is encountering a particular difficult internal complication arising from a mismatch between the demands of the treaties that provide the grounds for the further integration of the European Union and the weakening, popular support for them.

The provisions of the European Treaties from Rome (1957) to Maastricht (1992) and to Amsterdam (1997) are based on a principal assumption tracing back to the international circumstances of the first phase of the Cold War. The assumption at that time was to assure political and economic security by creating a super large state, namely Europe, as an entity. Particularly in good economic conditions, such logic enjoyed popular support, and where it did not so explicitly, perceived economic advantages that provided alternatives or start-up ground for consent. The last expression of such an evolution is clearly pronounced in the

Amsterdam Treaty with the introduction of the single currency and the common foreign and defense policy.

With these three pillars rending the entity sovereignty, the efforts to realize them in concrete terms are visibly facing obstacles. The common currency is still not inclusive, and after a weak start, hopes are high of keeping it healthy. The common foreign and security policy does not exist, though there were signs of materializing it during the Balkan crisis in the 1990s. These inherently difficult aspects have added to the concerns of governments which are encountering public objections even in core states as Germany and France, where a sense of loss of control along with on-doing high unemployment rates have led to a series of public discontent.

This evolution, with the difficulties surrounding the process of enlarging the European Union, might be interpreted as the result of the surviving strength of states and their persisting political legitimacy. But a deeper examination points that societies do not see enough benefit emerging from *sinking* individual identities into a larger whole because larger entities–themselves–are not doing quite well in the global environment. Consider here the rotting figures at elections and referendums, with a growing atmosphere of contempt for the institutions and at times formerly revered traditions of the state itself. This, indeed, represents a decline in political legitimacy and has been certainly leading to an increasing provincialization. The focus of relevant activity and sometimes a revived focus of ancient loyalties, as long submerged in the larger state for the sake of the advantage conferred by size of territory or population, can certainly often seem to lie in smaller units, even in substates, all proposing considerable less sovereignty for themselves but actually ensuring issues that matter.

Given the illustration of the European Union in view of its particularities, there are, however, other signs of similar tendencies elsewhere around the globe to give ground for assuming that Europe is not in fact different but merely demonstrating sharper cases of this problem. Take as evidence in this discussion, for instance, the Russian Federation, India, Indonesia, and China–countries representing examples of growing concerns of managing significant ethnically complex agglomerations of territory.

I.II.III. The Increasing Role of Non-State Actors and Globalization

However much governments try, both politically and diplomatically, to adapt to new conditions, the efforts still remain limited by the effective absence of a complementary side. Further factors of major influence have emerged as we enter the 21st century. The need to overcome and resolve the concerns surrounding the future of the global environment has created mixtures that require profoundly different initiators of international exchanges from those of the past. If previous circumstances had served to befog the familiar lines of responsibility for international negotiations between and within states, new areas of activity now seem set to erase them altogether. Moreover, they imply structuring new relationships between state governments and the private entities that have generated significant roles for themselves, seeking and gaining political support for their transnational activities.

I.II.III.I. Humanitarian-backed Initiatives

Since the end of the bipolar system in 1989, increasing involvement in the form of humanitarian intervention has emerged. The bipolar system rested on a tension that pushed the leaders of both poles into action of some sort if the domestic situation of a country or of a region began to run out of control. This willingness to re-act has now largely evaporated. Far from tension, societies and rulers are less willing to make sacrifices of people and money resources to maintain domestic or regional order elsewhere.

This evolution has also surfaced as we see an increasing number of crises caused by the collapse or near collapse of nations. States have been suffering a diminution of both internal and external authority because of the revolution guided by global communications. The webs of human activities that have resulted serve to erode the spiritual and practical bases of the state. At one end, the result is nervous discomfort along with uncertainty; and at the other, it is disaster and collapse. This vision, which seems to assure global security at the level of inter-state relations but leaving it threatened with many societies, has cut highways of global relationships.

With this evolution, recent events have proved that practical remedies and sources of help often come from private organizations, mostly from major charities such as Oxfam and *Médicins Sans Frontières (MSF)*, both who have graduated from local to global status. The reasons go beyond the nature of the problems on the ground. State collapse renders the traditional way in which states respond irrelevant, even useless. The same approach applies to the United Nations. The only proper channel for the United Nations to operate is via the government of a state, and when there is no effective existence of a government, the mechanisms of the United Nations encounter formal difficulties.[55] Governments may also see the direct use of tax revenues for external actions as politically infeasible. Here, the *privatization* of humanitarian efforts relieves this issue, allowing charitable actors to multiply.

Once dealing inside a given region or country, providing anything other than direct assistance to individuals, carries a political message of some type to one group–leading intentions to be badly-interpreted, either accidentally or deliberately. In such incidents, the private actors concerned may find themselves distant from the neutral status,[56] whether knowingly or not, and hence put themselves and their staff at safety risk. Changes as these can become both dramatic and harmful. They have brought forward issues of principle specifically regarding the degree to which private entities should or may be involved in raw politics, where this can eventually mean assisting one party in a domestic dispute to advance its own ends in a situation. Such cases constitute an unavoidable consequence of humanitarian crises arising out of state collapses rather than

---

[55] The United Nations may, however, consider a coordinating role to operate through established or already existing local and international private actors.

[56] For a view of the overlapping political and humanitarian role of organizations in Kenya, Rwanda, Burundi, Chechnya and Georgia, for example, see Langhorne (2001, pp. 84-85).

national disasters.[57] And in some, it can lead to a private actor withdrawing from a position where it either knows or fears that it is being used by a particular party for certain political advantages.

Furthermore, events following a state collapse most often involve serious violations of human rights, and eventually puzzle humanitarian private actors over their limits in publicizing such violations as part of their contribution. The attempts to avoid grave misuses of assistance by benefiting parties, accompanied with frequent needs to provide administrative and infrastructure services as a major part of humanitarian assistance, heads towards uneasy diplomacy.

Obviously then, the levels of activity range in scope from medical to essential administrative services. These aspects are pushing private actors to recruit staff with professional and political skill, along with the provision of training. The previous short-tem engagement of amateur officers is currently giving way to longer-term contracts for professional qualified personnel (see 'Greenpeace' job advertisement in Illustration 1.2.). Having joined a certain humanitarian organization out of enthusiasm and particular skill–in a branch of medicine, for instance, staff members find themselves turned by experience (and probably even by formal training) into perhaps unwilling *de facto* diplomats and administrators.[58]

Without doubt, a new layer in the global systems of relations has emerged, evolving from major changes and needs in the machinery of world politics. Reflecting more than a quantitative change, both the level and the manner of its contemporary application have altered in a qualitative way. The equilibrium of power among the entities concerned has drifted from state governments and state organs towards private actors.

---

[57] The attacks in Baghdad in 2003 on the offices of the United Nations (in August) and of the International Committee of the Red Cross (in October) reflect both the risks and possible tragedy of engagement.

[58] Langhorne (2001, p. 88) reviews the importance of the private organizations' perspectives in political forums, which have been demonstrated by their increasing relevance in official delegations or in humanitarian missions in capitals.

Greenpeace is the world's leading environmental campaigning organisation, using non-violent action to confront global problems and force through solutions.

Political Advisor
on Nuclear and Disarmament
Provide the strategic direction for Greenpeace's campaigns on nuclear and disarmament issues.

With 3+ years experience and proven expertise in high level political negotiation, policy development and working on nuclear issues, you could make a huge impact on the effective delivery of our campaigns on a global scale. You will be **BASED IN AMSTERDAM** for one or two years and travel frequently, but then have the opportunity to transfer to another part of the world.

As well as having a strong belief in our aims and an established network of international, political and media contacts, you must be able to call upon the strength of character, intellect, strategic ability and drive to make things happen. Excellent communication skills are essential, including fluency in English and at least one other language.

For a job description and competency profile search JOBS on the Greenpeace International website:

http://www.greenpeace.org/international_en/jobs

Please send your application, consisting of a covering letter stating how you meet the profile, with your cv to Charlotte Beal, Human Resources at the following email address

Int.recruitment@int.greenpeace.org
Application deadline: 15th May 2005

Illustration 1. 2. Greenpeace job advertisement for professional activists (published in *IHT*, April 25, 2005, 12)

I.II.III.II. International Organizations of Economic and Trade Nature

Organizations with a global economic function have been, too, profoundly affected by globalization. Existing economic organizations have their roots in a former international economic environment in which national governments were the primary cooperative actors, and multinational companies were the primary competitive agents. Today, these roles are becoming reversed. International economic organizations, in the past, were there to make sure that states and their societies gained the best deal that benevolent corporation could impose on private economic competition.

This meant that the main organizations, or measured decisions like the post-Second World War Bretton Woods Agreement on currencies, represented the wishes and actions of states. The International Monetary Fund (IMF), the World Bank, the General Agreement on Trade and Tariffs (GATT)–now the World Trade Organization (WTO)–and the International Labor Organization (ILO) are all associations of states. As decolonization left many new and often less economically developed countries, with a sentiment of discontent towards the world economic order, they created organizations to reflect that view. The result was also association of states in the form of trade blocs. Take, for instance, the European Economic Community (EEC) in Western Europe, the Association of South-East Asian Nations (ASEAN) in Southeast Asia, the North American Free Trade Agreement (NAFTA) in Northern America, and MERCOSUR in South America.

At present, concerns have risen for these organs due to the extent to which their roles have been overtaken by events, emphasizes Langhorne (2001, p. 33). With states no longer beneficiaries of economic globalization, the gainers now are the great global companies as competition alters. Consider the current position of the World Health Organization (WHO). Part of its original purpose was to advance the interests of its member states in health issues and to restrain the disadvantage that followed from the commercial priorities of drug firms. Recent developments now mean that world health may be best improved thanks to cooperation between the Organization acting globally along with drug firms equally acting globally over both research & development and manufacture. This implies, accordingly, abandoning the basic assumption of an inevitable conflict between government and drug manufacturers and, consequently, the idea that the Organization is there to represent the immediate interests of its members rather than the health of individuals.

With the economic structure of the world now different, unstable global markets in stocks, currencies and capital require regulation. Governments, to who regulation or advice or assistance was always applied, may not be able to respond to such treatment. Langhorne (2001, p. 33) illustrates this by referring to the 1998/1999 crisis in Indonesia, attributing the crisis to:

the activities of currency speculators, who hunt in their own global jungle and who are moving on from a killing in Thailand to a new victim.... The element of Greek tragedy in the whole affair came from the fact that the agency whose task was to relieve the crisis, the IMF, could work only according to rules which derived from its origins as an association of state.

The gross sums subject to speculation mounting to more than a trillion dollars a day are, therefore, capable of destabilizing the efforts of both the IMF and the World Bank. Governments have not been successful in introducing schemes to control, rigid enough, capital flows nor trade in goods and services. This may partly be because of the risk of market failure, on the one hand, and because recipient countries may not be even able to absorb such flows, on the other hand.

In addition, general issue-based entities prevail that essentially coordinate action conducted by regional or national institutions in the fields of, for instance, environment, air traffic control and health–with hopes of emerging globally envisioned strategies. Others are basically information gatherers and holders. The United Nations and the Organization for Economic Cooperation and Development (OECD) are examples of such bodies that can act as initiators of international discussions.

Finally, there are those organizations like the WTO that are essentially rule settlers. The task of the WTO has been extended to include foreign direct investment, intellectual property rights, environment and competition policies as well as cross-border trade in goods and services. Its global scope means that it will have to deal with disputes on these issues between international organs (such as the European Union and ASEAN) as well as disputes between states and such organs, or between state and state.

Effective management of a global economy in the interest of its increasingly numerous and vocal participants can only be derived from a balanced mixture of sub-national, national and global representation in fully global organizations. With the creation of such a hybrid being the task of the current century, what we now have is an irreversibly global economic context, lacking any machinery for managing it. If it evolves, the benefits of globalization will predominate, but if it does not, then the inherent risk of economic and political chaos could become a reality.

In any reform there will continue to be a significant, though perhaps lesser, role for national governments to play, at least as guardians of local economic rules and transparent and uncorrupt domestic administration. Even more seriously, they will seek out ways of engaging with the new sources of economic power and influence which globalization has created. This is not easy since the global markets are just beginning to see that their own effectiveness and convenience can only be secured if they generate their own cooperative systems to regulation and possession of legitimate authority, in order to combat their chaotic volatility.

Hence, when this does happen a role reversal will have taken place. National governments, who used to be the source of cooperation, have already become serious competitors at many levels for the inward investment made available, while companies and the global markets in which they operate, who used to compete, have become the more ready source of much effective cooperation. With tentative signs of this development in the global stock market, in global banking and in the management of the Internet, none has yet surfaced in the currency markets.

I.II.III.III. <u>Private Profitable Enterprises</u>

An entity functioning globally has become even more desirable than a multinational corporation once was. In the 1950s, multinational corporations were generally national-based concerns, with distinctively national characteristics. They operated multinationally, but there was little intra-firm trade or foreign direct investment between the subsidiaries. They dealt straightforwardly in the economic landscape and worked with each other and national governments from that posture. Now, that posture has changed.

Consider, for example, the tendency of formerly national airlines to go global in their cooperative partnerships and to compete by putting emphasis on the global reach which those associations give them. Their symbols as well tend to drop the resonance with a national tradition and substitute motifs which are either global in significance or have none at all. A particular illustration of this is the redesign of the tail planes of the British Airways aircraft in the late 1990s, where the distinctively British national marking gave way to a wide range of colorful but entirely abstract designs.[59]

Multinational entities increasingly view the world as a single entity for obtaining suppliers, finance and for providing them with markets. The global company has subsumed the multinational both in its style and operationally because of the arrival of fully global markets, the availability of a global labor force, the emergence of global electronic commerce and, with some commodities, the existence of a global culture creating global fashions. Furthermore, there is no longer any need for a solidly hierarchical structure of administration, as links are created horizontally rather than vertically—in a feature that tends to flatten out the systems and greatly reduce the size of the central offices of major corporations.

Likewise, there is a conjunction between the development of regionalism and the desire for global companies to have manufacture done in the most advantageous place, wherever it may. Communication and administration flexibility now means that it is better to create global coalitions of regionally based firms, whose local existence is socially desirable and political acceptable as well as be the object of locally decided advantages—in tax breaks of favorable variations in zoning regulations, for instance. It is here possible to assemble the needs of the global company and rising significance of regional and local activities, cultural, economic and political. The capacity to *think global and act local* also affects what is produced in addition to where and how it is produced.[60]

The emergence of a global culture is balanced by reaction to it, and to global economic and political power, which emphasizes local particularities: of tradition,

---

[59] Example cited from Richard Langhorne, *The Coming of Globalization*, 2001, p. 28.

[60] Marketers learn to weave their products into the local culture by hiring local managers and adapting everything from packaging, to serving sizes, to flavors, and even to the traditions of the local market. McDonald's Corporation, thus, for example, sells *Aloo tikka* in Bombay, *Teriyaki* burgers in Tokyo, flatbread *McArabia* in Amman, and *Kosher* McNuggets in Tel Aviv.

of taste, of expectation. The flexibility of the contemporary global firm allow it to produce goods and services that are tailored to local preferences, and gain competitive advantage thereby, while also serving global markets with other products. Another example of the contemporary economic paradoxes at work is the effect this has had to create a renaissance of the small to medium-size firm, in a world that also sees a procession of major global mergers, by which the giant becomes even more dominant in the market for high technology and branded goods and services.

This emergence of the new-style global firm with its concentration on core activities has changed the essentially adversarial nature of the previous competition between international companies. One result has been the birth of inter-firm alliances. With this rapid increase, the intention is to improve penetration of new markets, share costs and speed up innovation process. The same feature is seen in research & development. At a time of vastly accelerated technological obsolescence, guiding to closer interdependence between cutting edge technologies and more immediate effects of research & development» on manufacturing processes, both the importance and the cost of the exercise have risen. The result here has been wide cooperation in the field of research & development between firms, despite the fact that their ultimate fate is to be commercial rivals. The developments do certainly pose difficult problems–over concerns when to cooperate and when to compete. Yet the plasticity in these notions is creating a new kind of alliance capitalism in which there is no mutual exclusivity between them, but a synergy of competition and cooperation.

Respectively here, Chaigneau outlines the importance of "risk managers" in mastering and signaling out four types of risks: *le risque politique, le risque de marché, le risque de liquidité et le risque de change.*[61] In that context, the eventual adjustments to new global conditions being made by multinational firms are more

---

[61] That is: 'the political risk, the market risk, the capital risk, and the change risk'. Pascal CHAIGNEAU, «Le nouveau profil du risque international» in *Gestion des risques internationaux,* ('The New Profile of International Risk', published in *Management of International Risks*), sous la direction de Pascal CHAIGNEAU (Administrateur Général du Centre d'Etudes Diplomatiques et Stratégiques), Paris: Economica, 2001, pp. 11-12.

sensitive and successful than the more stumbling responses being made by national governments.

A remarkable aspect of this tendency arises out of the problem of corruption, where some degree of it has always been endemic in both government and commerce throughout history. The more societies became economically and politically developed, the more damaging and inconvenient extensive corruption appeared to be. It accordingly became part of the modern state's duty to legislate against it (and enforce that legislation). Corruption, in its traditional form, continued and continues in less developed areas, where, as globalization brings brisk business opportunities, it becomes less and less acceptable and a perceptible hindrance both to a genuine free market and to the rule of law in the Western sense, which itself is a crucial contribution to the context for successful economic development.

For the national governments concerned, weakened by other aspects of globalization, the reforms of corruption prove to be too difficult to achieve in any adequate extent. In an attempt to limit bribery, all thirty members of the OECD, along with Argentina, Brazil, Bulgaria and Chile, signed the Convention on Combating Bribery of Foreign Public Officials in International Business Transactions. The Bribery Convention[62] was adopted in 1997 and came into force on February 15, 1999.

I.II.III.IV. The Growth and Influence of Capitalism

One important way in which contemporary globalization is different from the emergence of the globally interdependent economy of around the year 1900 is the fundamental fact that the routine use of global communication has passed out of the sole control or regulation of governments and companies. This means that the relationship between individuals has now become direct and horizontally expressed

---

[62] See: *Addressing the Challenges of International Bribery and Fair Competition 2001: The Third Annual Report Under Section Six of the International Anti-Bribery and Fair Competition Act of 1998.* Executive Summary. U.S. Department of Commerce: International Trade Administration, July 2001, at: http://www.mac.doc.gov/tcc.

across the world. The new beneficiaries are their activities, not their authorities. Yet, the process is far from complete. There are more people in the world who do not have access to the Internet than those who do; at a time the activities of those who do have become so compellingly important that a sort of revolution has occurred.

Among the main characteristics of that revolution are the highly contradictory results. At the basic level, there is a growing contradiction between the huge benefits enjoyed by those who are wired and the loss of opportunity enforced on those who are not. Another contradiction is that the creation of a single world based on an integrated and comprehensive communications systems creates pressure and opportunities both being felt and require to be managed at a global level. This, in return, has important implications on future world governance, as well as on global markets, government economic policies and multinational organization structures.

The emergence of a large number of states almost universally pursuing market-oriented policies accompanied by liberalization and deregulation has produced a remarkable platform of shared attitudes and policies. The reduction of barriers to cross-border transactions and the deregulation and privatization of a variety of domestic markets have been significant. Between 1991 and 1997, for instance, of the 151 countries reported by the United Nations Conference on Trade and Development (UNCTAD) to have made changes to their internal systems, 135 introduced fewer regulations and only 16 increased them.[63]

Obviously, this is not to say that different societies and geographical areas do not pursue different forms of capitalism. To take two widely separated examples: that of Malaysia is not the same as that of Argentina. Nor has every society embraced the market with full-hearted assent. The Russian Federation is a noteworthy example of pervasive doubt about the benefits of global capitalism, as it is equally an example of the apparent impossibility of a government escaping from it.

---

[63] Stated in Richard Langhorne, *The Coming of Globalization*, 2001, p. 16.

Langhorne (2001, p. 17) lists the most significant features of global capitalism. Cross-border transactions have become "deeper, more extensive and more interconnected than ever before." Resources, capabilities, goods and services have become more mobile than ever before. Multinational enterprises create and disseminate more wealth, as well as originate and produce in more countries than ever before. Consider, for instance, the fact that at least a dozen transnational corporations have annual sales that are greater than the gross national products (GNP) of more than half the states in the world. The sales of Mitsubishi are larger than the GNP of Vietnam, the sales of Shell are three times the GNP of Guatemala, and those of Siemens are six times the GNP of Jamaica.[64]

Accordingly, an increasing real and financial volatility in cross-border markets is resulting–particularly clear in capital and currency markets. The character of cross-border transactions, notably in services, has been permanently changed by digital environment and the onset of e-commerce.

In view of the technological basis that globalization has brought, global capitalism, furthermore, has other distinctive features. The technological advances in communications have vastly increased the significance of the economic asset represented by "knowledge" and downgraded the importance of "things" in the global economy. This shift has been the chief motor of contemporary development. A computing skill may be more precious than auto engines. This is partly because of the needs of the system itself: to use it, operate, administer and to improve it have evoked both a new era of highly technical knowledge and a new manufacturing industry to support it. It is also important because the very existence of the system makes the diffusion of all forms of knowledge more or less immediate. Except in training and education with highly advantageous effects, knowledge is no longer limited to a territorial location in terms of access or use

A further notable feature is that although the production of many enterprises spreads across the globe, a greater concentration of some kinds of economic activity has appeared both between and within some countries than has before. And

---

[64] Data based on the *CIA World Factbook 2000*, at: http://www.cia.gov/cia/publications/factbook, and *Hoover's Handbook of World Business 2001*, Austin: Reference Press, 2001.

last, all forms of alliance and cooperative ventures, within and between firms, between governments and between firms and non-market institutions have become more important elements in the global economic system than ever. Transactional flows of capital, goods, services, technology and information have now acquired speed, intensity, comprehensive and self-reinforcing relevance and a fully global reach that make them qualitatively different from their precursors of even recent decades.

In earlier conditions, different economic units, blocs or states could not completely evade the effects of what was going on by the others, and were inextricably linked to a financial system based on the single currency of the Gold Standard. During the great depression of the 1930s, it was discovered that attempting a controlled economic isolation failed to work. Meanwhile during the post-war period, the capitalist world moved gradually but with increasing speed towards the general deregulation of the 1980s. The implosion of the communist bloc after 1989 globalized the pursuit of basically capitalist economic policy, though causing some parallel economic collapses in doing so. The enduring nature of capitalism has not, however, been solely the result of the collapse of communism, nor was the collapse of communism solely caused by the advance of global capitalism. Global capitalism has also demanded the effects of the current communications revolution to come into existence.

This can clearly be seen in the emergence of the global markets–in stocks, in currencies, in banking–and in the changing structures of multinational entities. A substantial de-territorialization of the labor market has mainly taken place, where there is no necessary connection between the points of ownership of a company, the point of manufacture of its goods–in whole or in part–and the point of their sale. Even the point of acquisition is nearly globalized thanks to electronic consumer purchasing. One may now manufacture where it is cheapest and most convenient to do so, administer in the same way, buy and pay similarly.[65]

---

[65] Consider, for instance, an American personal computer (PC) sold in Europe, with its memory chips from Japan and South Korea, a microprocessor from Costa Rico, a disk drive from Singapore, and a keyboard from Taiwan–all assembled in Ireland.

This emergence of a global labor market is the nearly wholesale departure of clothing manufacture to Asian sites, attracted by less regulated conditions and cheaper labor. Also, the ability of Indian educated computer programmers to deal with the 2K problem effectively transfers most of the work from the highly developed economies that most require it to India, which in practice needs it somewhat less, yet nonetheless, profits greatly. Other forms of manufacture show similar signs. The trend towards highly subsidiarized operations, in which quite small parts of a mechanism made on the opposite side of the world and then assembled in another different place under the management of a company physically based in yet another location, is significant in this regard.

This is an example of a commonly observed contemporary phenomenon; and with the pressures coming globally, the response is often paradoxically local or regional. In economic terms, this means the conditions an investing company regards as most attractive are likely to be set by factors that are highly localized: wage levels, environmental conditions, taxation, workforce education level, building standards.

In general terms, the effects of all this have been favorable. For less developed societies in particular, globalization introduces a wide range of opportunities in respect of employment and investment, and perhaps in the longer term, some leveling in comparative knowledge. What is globally accessible can be available to everyone and enables some remarkably rapid catching up to take place. Available capital and electronic information can be a sort of leveler, and, in less developed societies, they can level up. Rapid expansion, on the other hand, puts huge strains on underdeveloped infrastructures, underdeveloped financial systems and on inefficient domestic administration. The cumulative effect of this and often-endemic corruption can lead to crises. For more developed societies, these factors may not apply, but the short-term impacts, mainly on employment, may be more damaging.

I.II.IV. Globalization and U.S. Power

The United States plays a central role in all dimensions of contemporary globalization. At its core, globalization refers to worldwide networks of interdependence. And a network is simply a series of connections of points in a system, but can take a number of shapes and architectures. An airline hub and spokes, a spider web, an electricity grid, a metropolitan bus system, and the Internet are all networks, though they vary in terms of connection centralization and complexity. Network theorists argue that, under most conditions, centrality in networks convey power. That is, the hub controls the spokes.[66] Some see globalization as a network with an American hub and spokes reaching out to the rest of the world.

There is some truth in this illustration, as the United States is central to all four forms of globalization: economic (with the largest capital market), military (the only country with global reach), social (the heart of pop culture), and environmental (the biggest polluter, where its political support is necessary for effective action on environmental issues). On American's influence on globalization, Zakaria describes it as following:

> American stands at the center of this world of globalization. It seems unstoppable. If you close the borders, America comes in through the mail. If you censor the mail, it appears in the fast food and faded jeans. If you ban the products, it seeps in through satellite television. Americans are so comfortable with global capitalism and consumer culture that we cannot fathom just how revolutionary these forces are.[67]

While globalization has contributed to that current position of the United States, if may not continue to do so throughout the century. Today globalization reinforces American power; overtime it may weaken that power.

---

[66] See: Daniel Brass and Marlene Burckhardt, "Centrality and Power in Organizations" in Nitin Nohria and Robert Eccles, eds., *Networks and Organizations,* Boston: Harvard Business School Press, 1992.

[67] Fareed Zakaria, "Islam and the West: The Roots of Rage," *Newsweek*, October 15, 2001, 24.

Those who advocate a hegemonic or unilateralist foreign policy are attracted to this image of global networks. Yet there are at least four reasons, according to Nye (2002, p. 92), where it would be a mistake to envisage contemporary networks of globalization simply in terms of the hub and spokes of an American empire that creates dependency for smaller countries. The metaphor below is useful as one perspective on globalization, although it does not provide the whole picture.

First, the architecture of interdependence networks varies according to the different dimensions of globalization. The hub-and-spokes metaphor fits military globalization more closely than economic, environmental, or social globalization because American dominance is so much greater in that domain. Even in the military area, most countries are more concerned about threat from neighbors than from the United States, a fact that leads many to call in American global power to redress local balances. The American presence, for instance, is welcome in most of East Asia as a balance to rising Chinese power. That is, the hub-and-spokes metaphor fits power relations better than it portrays threat relation, and balancing behavior is heavily influenced by perceptions of threats. If instead of the role of welcome balancer, the United States came to be seen as a threat, it would lose the influence that stems from providing military protection to balance others.

At the same time, in economic networks a hub-and-spokes image is inaccurate. In trade, for example, Europe and Japan are significant alternative nodes in the global network. Environmental globalization–as in the future of endangered species in Africa or the Amazonian rain forest in Brazil–is also less centered on the United States. Where the United States is seen as a major ecological threat, as in production of carbon dioxide, it is less welcome, and there is often resistance to American policies.

Second, the hub-and-spokes image may mislead about an apparent absence of reciprocity or two-way vulnerability. Even militarily, the ability of the United States to strike any place in the world does not make it invulnerable, as learned on September 11, 2001. Other countries, groups and even individuals can employ unconventional use of force or, in the long term, develop weapons of mass destruction with delivery systems that would enable them to threaten the United

States (where nuclear or mass biological attacks would be more lethal than hijacked aircraft).

Global economic and social transactions, as explained earlier, are making it increasingly difficult to control borders. Opening to economic flows simultaneously implies opening to new forms of dangers. And while the United States has the largest economy, it is both sensitive and potentially vulnerable to the spread of contagious in global capital markets, as discovered in the 1997 Asian financial crisis. In the social dimension, the United States may export more popular culture than any other country, but it also imports more ideas and immigrants than most countries.

Environmentally, the country is sensitive and vulnerable to actions abroad that it cannot control. Even if the United States took costly measures to reduce emissions of carbon dioxide at home, it would still be vulnerable to climate change induced by coal-fired power plants in China.

A third problem with the simply hub-and-spokes dependency image which is common among hegemonists is that it fails to identify other important connections and nodes in global networks. New York is important in the flows of capital to emerging markets, but so are London, Frankfurt and Tokyo. In terms of social and political globalization, Paris is more important to Gabon than Washington is; Moscow is more important in Central Asia. In such situations, American influence is often limited.

Only a few feet above the sea level in the Indian Ocean, the Maldives Islands, in another example, are particularly sensitive to the potential effects of producing carbon dioxide in the rest of the world. They are also completely vulnerable, since their sensitivity has to do with geography, not policy. Sometime in the future China will become more relevant to the Maldives than the United States is, because they will eventually overgrow the United States in the production of greenhouse gases. And therefore, the United States will not be the center of the world for several countries.

Finally, Nye (2002, p. 94) states, the hub-and-spokes model may blind the United States to the changes that are taking place in the architecture of the global markets. Network theorists again argue that central players gain power most when there are structural holes–gaps in communications–between other participants. When the spokes cannot communicate with each other without going through the hub, the central position of the hub provides power. On the other hand, when the spokes can communicate and coordinate directly with each other, the hub becomes less powerful. The growth of the Internet provides these inexpensive alternatives connections that fill the gaps.[68] As the architecture of global networks evolves from a hub-and-spokes model to a widely distributed form similar to that of the Internet, the structural holes shrink, reducing the structural power of the central state.

The United States still promotes and benefits, for the meantime, from economic globalization where trade policy remains an area that touches a broad range of American interests. Trade no longer follows the flag, but rather electronic pathways that have largely been created and exploited by American businesses from satellites to high-capacity undersea cables and wireless telephones.

The American economy not only exports internationally; it has moved its operations overseas. For instance, America Online (AOL) markets its services in eight languages on all continents; General Motors has more employees in India than in the United States; London has more American banks than New York City; and the largest retail chain in Japan is Seven Eleven.[69] Among the 100 global brands that had a value greater than $1 billion in 2001, 62 came from the United States in terms of ownership, 27 from Europe, 6 from Japan, 3 from Switzerland,

---

[68] See: Ronald Burt, *Structural Holes: The Social Structure of Competition*, Cambridge, MA: Harvard University Press, 1992, Chapter 1.

[69] Examples taken from Wilson Dizard, Jr., "Digital Diplomats," in *iMP Magazine*, July 23, 2001. Also, while restrictions against marketing cigarettes to teenagers have been tightened severely in the U.S. and other major industrial nations, many tobacco companies, including the American giant Philip Morris, have continued practices in several countries such as Jordan, Russia, South Africa, Costa Rica, and Albania, that make it relatively easy for children to obtain cigarettes by offering free packages and samples–in an aim "to increase the number of smokers in developing countries and elsewhere aboard because in the United States they are losing their market." See: Greg Winter, "Tobacco Lures World's Teens: Free Cigarettes Find Their Way to Underage Smokers," *IHT*, August 25-26, 2001, 1.

and 1 from each South Korea and Bermuda.[70] Three years later, in 2004, some 58 brands were American, 30 were European, 7 were Japanese, 4 Swiss, and 1 South Korean.[71]

The first 20 top brands in 2004 were, in order: *Coca-Cola* (U.S.), *Microsoft* (U.S.), *IBM* (U.S.), *GE* (U.S.), *Intel* (U.S.), *Disney* (U.S.), *McDonald's* (U.S.), *Nokia* (Finland), *Toyota* (Japan), *Marlboro* (U.S.), *Mercedes* (Germany), *Hewlett-Packard* (U.S.), *Citibank* (U.S.), *American Express* (U.S.), *Gillette* (U.S.), *Cisco* (U.S.), *BMW* (Germany), *Honda* (Japan), *Ford* (U.S.), and *Sony* (Japan).

I.II.V. The Anti-Globalization Current

Throughout history, successful social protest movements have had one thing in common–a clear, simple message and objective. Whether it was a women's rights movement or an anti-Vietnam War movement, the naming itself immediately signified who the protesters were and what their objective was.

Yet, the striking thing about the protesters at gatherings starting from the Seattle WTO meeting in 1999–inaugurating a long string of street protests–to the G-8 summits in Washington, Davos, Prague, Nice, Gothenburg, Salzburg, Genoa (and elsewhere) is that they tend to be called simply "the protesters" or the "anti-globalization protesters," which in neither case conjures up much of anything. They seek to change the agenda of World Summits and the mode of international economic cooperation, but only agree so far on anti-corporate globalization.

Unlike the mass working-class movements of socialism in the 19th and early 20th centuries, *the protesters* tend to be elites rather than mass movements. They have "mobilization networks," which carefully plan their targets and move their attacks from one place to another, along with activist centers in the United States, France, Britain and Germany, and even a group called "Third World Network" in

---

[70] "The 100 Top Brands," *Businessweek,* (European Edition), August 6, 2001, 52.

[71] "The 100 Top Brands," *Businessweek,* (European Edition), August 2, 2004, 68.

Malaysia and another called "Focus on the Global South" in the Philippines (among several others worldwide).

Money, *the fuel*, comes from widespread subscription as well as from a few rich individuals. Greenpeace is an important contributor, and the World Wildlife Fund, for instance, has three times the resources of the WTO. Assorted representatives of interests who claim to be "injured" by the mere expansion of the world trade and business join in the demonstrations.[72] While their leaders and organizers often seek to speak on behalf of the poor and to represent global civil society, they tend to be relatively well-off self-selected groups from wealthy countries. Among them are leftist opponents of capitalism, trade unionists trying to protect well-paid jobs against competition from poor countries, sovereignists (in reference to nationalists opposed to removing barriers to movement of people and goods), environmentalists claiming stronger international regulations, young idealists wishing to show solidarity with the poor, and young anarchists simply rioting for fun and profit.

For some participants in the demonstrations, "it is an exhilarating adventure, a revel with the added spice of defiance to attempts to maintain order," while for most governments "it is a distressing challenge, very costly in terms of great numbers of police to deploy and sometimes damage alone."[73] The *antis* struggle to make it as difficult as they can for major international conferences to be held. In this regard, they are effective. And even if officials do try to substitute virtual conferences for meetings, then the activists are ready to disrupt them with computer skills.

When asked "who bears main responsibility for the violence that occurred during the G-8 summit in Genoa in July 2001," poll results in France showed that 43% answered "the Italian police," 33% "the protesters," while 24% did not reply. Also, some 15% of those surveyed (compared to 26% in November 1999) were

---

[72] Some groups, such as Friends of the Earth, Christian Aid, Jubilee 2000 and Oxfam, have distanced themselves from violent protest and have been insisting on codes of conduct.

[73] Flora Lewis, "The Anti-Globalization Spoilers are Going Global," *IHT*, July 6, 2001, 4. For a look at the demonstrations and costly efforts of the G-8 Summit in Genoa, see: "Death in Genoa," *Time*, July 30, 2001, 14-17.

"confident" or "enthusiastic" in respect of globalization, 17% were indifferent (11% in November 1999), and some 66% were "worried" or "hostile," (another 1% expressed no feelings, while 1% did not reply).[74]

In terms of view, these protesters actually fall into two broad categories: those who think the issue is whether or not to globalize and want to stop globalization in its tracks, and those who understand that globalization is largely driven by technology that is shrinking the world from a size medium to a size small–whether we like it or not–and therefore, the issue is how to globalize. A third "paradoxical" category may also stem from those who do not make a distinction between *anti-Americanism* and *anti-globalization*, such as a 23-year-old salesman who "may insist that he will never ingest a Big Mac because 'McDonald's stands for American imperialism,' but he seems oblivious to the origin of the Nike sneakers on his feet or the pack of Marlboro Lights in his hands."[75]

Up to now, these groups have been mixed together. Because the whether to globalize groups tend to be more noisy and violent, they have increasingly drowned out the how to globalize groups. In doing so, they have created the mis-impression that *the people* believe globalization is all bad when, in fact, it has both empowering and enriching features as well as dis-empowering and impoverishing features, all depending on how one manages it. In other words, if globalization is thought to be *all good* or *all bad*, then there is a lack of understanding to reality.

But, in fact, globalization has already affected different regions in different ways, when every part of the world is already being globalized directly or indirectly, in one way or another. In Asia, where autocratic rulings prevailed for decades, leaders tended to justify their rule with a simple trade-off: democracy for prosperity. Hence, people gave up many democratic rights and got prosperity. The more prosperous they became, the more the relationship between them and the

---

[74] «Les deux tiers des français contre la mondialisation», ('Two-thirds of French Against Globalization'), *Agence France Presse* (AFP), Paris, August 2, 2001.

[75] Example quoted from: "Brands in an Age of Anti-Americanism," *Businessweek*, online edition at: www.businessweek.com, August 4, 2003.

rulers changed, until eventually, turning into so-called "democratic" countries in most cases. In contrast, consider Egypt. The leader there is not judged on whether or not he has brought a better standard of living, but rather on how he confronts the British, Americans, and the Israelis. There the trade-off is: rights for the Arab-Israeli conflict. As a result, such a trade-off has led to a vast gap between the two.

Another fear among the antis camp arises from globalization turning out to be sheer "Americanization." Some believe globalization may homogenize the world only on the surface, while others argue that it is going to homogenize people to their very own roots–and perhaps cause cultural death. Addressing this unanswerable concern at the moment, Friedman states that there are two ways to make people homeless: one by taking away their home, and the other by making their home look like everybody else's home.[76] He illustrates that the most popular food in the world today is not the *hamburger* (or the *Big Mac*), but in fact, *pizza*. And a pizza is a simple "flat piece of bread that every society has, on which every society and every community throws its own local ingredients and culture." In India, for example, you would taste a *tandoori* pizza; in Japan, a *sushi* pizza; in Mexico, a *salsa* pizza; and in Turkey, a *lahambilajeen*.

Similarly, it is hoped that the Internet becomes an instrument for sharing cultures, not for spreading some kind of American cultural dominance to the world; and in this respect, how global information is "downloaded" in different countries is subject to domestic politics.

Finally, globalization may seem to be too vast a concept to be fully captured by today's limited set of statistical measurements to help determine which countries have become more global than the others; or to determine the extent to which a country has become embedded within the global economy; to realize if globalization is moving ahead or not; or to know if the levels of interdependence among broad distances are increasing or not. In other words, without certain means to quantify the scope of globalization, any meaningful evaluation of its effects remains elusive.

---

[76] Thomas Friedman, "States of Discord," *Foreign Policy*, online edition at: www.foreignpolicy.com, April 2, 2002.

In this concern, some attempts have been initiated to measure globalization and to express it in numbers. The A.T. Kearney/Foreign Policy Globalization Index, as one example, tries to track and assess changes in four key components of global integration incorporating such measures as trade and financial flows, movement of people across borders, international telephone traffic, Internet usage, and participation in international treaties and peace-keeping operations. Illustration 1.3. presents a detailed description of the criteria considered in the Globalization Index.

Illustration 1. 3. Measuring Globalization Criteria according to Foreign Policy magazine

Although the Annual Index may not settle the question of whether globalization does more good than harm, it does seek to provide an objective starting point for a debate that has often relied more on sketchy evidence than empirical facts. As reported in the Foreign Policy (May-June 2005 edition), the top 20 countries in the 2005 Globalization Index were respectively: Singapore, Ireland, Switzerland, United States, Netherlands, Canada, Denmark, Sweden, Austria,

Finland, New Zealand, United Kingdom, Australia, Norway, Czech Republic, Croatia, Israel, France, Malaysia, and Slovenia

I.II.VI. <u>The Course of Globalization to the Year 2015</u>

While globalization has been going on for centuries, its contemporary form and current revolutionary force have distinct characteristics. Virtually as old as human history, today globalization is different from how it was in the 19th century, when European imperialism provided much of its political structure, and higher transport and communications costs meant fewer people were involved directly with people and ideas from other cultures. The ancient Silk Road that linked medieval Europe and Asia is also an example of the *narrow* globalization that engaged small amounts of luxury goods and elite customers. Yet many of the most important differences are closely associated with the Information Revolution. In brief, contemporary globalization–the growth of worldwide networks of interdependence–is moving *further, faster, cheaper and deeper.*

The term "network effects" is used to refer to situations where a product becomes more valuable once many other people also use it. For example, one computer set is useless, but its value increases as the network grows. As interdependence becomes more interlinked, the relationships among the different networks become more important, and the interconnections among them ever more numerous. Accordingly, system effects, where small perturbations in one area can spread throughout a whole system, become more important.

In illustrating the impact of system effects, Nye (2002, p. 87) gives the example of financial markets and refers, once again, to the 1997 Asian crisis that affected markets on several continents. The crisis caught economists, governments, and international financial institutions 'by surprise,' and complex new financial instruments made it difficult to understand. Magnitude, complexity and speed now distinguish contemporary economic globalization from earlier periods and increase the challenges it presents worldwide.

Military globalization is also becoming more complex. The end of the Cold War has led to military de-globalization, that is, distant disputes between the superpowers become less relevant to the balance of power. However, the increase in social globalization over the past several decades has had the opposite effect and has introduced new dimensions of military globalization: humanitarian intervention and, more recently, the so-called "war on terrorism." Humanitarian concerns interacting with global communications evoked military interventions in Somalia, Bosnia, and Kosovo–as did the "war on terror" in Afghanistan and Iraq. Thus, fundamentalist reactions to modern culture interact with technology to create new alternatives for their strikes and for asymmetrical warfare.

Global Trends 2015 (2000, p. 10) concludes likewise:

> In contrast to the Industrial Revolution, the process of globalization is more compressed. Its evolution will be rocky, marked by chronic financial volatility and widening economic divide.... Regions, countries, and groups feeling left behind will face deepening economic stagnation, political instability, and cultural alienation. They will foster political, ethnic, ideological, and religious extremism, along with the violence that often accompanies it. They will force the United States and other developed countries to remain focused on "old-world" challenges while concentrating on the implications of "new-world" technologies at the same time.

In human systems, furthermore, people are often engaged in trying to outwit each other so as to gain an economic or social advantage precisely by acting in an unpredictable way. This results to a sense of pervasive uncertainty that accompanies globalization. There will be a continual competition between expanding complexities and uncertainty, and between efforts by governments, corporations, and others to comprehend and manipulate to their benefits these increasingly complex interconnected systems. Frequent financial crises and/or sharp rises in unemployment may lead to popular and organized movements to limit interdependence and, consequently, to a reversal of economic globalization. "Chaotic uncertainty," stresses Nye (2002, p. 87), "is too high a price for most people to pay for somewhat higher average levels of prosperity. Unless some aspects of globalization can be effectively governed, it may not be sustainable in its current form."

The feature of rapidity in contemporary globalization also adds to uncertainty and to the difficulties of shaping policy responses. At the present time, globalization operates at a much quicker pace than its earlier forms. Smallpox took nearly three millennia to conquer all inhabited continents, until finally reaching Australia in 1775. The AIDS virus took around three decades to spread all around the world. And a metaphorical virus, the Love Bug computer virus in 2000, needed only three days to tackle the globe. Also recall here the quick spread of the Severe Acute Respiratory Syndrome (SARS) in Southeast Asia in 2003, and the heat wave that hit several parts of the globe during that same year. Consider the speed of globalization–from three millennia to three decades to three days.

In view of the sweeping global changes to nearly every aspect of life, RAND's National Defense Research Institute (NDRI) attempts to forecast the future course of these changes over the next 10-20 years in the political/governmental, business/financial, and social/cultural dimensions throughout the world. It predicts:

- a rise in information work and information workers;

- new business models for the internal organization and functioning of business enterprises and for their external interactions with customers, suppliers and competitors;

- the rise of electronic commerce;

- challenges to the power and authority of the nation-state;

- the creation and empowerment of a wide variety of new, non-state (often global) political actors;

- an ever increasing porosity of national borders;

- many new winners, and also many new losers; and,

- new fault lines, within and between nations.[77]

---

[77] *Charting the Global Course of the Information Revolution,* RAND's National Defense Research Institute (NDRI), sponsored by the NIC, Points of an International Conference held in Pittsburgh, PA, May 2000.

In North America, the Information Revolution is viewed as *inevitable*, where backlashes of various forms may occur but not expected to sufficiently retard or modify the process.[78] After all, it will be "socially and economically beneficial."

In Europe, focus is on realizing economic value, while at the same time "maintaining and protecting existing cultural and social values." Europeans believe that they can and must actively shape the course to achieve these ends, with particular reference to the alleviation of disparities between winners and losers.

In the Asia Pacific region, emphasis is primarily on economic value, where the prevailing attitude is "Don't worry about losers; concentrate on becoming a winner." And there is widespread confidence that many Asian countries can become winners.

Finally, in the Middle East, Africa, and South Asia, many like to use the Information Revolution to better themselves and their countries–albeit with widely varying abilities to do so. Strong differences in focus between leadership/elite groups and mass citizenry are common feature in these parts of the world. In spite of the willingness of the leaders/elites to benefit from the technology, they are concerned over its influences on the citizenry. In other words, globalization is not necessarily an opportunity–but could be a threat.

---

[78] The fact that the United States is a giant in the contemporary phase of globalization is stressed in the words of former French foreign minister Huber Védrine, who states: "The United States is a very big fish that swims easily and rules supreme in the waters of globalization. Americans get great benefits from this for a large number of reasons: because of their economic size; because globalization takes place in their language; because it is organized along neo-liberal economic principles; because they impose their legal, accounting and technical practices; and because they are advocates of individualism." See: Hubert Védrine with Dominique Moisi, *France in an Age of Globalization*, Washington, DC: Brookings Institution Press, 2001, p. 3.

I.III. The Significance and Force of the Internet

Most experts agree today that the 21ˢᵗ century has brought along with it a turn of fundamental change, although there is, understandably, much uncertainty about what kind of a world the current global transformation may produce. In order to comprehend these changes and accordingly adapt to them, new conceptual repertories need to be developed to meet the challenges posed by the speed the world is evolving and the extreme global complexity that is emerging. One factor that is pushing towards this new environment is IT and, most significantly, the Internet. A look into the conventional approaches that have so far inspired theoreticians and practitioners may better help explain how the Internet has had an influence in shaping both local and world politics.

I.III.I. The Theoretical and Practical Impacts of the Internet

Since its introduction, the discipline of international relations has been based on a separation between internal and external state relations. This separation was forwarded to the modern state system by the Treaty of Westphalia in 1648, which attempted to resolve the religions conflicts of the Thirty Years' War by replacing a universal religious authority that acted as the arbiter of Christendom with the state-sovereign within its own territory and with the right to non-intervention in its affairs by any other state. After 1648, the internal affairs of states were thus conceptually separated from the external arena of interstate relations.[79] Yet, at the beginning of the 21ˢᵗ century, the traditional *domestic-international* framework no longer holds.

The division between internal affairs and foreign affairs is becoming untenable in an environment where world politics are increasingly driven by the forces of *globalization* and *localization*. Information Technology has dramatically accelerated the cross-border movement of goods, services, ideas, and capital, resulting eventually in a huge increase in transnational cultural and political

---

[79] Andreas Wenger, "The Internet and the Changing Face of International Relations and Security," in *Information Security: An International Journal*, Vol. 7, 2001, Sofia: ProCon Ltd., 5-11.

exchanges and in the emergence of many new institutions and structures that transcend state borders. Modern information technologies have minimized the previous limitations imposed by space and time on the mobility of worldwide capital and industry, and have created an environment for global trade and investment decisions. Meanwhile, local factors such as workforce skills, hard and soft infrastructure, legal norms, and political institutions allow local communities and actors to attract mobile capital, human resources, business deals, and multinational firms. The outcoming web of relations, thus, simply cannot be characterized as either domestic or international.

Despite the widespread belief that the IT revolution is restructuring the international system, there is far less consensus about the theoretical and practical impact of the often contradictory developments in international politics. With the diffusion of territorial, societal, and economic space, the debate initially centered on the redistribution and the changing nature of power. The distribution of power has become increasingly unstable and complex, and traditional political and cultural boundaries that once defined distinct worlds are being reshaped. The transformational architecture of global information networks has made territorial borders less significant to a certain extent (state borders are still highly significant when it comes to national security concerns). At the same time, war and peace are evolving in an environment where boundaries between the political space and the military space are increasingly indistinct, as between the civilian domain and the military domain.

Power in the global information society, as explained earlier, depends less on territory and military puissance. Information, technology and institutional flexibility have rather gained importance in international relations. In an unpredictable and highly turbulent international environment, the soft powers of knowledge, beliefs and ideas allow political actors to achieve their goals. Opposing powers these days are less inclined to battle out their differences in the physical arena. Rather again, they focus on the information domain, where getting access to information is now the central strategic principle. Networks wage wars, and small players can now outsmart huge opponents by using asymmetrical strategies.

Nevertheless, the understanding of such conflicts and their multifaceted dynamics remains limited in scope.

States are traditionally the exclusive holders of power and authority. But the importance of information and knowledge–with the advent of the Internet–have paved the way for new and diverse actors to engage in international relations. Simultaneously, the speed, the capacity, and the flexibility in the collection, production as well as dissemination of information have increased. As decentralized network-based soft power structures have gained in importance, the state's monopoly on authority has become fragmented. Countless number of non-governmental organizations, social movements, among other transnational non-state networks, now compete with states for influence.

These emerging contenders rely on the power to persuade a public that is increasingly global, and they are now able to mobilize support for an array of issues, with clashing intentions. And it is this huge increase in the number of actors and the potential fluidity of the international political agenda that complicate considerably the conduct of statecraft and the formation of foreign policy.

As a consequence of the fragmentation of authority and the transforming quality of power, the classic foundations of security have also altered. While the object of security is no longer simply the territorial integrity of the state, the Information Revolution has dramatically increased the dependence of developed countries on efficient national and transnational information infrastructures. In developed societies, key critical infrastructures–electricity production and distribution, transportation, financial services, telecommunications, and water supply–are reliant on information systems and are highly vulnerable and subject to risks. Threats to these structures are less likely to come from so-called "rogue states" (later referred to by the United States as "states of concern") than from hostile non-state actors operating on land or in a relatively opaque cyberspace that has yet to be regulated effectively.

I.III.II. The Advantages and Disadvantages of the Internet in Fostering Activism

Several case studies, along with an Internet activist survey[80] indicate that the Internet, including electronic mail, the Web, and its other facets, gives grassroots groups an essential new tool for attempting to foster political change. Some of these advantages appear to be merely evolutionary improvements in terms of speed and cost on older technologies such as the telephone and facsimile machines. Their advantages appear to be truly revolutionary, reflecting the unique nature of the Internet. No technology by itself, of course, guarantees a successful campaign, but when other forces come into play the Internet does give its users more power.

The following presentation summarizes the advantages the Internet enjoys in fostering activism (Danitz & Strobel).

*   *The Internet is inexpensive and convenient:*

Sending messages via electronic mail is far less expensive than using the telephone, facsimile machine, or other technologies, especially when activists must communicate over long distances and need to reach members of the network in remote areas. Furthermore, organizers can distribute campaign materials (posters, photographs, recordings, and the like), far more cheaply–and, surely, more rapidly and easily–than would be the case if they used the postal mail or other means to distribute physical copies of the materials. While some start-up costs are required (a computer, a modem, an Internet account), these are not beyond individuals' means. Not surprisingly, the survey revealed that many activists make use of freely provided university email accounts.

---

[80] Tiffany Danitz and Warren P. Strobel, "Networking Dissent: Cyber Activists Use the Internet to Promote Democracy in Burma," in *Networks and Netwars: The Future of Terror, Crime, and Militancy,* John Arquilla and David Ronfeldt, RAND, 2001, Chapter Five, pp. 129-69.

*   *The Internet is an organization tool 'par excellence':*

Without the Internet, it would be virtually impossible for activists to coordinate their moves and actions (such as for the anti-globalization protesters who move from one world city to another). The Internet has facilitated remarkably any coordination for a campaign demanding quick action and involving physical distances.

This feature is a revolutionary state of affairs. The Internet has allowed members of the international community, in a much wider scope, to comment on and affect domestic, local legislation, in a privilege once reserved for lobbyists or for registered voters. Even diplomatically, this aspect of the Internet along with its cost-effectiveness has led some governments to employ it for their embassies. Portuguese officials claim to have been among the early adopters of encrypted email for diplomatic messages, where in 1995 Lisbon's envoys around the world were advised to scan the Internet for news from and about home. Canada and Greece were among the early adopters of another Internet technology, namely Web casting.[81]

*   *The Internet allows rapid replication of successful efforts:*

Organizers of a successful Internet campaign can immediately share their winnings (or failing) strategies with cohorts anywhere on the globe. Yet, and due to local conditions and factors, a success or a failure in one locale does not automatically translate likewise in another,. And there seems little doubt that the Internet has helped activists broadcast news around the world about their campaign and about a given situation.

However, there are as well several potential disadvantages to using the Internet that can limit its usefulness to grass roots groups engaged in political action. Many of these *downsides* depends on how the Internet is used; and like the

---

[81] Adam Clayton Powell, III, "New Media: How They Are Changing Diplomacy," *iMP Magazine,* July 23, 2001.

advantages above, some are related to the medium's unique characteristics. Consider the disadvantages noted next:

*   *It is a risk to rely solely on a single source of communication:*

Although the Internet was designed for robustness during an emergency, disruptions can and have occurred. In July 1997, Internet traffic "ground to a halt" across much of the United States because of an odd combination of technical and human errors, signaling what some Internet experts believe could someday be a more catastrophic meltdown.[82]

Also, the break in a key undersea cable link between Australia and Singapore in November 2000 underlined the vulnerability of the Internet, and the need for access to alternatives in case of emergencies. More than 80 main telecommunications operators own the damaged 39,000-kilometer SEA-ME-WE3 fiber optic cable, which links Australia, Asia, the Middle East and Europe. With the region dependent on increasingly powerful fiber optic cables laid on the seabed to meet the surging demand for high-speed Internet access, the enormous traffic pile-up caused by the cut jammed connections to the Internet, an incident that occurs several times a year.[83]

Even more serious, the Internet Corporation for Assigned Names and Numbers (ICANN) emphasizes its concern over attempts to shut down the Internet by malicious hackers. The body that oversees Web address allocation worries that any 'mad' teenager with a $300 computer may attack the few "root" servers which direct computers to Web addresses, or domain names or the ten top-level domain servers, all of which serve as a kind of directory for the Internet.[84] In fact, that has already happened. Four Israeli teenagers, ages 15 and 16 from the same school,

---

[82] Rajiv Chandrasekaran and Elizabeth Corcoran, "Human Errors Block E-mails, Websites in Internet Failure: Garbled Address Files from Va. Firm Blamed," *The Washington Post*, July 18, 1997, A1.

[83] Michael Richardson and Thomas Crampton, "Undersea Cable Break Shows Internet Vulnerability," *IHT*, November 23, 2000, 8.

[84] Experts Say Key Internet Servers Vulnerable to Attack," *Reuters* (published in 'The New York Times'), November 13, 2001.

admitted they wrote and spread the computer virus "Goner" that wreaked havoc worldwide in December 2001. With computer users in North America, Australia and Western Europe hit the hardest, the four teenagers were simply placed under "house arrest" as they "made the virus delete files and clogged email in-boxes around the world."[85]

In view of the vulnerability of the Internet, other technologies such as the telephone and the facsimile machine still enjoy advantages in certain situations, notably if the sender needs immediate confirmation that the information has been received, or during conflicts where leaders would fear of being traced or intercepted while employing modern technology.

*   *Communications over the Internet can be easily monitored:*

As some activists do not see this monitoring as necessarily a bad aspect, private one-to-one electronic mail messages are slightly more secure although they can be hacked by anyone with sufficient technical knowledge. A more potent option is strong encryption, which, in theory, allows only sender and receiver to read the decoded message (like the system known as Pretty Good Privacy 'PGP'). A more recent development is the construction of secure Web pages that require passwords for users to enter secure "chat rooms" with real-time conversations (technologies, like these, are still out of reach of many Internet users).

The need to administer the Web has led the Web's *unelected government*, the World Wide Web Consortium (W3C), to respond. The Consortium, based at the Massachusetts Institute of Technology (MIT), is "an international collective of 275 companies, non-profit organizations, industry groups and government agencies that was created to set technical standards for the Web." Among its activities are "PICS, a series of codes designed to help parents screen out objectionable material

---

[85] "3 Israelis Spread E-mail Virus," *IHT*, December 11, 2001, 7.

while their children surf the Net, and P3P, a system designed to protect privacy online."[86]

Activists now refer to ancient methods as they communicate. Steganography, Greek for "hidden writing," is one of the most ancient ways of passing secret messages, but until very recently received attention from computer scientists. "The ancient Greek used it, writing a message on a wooden tablet and covering the wood with wax. Sentries would think the tablets were blank, but when they were delivered, their recipients would simply scrape off the wax and read the message."[87]

During World War II, as well, the Allies became suspicious about hidden messages, leading the U.S. Office of Censorship to take "extreme actions, such as banning flowers deliveries which contained delivery dates, crossword puzzles and even report cards."[88] More recently, steganography has arrived on the Internet with free and easy-to-use programs to insert messages and pictures on digital files (e.g., photographs or music files) that can be slightly altered and still look the same to the human eye or sound the same to the human ear.

*   *Information transmitted on the Internet is unmediated and can sometimes be of questionable accuracy:*

An advantage of the Internet for activists and for the majority of users is the fact that it allows them to dispense with the 'traditional filters' for news, even by reporters and government officials. It enables users to self-select information they are interested in and to retrieve data in far more depth than in a newspaper or television program.

---

[86] Richard Langhorne, *The Coming of Globalization*, 2001, p. 91.

[87] Gina Kolata, "Veiled Messages of Terrorists May Lurk in Cyberspace," *The New York Times,* online edition, October 30, 2001.

[88] *Ibid.*

For example, in 2001 the Indian government lost several ministers and nearly collapsed after reports of corruption appeared on the Internet, as scandals that were once more easily contained in New Delhi now impossible to control. "Not only did Tehelka.com reveal the corrupt underbelly of the Indian military: it also helped fan the controversy by serving as a bulletin board for readers and politicians to air their views."[89] With corruption remaining a problem in several countries, it is no longer solely a domestic affair, at a time non-governmental organizations publish corruption rankings of countries and leaders on the Internet.[90] And while foreign capital nowadays demands increasing transparency, governments that are not transparent (or pretend to be transparent in front of their public opinion or to the international media) are less credible, since the information they provide is considered biased and selective.

However, this openness Internet platform can also present dangers, allowing for wide and rapid dissemination of information that is factually incorrect or propagandistic, including material considered racist, sexist or hateful and incendiary–especially when the source of information is anonymous.[91]

*   *Access to the Internet is not equal and can highlight divisions between the 'haves' and 'have-nots':*

Not everyone has access to the modern tools of communication, including computers, modems, and the necessary telephone lines or other means to connect to the Internet. Worldwide in the first quarter of 2005, only around 14% people had access to the Internet. As noted, even access to encryption methods that allow for more secure communication remains limited. Language competence, in addition to computer literacy, may turn out to be other barriers to connection. Table 1.1. presents an overall view of the percentage of people with Internet access.

---

[89] John Thornhill, "Asia's Old Order Falls into the Net," *Financial Times*, March 17, 2001, 7.

[90] One example is "Transparency International," a major international non-governmental organization devoted to combating corruption. Its secretariat is based in Germany. See: www.transparency.org.

[91] See: Graeme Browning, *Electronic Democracy: Using the Internet to Influence American Politics*, Wilton, CT: Pemberton Press, 1996, pp. 79-81.

World Regions	Population (2005 Est.)	Population % of World	Internet Usage	Usage Growth 2000-2005	Penetration (% Population)	World Users %
Africa	900,465,411	14.0 %	13,468,600	198.3 %	1.5 %	1.5 %
Asia	3,612,363,165	56.3 %	302,257,003	164.4 %	8.4 %	34.0 %
Europe	730,991,138	11.4 %	259,653,144	151.9 %	35.5 %	29.2 %
Middle East	259,499,772	4.0 %	19,370,700	266.5 %	7.5 %	2.2 %
North America	328,387,059	5.1 %	221,437,647	104.9 %	67.4 %	24.9 %
Latin America/Caribbean	546,917,192	8.5 %	56,224,957	211.2 %	10.3 %	6.3 %
Oceania / Australia	33,443,448	0.5 %	16,269,080	113.5 %	48.6 %	1.8 %
WORLD TOTAL	6,412,067,185	100.0 %	888,681,131	146.2 %	13.9 %	100.0 %

Table 1. 1. World Internet Usage and Population Statistics
(Source: www.internetworldstats.com, March 31, 2005)

*   *The Internet does not replace human contact:*

The Internet, along with other communications media, cannot replace human interaction in all its uniqueness. It may, however, be considered as more of a complement rather than an alternative when it comes to contact. With its own distinct advantages and disadvantages, the Internet is only one of the *arrows* in an activist's *quiver*. A campaign activity, or lobbying, that focuses on virtual external communication and publicity–rather than on human contact and physical organization–may not assure its overall success.

Noteworthy in respect of e-commerce, airlines (such as Delta Air Lines and American Airlines) encourage their customers to buy online and reward those who do so. They offer, for example, 20% discount for Web site purchases, while other airlines have lured passengers with last minute specials and bonus miles in an aim to drive people from *offline* to *online*. Yet, and as only one-third of bank customers still prefer *human tellers* to *automated teller machines*, airlines are convinced that a significant number of travelers will continue to use travel agents.[92] In Europe, the aging populations are still accustomed to direct customer services, partly because of their unfamiliarity with modern technologies and also due to financial security concerns when paying online.

*   *The Internet can be exploited for sabotage and crime:*

Since the Internet allows for anonymity, it is possible for provocateurs posing as someone or something else to cause much harm–both personal and to the system as a whole. As a measure of precaution, for example, the site *www.georgewbush.com* was inaccessible to visitors outside the United States during the last few days before the Election Day on November 2, 2004. Such mounting danger, among others, pushed the member states of the Council of Europe (along with four non-member states: Canada, Japan, South Africa, and the United States) to adopt the Convention on Cybercrime in Budapest on November 23, 2001. The Convention,[93] which aims to combat online crime, covers three main topics: harmonization of the national laws that define offences, definition of investigation and prosecution procedures to cope with global networks, and establishment of a rapid and effective system of international cooperation.

The criminal offences implied are (to qualify as criminal, offences must be committed deliberately and 'without right' so that legal responsibilities may be considered):

- *offences against the confidentiality, integrity and availability of computer data and systems:* illegal access, illegal interception, data interference, system interference, misuse of devices;

- *computer-related offences:* forgery and computer fraud;

---

[92] Saul Hansell, "Internet Airline Tickets Sales Soar," *IHT,* July 5, 2001, 11.

[93] Extracts quoted from the official Web site of the Council of Europe, "The Convention on Cybercrime, a Unique Instrument for International Cooperation," at: http://press.coe.int/cp/2001/893a(2001).htm.

- *content-related offences:* production, dissemination and possession of child pornography. A protocol is to cover the propagation of racist and xenophobic ideas over the Web;

- *offences related to infringement of copyright and related rights:* the wide-scale distribution of pirated copies of protected work, etc.

Another objective of the Convention is to facilitate the conduct of cyberspace criminal investigations, with the help of several procedural powers, such as the powers to preserve data, to search and seize, to collect traffic data and to intercept communications.[94]

Countries that have strong laws and traditions against so-called 'hate speech', such as Germany and France, are growing even more alarmed about inflammatory expression which they fear could lead to racial or religious violence. The precedent case "Licra vs. Yahoo" is worth recalling here, where in April 2000 three anti-racist and Jewish associations (Licra, Mrap, and UEJP) lodged a complaint against a French court for hosting online auctions of Nazi memorabilia. The French court ruled that the American Web company had violated French law by allowing French citizens to view auction sites displaying Nazi memorabilia, and eventually ordered Yahoo! to take action to "render impossible" the ability of French Internet users to gain access to such related sites. But across the Atlantic, American civil libertarians were satisfied with a U.S. court ruling that the French court's orders and fine would not be enforced against Yahoo! in the United States in view of the provisions of the First Amendment of the U.S. Constitution, and on the basis that the Web site is used primarily by American Internet surfers and is based in the States.

Regardless of the outcomes of the two Courts, the question raised is whether or not the Internet is unregulated, free-wheeling, and a free-market

---

[94] Privacy and human rights groups are harshly critical of the Convention, saying it "gives police overly broad powers" and has been drafted in a process that has "excluded democratic controls." Also, some Internet service providers express discontent with the measures, which they claim, include "vague definitions" and could impose heavy burdens on providers that may not be reimbursed for their expenses when meeting law enforcement demands. Source: Rick Perera, "Cybercrime Treaty Ready for Signatures," November 12, 2001,
at: http://www.cnn.com/2001/TECH/internet/11/12/cybercrime.treaty.idg/index.html.

communications frontier. This case highlights two differing legal and cultural sensitivities. Where several European countries enforce several laws against issues dealing with inciting racism and neo-Nazi activities, the U.S. Constitution protects such speech on the underlying principle that 'good' speech will prevail. Here, the two views collide, as do the moral and legal aspects of the case.[95]

While observers worry that the proliferation of independent Web sites, media monitors, and lobbying campaigns may have a polarizing effect on conflicts, the Internet can be a conduit for friendship and reconciliation, allowing the like-minded to communicate across the divide. The quotation below illustrates this point:

> "In early January, Surinamese president Runaldo Ronald Venetiaan logged onto a small-nations chat room on Yahoo! and came across Estonian president Arnold Ruutel," U.N. Secretary-General Kofi Annan said. "The two exchanged messages and, before long, became Internet friends, bonding over their shared experiences as leaders of tiny republics."
>
> Despite their vast cultural differences and geographical distance, the Surinamese and Estonian leaders forged a strong alliance, granting each other most-favored-nation status and signing numerous trade pacts.[96]

I.III.III. Restricting the Flow of Information on the Internet in a Knowledge-based Society

Most governments find their control loosening in the 21st century as IT gradually spreads to the parts of the world that still lacks phones, computers, and electricity. Even the U.S. government finds some taxes harder to collect and some regulations (particularly those related to gambling or prescription drugs) harder to enforce. Today, many governments control the Internet access of their citizens by

---

[95] Victoria Shannon, "Yahoo Faces Deadline to Block Nazi Items," *IHT*, November 21, 2001, 1; and Carl S. Kaplan, "French Decision Prompts Questions about Free Speech and Cyberspace," *The New York Times,* online edition, February 11, 2002.

[96] The accuracy of the information remains to be verified. Quoted from: "Countries Who Met Over Internet Go To War," *www.theonion.com*, April 3, 2002. Among Kofi Annan's 10 recommended Web sites are: www.cite-sciences.fr (Cité des Sciences et de l'Industrie in Paris); www.smallarmssurvey.org (on the global flow of small arms); www.oneworld.net (on social justice worldwide); and www.hri.ca (on human rights). See: "Expert Sitings: Kofi A. Annan," at: http://www.foreignpolicy.com/issue_mayjune_2002/expert_sitings.html.

controlling Internet Service Providers (ISP). Skilled individuals, in both possible and affordable means, route around such restrictions.

As societies develop, they face the dilemma of trying to protect their sovereign control over information. And as they reach levels of development where their knowledge workers and general public demand free access to the Internet, they run the risk of losing their scarcest resource for competing in the information society. Closed systems may become costly, at a time openness turns out to be worth the price.

I.III.III.I. In Authoritarian States

The Internet poses a crucial threat to authoritarian rule. In those political systems, the state has often exercised a tough historical role in the development and control of ICTs and of the mass media. This legacy of control has morphed into a similar rigid role in Internet development. Western governments may find themselves struggling to impose effective regulation on a medium that has grown rapidly without their immediate oversight. Authoritarian rulings typically dominate the Internet from its beginnings and shape its growth and diffusion.

The impact of the Internet on authoritarian political systems, and on 'one-party states' (i.e., states ruled by the same party continuously for at least one generation), raises questions. Among them: Who is using the Internet, and for what purposes? What challenges to the state are likely to arise from this use, and how is the state likely to respond? And, to what extent is such a state proactively guiding Internet development so that the medium serves state interests?

Examine the potential challenges that arise from Internet use in four aspects.[97]

---

[97] Shanthi Kalathil and Taylor C. Boas, *The Internet and State Control in Authoritarian Regimes: China, Cuba, and the Counterrevolution*, Carnegie Endowment Working Papers, Carnegie Endowment for International Peace, Washington, DC, July 2001, pp. 2-4.

- *Mass Public*: Public access to ICTs may facilitate a 'demonstration effect', where exposure to outside ideas or images of transitions in other countries spurs a revolution of rising expectations and, perhaps, the eventual overthrow of the authoritarian regime. The use of e-mail, Internet chat rooms, bulletin boards and the World Wide Web may, alternatively, contribute to 'ideational pluralism' and a more gradual liberalization of the public sphere in authoritarian societies.

- *Civil Society Organizations*: Such organizations may use the Internet to support their activities in a variety of ways, including logistical organizations and the public dissemination of information. In many cases, such organizations play a crucial role in undermining authoritarian governments, either by calling for an initial political opening or by triggering scandals that attempt to de-legitimize authoritarian rule.

- *Economy*: Internet use in the economic sphere may pose multiple challenges to authoritarian rule. It may, for example, present significant opportunities for entrepreneurship in a developing economy, possibly leading to the emergence of new domestic business elite. If the Internet contributes to economic growth more generally, it may facilitate the growth of a middle class. These two forces, a business elite and a middle class, may place increasing demands on the rule that challenge its control of society.

- *International Community*: The coercive efforts of foreign governments and multilateral institutions through such measures as the imposition of sanctions, the extension of conditional loans and aid, or even in the form of compensations (such as hosting the Olympics Games or admission to certain world organizations) are all frequently influential factors in the opening process of authoritarian rule. Transnational advocacy networks, social movements, the media, and other actors outside of the target country usually play a key role in mounting campaigns for such decisive action. Obviously, Internet use is often crucial to the success of their activities. The case of China is interesting to observe, with street demonstrations recently becoming daily events, and activists likely to get more feverish as the 2008 Games approach, bringing some 30,000 international journalists to Beijing.[98]

These eventual Internet uses have the potential to challenge the stability of authoritarian governments. In cases where Internet use seems threatening, states will respond and even try to preempt such challenges, seeking to maintain control over the Internet as they have with other media channels in the past. Any given response is likely to involve a combination of two-types of strategies: *reactive* and *proactive* (Kalathil & Boas).

The most visible, **reactive strategies**, involve direct efforts to either counter or circumscribe existing or potential hazards signaled above by simply clamping down on Internet use. Tactics include limiting access to networked computers, filtering content or blocking Web sites with software tools, monitoring users' on-line behaviors, and entirely prohibiting Internet usage.

Another approach to exert control over the Internet is by proactively guiding Internet development and usage to promote particular interests and priorities. While reactive strategies respond to already existing or potential risks of Internet use, **proactive strategies** attempt to structure an Internet that is free from such challenges as it–at the same time–consolidates or extends state authority. Tactics, in this respect, may involve efforts to distribute propaganda on the Internet, create state-controlled national Intranets that serve as substitute for global Internet, implement e-government services that increase citizen satisfaction with the government, and strengthen state power on a world-wide scale by engaging in information warfare (such as hacking into Web sites and spreading viruses). Also,

---

[98] Another example is Iran, as members of the World Trade Organization agreed on May 26, 2005 to allow the country to open negotiations to join the body. WTO membership was one of the rewards European Union negotiators offered to Iran if it agreed to curb its nuclear program to ensure that it produces only electricity and not weapons. The United States previously blocked Iran's application 22 times ever since it had first applied to join the Organization in 1996.

governments may make use of the Internet to serve economic development goals, based on an understanding that economic growth–along with a general improvement in the living standards–may also help assure continuing support for the ruling political system.

In the East Asia region, Hachigian and Wu rank a number of countries according to Internet access restrictions and on online political content and usage. The four categories are: severe, significant, moderate, and negligible.[99]

Two countries with closed economies and military rulings, North Korea and Myanmar (Burma) fall at one end of the spectrum, as they *severely* restrict virtually all public Internet access. A national Intranet, known as the Kwang Myong network, reportedly links a few hundred North Korean computers in government departments, research institutes, industrial complexes, and universities.

Communist China and Vietnam place *significant* restrictions on Internet access. In 1998, the Vietnam government built a firewall to block more than 3,000 pornography sites and thousands of political sites, in addition to the proxy sites that allow circumvention of the blocks.

Singapore promotes public Internet access and sets *moderate* restrictions on political content and use. Noting that Singapore is a *de facto* one-party state (run by the People's Action Party since 1959), it essentially focuses on the Internet's commercial potential, while worrying less about the political consequences. By 2002, every school in the country was supposed to have one computer for every two students and 12 Internet connections per classroom. Singapore's e-government system, as well, is one of the most sophisticated and advanced in the world, allowing most transactions with the government to pass online.

---

[99] Nina Hachigian and Lily Wu, *The Information Revolution in Asia*, RAND Corporation, Santa Monica, CA, 2003; and also: Nina Hachigian, "The Internet and Power in One-Party East Asian States," *The Washington Quarterly 25*, no. 3, Summer 2002, 41-58.

Countries with *negligible* restrictions include Australia, India, Indonesia, Japan, Malaysia, Philippines, South Korea, and Thailand. Attempting to promote and enable Internet access, even for the poor, Malaysia places few to no restrictions on online political content. Its leadership, the *Barisan Nasional* (the National Front, which has ruled since 1969), is gambling on the hopes that being in the forefront of IT development and investment is more feasible than controlling political use, in spite of the political price.

A remarkable example of the political influence of IT in the East Asian region is in Indonesia, where IT contributed to the end of the 30-year reign of president Mohamed Suharto. According to Sen and Hill, during the last few years of Suharto's rule that started in 1967, the Internet was used extensively by the urban middle-class opposition to get around the government's censorship of broadcast media.[100] To take an example, the news magazine "Tempo," which was banned in 1994, found an eager online audience for the Web site it initiated in 1996, "Tempo Interaktif," (at: http:www.tempo.co.id). In the first six months of the site, estimated reports revealed that some 10% of the Indonesians online had logged in (Hachigian & Wu, 2003, p. 57).

Sen and Hill (2000, p. 210) stress that the utility of the Internet as a political platform render it a common tool for opposition groups. Even more importantly, it has led to the notion that "the very freedom of the Internet [has become] a constant reminder of the absence of openness and freedom in other media." Hachigian and Wu (2003, pp. 58-59) recall four particular factors that allowed the Internet to empower opposition groups to Suharto, eventually contributing to his resignation on May 21, 1998.

First, many Indonesians shared accounts and passwords, and by so reduced costs to get online. Internet cafes, second, became both more popular and affordable, and some proprietors even guided their clientele to locate the sites of opposition parties. Third, the traditional media covered much of the online political discussions, and thus advertised the existence of such sites and forums, as well as

---

[100] Sen, Krishna and David Hill, *Media, Culture and Politics in Indonesia*, Melbourne, Australia: Oxford University Press, 2000, p. 194.

conveyed their designated messages. Finally, the Indonesian government was not willing or able to censor online political activity. As several other countries in the region, it wanted to encourage the information economy, but did not have the technical or legal structures in place at that time to block certain undesired sites or to monitor e-mail traffic.

In China, the government screens information depending on bureaucratic rank and discourages the flow of information among individuals. It is seeking to profit from the economic benefits of the Internet with the hopes of not letting it shake political control. The government currently sponsors Internet contests and offers tax breaks to those IT companies considered to be engines of economic growth. The typical user there tends to be urban, male, single, educated and young.

The Chinese government does exert some control over the information posted online by blocking sites and enforcing censorship regulations. For instance, it only authorizes a handful of networks international access and forbids Chinese Web sites from using news from sites outside the country, with particular reference to sources that offer alternative ideologies to the Chinese Communist Party.

In a new system called the "Night Crawler" (*Pa Chong* in Chinese) expected to allow authorities to locate and block unregistered sites, the Chinese Ministry for the Information Industry (MII) on March 20, 2005 issued a decree obliging all China-based Web sites and blogs, whether commercial or not, to register by June 30, 2005, providing the complete identity of the persons responsible for the sites. Thought of as a concession to the Chinese government, Weblog entries on some parts of Microsoft's MSN site in the country are already being blocked once using words like *'freedom', 'democracy', 'human rights', 'demonstration',* and *'Taiwan independence'*. Anyone using these entries would get a pop-up that reads: *"This item should not contain forbidden speech such as profanity. Please enter a different word for this item."* [101]

---

[101] "Microsoft censors Chinese blogs," *BBC News*, June 14, 2005, at: http://news.bbc.co.uk/go/pr/fr/-/2/hi/technology/4088702.stm; and also: "China: Authorities declare war on unregistered websites and blogs," *Reporters Without Borders*, June 6, 2005.

Other sources also banned include the banned spiritual movement of Falun Gong,[102] Taiwan and Hong Kong newspapers, and human rights groups. Some sites and issues are quickly suppressed, pointing that general critiques of communist leaders and the Party's monopoly on power are commonly noticed—as are debates about the growing gap between the rich and the poor in China.[103] But even so, state control is diminishing, and for every Web site shut down, several others open up.

Although the Chinese leadership is aware of its success in restricting the flow of information or access to it, it chooses to lay down warnings about limits. Not to forget that the Chinese public security authorities, ever since the early Internet age, had already employed such technology in their internal coded communications. That is, it is betting on having the Internet *à la carte*, as it aims for economic benefits and avoids political backlash. While the country's leadership may assume to be on the right track for the next few years, the long term remains much more doubtful.

Consider another conclusion in regard of China's Internet policy:

> Since the Internet is changing and growing by leaps and bounds, China's task of blocking Websites is not unlike Sisyphus's work of pushing a stone up a hill only to have it fall back down again and again. China is finding it hard to keep up with the Internet's continual evolution, as well as technologies such as proxy servers and peer-to-peer networking that allows sites to circumvent blocks.[104]

---

[102] Started by a former clerk named Li Hongzhi in 1992, Falun Gong combines elements of traditional 'qigong', the harnessing of supernatural forces, with Buddhism and Taoism. It spread rapidly, especially among retirees who enjoyed group exercises in parks, and who were attracted by promises of good health and spiritual salvation. The group was banned in China in 1999 after followers staged a huge unauthorized demonstration in Beijing calling for official recognition. The Falun Gong Web site is www.faluninfo.net, and www.falundata.org. It should not be excluded that the United States is probably instrumentalizing Falun Gong as a means to destabilize and disturb Chinese authorities and certain sectors of the population. The leaders of the Falun Gong, based in New York, encourage activists in underground dissident journals (such as the *Tunnel* and *VIP Reference)* to send their publications to hundreds of thousands of Chinese e-mail accounts from the United States. (Refer to Nina Hachigian, 2002, 50.)

[103] As the Internet contributes to the economic independence and wealth of the people of China, the entrepreneurial, individualistic understandings that the growth of Internet commerce engenders would seem to contradict Communist principles.

[104] Nina Hachigian, "The Political Implications of the Internet in China," RAND Seminar, Center for Asia-Pacific Policy (CAPP), Santa Monica, CA, September 15, 2000.

In contrast to China's sharp growth in Internet access, the Internet in Cuba has grown slowly but steadily since the country had its first direct connection in 1996. Internet diffusion in Cuba is limited by the country's economic situation, the U.S. embargo, and the government's strategy of limiting public access. Without any significant change in one or another of these variables, the Internet in Cuba is likely to continue its slow but steady pattern of growth.

Cuba has noticeably promoted Internet development in areas it considers priorities. The government seeks to guide and channel the growth of the Internet so that like other media its principal impact is to serve the political goals of the Cuban revolution. And since these goals imply continued control by the current government, Cuba's proactive approach towards the Internet also serves to strengthen and extend state authority. Part of this strategy involves Internet propaganda. The successes and efficiency of such a policy still remain in doubt.

For instance, the leadership in Cuba has taken a keen interest in employing the Internet to counter its negative image in international media. Various government-affiliated organizations provide official perspectives on current events, all with frequent criticism of the United States. One site, namely *cubavsbloqueo.cu* (Cuba versus the blockade), rallies opposition to the American embargo imposed on the country. While much of the government's on-line propaganda is oriented towards a foreign audience, computer networking may come to enjoy a greater role in domestic politics as Cuba moves ahead in its plans for a national Intranet.

In 2000, the Cuban government began to implement its plans for public access to a national Intranet through some 300 youth computer clubs and through several thousand post offices in the country. Through Intranet, the government would encourage public use and access to national e-mail and Web pages hosted within the country. Any outside access would almost certainly be pre-approved. In addition to opening network access to a wider segment of the population, the Intranet is also sought to create a politically safe substitute for the Internet. On the political level, the leadership can also channel discourse and exercise editorial control over content. In the future, it may as well incorporate the Intranet into its long-standing practice of using the mass media for top-down political mobilization.[105]

Yet, the Cuban government's access controls are not perfect. A growing number of users manage to connect to the Internet *illegally* from home, using workplace passwords, black market accounts or personal connections. The potential for underground Internet access is likely to grow and increasingly become more of a challenge to state control. The Cuban government now needs to face an emerging 'rebel force', an 'Internet guerrilla', known as *informaticos,* which struggles to get access to and assure the flow of information.[106]

I.III.III.II. The Arab Region

The emergence of Internet as a major vehicle of communication raises several questions for Muslim countries. The range and nature of these questions–from religious to political to economic–entitle the Internet to an open-ended system of communication that many of these countries are not ready and/or willing to take the risks of. Henry describes Arab governments as "information-shy" in reference to their fear of the free flow of information. He notes the problematic status of the 'public' versus the 'private' sphere in the region:

> Even the distinction between the "public" and the "private" sectors of most countries in the region is problematic; public officials may be less informed than ostensibly private actors enjoying close personal relations with government officials. Most economic as well as political information is kept out of any public domain, even that of government officials.[107]

---

[105] Those granted access to the Internet are generally sympathetic to the government's points of view, and so their use of the medium poses little threat to the state security of Cuba (Kalathil & Boas, 2001, p. 12-13).

[106] Scott Wilson, "Laptop Brigade: Cuba's New Rebels," *IHT*, December 27, 2000, 1.

[107] Clement M. Henry, *Challenge of Global Capital Markets to Information-Shy Regimes: The Case of Tunisia*, UAE: The Emirates Center for Strategic Studies and Research, Occasional Papers no. 19, 1998.

The emergence of the Internet and the World Wide Web has radically altered the world of communications and placed powerful new constraints on information-shy governments. Yet, this is not to suggest that Internet development in Arab countries has stagnated but rather is developing at a much slower pace than other parts of the world. With a population 55 times that of Finland, for example, the region covers around 5% of the world population but only 0.7% of the Internet connections.[108]

Some of these impediments involve deeper issues of political culture that concern the public sphere, that zone of public access in which people are free to discuss and debate matters of public interest, moral issues, and collective destinies without fear of reprisal. In some cases there are troubling international issues, as in for example Syria. Although Syria had connected all of its major cities with fiber optic cables, in January 2000 nothing was connected to the fiber optic ring. That Syria had no Internet Service Provider at this time was partly because the country was on the U.S. list of countries "sponsoring terrorism," and consequently, was ineligible to purchase Internet routers and servers (out of fears that such technology may be of 'double-use,' in addition to the policy of containment and isolation). Iraq and Libya also ran into similar obstacles.

In the Arab region, the development and employment of advanced ICTs are critically dependent on economic means and government backing. Every country in the region is deficient in necessary economic factors and/or government involvement.

With the factors underlining revolution being several, complex, and interrelated, a recent U.S. study points to three particular aspects of concern in respect to the region:[109]

---

[108] "World Bank Supports the Knowledge and Learning Needs of the Middle East and North Africa Region," *The World Bank*, News Release no. 2004/262/WBI, March 15, 2004.

[109] Grey E. Burkhart and Susan Older, *The Information Revolution in the Middle East and North Africa*, RAND, Santa Monica, CA, 2003, pp. ix-x.

- The likelihood that most of the countries in the region will miss the information revolution altogether, while others experience a belated *information evolution.* This will, as a consequence, increase the development gap between the region and the countries members of the OECD, for instance.[110]

- The generally low level of ICT penetration in most of the region, independent of any consideration of an information revolution. This will further widen the gap between the countries in the region and the modern world.

- The irregular pattern of diffusion and use of such technologies favoring the wealthy and privileged. This pattern will further distance the standard of living and opportunity gaps between the richest and the poorest sectors within the same societies of any given country in the region.

The study conducted by Burkhart and Older (pp. 48-52) divides Internet development in the region into three categories: 'driven' countries that have allowed the Internet to develop essentially freely for the economic benefits it would bring, countries 'fearful' of potential adverse consequences to the extent that they banned the Internet, and last, countries that try to have it 'both ways' by fostering acceptable and tolerant activity while tightly controlling the rest.

→ **Driven**: This category includes countries as different as Bahrain, Lebanon and Yemen–all of whom were driven by economic imperatives. The greatest differentiator with respect to Internet development, among these 'driven countries', is the country's wealth. Here, wealthy countries did more, and faster (speaking relatively in terms of the region).

---

[110] It is recalled that more basic information infrastructure issues, such as ground-transport networks, electrical-power generation and distribution, and the availability, extent and use of water supplies occupy the time, attention, efforts and funds of all the countries in the Arab region.

The future for the 'driven countries' promises more of the same, as each country invests as much as it can and seeks to grow as rapidly as possible to benefit from globalization. The main limiting factor will be money, though the Internet has already expanded wide enough to begin providing economic benefits. Private-sector investments are expected to be the main source of capital in this field.

Morocco uses the Internet strategically in the form of an economic incentive and source of human revenue generation. Maroc Telecom retains primary ownership of the telecommunications systems while it leases use of its lines to private entrepreneurs who are able to provide Internet services. The Moroccan government, in addition, is aware of the manpower difficulties, both in the failure of the universities to graduate adequately trained IT workers, and in terms of the intense competition for such workers globally–which may eventually lead to 'brain drain' in the country and elsewhere.

In an effort to deal with that issue, an initiated agency, la *Confederation générale des enterprises marocaines (CGEM)*, launched a program for university-trained individuals who are unemployed and who are willing to undergo IT training. They are given a minimal salary and start-up funds to open a cyber café or some other sort of Internet service. And within two years, they are expected to be self-sufficient.

For these 'driven countries', a major question is whether the government or private interest groups should be in charge of Internet infrastructure development. Setting up such infrastructure is a very costly endeavor, and most governments in this region may not be in a position to afford it. If they privatize the telecommunications system to draw upon the resources of private enterprise, then they are likely to lose control of Internet development. They are, even more likely to lose control of the flow of information in general, and along with that, virtually all aspects of life, not excluding domestic politics.

➜ **Best of Both**: Success and growth in this category will depend on the strength of the ruling governments and resistance to internal pressures. As far as these countries are concerned, a number of observations are worth mentioning.

In Saudi Arabia, Internet access remains strictly controlled by the state, which maintains the only international gateway.[111] Allowing public access to the Web in 1999, this gateway is "heavily guarded by multiple, redundant firewalls in what must be the most complex and expensive attempt at content filtering in the world" (Burkhart & Older, p. 50).

But even so, some Saudi residents were able to find a crack in the government wall. By masking the online destination of the surfer, 'Safeweb', a small California-based company, enabled people in Saudi Arabia (and perhaps in other restrictive countries) to view any Web site. After thousands of surfers got access to the back door, the government was forced to cut access to it. And once again, Safeweb then pointed Saudi users to a new technology that helped them go around the blockade in the same kind of *cat-and-mouse* struggle over Web access.[112]

The Tunisian government, in a similar approach, wanted the IPSs to guarantee that nothing being transmitted over the Web could be morally offensive to the country's values, and that access to all networked computers be rigorously supervised (a policy that human rights organizations oppose).[113]

---

[111] Some sites, such as Internet telephony, are blocked for financial reasons to favor state-run telephone monopoly.

[112] Companies such as *Safeweb, Anonymizer,* and *Silentsurf.com* offer services– some even free– to counter such government restrictions. During the conflict in Kosovo in 1999, for instance, Anonymizer (also based in California) set up free services so that Kosovo residents could communicate with less fear. See: Jennifer Lee, "Web Firms Strive to Get Around Governments' Internet Bans," *IHT*, April 27, 2001, 1. The same author also stated that U.S. government agencies and Safeweb were in advanced discussions to design an American-based network to thwart attempts by the Chinese government to censor the Web for users in China. In "VOA Plans Internet Café for China," *IHT*, August 31, 2001, 13.

[113] Toby E. Huff, "Globalization and the Internet: Comparing the Middle Eastern and Malaysian Experiences," in *The Middle East Journal*, Summer 2001, Vol. 55, no. 3, published by the Middle East Institute, Washington, DC, 445.

Iran, though not an Arab country but placed in this group, is seeing how the Internet is gradually transforming personal lifestyles and opening public expression at a pace where a technologically handicapped bureaucracy has been unable to control. In 2001, Iranian officials were reported to be drafting rules and preparing equipment for Internet access and services–although it was not clear whether or not those restrictions would be implemented and how effectively they might be.[114] Rather than blast out at the potential harm of the Internet, many of the country's ranking clerics have created their own Web sites to "answer religious questions" and to offer their own interpretation of Islam. Nevertheless, and in view of the outcomes of the presidential elections in June 2005, it will be interesting to observe how the conservatives deal with the use of the Internet in the country.

→ **Fearful**: To the point of this writing, recent developments in Iraq, Libya and Syria render it difficult to predict any outcomes or orientations in the near future. Iraq is still in conflict. There are attempts, though perceived with varying degrees by the Iraqis, to transform the country from a closed-information society to a broad-information access society *all at once*. Consider, for example, the current situation of the country moving–all of a sudden–from one major political ruling party for decades to more than 200 parties in less than two years (March 2003-January 2005).

Libya is seeking to recover from its international isolation after the sanctions on it were lifted in 2004. How Libya intends to use its oil revenues and invest in ICTs still remains to be seen. As foreign companies start to pour into the country once again, there will certainly be more pressure on the government to ease its limitations on access to the outside world. In this respect, it is not excluded that certain developments in ICTs may soon be tailored to encounter certain connection difficulties (namely, state control or network capacity).

---

[114] Molly More, "Internet Boom Transforms Lifestyle in Iran," *IHT*, July 5, 2001, 2.

Syria recently suffers from U.S. sanctions, at a time regional peace concerns continue to hinder foreign investment and already cause the government security headaches, along with other priorities. Nevertheless, in addressing the 10th Congress of the ruling Arab Ba'ath Socialist Party on June 6, 2005, President Bashar Al Assad made clear reference to the impacts of the evolution of ICTs on his country. He stated that such developments have rendered "the society wide-open," while "creating a sense of confusion and suspicion in the minds of the Arab youth." He also blamed "forces behind" the modern trends that seek to exploit and generate societal upheaval in the Arab region, eventually leading to "the cultural, political and moral collapse of the Arab individual and his ultimate defeat without a battle."[115]

The wealthiest countries in the region will most likely continue to expand their already-substantial networks and offer a wider variety of value-added services to increase their profitability. Unconstrained by financial resources, the ultimate shapes and uses of these networks will depend almost entirely on the governments' continued efforts to control information access. The major exception, among the wealthiest countries here, is Saudi Arabia. The ruling monarchy of Al Saud is in little danger of being overthrown. Yet, the combination of relative economic hardship (due to the reductions or elimination of personal subsidies as a result of lower oil earnings), increased exposure to foreign cultures, in addition to a Western-educated and information technology-savvy middle class may put pressure on the government.

Middle-tier countries in the region will continue to expand their physical infrastructures, with hopes that ICTs continue to penetrate without any fundamental changes in those societies.

Yemen, at the other extreme, is still in need for every manifestation of modernity, starting with clean water and stable electrical power. Yemen's national

---

[115] "Al Assad calls for wider popular participation," *Elaph* news Web site, June 6, 2005, at: http://www.elaph.com/ElaphWeb/Politics/2005/6/67293.htm.

heritage can be described as *change without progress,* whereas that of Saudi Arabia is *progress without change.* And while the former could be said to be something of a steady state, Burkhart and Older (2003, p. 14) emphasize that "the latter cannot continue forever."

I.III.III.III. <u>Malaysia: A Modern Islamic View of the Internet</u>

In comparison, Malaysia represents a different case—not to forget that it, too, is a Muslim country. It has embarked upon a program of implementing all the political, economic, and social possibilities of the Web by committing itself to building an internal infrastructure that it calls the "Multimedia Super Corridor" (MSC). The MSC entails both a physical location and an electronic "cyberspace" which the government began building in 1996. With the construction of this Corridor in its three phases, Malaysians will have complete and full access to the Internet—nationally and internationally.

The project intends to provide all the technology and access points that any individual, educational institution, or business enterprise would need to have to the Web. The Malaysian government considers joining the ranks of the global "information society" in terms of a completely open-ended and unknown terrain, and thus, rendering unfettered Web access is a sort of experimental encounter with a unique vision.

Parallel to the country's ambitions to attain the status of a fully 'developed' nation by the year 2020, the Malaysians have adopted this high-tech 20-year project, which they believe will entitle them to the cutting edge of social, economic and technological development in the early 21st century. According to official statements,[116] the MSC aims to be:

---

[116] The MSC Web site is: www.mdc.my/index.html.

- a vehicle for attracting world-class technology-led companies to Malaysia, and developing local industries;

- a multimedia Utopia offering a productive, intelligent environment within which a multimedia value chain of goods and services will be produced and delivered across the globe;

- an island of excellence with multimedia-specific capabilities, technologies, infrastructure, legislation, policies, and systems for competitive advantage;

- a test bed for invention, research, and other ground-breaking multimedia developments spearheaded by seven multimedia applications;

- a global community living on the leading edge of the Information Society; and,

- a world of *Smart Homes, Smart Cities, Smart Schools, Smart Cards* and *Smart Partnerships.*

The shortage of knowledge workers is resolved by allowing the free movement in and out of Malaysia, realizing that the country itself alone cannot assure the vastly expanded pool of workers required for the coming society based on IT use. In other words, the country appears to be at peace with its neighbors and has left aside eventual fears of 'cultural pollution' arising from the immigration of foreign nationals who come, join, and contribute to the new information-based society of Southeast Asia.[117]

The 'multiple versions' of the information society will also be interesting to observe. Just as there are many cultures, languages, and civilizations, Azzman envisions the emergence of different kinds of information society.[118] That is, each society is in need of an *infostructure*, a technical human infrastructure that maximizes the human potential to access information and to create value-added commodities and services. He adds that with the new global market place based on the flow of information, individuals, corporations, and governments can obtain the information they need from any service provider, located anywhere in the world. Such an assumption signals that all potential local providers are put on notice that

[117] Economically speaking, the traditional paradigm centered on land, labor and capital has undergone a radical shift, where *information* is now the underlying source of value–not land nor labor. This contemporary shift highlights the emerging 'new growth theory' in economics. Supporting this view is the deeper insight that *ideas are commodities* and that since *ideas* are basically *infinite* in supply, the so-called 'law of diminishing returns' no longer applies.

[118] Tengku Mohd. Azzman Shariffadeen, "Moving Toward a More Intelligent Use of Human Intelligence," presented at INFOTECH 95 Malaysia, Kuala Lumpur, November 1-5, 1999, p. 4.

they must compete on a level set by international, global standards, and not by those of any one country.

To sum up, political leaders have revealed obvious worries about the potential political uses of the Internet. With the study of the political uses of the Internet still in its early stages, initial indications suggest that the Internet is a means for many individuals to express political and anti-government sentiments.

In an inquiry based on the analysis of messages posted on the various "Usenet" news groups by country, Hill and Hughes found that only 33% of all messages posted could be considered as 'political'.[119] Of these messages that were political in nature, around 24% were anti-government, while 19% were pro-government. Of all messages posted in the Usenet groups, only 8.5% were accounted as anti-government, with another 6.4% as pro-government. Since the Internet has been used as a medium for anti-government expression, anti-political messages have not constituted a major portion of all the messages posted–as illustrated by these results. Respectively, this leads to wonder how much public expression of political nature–especially negative one–can governments in transition in an Information Society withstand?

On a more practical level, there are essential technical issues to resolve. The Internet cannot operate, technically speaking, without an efficient telecommunications system, and more and more, without wide bandwidth or fiber optic cable networking. Installing such a system is not only costly but also relies on the resources of private industry to ensure it. Privatizing the telecommunications system poses a major hurdle for developing countries.

---

[119] Kevin Hill and John E. Hughes, *Cyberpolitics. Citizens Activism in the Age of the Internet*, Lanham, MD: Roman and Littlefield, 1998, pp. 81, 84.

I.III.III.IV. Global Access to the Internet

The first global index to rank ICT issued by the International Telecommunications Union (ITU) in November 2003 classifies countries into one of four digital access categories: **high**, **upper**, **medium**, and **low**.[120] In an aim to provide an overall country score, the Digital Access Index (DAI) covers five areas, namely: availability of infrastructure, affordability of access, educational level, quality of ICT services, and Internet usage.

Among the findings of the DAI, which covers around 180 economies, Slovenia ties France (ranked 23rd); and the Republic of Korea, usually not among the top ten in international ICT rankings, comes in fourth. Other than Canada, the top ten economies are exclusively Asian and European. In order, they are: Sweden, Denmark, Iceland, Republic of Korea, Norway, Netherlands, Hong Kong (China), Finland, Taiwan (China), and Canada. A number of countries have used ICTs as a development enabler, where government policies have helped them reach an impressive level of ICT access. This includes major ICT projects such as the Dubai Internet City in the United Arab Emirates (the highest ranked Arab country in the Index), the Multimedia Super Corridor in Malaysia (the highest ranked developing Asian country), and the Cyber City in Mauritius (along with Seychelles, the highest ranked African country).

Finally, there is the global problem of manpower demands and recruitment of the new information-based economy. Even American corporations, representing the largest economy in the world, recruit IT workers from elsewhere (as do the European), especially from India.[121]

Realizing the importance of timing in recruiting, the U.S. Immigration and Naturalization Services (INS) in June 2001 began to allow foreigners to pay $1000 to get work-visa applications processed within 15 days, instead of waiting for the

---

[120] "ITU Digital Access Index: World's First Global ICT Ranking," *ITU*, November 19, 2003, at: http://www.itu.int/newsarchive/press_releases/2003/30.html.

[121] See: Ann Lee Saxenian, "Silicon Valley's New Immigrant Entrepreneurs," June 1999, at: www.ppic.org/publications/PPIC120/index.html.

usual three months or more. The 'Premium Processing Program', which enables citizens of other countries to work in the States for limited periods, applies to a wide range of celebrities, athletes, executives, scientists, as well as to those with specialized skills.[122] Although the fee does not guarantee approval, the money is returned if the applicant does not receive a response from the agency within that delay.

Malaysia has to compete in its own regional *niche* against Singapore's high demand for IT and knowledge workers and its program of recruiting high school students in India before they are recruited by American corporations.[123]

The German government in 2000, under pressure from its industry, offered five-year residence permits to 20,000 foreign computer experts. Only 8,000 people took up the offer, and advocates of increased immigration to Germany stated that limited visas encouraged skilled people to look instead to the United States where they could become legal permanent residents and, eventually, American citizens.

---

[122] Dan Eggen, "Rich? Famous? America Wants You," *IHT*, June 1, 2001, 1.

[123] Huff in "Globalization and the Internet" (2001, p. 450) points to political tensions between Malaysia and Singapore, generated largely by the desire of the Singaporean leadership to keep an external threat alive to fuel its 'survivalist' ideology. See also: Beng Huat Chua, *Communitarian Ideology and Democracy in Singapore*, London: Routledge, 1995; and Michael Haas, ed., *The Singapore Puzzle*, Westport, CT: Praeger Press, 1999.

I.IV. The Course of Development in Military Warfare
and Space Weapons

This section explores the important trends and achievements in the military field, where such developments in terms of the doctrine, technology, and employment have all come forward throughout the course of the Information Age. It outlines essential features of the association between technological advancement and military dominance. It also envisions possible scenarios of conflict, whether conventional or not, and their respective battlefields in the years to come, both on ground or in space.

I.IV.I. Tracing the Contribution of Warfare to the Information Age

The rise of agriculture, along with the domestication of animals in the fifth millennium B.C., is acknowledged as the early initiatives that set the stage for the emergence of the first large-scale, complex urban societies. Those societies, evolving almost simultaneously around 4000 B.C. in both Mesopotamia and in the Nile, used stone tools. Within 500 years stone tools and weapons paved way to bronze, leading to a revolution in warfare.[124]

The two city-states that produced the most sophisticated armies of the Bronze Age are the sites of ancient Sumer and Akkad, in the area of present-day Iraq. In terms of effectiveness and weaponry, the armies of Sumer and Akkad represented the height of military development in the Bronze Age; recalling here that the Sumerian civilization invented no fewer than six major weapons and defensive systems, all of which set the standards for the armies of the Bronze Age and, later on, for the Iron Ages.

---

[124] The following summary and documented information is based on: Richard A. Gabriel and Karen S. Metz, *A Short History of War: The Evolution of Warfare and Weapons*, Professional Readings in Military Strategy, No. 5, June 30, 1992, U.S. Army War College: Strategic Studies Institute, Carlisle Barracks, Pennsylvania. A word of thanks is due to Dr. Jean-Jacques PATRY of C.E.D.S. for drawing attention to the reference material.

The military innovation of the ancient world did not, as in modern times, emerge independent of need. In Sumer, two thousand years of wars among the city-states provided the opportunity for constant military *modernizing*. In other parts of the globe, as in the Nile (now Egypt), which were sealed off from major enemies by geography and culture, military weaponry demanded little change–leaving it (the weaponry) far behind developments in Sumer.

Accordingly, with sophisticated weaponry and tactics requiring some form of social organization, the period from 1500 B.C. to A.D. 100 witnessed a veritable evolution in most aspects of people's existence and life style. Those years were also characterized by a transformation in the manner and means of conducting warfare, thanks to the discovery and use of iron first employed in war around 1300 B.C. The Iron Age was marked by nearly constant war, when states of all sizes emerged only to be extinguished by the rise of still more powerful empires. In addition, that period saw the practice of war firmly rooted in man's societies and experience, and even more significantly, in his psychology. *War, warriors,* and *weapons* had then become a normal component of human existence.

From the 1860s, the pace of weapons development increased enormously with the Industrial Revolution producing one advance after the other. The French, in 1870, deployed the *mitrailleuse*, a highly reliable 25-barrel machine gun capable of firing 125 rounds a minute while accurate at 2000 yards (1800 meters). And again in France in 1877, time fuses were developed and served to make overhead artillery more lethal than ever before.

The most essential consequences of the factory system, mass productions, and machine manufacture were, among others, the immense reduction in time required between new ideas and the manufacture of production prototypes (compared to the Iron Age, when armies produced the prototype of every weapon that was developed for the following three thousand years). New concepts were quickly translated into drawings, then to models, then prototypes, and finally to full-scale implementation within very short periods of time.

The increasing volumes of technical journals and their wide-scale circulation shortened the time it took for innovations in one discipline to have an impact in another related field. While the immediate result was a rapid increase in *information transfer*, the overall consequence of these circumstances was the fast application of new weapons and war technologies to the battlefield at a pace never known before in history–and, of course, with the corresponding impact that weapons became once again even more lethal.

Yet, if the Information Age and knowledge-society make sharing and cooperation more beneficial, Ury (1999, p. 86) argues that they also make fighting more harmful. Weapons have become not only deadlier, but also cheaper and more accessible to anyone. Automatic weapons can be purchased on many street corners (at times, even offered free), land mines can be acquired for a few dollars each, and bombs able to kill hundreds–as we have seen most recently–can be assembled from store-bought items. With modern weapons changing the very nature of what it means to fight, the evolution of logic in warfare has shifted from *arrows* (seen as a warning or lesson), to *guns* (fatal), to *nuclear war* (as total destruction).

Therefore, the study of history has great functional significance for comprehending the future. Since men think in analogies, many of the problems of the past are quite analogously alike to those of today. Consider, for instance, the fact that with the exception of the United States and the powers in Western Europe (none of which were in existence at that time), the coalition of nations that launched the attack on Iraq in the Iraq-Kuwait conflict were the same coalition of powers that attacked the Assyrian Empire–in Mesopotamia–in 612 B.C. (Gabriel & Metz, p. 114).

Examine, as well, the problem of mass migration due to tragic economic circumstances that are provoked from Eastern Europe and currently confronting the Western European states, and how that same problem was encountered by similar migrations from the same region into the Roman Empire in the 3rd century. To conclude, the study of historical situations that are truly analogous to recent incidents faced by political actors expands the analyst's frame of reference when attending to the solutions of such cases.

I.IV.II. **Military Force and Technology in the Information Age**

A new era in military planning is underway, one that has already involved dramatic changes. As defense leaderships attempt to define and prepare a more efficient and effective military from the top down, military services are selectively transforming key capabilities to meet the anticipated needs for warfare in the present millennium. This broad-level change is continuing at a speed faster than some might have expected, with both derivation and entirely new capabilities becoming available. But what makes challenges in this era remarkably different from those planners confronted in the past?

In the past, the primacy of planning involved countering the single major threat to national interests. At that time, the questions of "who" and "where" were known, and the challenge was less about understanding the problem than about providing the solution. That in mind, the answer appeared to be linked to developing a superior military capability by sources of manpower and material that would in large part already be in place. And where equality in manpower could not be achieved, technology was employed to level the battlefield. Many *force multipliers* were designed and stationed, including the first generation of so-called "smart" and precision-guided weapons. Accordingly, all the services collectively did their part, resulting in a highly effective military.

Military reflections of the 1970s, along with the evolutions in military warfare of the 1980s, explains Garcin,[125] led to a series of interlinked–but decentralized–combat options. That included launching fire from distance positions, ability to penetrate deep in enemy field, and capacity to strike targets with significant precision (causing maximum damage but minimal human casualties). The targets sought implied both civilian (such as cities and vital installations) and military (forces).

---

[125] Thierry GARCIN, *Les enjeux stratégiques de l'espace*, ('The Strategic Stakes of Space'), Brussels: Bruylant, 2001, p. 100. The geopolitical, socio-political, and military aspects that have contributed to the evolution of the RMA are well treated by the same author (pp. 99-107).

Yet, in contrast to the previous era, the immediate challenge for today's planning is about understanding the problem, not just in terms of the *who* and the *where*, but also the *why* and *to what extent*. To a certain measure, the critical challenge is less about providing manpower and material *en masse*, and more about providing the right combination (noting that defense spending remains a principle constraining factor).

In examining what military capabilities are essential for 2015, a RAND study defines three broad priorities driven by future technology options: remote fires, rapidly deployable ground forces, and a joint capability that integrates the two.[126]

I.IV.II.I. Improvements for the Remote-Fires Options

Programmed advances in Command, Control, Communications, Computers, Intelligence, Surveillance, and Reconnaissance (C4ISR) provide greater levels of situational awareness to friendly forces and offers the potential to improve knowledge of enemy actions. *Smart* munitions become *smarter*, and guided munitions become even more accurate (with a maximum three-meter circular error probability). All that implies distancing standoff ranges significantly.

The Revolution in Military Affairs has introduced an array of sensors, vehicles and weapons that can be operated by remote control or are totally autonomous. Within a decade, those machines are expected to be able to perform many of the most dangerous, effort-demanding, or boring tasks now assigned to a typical soldier.[127] The rapid shift away from people, referred to as manned units, to automation has several objectives.

Several new devices will be much smaller and lighter, making them cheaper, more fuel efficient, and easier to move. Thanks to their unlimited attention spans,

---

[126] John Matsumara et al., *Preparing for Future Warfare with Advanced Technologies: Prioritizing the Next Generation of Capabilities*, RAND, Santa Monica, CA, 2002.

[127] Read: James Dao and Andrew C. Revkin, "A Revolution in Warfare: Machines Are Filling In for Troops," *The New York Times*, online edition, April 16, 2002.

machines should function better at tedious, time-consuming duties that human warriors detest, such as standing guard or monitoring mountain passes.

Most importantly, however, remote technology is to shield and aid the flesh-and-blood soldier. By the year 2020, pilotless aircrafts (e.g., the Predator, Global Hawk, the Dragon Fly) and driverless vehicles will direct remote-controlled bombers towards targets, pilotless helicopters will coordinate driverless convoys and unmanned submarines will clear mines and launch cruise missiles. Indeed, the United States did fly for the first time the armed, unmanned RQ-1 Predator into combat and guided them with operators in its country thousands of miles from the battlefield in Afghanistan in late 2001.[128]

Last, the Pentagon predicts that robots will constitute a major fighting force in the American military in less than a decade. A $127 billion project, called Future Combat Systems, is considered the biggest military contract in American history. According to military planners, robot soldiers will think, see, and react increasingly like humans. Although they will be remote-controlled in the beginning, robot soldiers will take many shapes, grow in intelligence and extend in autonomy as the technology develops.

The hunter-killer robot is only one of five broad categories of military robots under development. Another type of robots is to scout buildings, tunnels and caves. A third is to haul tons of weapons and gear, and perform searches and reconnaissance. A fourth is a drone in flight. And the fifth, designed originally as a security guard, is soon to be able to launch drones to conduct surveillance, psychological warfare along with other missions.

Noting that the Future Combat Systems is still in its first stages (where it may take at least another 30 years to realize in full), a typical military unit is intended to include around 2,245 soldiers and some 151 military robots. However, there will

---

[128] See also: Thomas E. Ricks, "Waging war by remote control," *www.msnbc.com*, October 18, 2001.

be much work to do before a robot can be trusted in distinguishing friend from foe, and also combatant from bystander.[129]

I.IV.II.II. Improvements for the Rapidly Deploying Ground Forces Options

Improved deployability and greater effectiveness are the two major factors that are to distinguish the current forces from now up to 2015. The American army demonstrated for the first time in an exercise the concept of a 'digital' army, a radical new idea to transform the military into a "faster, lighter, and smarter" force.[130] This reflects, according to analysts, post-Cold War realities, in which troops are expected to engage in swift skirmishes rather than set battles with heavy equipment.

The system relies on a complex network of wireless modems, satellite links and traditional human scouts to compile a computerized overview of a battlefield. Army tanks and armored personnel carriers are equipped with 25-centimeter computer monitors that instantly locate where they are, where they should go, and where the enemy might be–reflecting the importance and power of *information* as an element of combat. To reduce "friendly fire" incidents (a major source of concern during combats), a battlefield identification program is being developed to electronically identify a soldier or vehicle and instantly distinguish them from that of the enemy.

Accordingly, to give all American commanders and troops a moving picture of all foreign enemies and threats, the Pentagon is already building its own Internet–the military's World Wide Web for the wars in the future. The secure network, called the Global Information Grid (GID), had its first connections laid in late 2004. A persistent problem to solve is bandwidth, where the military will need 40 or 50 times what was used at the height of the invasion in Iraq in 2003,

---

[129] Tim Weiner, "A New Model Army Soldier Rolls Closer to the Battlefield," *The New York Times*, online edition, February 16, 2005.

[130] Peter Pae, "On the Battlefield of the Future, War Is Handheld," *IHT,* May 5-6, 2001, 1. Also: Dainty Duffy, "Information as weapon: Military IT," *CNN,* online edition, (Sci-Tech), November 5, 2001.

something enough to provide front-line soldiers bandwidth equal to download three feature-length movies a second. Pentagon documents suggest it may take 200 billion dollars or more to construct the military Internet hardware and software in the next decade or so.[131]

Moving to the so-called *digital force*, however, could mean dramatic changes for the army's traditional command structure, where future battles may occur so rapidly that a tank lieutenant may find himself making critical decisions usually reserved for higher-level commanders. A bigger challenge may also arise for the soldiers who may not know what to do with all the information they receive, while commanders, on the other hand, may be reluctant to assume authority. Even worse, soldiers may confront the psychological factor of becoming too reliant on the computer and less on their own individual decision-making process. Also consider what would happen when the network that supports these technologies goes down or is hacked, or if the technology falls into enemy's hand.

I.IV.II.III. <u>A Combined Approach Through a Joint Rapidly Responsive Force</u>

By combining the first capabilities, it is possible to leverage each one's areas of strength and minimize areas of weakness. Resembling a war room that seemed modeled after a "Star Wars" movie, in early 2002 engineers at Boeing Co. displayed three screens: the first featuring a satellite image of a region, with moving squares and triangles identifying fighter jets, bombers and spy planes; the second showing detailed infrared images of a building targeted for possible attack; and the third screen providing a live feed from a foot soldier wearing a small video camera on his helmet.

The images were part of a mock military operation in an unidentified Middle Eastern region, providing a glimpse at what Boeing believed to correspond to the methods of war for the 21st century.

---

[131] Tim Weiner, "Pentagon Envisioning a Costly Internet for War," *The New York Times*, online edition, November 13, 2004.

It represents a fundamental reversal of the way wars have been fought for the past 2 ½ centuries. Ten years ago, Norman Schwarzkopf had to pack up a small town and move it to Saudi Arabia to fight the Gulf War. You won't have to do that anymore. It'll be a lot like telecommuting.[132]

In terms of nuclear arms, since the end of the Cold War the United States has been re-examining the role of nuclear forces in its national security policy. Among other objectives, traditional U.S. nuclear strategy was essentially intended to deter a Soviet attack against the United States. That strategy called for a nuclear arsenal held at constant high alert and a Single Integrated Operation Plan (SIOP) that would make the execution of a retaliatory strike as simple, quick, and effective as possible.

Respectively, the classified Pentagon report "Nuclear Posture Review" (provided to the Congress in January 2002) states that the Bush administration has directed the military to prepare contingency plans to use nuclear weapons against at least seven countries and to build smaller nuclear weapons for use in certain battlefield situations. While no longer officially naming Russia as an 'enemy', the report emphasizes that the Pentagon needs to be prepared to use nuclear weapons against China, Russia, Iraq, North Korea, Iran, Libya and Syria.

In apparently the first time that an official list of potential target countries comes to light, the reports adds that "the weapons could be used in three types of situations: against targets able to withstand non-nuclear attack, in retaliation for attack with nuclear, biological or chemical weapons, or in the event of surprising military developments."[133] More specifically, the reports says the Pentagon should be prepared to use nuclear weapons in an Arab-Israeli conflict, in a war between China and Taiwan, or in an attack from North Korea on the South. Nuclear

---

[132]   Peter Pae, "Ushering In the Warfare Information Age," *Los Angeles Times*, online edition, March 16, 2002.

[133] Paul Richter, "U.S. Works Up Plan for Using Nuclear Arms," *Los Angeles Times*, online edition, March 9, 2002.

weapons might also become necessary in an attack by Iraq on Israel or another neighbor, the Report mentions.

The United States, therefore, today faces a more diverse set of potential threats. Political instability in established nuclear countries, such as Russia and Pakistan, is a major concern.[134] The deterioration of military command and control in Russia increases the chances of accidental or unauthorized launch. In addition, nuclear weapons may become instruments of the weak rather than of the strong. Weak parties opposed to the United States may attempt to deliver nuclear warheads on trucks or ships, hence, eluding U.S. tactical warning systems. States or groups that embrace radical, anti-American ideologies and feel they have nothing left to lose may not be deterred by the threat of nuclear retaliation.

To conclude, a research paper titled *Future Roles of U.S. Nuclear Forces: Implications for U.S. Strategy* examines a range of strategies and force postures that the United States could adopt to make the most effective use of its nuclear forces in an uncertain world.[135] Key observations include the following:

- the need for the United States to retain nuclear weapons is much less compelling than in the past;

- a much smaller nuclear force could fulfill all U.S. political and military needs; and,

- reducing the risk of nuclear war due to accidents or mistakes is even more important than in the past.

I.IV.II.IV. The Gap in RMA among Western Countries

The key to military power in the Information Age, as recalled, depends on the ability to collect, process, disseminate, and integrate data from complex systems of space-based surveillance, high-speed computers, and 'smart' weapons. The conflict in Kosovo in 1999 signaled the concerns of European governments in increasingly

---

[134] According to Project Ploughshares (a Canadian ecumenical peace center), over 700 incidents of illicit trafficking in nuclear materials have been recorded since 1991. See: "Swords and Ploughshares 2003," at: www.ploughshares.ca.

[135] Glenn C. Buchan et al., *Future Roles of U.S. Nuclear Forces: Implications for U.S. Strategy*, RAND, MR-1231-AF, 2003.

becoming *second-rank* powers, unable to affect American foreign policy goals because they cannot bring forward neither efficient nor sufficient military assets.

This observation was pointed out by NATO's former secretary general Lord Robertson who warned the European countries of a choice between "modernization or marginalization," and expressed more directly by the U.S. Ambassador to NATO who reiterated that "without dramatic action to close the capabilities gap, we [the Americans] face the real prospect of a two-tiered alliance [with a risk that the alliance] is so unbalanced that we may no longer have the ability to fight together in the future."[136]

Among the obvious improvements the Europeans need to focus on include quicker troops deployment by air, mid-air refueling, precision-guided munitions, and ability to operate with battlefield radars from the sky. Europe, devastated by military conflicts in the 20th century, prefers to spend its resources on social welfare at home and on aid to countries in need abroad. The countries of the European Union altogether provide around 56% of the world's aid and about 36% of the United Nations budget.

Noteworthy in this context is the Commitment to Development Index 2004 conducted by the Center for Global Development and Foreign Policy magazine. The Index ranks rich countries on how their policies help or harm prospects for development in poor nations in terms of trade, technology, security, environment, migration, investment, and aid. The leading countries in the Index, published in the May-June 2004 edition of Foreign Policy, were respectively: Netherlands, Denmark, Sweden, Australia, United Kingdom, Canada, United States, Germany, Norway, France, Finland, Austria, Belgium, Portugal, Italy, New Zealand, Greece, Ireland, Switzerland, Spain, and Japan.

In the coming years, Pentagon's budget is expected to exceed the overall military budgets of the world's next 14 biggest defense spenders put together.

---

[136] Steven Erlanger, "Military Gulf Separates U.S. and European Allies," *The New York Times*, online edition, March 16, 2002. See also: Michel R. Gordon, "Military Gap Growing Between U.S. and Allies," *IHT*, June 7, 2001, 7.

More in details, Europe spends about \$140 billion a year on the military, with an average of only around \$7,000 per soldier–compared with \$28,000 per American soldier–on research & development.[137]

Yet, budget allocations are not the only hindrance to the enlarging gap. Another problem can be as basic as transportation. For instance, Germany was unable to deliver *on schedule* more than a third of the troops it committed for peacekeeping in Kabul simply because it had to rent Russian or Ukrainian transport planes on the commercial market.

And then, there are the Americans who would prefer to keep a serious military power, such as France, away from any significant cooperation or engagement to avoid any sharing of strategic, political or operational information in a collective command.[138] Consider and compare, as well, the nature and volume of forces participating in the coalition along with the United States during the 1991 Iraq-Kuwait conflict, to that during the 1999 Kosovo conflict, to the 2001 coalition against Afghanistan, and most recently, to the participating troops during the American invasion in Iraq in 2003.

In a few words voiced more commonly, the United States is seen as the power that fights, while the United Nations feeds, the European Union finances, and European soldiers maintain peace.

I.IV.III. Conquering No Man's Zone: Striving for Space Weapons

The concept of space weapons is not new, as it had already been debated in the modern history of space. At the start of the Cold War, the issue was the

---

[137] The figures are cited from Erlanger (*Ibid.*). The U.S. Senate approved a \$447 billion defense bill for 2005, with \$68.6 billion allocated for research & development. See allocations at: "US approves \$447 bn defense bill," *www.bbc.co.uk*, June 24, 2004.

[138] On the tense sentiments regarding the U.S.-French military cooperation, see: Philippe Chatenay, «L'Amérique veut bien de nos diplomates, mais pas de nos soldats», ('America well wants our diplomats, but not our soldiers'), *Marianne*, no. 235, October 22-28, 2001, 35; and also: Jacques Isnard, « La délicate coopération militaire franco-américaine », ('The delicate French-American military cooperation'), *Le Monde*, Tuesday, July 9, 2002, 2.

possibility of bombardment satellites carrying nuclear weapons. At the end of the Cold War, the issue then was the possibility of space-based defenses against nuclear missiles. After the Cold War became history, the topic of space weapons is now once again surfacing.

Reference to "space weapons" is meant to cover "things intended to cause harm that are based in space or that have an essential element based in space." The degree of harm implicitly included in the definition of space weapons may range from temporary disruption to permanent destruction or death. Accordingly, the definition does not include things that are based on the earth and transit space without achieving orbit, such as ballistic missiles.[139]

The importance of examining space weapons here arises from the possibilities that countries may–or already have–decide(d) to acquire them. A modest number of space-based weapons with limited space-based support could deny any country of its maritime means for power projection. Such weapons, reasonably available to *space faring* countries having even the humble capabilities of India or China, could even result to a high-leverage, asymmetric response to U.S. military strengths.

A distinction is deemed necessary between the issue of space weapons in terrestrial conflict, as opposed to uses of space in conflict or weapons in space conflict. Focus is devoted on space weapons in terrestrial conflict because they constitute an emerging decision subject. Meanwhile, the use of space in conflict and the employment of weapons against space systems are both historical fact and current reality. Ever since its early beginning, the use of space has not exempted conflict and tension: locating targets, signaling threats, relaying commands, aiding navigation, and forecasting weather. Such vital significance and use in wartime has long rendered the space zone a military objective.

Throughout the Cold War, starting with the race to the space and the moon, both sides developed, tested, and deployed weapons against satellites. Numerous countries have weapons that can be used against space systems, whether to jam

---

[139] This definition of "space weapons" is adopted from: Bob Preston et al., *Space Weapons Earth Wars*, RAND, Santa Monica, CA, 2002, p. 23.

links, blink sensors, or disable ground stations. Certain among them have already used them, including Russia's jamming of telecommunications satellites during its war in Chechnya.[140]

A Congress Report, as well, has warned that the some 600 satellites the U.S. military depends on "for photo reconnaissance, targeting, communications, weather forecasting, early warning and intelligence gathering are highly vulnerable to attack from adversaries."[141] The report does not exclude an anticipated "Space Pearl Harbor" attack against American satellites orbiting the planet.

Therefore, the U.S. national space policy embodies explicit goals for strengthening and maintaining national security and promoting international cooperation to further U.S. national security and foreign policy. The national space policy directs the conduct of specific space activities considered necessary for national defense, with particular emphasis on activities that support military operations around the globe, monitor and respond to threats, and oversee arms control and non-proliferation agreements. The emphasis outlined in the language is on support, without specifically precluding the possibility of space weapons. The broad interpretation is to provide support for the inherent rights of self-defense, within the below details:

- deter; warn; and, if necessary, defend against enemy attack;

- ensure that hostile forces cannot prevent U.S. use of space;

- if necessary, counter the hostile use of force;

- maintain the capability to execute mission areas of space control and force application;

- consistent with treaty obligations, develop, operate, and maintain space-control capabilities to ensure freedom of action for the United States and to deny freedom of action to U.S. adversaries; and,

---

[140] "Military Spokesman Admits Phone Jamming in N. Caucus," *Agence France Press*, FBIS AU2411101599, Paris, 1999.

[141] Jonathan Broder, "Pentagon has big plans for combat in the cosmos," *www.msnbc.com*, September 20, 2001.

- pursue a ballistic missile defense program to enhance theater missile defenses, to provide readiness for national missile defense as a hedge against emergence of a long-range threat, and to develop advanced technology options to improve planned and deployed defenses.[142]

I.IV.IV. <u>The Needs and Means of Acquiring Space Weapons</u>

A number of hypothetical ways prevail determining whether or not a country decides to acquire space weapons. A conscious or deliberate decision to do so may be considered, in contrast to an incidental or accidental decision where related technologies and systems developed for commercial or other purposes then become available for or are applied to military operations. Without neglecting any incidental outcomes in the foreseeable future, the section below essentially deals with deliberate decisions.

To start with the United States, there is currently no compelling threat to its national security that could not be deterred or addressed by means other than space weapons. A decision by the United States to acquire such weapons could result out of a variety of circumstance, among of which are:

- defending against a threat to national security posed by an adversary who is undeterred by other capabilities;

- responding in kind to the acquisition of space weapons by another country, whether ally or adversary;

- acquiring space weapons in coordination with another country or with several countries to forestall, control, or influence their independent acquisition or space weapons; and,

- unilaterally undertaking the acquisition of space weapons on the basis of any one of several purposes, for instance, to demonstrate global leadership, to protect American and allied economic investments, or to impose the efficiency and effectiveness of military capability.[143]

The United States could consider the last point as a component of its vision of global power projection for the year 2010 and beyond. In part, the decision to acquire space-based weapons for use against territorial targets depends on another

---

[142] *Space Weapons Earth Wars*, 2002, pp. 15-16.

[143] *Space Weapons Earth Wars*, 2002, p. xxii.

country's decision to acquire similar weapons. Yet, alternatives and responses by the United States could vary according to the nature and decision of the other country.

Based on the strategic vision above, and given the current U.S. technological and economic potential capacity, the United States may find itself not alone in the opportunity and ambition to acquire space-based weapons. The presentation next demonstrates *whom*, *why* and *how* other states may join the race.

- **Peer Competitors:**

While the United States throughout the Cold War had only one peer competitor, namely, the Soviet Union, it does not–in a military sense– have one at the moment. But, that may change. As noted, the military sense is not the only field of competition that matters for a decision to acquire space weapons, where a peer may simply decide to acquire them to *reduce* or *bypass* American military advantages. Also, an economic competitor might decide to acquire them to gain an independent ability to protect its own global interests, not out of a desire for a confrontation with the United States.

Though it might be common to think of future peers in the same terms once referred to the Soviet Union, that seems to be two narrow here. A striving Russia or an economically maturing China can be seen as potential examples of a future peer competitor, as may a *political cohesive* European Union. Such possibilities would demand a more in-depth definition and comprehension of what the reference to "peer competitor" may imply, outlining national capabilities and interests. In this context, capabilities would include both technical abilities (technology and facilities) and economic resources.

- **Friend or Ally:**

The defining element of friendly or allied nations considered here stems from the understanding that solid common interests have established a mutual relationship–either formalized by treaty or set in place over time by custom. Since the United States would not normally perceive these countries as threats to its interests, their decision to acquire weapons would not evoke the adversarial response that a competitor's decision might (leading, perhaps, the United States to re-act in a different manner).

Importantly to observe as well, most mutual relationships include a security element between the two sides. Among the group of friends or allies to examine include any of the NATO members, Israel, Australia, Saudi Arabia (as an example of one of the Gulf States that share American interests in regional stability and security), Taiwan, South Korea and Japan. The list is even more narrowed if we consider the means available to them to acquire some sort of space weapons.

Access to space is clearly the first prerequisite for such weapons, with potential candidates as France, Japan and Israel already enjoying space-launch capabilities. *Satellite technology* is the second prerequisite, where France, the United Kingdom, Germany, Italy, Japan, and Israel possessing adequate satellite industries and technology for the development of some kinds of space weapons. *Resources* complete the set of prerequisites needed to acquire space weapons. "If the need is for immediate response, global reach, and many targets, the resources needed would be large. However, if the urgency, coverage, and quantities are relaxed, the resources could fit within national security budgets," the study assumes.[144]

Nevertheless, the acquisition of space weapons by European countries (with the leading role of France) has seen certain drawbacks. Among them, clarifies Garcin (2001, pp. 105-07), include abandoning certain projects (e.g., space ships), the respective needs and ends of the parties

---

[144] *Space Weapons Earth Wars*, 2002, p. 92.

involved are not identical or synchronic, a number of essential projects (e.g., missiles and military satellites) are subject to debate, cooperation with the United States is often engaged by other countries in the continent (the United Kingdom, Germany, Italy), and budget allocations (which are poor, or even reduced) for such projects are neither comparable nor assured in the long-term.

- **Neither Ally nor Adversary:**

Many states are obviously neither peer competitors nor friends or allies. Such states do not generally have the scope of global interests that might accordingly motivate a preference for space weapons–although they may have regional security concerns that could provoke the motivation. Enjoying its own access to space, the Indian subcontinent, for example, is one possible region for interest in space weapons, with probably unpleasant consequences for the United States.

While states that fall into this group may not be adversaries to the United States *for the moment*, their acquisition of space weapons might increase the possibility of bringing them into conflict with the United States. Since such countries do not have the capacity to threaten that a peer competitor would have, the United States might have more possible responses then it would with a peer. And because of missile technology proliferation controls, it becomes more difficult for these countries to acquire space-based weapons even in the manner described for friends or allies. Yet, these controls have proven to be fruitless several times.

Pakistan, for example, has already acquired the beginnings of launch technology by buying missiles from North Korea. Brazil has had its own space launch developments with assistance, ranging in time and occasion, from the United States, Russia, and China. Among these states, the second prerequisite for space weapons, that is, a well-developed indigenous satellite industry, applies only to India.

- **Non-Peer Adversary:**

Small, less-capable, isolated countries may fall into this category. The United States considers these countries adversaries, such as North Korea, Iran,[145] Cuba, and Syria (including Iraq before March 2003). They have limited ability to acquire space weapons independently and are restrained even more by rigid trade and non-proliferation controls. However, this does not exclude the possibility that a small adversary may not become a client state of a U.S. peer competitor, or at the very least, a customer for the elements of space weapons.

Through non-proliferation controls, the United States intends to convert these so-called "rogue states" (or "states of concern") from adversary to friendly—or at least to non-aligned status (as it did with Libya). The *over significant* concern here is the likely willingness of one of these states to use any acquired space weapons for mass-destruction.

- **Non-state Coalition:**

The last set among those who *might* be able to place weapons in space to use at some point in time is a coalition of actors. Though this is a possible case, such interested parties have proven to be more attracted to car bombs and hand-made explosives (such as Al Qaida), and to the development of chemical weapons and more effective ways to deliver them (such as Aum Shinri Kyo and its sarin gas release in Tokyo's subway).

---

[145] Since the Islamic Revolution in 1979, Iran's geopolitical environment has changed dramatically. With the collapse of the Soviet Union, the military defeat of Iraq twice (in 1991 and 2003) and the large U.S. military presence in its region, all these factors have altered Iran's basic strategic outlook—making the state far more secure. However, another feature of Iran's geopolitical situation is the rampant instability that characterizes its even immediate neighbors. In brief: Iraq is already in real danger of fragmenting; Turkey has been fighting an insurgency under a national emergency for nearly two decades; Pakistan suffers intermittent civil conflict, repeated ruling changes, and a military coup; Azerbaijan and Armenia have not yet settled their territorial disputes (including borders along Iran); Afghanistan enters three decades of civil war and instability; and the civil war of Tajikistan has destabilized several neighbors. One may also wonder to what extent is the United States making use of such an environment to weaken Iran in the region. Refer to: Daniel L. Byman et al., *Iran's Security Policy in the Post-Revolution Era*, RAND, Santa Monica, CA, 2001.

Characterized by the international community and by the United States as criminals and terrorists, concern arises not with the precedent action or scope of competition–but rather with the nature of an eventual hostile act. *Space Weapons Earth Wars* concludes (2002, p. 98) that if and once incidental development via commercial, reusable space systems is taken into serious account, the difference between a truck bomb (or gas diffusion techniques) and a space cargo recovery module bomb might only be merely a question of time and selection of convenient ordnance.

To sum up, in view of the advantages American armed forces enjoy as a result of the unrestricted use of space, it is shortsighted to expect any potential adversary to refrain from attempting to offset or disable U.S. space capabilities. With the proliferation of space know-how and related technology around the world, adversaries will inevitably seek to make use of many of the same space advantages in the future. Not to forget in this respect that *space commerce* is a growing part of the global economy.

Consider for instance the year 1996, when commercial launches exceeded military launches in the United States, and commercial revenues exceeded government expenditures on space. At present, more than 1,100 commercial companies across more than 50 countries are developing, building, and operating space systems.[146]

Not surprisingly, several of these commercial space systems imply direct military applications, including information from global positioning system constellations and better-than-one-meter resolution imaging satellites. And indeed, some 95% of current U.S. military communications are conducted over commercial circuits, including commercial communications satellites. The U.S. Space Command envisions that in the coming decades (*Ibid.*):

---

[146] "Rebuilding America's Defenses: Strategy, Forces and Resources for a New Century," A Report of the Project for the New American Century, Washington, DC, September 2000, pp. 54-55.

> An adversary will have sophisticated regional situational awareness.
> Enemies may very well know, in near-real time, the disposition of all
> forces.... In fact, national military forces, paramilitary units, terrorists,
> and any other potential adversaries will share the high ground of space
> with the United States and its allies.
>
> Adversaries may also share the same commercial satellite services for
> communications, imagery, and navigation.... The space "playing field" is
> leveling rapidly, so U.S. forces will be increasingly vulnerable. Though
> adversaries will benefit greatly from space, losing the use of space may
> be more devastating to the United States. It would be intolerable for U.S.
> forces...to be deprived of capabilities in space.

In other words, the unequivocal supremacy in space enjoyed by the United States today is subject to increasing risk. On the other hand, Pentagon officials regularly need to demonstrate potential risks and threats facing the country as a means for higher budget demands.

I.IV.V. Space Wars: From Science Fiction to Non-Fiction

As World War I introduced new weaponry and modern combat to the 20th century, the Information Age is currently revolutionizing warfare in the 21st century. All over the world, the scope of IT has diffused weapons systems and defense infrastructures, and as a result, renders *cyberspace* a new global battlefield.

More than a decade after the end of the Cold War, the U.S. military stands as an uncontested superpower in both conventional and nuclear force. Yet ironically, the overwhelming military superiority and the leading edge in IT has also made the U.S. the country more vulnerable to cyber-attack. While other countries have recognized they have fallen behind in the military race, they have begun to explore other methods for enhancing their war-fighting and defense capacities, namely, *asymmetrical warfare*, characterized as countering an adversary's strengths by focusing on its weaknesses.

Americans celebrated the Iraq-Kuwait conflict in 1991 as a major triumph for U.S. military forces and as justification for the nation's defense structure (despite all the deficiencies and poor precision results, particularly in missile strikes). But elsewhere around the globe, the conflict drew attention to the fact that a direct military confrontation with the United States would inevitably lead to defeat. As the United States continues to develop its conventional forces, other countries are in the meantime seeking asymmetric advantage. In other words, the world has realized that a military confrontation with the United States makes no sense, at a time when one can most probably bring it down or cause it severe damage in a more oblique manner. This is where the vulnerability of the United States remains.

With RMA plans ranging from computer-based weapons research programs to software that encrypt classified military data, from computer-guided *smart* bombs, to a space-based missile defense, America's military forces are depending more and more on computers and information networks. As a consequence, the IT dominance of American conventional forces, along with the military's already extensive and growing use of it, make cyber-attack an increasingly attractive and effective weapon to employ against the United States.

Aware of its own vulnerability, American intelligence sources have been closely monitoring China out of fears that it might make use of such weaknesses. Since Beijing sees Washington its principal antagonist in the present era, Chinese military leaders and policy makers devote intensive effort to apply the lessons from the Cold War arms race and from the even more recent shows of American military might. After thorough examination, they consider the American engagement in the 1991 Iraq-Kuwait conflict the last demonstration for the traditional style of battles.[147] The following conclusion by two Chinese People's Liberation Army (PLA) colonels serves to the point:[148]

---

[147] Thierry GARCIN, in *Les enjeux stratégiques de l'espace* (pp. 30-34), reviews the early signs of the overwhelming U.S. military might, as demonstrated in the 1991 conflict.

[148] Qiao Liang and Wang Xiangsui, "Unrestricted Warfare," stated in "Virtual Defense," James Adams, *Foreign Affairs*, Vol. 80, no. 3, May/June 2001, 103.

> The age of technology integration and globalization...has realigned the
> relationship of weapons to war... Does a single "hacker" attack count as
> a hostile act or not? Can using financial instruments to destroy a
> country's economy be seen as a battle? Did CNN's broadcast of an
> exposed corpse of a U.S. soldier in the streets of Mogadishu shake the
> determination of the Americans to act as the world's policeman, thereby
> altering the world's strategic situation?... When we suddenly realize that
> all these non-war actions may be the new factors constituting future
> warfare, we have to come up with a new name for this new form of war:
> Warfare which transcends all boundaries and limits–in short, unrestricted
> warfare.

The two colonels are convinced their country will never be able to match American's technological superiority, and hence, believe that a digital attack will give China a significant asymmetric advantage. Hence, China has invested enormously in new technology for the PLA and has established a special information-warfare group to coordinate national offence and defense. Pentagon monitors refer to these efforts as the creation of the "Great Firewall of China."

More precisely, during its first decade of development in the 1980s, China 'quietly' supported (or at least did not stand against) American policies in what may be considered as a 'non-confrontational approach.' It is gradually expanding its economic ties, ceaselessly searching for continued supplies of oil and energy resources, acting calmly and moderately in concern of global issues, slowly but soundly enlarging its sphere of influence, and seeking to wear out America's patience and endurance as much as possible.

In respect of Taiwan, China is more likely to keep undermining the Taiwan independence movement, as Beijing attempts to accumulate advantage and gradually wear out the opponent. Consider, for example, the weeklong historic visit (the first in 56 years) of the leader of Taiwan's largest opposition party nationalist Lien Chan to Beijing in late April 2005, in what was described as a major attempt at improving relations between the two sides. At the end of the visit, China offered to send two giant pandas to the island as a symbol of 'friendship and peace.'[149]

---

[149] During the Cold War, pandas were given as goodwill gestures, and hence came the term "panda diplomacy." While many monarchs and heads of states present birds, dogs or even racehorses to visiting dignitaries, the Chinese offer a giant panda as the ultimate gift. See the history of 'panda

Eventually in January 2001, the possibility of war in space moved from pure science fiction (as in the film "Star Wars") to realistic planning by the U.S. Air Force. Driven by the increased reliance of the American military and economy on satellites, the Space Warfare Center in Colorado staged the military's first major war game to focus on space as the primary theater of operations, rather than just a supporting arena for combat on earth. Not surprising, the scenario was growing tension between the United States and China in 2017.

Involving 250 participants for five days on an isolated, super secure base, the game was the most visible manifestation of a little-noticed but major shift in the armed forces over the last decade.[150] The conflict in the Arab Gulf in 1991 showed the U.S. military, for the first time, how important space could be to its combat operations–for communications, for the transmission of imagery and for global positioning satellites to inform ground troops where they are.

The end of the Cold War, for its part, allowed many satellites to be shifted from being used primarily for monitoring Soviet nuclear facilities to supporting the field operations of the U.S. military. But military thinkers worried that such new reliance on space had created new vulnerabilities. All of a sudden, an efficient way to disturb an American offensive against a given target appeared to be jamming the satellites on which the United States relied, or blowing up the ground station back in the United States that controlled the satellites transmitting targeting data.

Noteworthy here is Washington's increased focus on space–not just in terms of operating there, but also how to protect operations and attack others in space. To meet these challenges, it established a *Space Operations Directorate*, opened a *Space Warfare School*, and activated two new units, the 76th Space Control Squadron (for space battle), and the 527th Space Aggressor Squadron (to probe the U.S. military for new vulnerabilities). The military has a long tradition of conducting war games, not just to predict if a war may emerge, but more to figure

---

diplomacy' in: Kate McGeown, "China's panda ambassadors," *BBC News*, May 3, 2005, at: http://news.bbc.co.uk/go/pr/fr/-/2/hi/asia-pacific/4508873.stm.

[150] For a detailed review of the War Game, read: Thomas E. Ricks, "US Air Force Prepares Itself To Do Battle In Outer Space," *IHT*, January 30, 2001, 1.

out how to employ new weapons, how to best organize the military, and how political considerations might shape the conduct of war.

That space war game involved country *Red* massing its force for a possible attack on its small neighbor, *Brown*, which then asked *Blue* for help. Red stood for China, while Blue for the United States. Based on conventional wisdom, it was assumed that the heavens were full of weapons by the year 2017. Both Red and Blue possessed microsatellites that could maneuver against other satellites, blocking their view, jamming transmissions, or even frying their electronics with radiation. The two also enjoyed ground-based lasers that could temporarily dazzle or permanently blind satellite optics. The Blue side had a national missile defense system, as well as re-usable space planes that could be launched to quickly place new satellites in orbit, or repair and refuel ones already there. And finally, both sides were able to attack each other's computers. In other words, the two were in possession of *offensive information warfare capabilities.*

All along the tensed war game, the two sides came closer and closer to the edge of war, but never actually fired a shot–thanks to deterrence tactics that saved the planet from unforeseeable disaster.

In respect of Russia, political and military leaders are obviously convinced that they are losing the cyberspace war to the United States. This has forced the once-space mighty rival to seek for a possible international arms-control treaty for cyberspace. The United States dismisses any such initiative arising from a nation with a weak information economy already losing the cyber-war. That is, from the perspective of IT powers, an arms control treaty that will primarily benefit those nations falling behind in the information war makes no sense–this time for the Unites States.

In May 2001, tensions between Russian and American space officials resurfaced when the National Aeronautics and Space Administration (NASA) accused the Russian space agency, Rosaviakosmos, of not taking its obligations to the International Space Station seriously. NASA stated that the participation of the American space tourist Dennis Tito had set "enormous strain" on mission controllers and on the crew of the Station.[151] Though the Station is supposed to usher in an era of cooperation, the Russians are already evoking concerns over NASA's domination in the project. Neither party can afford to pull out now, since NASA contributes in power and money, and the Russians offer expertise in space-station operations.

Even though Moscow's idea of an international treaty to limit information warfare may seem not near from materializing, the concept of an effective deterrence regime for cyberspace is gaining voice in Washington itself. As the Information Revolution moves on in pace, so do the frequency and sophistication of the attacks on U.S. computers and communications networks, introducing two clear changes in American military and national security structures.

First, emphasizes Adams (2001, p. 104), during the Cold War Washington controlled the pace of U.S. technology development by directly funding approximately 70% of technology research. That figure is currently less than 5%. Private interests that refuse to depend on Washington's archaic acquisition systems now drive technological innovation. Instead, technological entrepreneurs strive incessantly to increase the speed of change. Unlike 20th century weapons innovations that took an average of 15 years to enter military service, today's newest versions of constantly updated computers and software—which constitute the tools of an information warrior—are available everywhere and accessible to everyone at the same time.

Second, the front line has also been transformed. In the last century, the transparent battlefield was generally marked as the place where soldiers, sailors and aviators met in combat. For the United States, with no 'aggressive' neighbors around its borders, homeland defense meant projecting power overseas when American interests were at stake. Unlike most modern great powers, the United States has rarely been invaded by foreign forces.

---

[151] See: "Space Tourist Denies Problems," *IHT*, May 5-6, 2001, 3; and Erika Check, "Warning: Craters Ahead; Will the International Space Station foster cooperation–or conflict?" *Newsweek*, international edition, March 19, 2001, 48-49.

With the cyber-world changing that paradigm, potential attackers now look instead to strike the United States in such a manner so that military retaliation (or by other means) becomes very difficult, either because the attack's origin is unknown or because the perpetrators have sabotaged civilian or military command networks. Before the September 11 attacks, and despite warning signs, the United States (as well as most countries) did not prioritize threats to the private sector or sufficiently emphasize cooperation between citizens and government in defense. In many cases, the United States still remains legally constrained from passing on information to the private sector about potential threats.

Eventually, the lack of an American (or international) strategy for deterrence in the virtual world, in addition to the absence of a clear legal regime for retaliation against cyber attacks encouraged (and still does) potential hackers to enter battle with impunity. Remember, for example, what happened in May 2000 when a hacker in the Philippines launched the *"Love Letter"* virus around the world. In the United States alone, "the Veterans Health Administration received 7 million 'I Love You' messages, 1000 files were damaged at NASA, and recovery from the attack at the Department of Labor required more than 1600 employee hours and 1200 contractor hours."[152] Despite the estimated cost of damage to the United States ranging from 4 to 15 billion dollars, Washington did nothing to prosecute the hacker or to recover damages. Although the hacker was arrested, he was later released–simply because Philippine law was not framed to prosecute such *crimes.*

Attempts to avoid such incidents in the future by creating an effective defense and deterrent policy does not seem to be so easy, even if the threat of retaliation turns out to be a sound preventative strategy. If a country is accordingly to respond effectively to cyber attack, it first needs to know who is responsible for the aggression. Tracing those (whether state agents or individuals) who act through computer networks is itself a challenge, since attacks in cyberspace can arise from multiple points simultaneously, with their origins disguised.

---

[152] James Adams, "Virtual Defense", 2001, pp. 106-07. Incidents of similar reported hackings continue worldwide.

Take another example. While tensions were mounting with Iraq in February 1998, the Pentagon discovered a sophisticated set of intrusions into a number of Defense Department information systems. Those attacks, code-named *Solar Sunrise*, seemed designed to gather intelligence on American plans for actions in Iraq and disrupt command-and-control and logistics systems. The hacks were assumed to have been organized by Iraq, and their origin was traced to Abu Dhabi.

A strike force was sent out there, and after receiving permission from its government, entered what was thought to be the building where the Iraqi computer team was hiding. In fact, the building housed not Iraqis–but mere computer services; the attacks were not ordered by Baghdad; and Abu Dhabi was simply a false trail laid by the hackers. Just shortly afterwards, two teenagers in California were arrested, and as it turned out, they and an Israeli hacker had launched Solar Sunrise, stressing that their motivation had nothing to do with Iraq (Adams, 2001, pp. 109-10).

Last but not least, and before concluding Chapter One, following is an overview presentation on the type of satellites already in orbit and that are currently being employed for military purposes.[153] To note first, "Spacecom" is the military jargon for the U.S. Space Command, which coordinates all military and civilian *space assets*, where *space* is defined as everything above 100 miles (160 kilometers). These assets include dozens of satellites that contribute directly or indirectly to American military efforts, with some ranging more than 22,000 miles (35,400 kms) above the surface.

Most missile warning and communication satellites operate in what are called *geosynchronous orbits*, perches that remain fixed over a given part of the planet by orbiting Earth once every 24 hours at altitudes from 22,300 miles (35,880 kms) up. Weather satellites share this region of space. The Geostationary Operational Environmental Satellite (GOES) of the National Oceanic and Atmospheric Administration, which are able to view half the globe, feed constant data about cloud cover and moisture into weather forecasting programs–information used as

---

[153] Summarized from: Robert Roy Britt, "Satellites Play Crucial Roles in Aid and Ground Battles," *www.space.com*, October 9, 2001.

well by the military. First launched in 1975 and witnessing 9 developed versions ever since, the GOES also tracks severe weather conditions such as tornadoes, flash floods, hail storms, and hurricanes. Satellite sensors detect, as well, ice fields and map the movements of sea and lake ice.

Some television satellites also operate at this altitude, where their fixed locations in the sky explains the fixed position of home satellite TV receiver dishes. Various types of military communication satellites also traverse this high ground.

Yet, more critical at this extreme height are a handful of Defense Support Program satellites, first launched in 1970. They are a key part of the military's early warning systems, using infrared sensors to detect heat from missiles or rockets (as the U.S. military claims being able to spot any missile launch over 90% of the Earth's surface). The inability to see anything with high resolution is taken as a trade-off for the wide view offered from 22,300 miles (35,900 kms) up in space, and so, a set of other satellites operate much closer to the planet.

These are some 24 satellites that comprise the Global Positioning System (GPS), orbiting around 10,900 miles (17,540 kms) above the surface. Each satellite circles the planet every 12 hours, as they combine to give near-total coverage of the globe. While GPS is absolutely critical to American military operations, the system is also used commercially by pilots, boaters and hikers (and eventually, contributes to many rescues each year). The GPS emits signals, which when picked up by receivers in the air or on the ground can, according to the U.S. Air Force, calculate time to within a billionth of a second, velocity within a fraction of a mile per hour, and location to within a few feet. Five ground stations and four ground antennas located around the world coordinate the satellites and their signals.

GPS has allowed for dramatic improvements over precise attempts, as in the 1991 Iraq-Kuwait conflict, to target missiles and bombs remotely. One modern bomb, called *Joint Direct Attack Munition* (JDAM), has a GPS receiver installed inside it and can be programmed to hit a target based on longitude and latitude.

Because the JDAM locates the target, the crew does not have to–enabling them to fly at higher and safer altitudes.

Another group of satellites float in *low* Earth orbit–typically between 100 and 300 miles (160-480 kms) up but as close as 8 miles (12 kms) and as far as 1,200 miles (1,930 kms). They provide intelligence imagery and weather data. Space shuttles and the International Space Station operate in low orbit. Also, several military spy satellites work in the 600-1200 mile (960-1,930 kms) range, as their acronyms reflect the types of data they collect: *Electronic Intelligence* (ELINT); *Signal Intelligence* (SIGINT); and *Radar Intelligence* (RADINT).

Orbiting at 25 times the speed of sound, spy satellites normally pass over a given location twice a day in a useful routine for spotting movements of entire encampments, single vehicles and groups of people. Experts state that spy satellites can see features as small as 4 or 5 inches (100-127 millimeters) across, identify people (but not faces), can spot a license plate on a car (and perhaps, even read it). A highly classified type of spy satellite known as *Keyhole-class* is thought to detect objects as tiny as a newspaper headline, with three of these satellites manufactured by Lockheed Martin already ranging over Earth's polar region.

To get an even closer look of what is on the ground, the military employs the U-2 spy aircraft at around 70,000 feet (21,330 meters), and pilotless drones at lower altitudes. The drones, with their nearly disposable low cost, are deployed to distinguish between a group of refugees and a group of terrorists.

Not all the *spy imaging* is done by the military. "Space Imaging," a private company, uses its Ikonos satellite to snap pictures from 423 miles (680 kms) above Earth, revealing features as small as 3.3 feet (1 meter) across (reminding that the company provided images of lower Manhattan after the September 11 attacks on the World Trade Center).

"Spot Image," a French project in collaboration with Sweden and Belgium, has been operational and offering satellite imagery since 1986. Based in Toulouse (France), and considered among the pioneer European providers of commercial satellite imagery, Spot Image already has five satellites in orbit, supplemented by a new generation of mini-satellites named Pléiades. Not to forget that the National Aeronautics and Space Administration (NASA), as well, regularly photographs the planet in the name of science.

II.   CHAPTER TWO:

DIPLOMACY IN THE INFORMATION AGE

II.I. The Evolution of Diplomacy

Diplomacy is an essentially political activity and a major element of power. Its chief purpose is to enable states to secure the objectives of their foreign policies without resort to force, propaganda, or law. That is, diplomacy consists of communication between officials designed to promote foreign policy either by formal agreement or tacit adjustment. Although diplomacy also implies such discrete activities as gathering information, clarifying intentions, and engendering goodwill, it is hence not surprising that until the label "diplomacy" was affixed to all of these activities by Edmund Burke in 1796, it was known most commonly as *negotiation,* and by Cardinal Richelieu, as *négociation continuelle.*[1] That was, permanent diplomacy "in all places," irrespective of friendship of religious hue. Diplomacy is not limited to/by what professional diplomatic agents do, but may rather as well be carried out by other officials and individuals under the direction of officials.

In the Middle Ages, diplomacy was chiefly assigned to a *nuncius* and a plenipotentiary. While the former was merely a "living letter," the latter had "full powers"–*plena potestas*–to negotiate on behalf of and bind his principal. The two were alike, however, as being temporary envoys with narrowly focused tasks. In the second half of the 15th century, these ad hoc envoys were replaced and/or supplemented by permanent or *resident* embassies with broad responsibilities.

This was the case because temporary embassies were expensive to dispatch, vulnerable on the road, and always likely to cause varying degrees of trouble over precedence and ceremonial (in view of the high status required by their leaders). Eventually, with diplomatic activity intensifying in Europe in the late 15th century, "it was discovered to be more practical and more economical to appoint an ambassador to remain at a much frequent court."[2] Even more, continuous representation produced greater familiarity with condition and personalities in the country concerned and was accordingly likely to generate a more authoritative flow of information home. It also

---

[1] The definition and following evolution of diplomacy is adopted (expect if noted otherwise) from: G.R. Berridge, *Diplomacy: Theory and Practice,* New York: Palgrave, 2002, pp. 1, 5-6, 105-12.

[2] D.E. Queller, *The Office of Ambassador in the Middle Ages*, New Jersey: Princeton University Press, 1967, p. 82.

simplified the preparation of an important negotiation, in addition to launching it without attracting the attention that would normally accompany the arrival of a special envoy. The spread of resident missions was also facilitated by the increasing strength of the doctrine of *raison d'état*, that is, the doctrine where standards of personal morality were irrelevant in statecraft. The only test then was what furthered state interests. As early as 1535, the most Christian King of France, François I, had established a resident embassy in Constantinople at the Court of the Ottoman Sultan.

Expectedly, resident missions were initially greeted in some areas with intense suspicion. Yet, their importance was such that they were steadily enforced by the customary "law of nations," which evolved in the region after the late 16th century. The premises rented by the envoy and his entourage soon began to acquire special immunities from local criminal and civil jurisdiction–reflecting a change in practice.[3] Obviously at the time, nevertheless, the more powerful and more relaxed states were slower to dispatch than to receive resident embassies.

Structurally speaking, responsibility for diplomacy in the states of Europe was routinely designated among different bureaucracies on a geographical basis (mixed at times with domestic matters). In France, in 1626, the first "Ministry of Foreign Affairs"–as known in its current form–was created by Cardinal Richelieu, the legendary chief minister of the French King Louis XIII. Increasing diplomacy raised the possibilities of inconsistency in both the formulation and execution of foreign policy, a concern demanding more unified guidance and better preserved archives. The fact that diplomacy was more and more conducted by representatives residing for long periods abroad eventually urged for a certain extent of organized communication with them, including ciphering and deciphering instructions and dispatches. These continuous negotiations abroad required not only standing bureaucracies at home but also one rather than several competing bureaucracies.

That said, only in the 18th century did the provision of advice on foreign policy and the administration of diplomacy by a single ministry headed by a "foreign ministry"

---

[3] E. Young, "The Development of the Law of Diplomatic Relations," *British Yearbook of International Law 1964,* Vol. 40, 1966, London: Oxford University Press, 141-82.

become the general rule in Europe.[4] Britain waited until 1782 before creating its Foreign Office, while the U.S. State Department was established a few years later, in 1789. China, Japan, and Turkey followed afterwards in the middle of the 19th century.

Continuity of diplomacy via the resident mission was not the only distinguished feature of the French experience. Another, points out Berridge (2002, p. 107) was *secrecy*. Currently, reference to "secret diplomacy" may mean keeping secret all or any of the following: either the contents of negotiation, knowledge that negotiations are going on at all, the content of any agreement issuing from negotiations, or the fact that any agreement at all has been concluded. In the French system, remarkably, secret diplomacy generally meant keeping either the fact or the content of negotiation secret. This was an important consideration mainly because a successful negotiation implied–by definition–each side battling for less than its ideal demands. Once certain parties, such as radical supporters of a government, some other domestic constituency, or a foreign friend, were aware of what was ahead at the time, the more likely the talks could be disturbed.

Furthermore, the French adopted the critical principle that deceit had no place in diplomacy. As the resident ambassador became more accepted, achieved a higher social standing, and gradually became part of a profession, he attached more importance to honesty in diplomacy. In "The Art of Diplomacy," Callières underlines that the purpose of negotiation was not to trick the other side but to reconcile states on the basis of true estimate of their enduring interests.[5] Since only if agreements are made on these bases are they likely to endure; otherwise they are not worth concluding in the first place. By contrast, if a state assures an agreement by deceit or subsequently renounces an agreement once it becomes inconvenient, it is likely to breed a desire for revenge. Not only so, other states will find themselves disinclined to enter negotiations with it in the future. And that is how *greater honesty* in diplomacy was a maturing sign of the diplomatic system.[6]

---

[4] D.B. Horn, *The British Diplomatic Service 1689-1789*, Oxford: Clarendon Press, 1961.

[5] F. de Callières, *The Art of Diplomacy*, ed. by H.M.A. Keens-Soper and K. Schweizer, New York: University Press of America, 1994, p. 83.

[6] «En toutes circonstances, le premier devoir du diplomate est d'être de bonne foi... Il doit d'autre part, en raison des intérêts importants dont il a la charge, avoir un esprit vigilant et objectif, un caractère

Another distinguished feature of the French system was the *professionalism* of diplomacy, with its controlled entry, proper training, clear ranks and regular payments. Callières (1994, pp. 99-100) estimated diplomacy was too important and too much in need of extensive knowledge and technical expertise to be treated otherwise. The transformation of diplomacy into profession was a slow process, and was not seriously under way until the 19th century.[7] However, signs towards this direction showed up before that by the emergence of the *corps diplomatique*. The evolution of this organ, with its own rules of procedures, such as the rule that the longest-serving *ambassadeur* should be the spokesman, or *doyen* (dean) of the *corps* on matters of common interest, was clear evidence of an emerging sense of professional identity among diplomats. In other words, diplomats in the French system came to recognize that they had professional interests that united them as diplomats, along with political and commercial interests that divided them. Among these professional interests–and perhaps the foremost–was defense of their immunities under the "law of nations."

Despite the fact that the earliest resident diplomats were not generally of the highest social standing, special envoys normally had considerable status. This was deemed necessary to maintain the prestige of the prince and flatter the party with whom he was dealing, as well as to make it easy for the diplomat to move in circles of influence.[8] As the French system matured, with the institutionalization of resident

---

prudent et réservé, un jugement sain et froid. Il doit s'être discipliné à toujours tenir un langage modéré.», ('In all circumstances, the first duty of a diplomat is to be in good faith... Furthermore, and due to the important interests in which he undertakes, he needs to enjoy a vigilant and objective spirit, a prudent and reserved character, a sound and cold judgement. He always has to keep a moderate language.'), Source: Marie-France Lecherbonnier, *Le Protocole: Histoire et coulisses*, ('Protocol: History and Secrets'), Paris: éditions Perrin, 2001, p. 22.

[7] M.S. Anderson, *The Rise of Modern Diplomacy*, London: Longman, 1993, pp. 80-96, 119-28.

[8] Speaking of flattering, when Queen Elizabeth I ascended the throne of England in 1558, there was much to-do about her finding a husband. By marrying and committing to an alliance with one party or nation, the queen believed she would become embroiled in conflicts that were not of her choosing, conflicts which might eventually overwhelm her or lead her into a futile war. Also, the husband becomes the *de facto* ruler, often trying to do away with his wife the queen. Hence, the queen had two goals as a ruler: to avoid marriage and to avoid war. And she managed to combine these two goals by dangling the possibility of marriage to forge alliances. She had to emanate mystery and desirability, never discouraging anyone's hopes but also never yielding. The queen mastered this lifelong game of flirting and withdrawing with excellence–whether it was with the king of Spain, the prince of Sweden, the archduke of Austria, or with the dukes of Anjou and Alençon, brothers of the French king. With this great diplomatic issue of Elizabeth's day, the queen dominated the country and every man who sought to conquer her. History reveals that the queen was accordingly able to live the rest of her life as she desired, and that she died the 'Virgin Queen'. She left no direct heir (as she became too old to bear children), but ruled through a period of incomparable peace and cultural fertility. From: Robert Greene and Joost Elffers, *The 48 Laws of Power*, New York: Viking, 1998, pp. 146-47.

diplomacy, permanent ambassadorships attracted leading notables. Likewise, the emerging foreign services of the various European states became the province of the traditional aristocracy, explains Anderson (1993, pp. 119-21). This aristocratic dominance of diplomacy was significant because of the considerable uniformity of outlook that it fostered across the diplomatic services of different states. A diplomat who spend most of his career in foreign capitals could easily feel himself part of an aristocratic international.

As the number of states increased, the complexity of the problems confronting them multiplied. With the urgency to attend the issues mounting, the French system of bilateral diplomacy became too slow "ordinary diplomatic channels" and no longer sufficient alone. According to Nicolson,[9] this was realized during World War I and was demonstrated by the large number of conferences, many of them achieving permanent status, which were hurriedly organized to cope with the events. Subsequently, *multilateral diplomacy* was initiated with the foundation of the League of Nations after World War I. The French system, however, remained at the core of the world diplomatic systems and it remains, asserts Berridge (2002, p. 112), at its core today.

This merit is once again well acknowledged by the comments of several American diplomats who dealt intensively with French officials in the course of their careers in France and elsewhere:

> Our American diplomats have great praise for the skill and superior quality of their French colleagues. These French officials are consistently described as first class, highly trained, intelligent public servants, well versed in French policy and capable of expressing it eloquently. While they have little flexibility in negotiations and can be expected to follow instructions meticulously, they are marvelously adroit in adapting quickly to any sudden change or reversal of policy dictated by higher authority.
>
> The French diplomat and senior administrator is one of France's elite government officials, a carefully selected, highly, trained graduate of a first rate French university, often l'École nationale d'administration, a prestigious institution whose graduates dominate the French administrative hierarchy. Unlike the United States where ambassadors and their high officials are often chosen

---

[9] H. Nicolson, *Diplomacy,* 3rd ed., London: Oxford University Press, 1963, pp. 84-85.

from the private sector, the French rarely look outside this special cadre for their top administrators and diplomats. [10]

Until 1961, diplomatic law, which provided diplomatic agents with immunities under local criminal and civil law, was mainly defined in the accumulated practice of states that had come to be accepted as binding upon them. Concluded in 1961, the Vienna Convention on Diplomatic Relations (VCDR) codified the customary law in diplomacy. That is, it clarified and tightened it, refined its content, and relaunched it in the form of a multilateral treaty. This was realized under the impetus of concerns felt most strongly by the states of the West at that time.

First, there was a sense of growing anxiety that looseness in the existing roles was enabling some states to use their embassies for illegitimate purposes. Second, there was a fear that traditional diplomatic institutions would be dismissed as part of the machinery of neo-colonialism if the new states of Asia and Africa were not allowed to give them official sanction. And third, cites Denza,[11] there was an apprehension that the prevailing rules were inadequate to cope with the huge increase in the "armies of privileged persons" in the major capital cities attendant upon the arrival of representatives from those cities. In fact, the move towards codification had begun in the late 19th century but was only formalized in 1949, when the U.N. International Law Commission (ILC) inscribed the issues on its agenda.[12] The matter was treated with more urgency after 1952 in view of strong complaints from the Yugoslav government about the activities of the Soviet embassy in Belgrade.

Furthermore to the inviolability of resident missions, the VCDR would continue to entitle diplomatic agents immunity from the criminal jurisdiction of the receiving state, and also from its civil and administrative jurisdiction–except in some matters where the diplomats were involved in an entirely private capacity. Certainly, the Convention

---

[10] Dayton S. Mak, "The Nature of French Diplomacy: Reflections of American Diplomats," *www.americandiplomacy.org,* September 22, 2003.

[11] E. Denza, "Diplomatic Law: Commentary on the Vienna Convention on Diplomatic Relations," London: British Institute of International and Comparative Law, 1976, 5.

[12] See: Richard Langhorne, "The Regulation of Diplomatic Practice: The Beginnings to the Vienna Convention of Diplomatic Relations, 1961," *Review of International Studies,* Vol. 18, no. 1, 1992.

reiterated the right of receiving states to expel diplomats whose actions were considered as harmful, rather than subject them to court proceedings.

Importantly, the Convention also pointed to the freedom of movement of the diplomatic agent–a vital aspect of his functions, not least that of information gathering. The necessity of this right was affirmed by the Soviet bloc policy to limit the travel of foreign diplomats to 50 kilometers from the capital unless they obtained special permission for longer destinations.[13]

Signed in Vienna on April 18, 1961, the Convention came into effect three years later, on April 24, 1964. It remains, describes Brown, "without doubt one of the surest and most widely based multilateral regimes in the field of international relations."[14] One of the reasons for its success is that the VCDR deals only with traditional bilateral diplomacy, and hence, excludes relations with international organizations and special missions. Another reason for its success, points Kerley,[15] is the fact "all states are both sending and receiving states."

Today however, not only the context but also the content of diplomacy has radically altered. The context of persuasion to advance national interests has expanded to include anyone anywhere connected to and affected by any of the information and communication media.[16] Even more disorienting, the realm of national interests now includes at the very least global economies, and, increasingly, international migration, environmental crises, terrorism, drug trafficking, weapons proliferation, and cyber

---

[13] In this respect, it is interesting to note to the U.S. State Department announcement of May 7, 1991 on the agreement to permit an Iraqi interests sections to operate from the former chancery building under the protection of Algeria. It was emphasized that this was designed to "facilitate maintenance of *minimal* communications between the United States and Iraq and provide *basic* consular services." The Iraqi Interests Section was to be staffed by only three Iraqi nationals (two diplomats and one of administrative and technical rank) and none of them would be allowed to travel, without special permission, beyond a 25-mile "zone of free movement." U.S. Department of State Dispatch, May 13, 1991, p. 347.

[14] J. Brown, "Diplomatic Immunity–state practice under the Vienna Convention," *International and Comparative Law Quarterly,* Vol. 37, 1988, 54.

[15] E.L. Kerley, "Some Aspects of the Vienna Conference on Diplomatic Intercourse and Immunities," *American Journal of International Law*, Vol. 56, 1962, 128. The full text of the Vienna Convention on Diplomatic Relations, 1961 is available at: http://www.un.org/law/ilc/texts/diplomat.htm.

[16] Canadian diplomat Gordon Smith defines traditional diplomacy as being the art of advancing national interests by the practice of persuasion. Source: "Reinvention Diplomacy: A Virtual Necessity, *"Virtual Diplomacy Series*, February 25, 1999, available at: http://www.usip.org/oc/vd/vdr/gsmithISA99.html.

harassment. All these issues pose global threats, but are also suffered immediately and most profoundly at the local level. Therefore, diplomacy, the practice of foreign affairs, is a subset of domestic policy, which has been itself shaped by the expanded agenda of national interests.

This new structure is undergoing a decentralized fusion of global and local interest, which Rosenau calls "fragmegration," a concept that juxtaposes the processes of fragmentation and integration occurring within and among organizations, communities, countries, and transnational systems to the extent that it is virtually impossible not to treat them interactively and causally linked.[17] Along with fragmegration comes the dispersion of authority away from states and the growing role of decentralized governments, non-governmental organizations, media, social movements, in addition to other transnational non-state networks as essential international actors. This transition period and perhaps the emerging paradigm is characterized by the profusion of asymmetrical relationships between state and non-state actors, including activities sponsored and carried out by diverse supra-individuals in the fields of politics, media, technology and business.

And although fragmegration threatens nation-states' conventional hold on power, savvy states should recognize these new conditions as an opportunity to implement revolutionary approaches to global affairs, strategies and management. "What states lose in control," stress Brown and Studemeister, "they could regain in influence."[18]

The Information-Age fostered "hard power" (or coercion) versus "soft power" (or persuasion) distinction has radically reformed conventional theories about national security. Popular persuasion *au lieu de* hardball coercion is neither an easy sell to nations-states nor once grasped, learned and implemented with simplicity. According to this perspective, having the means today to circulate the most persuasive information to the largest number of people the quickest becomes to be as important, if not more

---

[17] James N. Rosenau, "States, Sovereignty, and Diplomacy in the Information Age," *Virtual Diplomacy Series,* February 25, 1999, available at: http://www.usip.org/oc/vd/vdr/jrosenauISA99html.

[18] Sheryl J. Brown and Margarita S. Studemeister, "Virtual Diplomacy: Rethinking Foreign Policy Practice in the Information Age," *Information and Security: An International Journal.* Sofia: ProCon, Ltd., Vol. 7, 2001, 28-44.

important, than a striking weapon. That being said, access, information, and connectivity are all essential components of wielding influence to this power.

Explaining more precisely what "soft power" is, Nye writes:

> Military power and economic power are both examples of hard command power that can be used to induce others to change their position. Hard power can rest on inducement (carrots) or threats (sticks). But there is also an indirect way to exercise power. A country may obtain the outcomes it wants in world politics because other countries want to follow it, admiring its values, emulating its example, aspiring to its level of prosperity and openness. In this sense, it is just as important to set the agenda in world politics and attract others as it is to force them to change through the threat or use military or economic weapons. This aspect of power–getting others to want what you want–I call soft power. It co-opts people rather than coerces them.
>
> ...Soft power is not merely the same as influence, though it is one source of influence. After all, I can also influence you by threats or rewards. Soft power is also more than persuasion or the ability to move people by argument. It is the ability to entice and attract. And attraction often leads to acquiescence of imitation.
>
> Soft power arises in large part from our values. These values are expressed in our culture, in the policies we follow inside our country, and in the way we handle ourselves internationally.
>
> ... [All] these sources of soft power are likely to become increasingly important in the global information age of this new century. And, at the same time, the arrogance, indifference to the opinions of others, and narrow approach to our national interests advocated by the new unilateralists are a sure way to undermine our soft power.[19]

Respectively, Information Age analysts Arquilla and Ronfeldt observe that diplomats will have to realize that a new realm is emerging–the noosphere, a global "realm of mind"–that may have a profound effect on statecraft. Second, they see that the Information Age will continue to undermine the conditions for classic diplomacy based on realpolitik and hard power, and will instead favor the emergence of a new diplomacy based on what they call noopolilitik (nu-oh-poh-li-teek) and its preferences for soft power.[20]

---

[19] Joseph S. Nye Jr., *The Paradox of American Power*, 2002, pp. 8, 9, 11. See Table 2.1.

[20] John Arquilla and David Ronfeldt, "What if there is a Revolution in Diplomatic Affairs?" *Virtual Diplomacy Series,* February 25, 1999, available at: http://www.usip.org/oc/vd/vdr/ronaryISA99.html.

Period	State	Major Resources
16th century	Spain	Gold bullion, colonial trade, mercenary armies, dynastic ties
17th century	Netherlands	Trade, capital markets, navy
18th century	France	Population, rural industry, public administration, army, culture (soft power)
19th century	Britain	Industry, political cohesion, finance and credit, navy, liberal norms (soft power), island location (easy to defend)
20th century	United States	Economic scale, scientific and technical leadership, location, military forces and alliances, universalistic culture and liberal international regimes (soft power)
21st century	United States	Technological leadership, military and economic scale, soft power, hub of transnational communications

Table 2. 1. Leading States and Their Power Resources, 1500-2000 (Source: Joseph Nye, 2002: 13)

Noopolitik, they state, is an approach to diplomacy and strategy for the Information Age that emphasizes the shaping and sharing of ideas, values, norms, laws, and ethics through persuasion. "Both state and non-state actors may be guided, by noopolitik; rather than being state-centric," argue Arquilla and Ronfeldt (1999). Its strengths may well stem from enabling state and non-state actors to work conjointly." They stress the driving motivation of noopolitik cannot be national interests defined in static terms. Where "Realpolitik pits one state against another," the two Information Age analysts conclude saying, "noopolitik encourages states to cooperate in coalitions and other mutual frameworks." Table 2.2. summarizes the distinctive features of Realpolitik in contrast to Noopolitik in the Information Age.

Realpolitik	Noopolitik
States as the unit of analysis	Nodes, nonstate actors
Primacy of hard power (resources, etc)	Primacy of soft power
Power politics as zero-sum game	Win-win, lose-lose possible
System is anarchic, highly conflictual	Harmony of interests, cooperation
Alliance conditional (oriented of threat)	Ally webs vital to security
Primacy of national self-interest	Primacy of shared interests
Politics as unending quest for advantage	Explicitly seeking a *telos*
Ethos is amoral, if not immoral	Ethics crucially important
Behavior driven by threat and power	Common goals drive actors
Very guarded about information flows	Propensity for infosharing
Balance of power as the "steady-state"	Balance of responsibilities
Power embedded in nation-states	Power in "global fabric"

Table 2. 2. Contrasts between Realpolitik and Noopolitik (Source: Ronfeldt & Arquilla, 1999)

II.I.I. Contemporary Practices of Traditional Diplomacy

II.I.I.I. Telephone Diplomacy

Until the 19th century, diplomatic messages were carried by hand. Even at the beginning of the 21st century, diplomatic couriers are still being employed for the delivery of certain top-secret packages. Yet over the past 150 years, it is the domain of "telecommunication" that has such a profound impact on diplomacy.

With *tele* in Greek for 'far', telecommunication is any mode of communication over a long distance that requires human agency only in the sending and reception of the message it contains and not, as with a diplomatic courier, in its conveyance. The drums and smoke-signals that originated in ancient times, as well as the optical telegraph or "semaphore" devices introduced in Europe in the late 18th century, hence, were all forms of communication, just as much as the telegrams, radio and television broadcasts, facsimile, and e-mails of today. Not astonishingly, points out Berridge (2002, pp. 90-91), telecommunication did not make a major impact on diplomacy until the introduction of the electronic telegraph towards the middle of the 19th century. Shortly after using submarine and land cables, written messages sent by telegraph cut delivery times over some routes from weeks to hours–and they were relatively more reliable.

In the early 20th century, a further radical development occurred when the telephone and short wave radio made it possible to deliver the spoken word over vast distances. After World War II, additional refinements materialized, namely, the facsimile, electronic mail, and multi-media video-conferencing. Efficient and sophisticated communications improved with recent and imminent increases in cheap bandwidth, in the wires and cables through which all these information flow, and in the prospect of *wireless* communications via an increasing number of satellites. Also, latest developments in ITCs vastly enlarge the extent and mobility of the points from which messages may be transmitted and received, and surely their speed. This has eventually led to a new concept in diplomacy referred to *Virtual Diplomacy*, as defined by Brown and Studemeister:

> At is broadest, the term "virtual diplomacy" signifies the altered diplomacy associated with the emergence of a networked globe. At its narrowest, "virtual diplomacy" comprises the decision-making coordination, communication and practice of foreign affairs as they are conducted with the aid of information and telecommunications technologies in the wake of the changes brought about by the computer and telecommunications industries. (*op. cit.,* 2001)

However, doubts over security have traditionally caused government to employ these latest technology developments in exchanging classified messages only with great caution and after considerable hesitation. But even so, the use of the telephone still proves to be an unavoidable channel in diplomacy–especially in a crisis.

The prerequisite of a telephone connection as a means of eventual direct communication between governments over great distances is evident. Though other means of telecommunication may be as fast, the telephone is superior to them in some important respects. First, enumerates Berridge (2002, p. 91), it is easier to use. It is also more personal and therefore more flattering to the recipient, while written messages, especially at the highest level, are mostly drafted by someone else and recognized as such. This notion is also of particular observation when the addresser lacks certain language competence, and thus demands assistance in drafting correspondence.

The telephone, as well, assures "unrivalled certainty" that a message has been passed. A telephone call can generally be assumed to provide no verbatim transcript and therefore be deniable if that should prove expedient. Accordingly, it renders possible the immediate correction of a misunderstanding or instant adjustment of a statement that causes unintended offence. Last, the telephone offers the opportunity to extract an urgent response from the party at the other end of the line. For these reasons political leaders and senior officials attach increasing importance to the use of telephone diplomacy in maintaining their distant communications.

Obviously, telephone diplomacy is viewed more appropriate in certain circumstances and in some relationships than in others. For example, it turns out to be advantageous during a major international crisis–though more for framing the response of an alliance then for exploring the possibility of a settlement with an adversary.

In a vivid account of the effective use of the telephone in diplomacy, Sterns recalls the 40 telephone conversations between U.S. president George Bush and his Turkish counterpart Turgut Ozal, all done from the start of the Iraq-Kuwait conflict in August 1990 to the end of the year.[21] George Bush also used the telephone to contact the Malaysian prime minister in a Tokyo restaurant to assure his support for a vital Security Council resolution at that time. Noteworthy here, the absence of language barriers, and confidence that any slips of the tongue or ill-considered statements would be treated charitably favors use of the telephone as well.

Cautiously, the notion above perhaps explains why the telephone is rarely employed between hostile states or even among friendly states in tense circumstances. The establishment and eventual employment of a communications link, referred to as a "hotline," between two parties falls within the scope of Confidence-Building Measures (CBMs). These steps are taken by governments to avoid unnecessary conflict, develop confidence in each other and through such a process, build peace and harmonious relations between potential adversaries. These CBMs became more common with the emergence of the Cold War, and helped maintain relative peace and stability even as the Soviet Empire collapsed.

---

[21] M. Sterns, *Talking to Strangers: Improving American Diplomacy at Home and Abroad,* Princeton: Princeton University Press, 1996, p. 11.

As the Cuban missile crisis of October 1962 underscored the importance of prompt, direct communications between heads of states, U.S. and Soviet representatives signed in Geneva on June 20, 1963 the "Memorandum of Understanding Between the United States of America and the Union of Soviet Socialist Republics Regarding the Establishment of a Direct Communications Link."[22] This first bilateral agreement between the two superpowers provided concrete recognition to the dangers implicit in modern nuclear-weapons systems, although it was a limited but practical step to set those dangers under rational control.

That particular communications link did, whatsoever, perhaps prove its worth since its installation. For example, the United States used it to prevent possible misunderstanding of American fleet movements in the Mediterranean Sea during the Arab-Israeli War in 1967; and once again employed it during the Arab-Israeli War in 1973. The significance of the hotline is also attested by agreements signed in 1971, 1984, and 1984 to modernize it.

After their war in 1965 and as part of CBMs, India and Pakistan also established a hotline between their respective Directors General of Military Operations. Noting that the two countries have already been to war against each other three times since independence from Britain in 1947, both India and Pakistan carried out nuclear tests in May 1998, and came close to war once again in mid-2002 when India blamed Pakistan for an attack on its Parliament. In June 2004, the two nuclear powers agreed on a series of Nuclear Risk-Reduction Measures in an attempt to 'prevent misunderstandings and reduce risks relevant to nuclear issues.' They also agreed to establish a "dedicated and secure" hotline between their Foreign Secretaries, as well as to upgrade and secure the existing hotline between the Directors General of Military Operations.[23]

---

[22] The text of the Memorandum of Understanding, which entered force on the same day, is available at: http://www.fas.org/nuke/control/hotline/text/hotline1.htm.

[23] Significant as these measures may seem, those two Foreign Secretaries are not the decision-makers in nuclear/military issues, but perhaps seen as conveyors of information to their political leaderships. See: Praful Bidwai, "Talking Peace and Kashmir–Warily, Under a Nuclear Shadow," Washington, DC: Foreign Policy In Focus, July 6, 2004,
available at: http://www.fpif.org/commentary/2004/0407kashmir.html.

However, resort to a certain hotline may not be an appropriate or even a desired approach in resolving a given crisis. For instance in April 2001, during the critical period in the Sino-American relations provoked by the mid-air collision over the South China Sea between an American EP-3 spy plane and a Chinese jet fighter, President George W. Bush did not try to resolve the crisis by telephoning his Chinese counterpart Jiang Zemin. Although a hotline was formally established between Washington and Beijing in April 1998 (agreed upon in October 1997), Bush relied instead on traditional channels (Berridge, 2002, p. 95). Tactically important, traditional channels gain time in such a crisis.

Similarly in May 1999, in the wake of the bombings on the Chinese Embassy in Belgrade, CNN reported that Jiang Zemin refused to receive a call from Bill Clinton on the hotline. On that same day May 11, however, China Central Television (CCTV) reported that Zemin spoke to Boris Yeltsin of Russia on the Russia-China hotline (which was initiated in May 1998, in what is considered as the first hotline between a Chinese leader and a foreign leader).[24]

The fact that telecommunications are generally vulnerable to eavesdropping has made foreign ministries to proceed only with the widest circumspection in the introduction of electronic mail.[25] Mainly for this reason do the integral regulations of most ministries of foreign affairs expressly forbid the treatment of classified issues on the telephone at the subpolitical level. This anxiety about the security of telecommunications helps explain, furthermore, why states still depend at times on specials envoys and diplomatic couriers–who enjoy significant protection in international law–to deliver orally or hand-carry messages of a particularly sensitive nature (in additional to items that do not lend themselves to delivery by means of telecommunication). At the beginning of 2000, the U.S. Diplomatic Courier Service still

---

[24] *China News Digest*, Global News, no. GL99-063, May 12, 1999, at:
http://services.cnd.org/CND-Global.99.2nd/CND-Global.99-05-11.html.

[25] "Equipped for the Future: Managing US Foreign Affairs in the 21st Century," Stimson Center Project on the Advocacy of US Interests Abroad, Stimson Center, October 1998. Available at: www.stimson.org/pubs/ausia/ausr1.pdf.

had almost a hundred couriers and carried an average of ten tons of "classified and sensitive material for State and other US government agencies every day."[26]

II.I.I.II. Public Diplomacy

Foreign policy is being driven by the expectations and demands of audiences in an increasingly sophisticated world. That is, diplomats need to hold a combination of skills in both politics and communications as they address their message.[27] In an era where people are sensitized to perceptions of cultural imperialism and invasion, it is no longer enough to simply send out one-way messages about a country's expertise and attractions.

In developing and developed countries, audiences increasingly demand two-way communication and interaction through partnership. This comes at a time when diplomacy is more involved in engaging in dialogues and is acting as an agent to link groups with similar or differing interests together so that both parties can give and take from each other. Gradually, bilateral and multilateral partnerships between NGOs have risen to be a useful tool in international relations. While many construct their own alliances using their own networks and information sources, governments have only a small role to play in bridging them together. However, governments do need to exercise a more valuable role in helping NGOs from their respective countries gain credence in the eyes of foreign governments. This is of particular importance in countries like Japan, for example, where the voluntary or non profit sector is just recently developing and local and foreign NGOs do not yet have much standing or influence amongst government or society in general.[28]

---

[26] See: D. Miles, "Diplomatic Couriers: On the Road, from Rangoon to Russia and Back!" *State Magazine*, February-March 2000, available at:
www.state.gov/www/publications/statemag/statemag_feb2000/feature1.html.

[27] Taylor points that modern communication is indeed about technology, but it is also about human creativity. Because *something* is communicated to *someone*, an *impact* or an *influence* is likely to be the result, which often depends on how *creatively* the *content* of communications is *deployed*. Philip M. Taylor, *Global Communications, International Relations and the Media since 1945,* London: Routledge: 1997, p. 5.

[28] "Being Public: How diplomacy will need to change to cope with the information society," Mark Leonard and Liz Noble, *iMP Magazine*, July 23, 2001. Available at: http://www.cisp.org/imp/july_2001/07_01leonard.htm.

In developed countries, diplomacy needs to be more political. As countries increasingly unite into regional and global blocks and organs such as the EU, G-8, NAFTA, and the WTO, they realize that it is less necessary to try and install their values on those partners who already share them. In these organs, diplomacy becomes an extension of national politics. This implies having governments develop a new form of multilateral diplomacy–retooling embassies to become lobbying and policy-exchange organizations that link up political parties and think tanks across borders.

Eventually, this has dramatic consequences for foreign services. If a foreign policy is needed, one which cuts across government departments and focuses on networks and issues rather than just geography, then every government department becomes a foreign ministry and needs to join up with the others to tackle common issues, perhaps even creating temporary departments or units to focus on specific issues. Such a "joined-up approach should create a flatter, more flexible and entrepreneurial structure which draws on the best ideas and information sources of information from many more sources than are currently harnessed," (Leonard & Noble, 2001).

The economic arguments for public diplomacy are noteworthy as well. In a global economy, countries compete against each other for investment, trade and tourism. The success or failure in a market place obviously depends on the quality of the product, investment environment or tourist destination. Yet today, the products are becoming more alike to the extent that it is becoming difficult to be differentiated in terms of quality alone. Businessmen have long explored ways of tapping into a deeper sense of identity to develop brands as a way of selling products and distinguishing themselves from their competitors. The same is true of countries today. All things equal, identity can play a key role in deciding what products, destination or country people go for.

Many companies also realize this selling point. Opinion surveys show that three quarters of Fortune 500 companies actually see *national identity* or place of origin, as one of the key factors that influence their decision when buying goods and services.[29] In the 1990s, German AEG (Allgemeine Elektrische Gesellschaft) ran a publicity campaign in Britain based around redefining their initials as "Advanced Engineering from

---

[29] This figure and the examples following are taken from Leonard and Noble, "Being Public: How diplomacy will need to change to cope with the information society," 2001.

Germany." The centerpiece of their advertising was that the company was a 'German' one representing brand quality. Meanwhile, British companies, ranging from British Telecom to British home stores, were dropping the word 'British' from their names. Retail chain "Dixons," for example called its launched brand *Matsui* in an attempt to try to make it sound Japanese–merely because their market research suggested that people would not buy British-made television and radio sets.

Consider another illustration from Britain. The recent Foot and Mount Disease crisis in Britain demonstrated the catastrophic and costly consequences of not managing the message overseas with caution. Likely foreign visitors, especially Americans, quickly got the message that Britain was "closed," and so stayed far away. A single powerful image of the British Prime Minister on a farm in a yellow protection suit is said to have reinforced that misconception enormously overseas, although it was supposed to demonstrate to the domestic audience the Prime Minister's concern and involvement in the crisis.

On the impact of French cinema production abroad, a survey concluded some 80% of tourists in France had already watched at least one French film in their respective countries, and accordingly, had a feeling of enthusiasm to visit France.[30] That was simply because the films presented France, and particularly its capital Paris, as an interesting tourist destination. In terms of buying and consuming French products (namely, perfumes, alcohol, and cosmetics), around 60% of those surveyed stated that the French films they had seen had an influence on them when buying such goods.

Sports, a feature of public diplomacy, have become a non-threatening way to bridge political fissures between the East and West. After more than twenty years of bitterness and distrust, sporting events seemed to be the favored way to advance U.S.-Iran contacts. Under reformist President Mohammed Khatami, Iran's national basketball team hired an American coach as a step forward towards opening dialogue between the two governments, and among civilizations. Not only so; the game of the "Great Satan"

---

[30] «Impact du cinéma français à l'étranger», Rapport de synthèse, ('Impact of French cinema abroad', Synthesis report), Association des Exportateurs de Films (ADEF), no. 33949, Paris, September 2004, p. 34. Some 71% of the non-Europeans questioned stressed that French films had given the country a positive image (except for the Americans).

(in reference to the Iranian rhetorical designated to the United States) is taking root in Iran–as long as there is nothing "un-Islamic about baseball." With the aid of American coaches and advisers, Iran is trying to train a national baseball team and to encourage a network of local clubs. The long-range goal is to field a competitive team in international tournaments and in the Olympics, joining such other baseball newcomers as Greece and Russia.

The Americans sent to drill the players included retired umpires, college coaches, some former major leaguers, and Christian missionaries in a country where trying to convert Muslims is punishable by death. Although the motto of the missionary group "Unlimited Potential Inc." is 'Serving Christ through Baseball', it claims to restrict its activities to baseball.

Given the political animosity and personal anguish that have marked relations between the American and Iranian governments, and the two nations for a few decades, perhaps "all Americans in Iran won't any longer be considered spies, nor will all Iranians in the US be considered terrorists."[31] Some compare the efforts with the "Ping-Pong Diplomacy" of 1971, when a visit by American ping pong players to China helped lead to the establishment of U.S.-China relations. Of particular notice while reviewing historic trends is that two decades ago, in 1982/83, Iran was the leading country of origin in terms of international enrollment in U.S. colleges and universities, with 26,760 students in the United States (compared to only 2,258 in 2002/03).[32] This figure did not even entitle Iran to one of the top 20 sending countries today.

---

[31] Michael Nazir-Ali, "After the Revolution: A Christian report on Iran," *The Guardian*, November 25, 2000, 10; also John Ward Anderson, "New in Middle East: Hoops Diplomacy," *IHT*, December 7, 2002; and Brian Murphy, "The Crack of the Bat in Iran," *IHT*, June 25, 2001, 1. A number of American universities were reported to have provided the Iraqi Federation of Baseball (founded in July 2004) with the necessary equipment for the sport. Source: "Iraqis Play Baseball," *http://www.elaph.com/sports/2005/2/41442.htm*, February 17, 2005.

[32] "Open Doors 2003: International Students in the U.S.," *Institute of International Education,* Washington, DC, November 3, 2003, available at: http://opendoors.iienetwork.org/?p=36523.

II.I.I.III. Cultural Diplomacy

An invention of the French in the late 19th century, Taylor defines "cultural diplomacy" as "a governmental activity which attempts to by-pass commercial media images by appealing directly to the peoples of foreign societies on an ostensibly non-political level. Its principal instruments are language teaching, educational exchanges and other forms of cultural contact..."[33] It benefits the countries involved in the long-term, if somewhat in unformulated ways. If foreigners have direct experience of a nation's culture, through an ability to speak its language, read its literature, observe its cultural forms preferably in their natural surroundings or at least in their own localities, then those foreigners are more likely to understand and appreciate that any media images they are exposed to do not reveal the whole story about that particular nation. Even more, their appreciation may translate into empathy and friendship, paving the road for greater mutual understanding. Respectively, government-sponsored or supported organizations such as the British Council, the *Alliance Française*, the *Societa' Dante Alighieri*, the *Goethe Institut*, or the Tokyo Foundation all initiate cultural and educational exchanges, take part in international exhibitions, establish libraries in countries overseas, and sponsor traveling drama, music and lecture tours.

All these activities are conducted in an attempt to increase a level of international understanding and appreciation that can assist foreign policy in the long-term. Since these activities have proved vulnerable to political debate (as from taxpayers of a country that engages in it who wonder why they should subsidize an activity that does not directly benefit them), there is also an economic justification for them. This suggests that if Nation X subsidizes a student from Nation Y to study a subject like engineering for three years or more in X, then upon graduation he/she will return to Y in a fast-track career. That person may ultimately become in control of an engineering firm, and when the firm needs to consider a foreign order, he/she will automatically look to Nation X as a result of the goodwill generated towards that person's period of study. In other words, cultural diplomacy is thus good for business as well as for international cooperation.

---

[33] Philip M. Taylor, *Global Communications, International Affairs and the Media since 1945*, 1997, p. 79.

However, such engagement tends not to be a mass activity. Rather, it is directed at the future movers and shakers, the *elites*, of foreign societies, whether they be the political, military, economic, cultural or diplomatic leaderships of the future.[34] Cultural diplomacy is also very much an adjunct of conventional diplomacy. If the latter fails, the former suffers—though the former is considered worth trying in an attempt to lubricate the workings of the latter. Ever since the Revolution in 1789, the French have aspired to see their language achieve a sort of universal status. By the end of the 19th century, with France established as a colonial power second only to Britain and its language accepted as the *lingua franca* of diplomacy, they seemed to be on their way to reaching their goal. As the 20th century drew on, however, and English continued to trespass, French was driven onto the defensive.[35] France, at present, spends around $1 billion a year on various aid and other programs designed to promote its civilization abroad.

Accordingly, cultural diplomacy may be seen as a political activity designed to serve national interests in an ostensibly cultural guise. It is a reflection not only of the broadening popular base of the foreign-policy-making process but also of the growing role of ideology in international affairs. For example, the British Council was established in 1934 under the auspices of the Foreign Office as a direct response to the aggressive ideological circumstances of the pre-Second World War period. Essentially the same to this day, its role was defined as:

> To make the life and thought of the British peoples more widely known abroad; and to promote a mutual interchange of knowledge and ideas with other peoples. To encourage the study and use of the English language;...To bring other peoples into closer touch with British ideals and practice in education, industry and government; to make available to them the benefits of current British contributions to the sciences and

---

[34] On how to consider and select potential elites, refer to «La Stratégie de formation des élites: Comparaisons internationales», ('The strategy of training elites: international comparisons'), Frank BOURNOIS, Lecture presented for the Cycle d'enseignement diplomatique supérieur, C.E.D.S., Paris, March 27, 2002. A potential elite may be recognized as of 30 years of age (after having assumed two to three professional posts of around 2 years each).

[35] French had become the language of diplomacy on account of the intellectual hegemony France exercised over Europe in the 17th and 18th centuries. Furthermore, French possessed orderliness and clarity of expression that made it particularly suitable as a vehicle for international relations. For more on the rise and fall of the French and English languages in diplomacy, see: Keith Hamilton and Richard Langhorne, *The Practice of Diplomacy: its evolution, theory and administration*, London: Routledge, 1995, pp. 105-07.

technology; and to afford them opportunities of appreciating contemporary British works in literature, the fine arts, drama and music.[36]

The Americans engage in cultural diplomacy only through the U.S. Information Agency (USIA), originally founded in 1953 to serve Cold War objectives. The United States has no equivalent of the British Council. As defined under the 1961 Fulbright-Hayes Act, the aim of the USIA includes spreading information abroad about the United States, its people, culture, and policies, as well as conducting educational and cultural exchanges between the United States and other countries. Among the USIA programs are the Voice of America (broadcasting in several languages), Radio Liberty, Radio Free Europe, and the WORLDNET television services. It embraces the Fulbright Scholarship, International Visitors and other educational exchange programs, the American Speakers Abroad program, the Wireless File, in addition to a network of overseas operations, including libraries and cultural centers. The USIA also supports a number of private philanthropic organizations, such as the Carnegie Foundation, to promote educational exchanges.

It is worth reminding that international students studying in the United States contribute nearly $13 billion dollars to the American economy, through their expenditure on tuition and living expenses. U.S. Department of Commerce data describe higher education in the country as the 5th largest service sector export. Those students bring money into the national economy and provide revenue to their host states for living expenses, including room/board, books and supplies, transportation, health insurance, support for accompanying family members, and other miscellaneous items. Some 67% of all international students receive the majority of their funds from family and personal sources, and, when other sources of funding from their home countries, including assistance from their home-country governments or universities, are added in, a total of nearly 75% of all international students funding comes from sources outside of the United States.[37]

---

[36] Philip M. Taylor, *Global Communications, International Affairs and the Media since 1945*, 1997, p. 80.

[37] "Open Doors 2004: International Students in the U.S.," Institute of International Education (IIE), New York, November 10, 2004.

Yet, findings of the study stated that the number of international students enrolled in U.S. higher education institutions decreased by 2.4% for the academic year 2003/2004 to a total of 572,509. That 2.4% drop follows minimal increase the prior year (0.6%) in 2002/2003, preceded by five years of steady growth. The drop in enrollments in 2003/2004 is the first absolute decline in foreign enrollments since 1971/1972 (when enrollments dropped 3% to 140,126), although several years of minimal (less than 1%) growth were reported in the mid-1980s and in the mid-1990s.

The overall decline in international students enrolled in U.S. colleges and universities has been attributed to a variety of reasons. Among them are real and perceived difficulties in obtaining student visas (especially in scientific and technical fields),[38] rising U.S. tuition costs, vigorous recruitment activities by other English-speaking countries, and perceptions abroad that international students may no longer be welcomed in the United States.

India remains the largest sending country of origin for the 3rd year, up by 7% over the prior year, to a total of 79,736 in 2003/2004 (though India's rate of increase in that year slowed from the prior year's dramatic 12% growth). Among the leading five places of origin, total enrollments fell by 5% for students from China (still the second largest sending country with 61,765), down by 11% for Japan (ranked 4th with 40,835).

---

[38] Applicants from China face more visa difficulties than applicants from any other country outside the Middle East. This is partly because many Chinese students pursue the science disciplines that set off a screening process known as Visa Mantis (established in 1998), intended to prevent the transfer of sensitive technology out of the United States. A U.S. Congressional study found that during a three-month period in 2003 (April to June), more than half of all the 2,888 Visa Mantis investigations worldwide involved Chinese students (1,662 cases). Among the other nationalities involved were those of Russia (567 cases), the United Kingdom (75 cases), and India (51 cases). The report also found it took an average of 67 days for the security check to be processed and for the U.S. State Department to notify the consular post (see Figure 2.1.). Refer to: United States General Accounting Office (GAO), Report to the Chairman and Ranking Minority Member, Committee on Science, House of Representatives, *Border Security: Improvements Needed to Reduce Time Taken to Adjudicate Visas for Science Students and Scholars*, February 2004. Responding to concerns that onerous visa requirements are discouraging foreign students and scientists from coming to the United States, the State Department extended the validity of the clearance to up to four years for students, and two for scientists, making it easier to remain in the united States for the duration of work or study programs (before so, clearance had to be applied for each year). See: Kristen A. Lee, "State Dept. Relaxes Visa Rules for Some Scientists and Students," *The New York Times*, online edition, February 14, 2005.

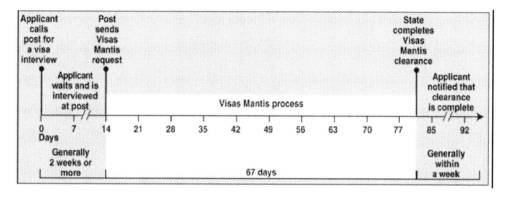

Figure 2. 1. Average Time Frames for Visas Mantis Adjudication Process, April to June 2003 (Source: GAO, February 2004)

The number of students rose by around 2% from the Republic of Korea (positioned 3rd with 52,484), and Canada (5th with 27,017). A decrease of 7% in students studying in U.S. institutions dropped Taiwan to 6th place (with 26,178), and moved Canada up to become the only non-Asian country among the top five. Additional sharp decreases in Asian student enrollments were reported from Thailand (down 10.5%), Indonesia (down 15%), Hong Kong (down 9%), and Pakistan (down 10%).

Students from the Middle East continued to decrease substantially, though the 9% rate of decrease in 2003/2004 is slightly less than the 10% decline for 2002/2003. Major decreases have been reported in the numbers of students from many countries of the region, including Saudi Arabia (down 16% to 3,521), Kuwait (down 17% to 1,846), Jordan (down 15% to 1,853), and the United Arab Emirates (down 30% to 1,248). The enrollment from the largest sender in the region, Turkey (ranked 8th with 11,398), has remained relatively steady, with a decrease of 2% for that year. Significant declines from other countries in the region only marginally affected the overall student totals, since absolute numbers of students coming from these countries are comparatively small.

The most popular fields of study for international students in the United States are business and management (19%), engineering (17%), and mathematics and computer science (12%). After two years of remarkable growth, the number of international students studying mathematics and computer sciences has declined by 6% in each of the past two years. The fields of Social Sciences (10%) and Physical and Life Sciences (8%) have seen increased growth of 18% and 2% respectively.

On the other hand, American students–more than ever–now recognize the importance of studying abroad in a globally interdependent world. In the first academic year after the September 11 attacks (year 2002/2003), the number of U.S. higher education students receiving credit for study abroad increased sharply by 8.5% from the previous year, reaching a record total of 174,629. This increase constitutes a strong indicator of the tremendous interest in studying abroad, both in spite of and in response to the changing geopolitical climate following the events.

As study abroad opportunities have become more plentiful, varied and more affordable, the number of students taking advantage of an academic experience abroad has increased dramatically. Since 1991/1992, the number of students studying abroad for credit has more than doubled (from 71,154 to 174,629, that is, an increase of 145%).

The United Kingdom continues to be the leading destination for U.S. students (up by 5.2% to 31,706), followed by Italy (up 10.3%, to 18,936), Spain (up 9.8%, to 18,865), and France (up 6.6%, to 13,080). Increases were also reported in students going to Eastern Europe, including the Czech Republic (1,997, up 20%), Russia (1,521, up 20%), and also Hungary (562, up 24%). Numbers of U.S. students studying in Latin America also continued to rise (up 14%, to 26,643), with Mexico continuing to be the largest host country in the region (up 9%, to 8,775).

Americans studying in the Middle East were down by 51% (to 648 students), reflecting a sharp decline in the number of students studying in the largest host country in the region, Israel (340, down 67%). Nevertheless, U.S. enrollments in Turkey grew sharply (228, up 77%), and in northern Africa (495, up 15%), with a 26% increase of U.S. students in Egypt (to 303), and a 12% increase in Morocco (to 191).

American students studying in Australia remained to expand (10,691, up 13%). Numbers were also growing sharply in New Zealand (1,917, up 45%), along with the Oceania (12,749, up 16%), and thus being the world region with the strongest growth in U.S. students abroad.

Finally, it is worth noting that American students continue to study abroad in larger numbers but for shorter time periods, with more than 50% of U.S. undergraduates and masters degree students preferring summer, January terms, and other programs of 8 weeks or less (with a continued decline in popularity of longer term programs).

In 2002/2003, the leading majors of Americans studying abroad were Social Science (21%), Business and Management (18%), Humanities (13%), Fine or Applied Arts (9%), and Foreign Languages (8%).

Based on comparable figures available for the year 2002, some 586,000 foreign students were enrolled in U.S. universities, compared with around 270,000 in Britain, the world's second destination for education, and 227,000 in Germany, the third-largest destination. As for France, there were more than 194,194 foreign students enrolled in French universities in 2003/2004 (compared to 128,141 in 1985/1986). Foreign students represented 13.6% of overall university students in France (a 1% increase from the year 2002/2003), noting that a grand majority of them (51.7%) come from Africa, while European students mounted to 24.2% and those from Asia to 17.2%.[39]

To end with an interesting observation on education and career choice, Japan's generation gap has for several years been visible on the streets of Tokyo. Walking beside the legions of salary men in dark suits rushing to fill 14-hour work days are wild-haired, brightly dressed young people, some even with artificial tans. When the two worlds interact, a new expression is sometimes invoked that perhaps best expresses the gap in understanding and communication between generations–as older Japanese, on occasion, refer to younger people as *uchu jin*, or space aliens.

Talented young Japanese are less and less drawn to science and engineering-related careers, such as manufacturing. With a steady 30-year decline in the number of students choosing engineering compared with liberal arts (the share of liberal arts students increased from 12.7% in 1970 to 16.6% in 2000, compared to engineering

---

[39] «Repères et références statistiques sur les enseignements, la formation et la recherche», Ministre de l'éducation nationale, ('Statistical Indicators and References on Education, Training and Research', Ministry of National Education), Paris, edition 2004, pp. 176-77.

students that slipped from 21.1% to 18.9% during the same period), these shifts–though small–have attracted the concern of the government.

In 2000, the top five professions for the Japanese teens were, in order of preference: television announcer, musician, athlete, video game creator and doctor. At the bottom of the list were politician, business executive and banker. Furthermore, the word "freeter," a combination of 'free' and the German word *arbeiter* (or worker), is now commonly used in the Japanese society. It describes young people who do not commit to one line of work, change jobs frequently and–importantly–will not take up a decent job unless they enjoy it. "It is this freeter phenomenon that confuses older Japanese, who cannot understand why in times of hardship and rising unemployment, jobs can be vacant," concluded one article.[40]

II.I.I.IV. Summits and Funerals

A great deal of both bilateral and multilateral diplomacy takes place today at the summit, that is, at the level of heads of governments or states. An example of such bilateral diplomacy is the Franco-German Summit that has been achieved formally at regular intervals five to six times a year since the signing of the Franco-German Treaty of Friendship and Cooperation in January 1963 (though the two leaders are supposed to meet at least twice a year).

Summitry had ancient origins, where at least by the Middle Ages it was indeed a usual method of conducting diplomacy. During that period, countries were little more than the private estates of their absolute rulers, when personal encounters were relatively easy to arrange as diplomatic relations were mostly confined to neighbor states.[41] Despite of that practice, French diplomat and historian Philippe de Commynes (1447-1511) asserted in his memoirs "Two great princes who wish to establish good personal relations should never meet each other face to face but ought to communicate through good and wise ambassadors." His view arose from his belief that great princes

---

[40] Thomas Fuller, "Work Hard? Young Japanese Have Other Ideas," *IHT,* April 11, 2001, 1.

[41] See: E. Goldstein, "The Origins of Summit Diplomacy," in David H. Dunn (ed.), *Diplomacy at the Highest Level: The Evolution of International Summitry,* Basingstoke: Macmillan, 1996, p. 23; and also: D.E. Queller, *The Office of Ambassador in the Middle Ages,* p. 225.

were in general spoiled, vain, and badly educated; in other words, they were poorly equipped for diplomacy.[42]

During the modern era, summitry gradually fell into disuse as the result of the rise of the modern state and the introduction and spread of resident embassies. In the 19th century, the Concert of Europe saw the revival of summit diplomacy–although it did not become significant once again until the first half of the 20th century. The firm course of summit diplomacy was confirmed by the Paris Peace Conference in 1919 that joined Lloyd George, Georges Clemenceau, and Woodrow Wilson, as well as by the wartime conferences grouping Roosevelt, Churchill, and Stalin.

Stimulated by the same political and technological trends promoting multilateral diplomacy, summitry increased as a result of concern over developments in the Cold War–leading rulers to believe "diplomacy in the nuclear age was too important to be left to the diplomats."[43] In addition, the decolonization of the European empires in the 1950s and 1960s multiplied summitry, as new states rarely possessed competent and extensive diplomatic services. Similar to the present case, regional organizations that were becoming fashionable gave (and still do give) summitry a natural focus.

An important and particular case of the ad hoc summit is the funeral of a major political figure that is attended by high-level delegations from the region concerned or, more recently, from all over the world. In fact, the *working funeral* resembles the serial summit to the extent that at least by the 1960s it had established a predictable pattern of procedure. It is a particular case, however, because it is rather useless for the diplomatic purpose for which the typical ad hoc summit is principally conceived (i.e., generating significant diplomatic momentum on a major issue). This is partly due to its theme and partly due to the unavoidable short notice the countries sending delegations receive. Of

---

[42] He also stated that leaders of his time were usually suspicious persons. A state of mind produced by the many false stories and groundless reports brought to their attention by court flatterers. Even more, summitry could place them in physical danger. And Commynes' attitude may not have been entirely unconnected to the role that he was required to play when his master, Louis XI, met Edward IV on a bridge over *la Somme* at Picquigny to discuss the peaceful retreat of the English invasion force of 1475. There and then, Louis instructed Commynes to wear identical clothes to his own as a precaution against assassination. Source: Philippe de Commynes, "The Memoirs of Philippe de Commynes," Vol. One, ed. Samuel Kisner, trsl. Isabelle Cazeau (Columbia, South Carolina: University of South Carolina Press, 1969).

[43] David H. Dunn, *Diplomacy at the Highest Level*, 1996, p. 5.

course, funeral summits carry risks as prior diplomatic schedules are upset, and decisions on attendance (and its level) have to be made in the absence of precise knowledge about the reactions of other states and of how the delegation will be received.

On the other hand, nevertheless, funeral summits can be of considerable value in diplomacy. Among the compensating advantages *mourners* have as a result of the short notice is that it provides heads of governments with an acceptable excuse to interrupt an existing schedule in order to have urgent discussions on a current problem with other leaders in circumstances that will not evoke public expectations. Another advantage implies a decision to attend that is unlikely to prove embarrassing as a result of changed circumstances by the funeral date. And finally, if attendance at the funeral is likely to cause controversy, there is little time available for domestic opposition to be mobilized.

In addition, a summit of this type is of special importance if it is the funeral of an incumbent head of government. This is because the funeral offers the first occasion both for the foreign friends of the deceased to confirm that the new leadership commits to their relationship, and also for foreign rivals to explore the possibility of opening a new page in their relationship. Berridge (2002, p. 80) notes that the state leaders of the Warsaw Pact always attended the funerals of Soviet leaders for the former purpose, while Western leaders attended them for the latter, at least in the 1980s. Consider as well the attendance of former U.S. secretary of state Madeleine Albright to the funeral of late Syrian president Hafez Al Assad in June 2000, when she met with his son– although Syria was on the U.S. list of states sponsoring terrorism. Such examples show a funeral summit may also provide a valuable cover for discreet consultations between rivals seeking to keep their conflict within peaceful bounds or striving for a way out of an impasse. "Funerals of this kind are times of political truce," concludes Berridge (*Ibid.*).

Recall, in this context, the widely-media covered funeral of Pope John Paul II on April 8, 2005, which was not only a unique moment in the history of the Catholic church, but also an opportunity for diplomatic contacts to be made and renewed. Some four kings, five queens, and 70 or more presidents and prime ministers attended the funeral in delegations of around 2500 dignitaries. President Chen Shui-bian of Taiwan went there with hopes of meeting foreign leaders—in a momentous chance for the leader of an island that is largely unrecognized by the rest of the world (noting that China did not send a representative because of Mr. Chen's presence, and because the Vatican maintains diplomatic ties with Taiwan). President Bashar Al Assad of Syria and President Mohammed Khatami of Iran (two Muslim countries) both attended in an attempt to ease international pressure on their countries.

Trends in international human rights law, which suggest that heads of states no longer enjoy immunity from charges of crimes against humanity, may in the future lower enthusiasm for summit travel. Summitry for certain leaders may also be restricted in terms of travel zone, or due to political circumstances. Saddam Hussein never traveled outside Iraq ever since the Iraq-Kuwait conflict, nor were state leaders—whether Arab or foreign—anxious to visit him in Baghdad. Yasser Arafat, another example, was confined in his headquarters in Ramallah for 3 years (from December 2001 until his death in November 2004). In contrast, President Robert Mugabe of Zimbabwe defied travel restrictions imposed by member nations of the European Union and attended the funeral of Pope John Paul II.

Last, reference is also made here to the diplomatic implications of natural disasters and catastrophes that are increasingly receiving the compassion of the international community at large. With some hope of easing the tension between Teheran and Washington, and in spite of the "axis of evil" notion pronounced by President Bush in January 2002, Iran's President Mohammad Khatami stated Iran would accept U.S. government's offer of humanitarian aid after a powerful earthquake had hit Iran less than six months after.[44]

Take, as another example, the deadly tsunami disaster that hit countries stretching from Malaysia to Tanzania on December 24, 2004. In an aim to keep up the role it seeks to develop in the region and in the world, India was quick to extend help to Sri Lanka, the Maldives, and to Indonesia. The Indian government was successful through its actions to improve its standing with its eastern neighbors, as well as in reaffirming its "Look East" policy. Furthermore and for the first time, the Indian navy

---

[44] Parisa Hafezi, "Iran Accepts US Aid Offer to Help Quake Victims," *The Washington Post*, online edition, June 25, 2002.

coordinated its humanitarian operations with American navy forces in the Indian Ocean region in what may be considered as another illustration of the deepening U.S.-Indian relations. This cooperation runs contrast with the Cold War era when India looked with suspicion on the American naval presence in the region, and while the United States looked on India's growing naval capabilities as a potential threat. Last, India's swift response to the tsunami catastrophe is expected to strengthen the country's track record and global role as it vies for a permanent seat on the U.N. Security Council.[45]

Another observed case related to the tsunami disaster concerns Sri Lanka, the country hit hardest in relation to its size and population. A substantial segment of the areas affected lies within the region claimed by the Liberation Tigers of Tamil Eelam (LTTE) as the "historical Tamil region." The Tigers' de facto administration in the predominately Tamil population in northeastern Sri Lanka sought to benefit from an unprecedented chance to work with the Colombo government, and perhaps move forward to a lasting peace. President Chandrika Kumaratunga's office invited Tamilselvan (the equivalent of the LTTE prime minister) to take part in top-level decisions about rehabilitating the impoverished northeast region. After being inoperative for years, a hotline between the government and the LTTE was also put back to service.

Britain, the United States and India consider the LTTE a "terrorist organization," and accordingly ban official contact. However, officials from the U.S. Agency for International Development were reported to have met with Tamil representatives. The Italian government was keen to speed relief to the region, and thus dispatched a number of diplomats along with trucks of humanitarian supplies into Tiger territory. Meanwhile, an increasing number of international donors, as well as the Australian government, connected directly with the Tigers' relief agency, the Tamil Rehabilitation Organization (TRO), a legally registered NGO in Sri Lanka. While the LTTE tried to use the relief efforts as a way to demonstrate its effective control of the Tamil areas, Colombo

---

[45] Read: "Tsunami Disaster's Diplomatic Implications," South East Monitor, no. 79, published by the South Asia Program, Center for Strategic and International Studies (CSIS), Washington, DC, February 1, 2005. Noting that China supports India's ambitions for a permanent seat on the U.N. Security Council, in April 2005 the two Asian powers signed an agreement to resolve the long-dispute over their Himalayan border. China accordingly gave over its claim to the state of Sikkim, which was referred to in the joint statement as 'the Sikkim State of the Republic of China.' See: "China and India sign border deal," BBC News, online edition, April 11, 2005.

remained sensitive about such contacts. It is not surprising, consequently, that Sri Lankan authorities blocked U.N. Secretary-General Kofi Amman from visiting the Tamil-controlled region out of 'security concerns,' a decision that certainly did not please the LTTE.[46]

II.I.I.V. Universal Jurisdiction

Human rights lawyers see that an age of justice without borders is dawning. The trend is being viewed as an alarming challenge to national sovereignty and a potentially unpredictable political tool. Some governments can also fear such a trend causes a potentially paralyzing effect on government decision-making, warning such prosecutions–which are jumping into other borders–will be even-handed, indicting the friends as well as foes of great powers.

Consider the following cases as examples: former Yugoslav president Slobodan Milosevic was handed over to an international tribunal in La Hague; Manuel Noriega of Panama was seized and convicted of drug trafficking by the United States in 1989; Augusto Pinochet of Chile spent a year and a half in British custody on a Spanish warrant before being allowed to return home (where his legal problems continued); Hassan Habre of Chad was under arrest in Senegal until being turned loose by a new government (though his fate remains uncertain); former Rwandan prime minister Jean Kambada went to jail for life in 2000 for committing genocides in 1994; and Peru demanded Japan to extradite its former president Alberto Fujimori.

The idea of universal jurisdiction, where officials are vulnerable to international prosecution, first arose in 1919 when there was an abortive attempt to put Kaiser Wilhelm on trial for World War I. After World War II, the Nuremberg trials of Nazi officials were the century's high point in the use of universal jurisdiction for war crimes. Afterwards, that kind of law became a narrow, specialized field. In recent years,

---

[46] Melinda Liu, "Worse than War," *Newsweek*, international edition, January 17, 2005, 23-25.

it has revived with the establishment of war crimes tribunals for the Balkans and Rwanda and with the inauguration of the International Criminal Court (ICC).[47]

Entered in force on July 1, 2002, the ICC is "the first ever permanent, treaty based, international criminal court established to promote the rule of law and ensure that the gravest international crimes do not go unpunished."[48] The ICC deals with genocide, war crimes, crimes against humanity and–eventually–*aggression*. Crimes against humanity include systematic murder or torture, rape and sexual slavery, noting that crimes committed before July 1, 2002 are not subject to prosecution.

Notably objectors to the ICC include the United States and Israel. The United States opposes the idea that Americans could be subjected to the court's jurisdiction if a crime is committed in a country that has ratified the Rome Statute establishing the ICC (initiated on July 17, 1998)–even if the United States is not a party. This concern led the U.N. Security Council in July 2002 to unanimously adopt a resolution effectively giving American peacekeepers a year's exception from prosecution by the ICC (the United States had threatened to withdraw its peacekeeping forces from Bosnia, from the Croatian peninsula of Prevlaka, and from East Timor if it were not granted such an exception).[49] As for Israel, concerns about potential vulnerability have been fueled by two separate cases: an attempt in Belgium to charge the Israeli Prime Minister Ariel Sharon for the 1982 invasion of Sabra and Chatila refugee camps;[50] and the second involved "unhappiness" in Demark for naming Carmi Gillon, a former chief of the Shin Bet security service in mid-1990s, as its new ambassador to Copenhagen. The latter outraged the Danish for endorsing the use of moderate physical pressure during police interrogations.

---

[47] Barbara Crosette, "New Anxiety Over Idea of a Borderless Justice," *IHT,* July 2, 2001, 1.

[48] According to the official Web site of the ICC, at: http://www.icc-cpi.int/php/show.php?id=history.

[49] See: "U.S. solos against war crimes court," July 1, 2002, *www.msnbc.com*; and Serge Schmemann, "U.S. Peacekeepers Given Year's Immunity from New Court," *The New York Times*, online edition, July 13, 2002.

[50] Adopted in 1993 and expanded in 1999, a Belgian law allows the country's courts to hear cases of atrocities, including genocide and other crimes against humanity that may have happened anywhere, without any connection to Belgium.

With powers to issue warrants and insist on individuals being delivered up to it for trial, the new court and its prosecutor could in theory be driven by quite different attitudes.[51] One country's *necessary* war measures or *unavoidable* self-defense, possibly bombing a village or moving a local population or simply attacking a power or radio station, could be seen from the other side as deliberate and inhuman conduct towards civilians, meriting the charges domestic courts were unwilling to pursue.

Some scholars and lawyers are even disturbed by the pressure of rich nations put on Yugoslavia, especially by the United States, through threats that money needed to rebuild the country could be withheld until former president Slobodan Milosevic was handed over to the ICC. The extradition led to the resignation of Yugoslav's prime minister Zoran Zizic, yet immediately secured Yugoslavia with $1.28 billion in aid for reconstruction. "The question remains: How cheap was he sold for?", concluded an article.[52] Also, there is Henry Kissinger who warns against a dangerous mix of law and politics in what he acknowledges has become a growing movement for universal jurisdiction.

Kissinger, whom some critics want to see face trial for his policies in Cambodia during the Vietnam War, writes a universal system "must now allow legal principles to be used to settle political scores."[53] He sees a possible chilling effect on makers of foreign policy, who would have to weigh whether they could be prosecuted for acting on behalf of what they see as their nation's interests.

---

[51] For a look at some leaders accused of crimes and their cases, see: *Courrier International*, no. 558, July 12-18, 2001, pp. 28-35; and, «Les fous du pouvoir», ('The Madmen of Power'), published in the sarcastic magazine *Les dossiers du Canard enchaîné*, no. 77, October 2000.

[52] Keith B. Richburg, "Milosevic in Hague Prison: Belgrade Gets Aid Package," *IHT*, June 30-July 1, 2001, 1. Also read: Ramesh Thakur, "Yes to International Justice, But It Won't Be Easy," *IHT*, July 17, 2001, 6.

[53] Henry Kissinger, *Does America Need a Foreign Policy? Towards a Diplomacy for the 21st Century*, New York: Simon Schuster, 2001, pp. 273-82. Kissinger was also asked to appear as a witness in an investigation concerning French citizens who disappeared under the 1973-1990 ruling of Augusto Pinochet. The lawyer for the families considered Kissinger's testimony "essential" to the case because of numerous exchanges between the security agencies of the United States and Chile after the 1973 coup that brought Pinochet to power. Kissinger was in Paris for a private visit when the summons was delivered to him at his hotel, and was under no legal obligation to answer it. See: "A Pinochet Inquiry Summons Kissinger," *IHT*, May 29, 2001, 3.

Another feature in diplomacy may be referred to as *biological foreign policy*. That is, a given state runs out of ideas or political room to maneuver on how to deal with a certain foreign leader, and so, the whole approach is to wait for the leader to pass away. In such cases, most policies involve doing nothing, simply because there is nothing to be done but to rely on biology, human nature and on time.

Cuba is one example, where nine U.S. presidents have boycotted the country as they still wait for President Fidel Castro to die. Only in May 2002 did Jimmy Carter become the first current or former U.S. president to visit Cuba since that of Calvin Coolidge back in 1928. Such an American foreign policy has also been adopted likewise in regards to Kim Jong II of North Korea (as well as President Saddam Hussein of Iraq from 1991-2003)–in the hopes that they be replaced by American-viewed more pragmatic leaders. Interestingly, reports and rumors on the arising health conditions of those leaders become a major interest to follow, particularly by the media and the states concerned.

Israel had also adopted a related approach in respect of Yasser Arafat:

> The agonizing answer is that Yasser Arafat did not prove to be a partner for peace and quite probably will not be one in the future....
> At some point in the future a new Palestinian leadership will emerge, capable of making the decisions that would make peace with Israel possible.[54]

The Israeli government has drawn up a list of Palestinian leaders who can be assassinated and is accordingly methodically carrying out targeted killings as its intelligence resources provide the opportunity. The assassination campaign replaces known Palestinian activists with new militants who are less known but are even more determined to escalate the *Intifadha*. Though targeted killings may satisfy a blood lust and perceived need for revenge, they are ineffective in achieving their stated objective of deterring retaliation.

---

[54] Ehud Barak, "It Seems Israel has to Wait for a New Palestinian Leadership," *IHT*, July 31, 2001, 6. Also see: Thomas L. Friedman, "Just Waiting for Some to Go Away," *IHT*, July 11, 2001, 6; and Vincent Cannistraro, "Assassinating Israeli Adversaries Is Wrong and Also Dumb," *IHT*, August 31, 2001, 4. Immediately after Palestinian leader Mahmoud Abbas was elected, Israeli Prime Minister Ariel Sharon stated conditions were right for a "historic breakthrough" between the two peoples. See: "Sharon praises Palestinian leader," *BBC News*, online edition, January 27, 2005.

II.I.II. Diplomats in the Information Age

A series of conferences around the turn of the millennium debated the future direction of diplomacy. Some questioned whether there was a place at all or a future for the profession, given the powerful march of global capital forces, the proliferation of non-state actors, and the revolution in communications. As the boundaries between *domestic* and *foreign*, and between *state* and *non-state* become increasingly blurred, the once-discrete functions of diplomats (foreign policy analysis, reporting, representing, negotiating) are now performed routinely by a large cast of others, including home civil servants, bankers, aid workers, civil society leaders, and a huge bunch of miscellaneous experts.

Even so, these discussions on the whole concluded there is likely to be a continuing role for diplomats. The state will also remain a key actor, even if increasingly in groups and jostled for space by private organizations, business and financial institutions. *Global Trends 2015* (2000, p. 10) concludes:

> States will continue to be the dominant players on the world stage, but governments will have less and less control over flows of information, technology, diseases, migrants, arms, and financial transactions, whether licit or illicit, across their borders. Nonstate actors ranging from business firms to non profit organizations will play increasingly larger roles in both national and international affairs. The quality of governance, both nationally and internationally, will substantially determine how well states and societies cope with these global forces.

Some of the traditional functions of the diplomats will still be needed, not least looking after their citizens abroad. Foreign ministries will continue to provide essential consular and–to a varying extent–commercial services. As the number of citizens traveling grows, so does the volume of consular work, demanding a comparably higher proportion of staff resources. In an attempt to assure that demand, an interesting evolution is a new emphasis on "American Presence Posts" (APPs), which can best be described as micro-consulates to meet information age societies.

APPs are small decentralized offices in provincial cities aboard consisting of a foreign service officer whose primary working tool is a computer linked to the embassy in the capital city. The first APPs were set up in France in 1999, beginning with Lyon; Noting that they (the APPs) are only one of the organizational reforms changing the ways in which American Foreign Service officers conduct business from now on. Those small posts have been hailed in some quarters as a move in the direction of *telediplomacy*, in which *virtual embassies* serve as electronic data-gathering outposts for computerized decision-making in Washington.[55]

Despite such changes in the way things are accomplished, more readily with e-mail and video conferencing, states still need to talk to one another. That means having people on the ground to assume the talking, thanks to whom have been there long enough to understand what is really being said. Noteworthy here are the Americans working overseas and the Arabs working in non-Arabic speaking countries, as they both tend to isolate themselves in "golden ghettos" and interact with each other rather than with the people of the host country. That approach and behavior simply renders the ability to adopt and learn the foreign culture even more difficult. Many executives (particularly the Americans and British), as well, are assigned aboard for short periods, usually two years, which is not enough time to both learn the language and integrate into the society.[56] Moreover, since they expect to be leaving back in two years, they may feel the effort of learning the language as a waste of time/effort, or even useless–demonstrating "another example of how the American short-term time orientation adversely affects business performance."[57]

However, the notion above runs counter to *localitis*. Now sometimes referred to as "going native," *localitis* is an occupational hazard experienced by the professional diplomat (and even senior executive) who has been posted for a long time in the same part of the world. Berridge (2002, p. 109) recalls it has been recognized since the birth of resident missions during the Italian Renaissance. "At best the diplomat loses touch with sentiments at home; at worst he becomes a mouthpiece for the government to which he is accredited rather than the one he nominally represents."

---

[55] Wilson Dizard, Jr., "Digital Diplomats," *iMP: The Magazine on Information Impacts,* July 23, 2001.

[56] Noting also that "Today the average overseas assignment for an agency spy-handler is three years, barely enough time to learn one's way around, let alone penetrate a terror cell." See: Massimo Calabresi and Romesh Ratnesar, "Can We Stop the Next Attack?" *Time,* online edition, March 3, 2002.

[57] Edward T. Hall and Mildred Reed Hall, *Understanding Cultural Differences: Germans, French and Americans,* Maine (U.S.A.): Intercultural Press, Inc., 1990, pp. 172-74.

Obviously then, it was considerably because of recognition of the possibility the resident diplomat might "go native" that it became normal to rotate diplomats between postings, typically after three or four years, in spite of "the costly sacrifice of hard-won area expertise that this involved," states Berridge (2002, p. 110).

The vestiges of 18th century protocol are still pertained to diplomacy and diplomats, though further diminished and practiced with widely varying degrees. Consequently, it continues to be necessary to acquaint diplomatic staff with the formal rules of procedure and precedence. As some of the rules are useful, ceremony will continue to matter to many–mostly to those who can afford the cost. But it is quite clear that the trend in diplomacy is away from prestige and protocol.[58]

Hemery outlines the reasons behind such an evolving trend in diplomacy.[59] One is because diplomacy is conducted by non-diplomats, without plumed hats or spurs, from other ministries or from outside government altogether. "An increasing proportion of diplomatic activity takes place in multilateral working institutions having neither historical baggage nor national image to project." Gradually, modern society itself becomes steadily less formal, and therefore, "by 2015 less time and money will be spent on the auto-erotic exchange of courtesies under the candelabra with *chers colleagues.*"

Diplomats still need to be trained how to write with clarity, brevity and precision, and how to structure a report. While diplomatic communication both within and between governments is conducted increasingly with informality by secure e-mails, there is little demand and less time for the elegant embellishments of traditional diplomatic prose. Yet, for those involved in text-based negotiations, as for example within a working group of the Council of the European Union, essentially important will be the ability to draft and redraft quickly, "with an eye both for the vital detail that preserves a position and for the creative ambiguity that breaks a deadlock."[60]

---

[58] For a review on the evolution of *Le Protocole*, also referred to as '*Le Cérémonial*', consult: Marie-France Lecherbonnier, *Le Protocole: Histoire et coulisses (op. cit.).*

[59] John Hemery, "Training Diplomats for 2015," *iMP: The Magazine on Information Impacts,* July 23, 2001.

[60] John Hemery, "Training Diplomats for 2015."

At a time certain aspects of diplomacy need to be modernized to cope with the evolving pace of the Information Age, some training for diplomats will be completely new. Developments in ICTs have introduced changes in both diplomatic practices and diplomatic training. Virtual teams of diplomats, for example, increasingly meet electronically to discuss and amend draft texts. Pre-negotiations are carried out more and more online. A large portion of the traffic between ministry and post is direct from *desk* to embassy *desktop*. The same is true of communications between ministries, and to an increasing extent between governments. All those skills involved in performing these arts have to be taught to enable diplomats to be as effective in cyberspaces as in person, to ensure a common ministry standard, and to safeguard the vital bureaucratic processes of filing, retrieval and archiving.

Impoverished in recent years by a failure to invest and sustain first-class Foreign Service, much criticism has been voiced on American diplomacy. Two American scholars write:

> U.S. diplomats need to be trained as conflict managers and mobilized to lead and coordinate action with key allies....
> America needs more effective negotiators, backed by economic assets and the military, to prevent international conflicts from turning violent and to make peace agreements stick. Military preponderance is central to global leadership, but it is not by itself a strategy.[61]

A number of fundamental reforms deemed necessary to equip the U.S. diplomatic system for the challenges of the 21st century were recently specified and analyzed in three perceptive and compatible studies prepared by distinguished American leaders. The recommendations of these reports can be set under the following 10 headings:

Security of American embassies and consulates; Information Technology; "Right-Sizing" of embassies; Managing Overseas Buildings; Relations with Congress;

---

[61] "Rethink U.S. Leadership for a Different World," Chester A. Crocker (Board Chairman of the United States Institute of Peace) and Richard H. Solomon (President of the Institute), *IHT*, January 26, 2001, 10. Also read: Stephanie Smith Kinney, "Developing Diplomats for 2010: If not now, when? The Challenges, Risks, Relevance, Resources and Renewals," *American Diplomacy,* Vol. V, no. 3, Summer 2000 (Durham: American Diplomacy Publishers).

Public Diplomacy; State Department Workforce Planning; Commercial Diplomacy; Decentralization and its implications; and Inter-Agency Coordination.[62]

Here, nevertheless, is a crucial aspect to consider. By the year 2015, the already significant gap in technical capacity between developed and less developed countries will have widened remarkably.[63] With the speed and complexity of diplomacy increasing within multilateral institutions, such as the European Union and even more in global markets, states with less sophisticated information and communications systems and less flexible and responsive management cultures will be progressively less able to advance and defend their national interests effectively in respect to the more developed countries. In other words, diplomats being trained in the Information Age should be aware of two different realities: one group of countries still operating in terms of and largely with means appropriate to the diplomacy of the mid 20th century; and the other, much smaller but with misappropriated influence, adapted to operate at high speed and with maximum communication and coordination between government departments, and between capital and missions.

II.I.II.I. <u>Information Gathering</u>

States continue to deal with one another in many traditional ways and at a variety of different levels, but all these dealings involve communication of a certain sort. It is hence misleading to identify communications as a specific and separate element of inter-state relations that also embrace diplomatic, military and economic affairs. Yet, communications have become so important in the way states perceive and deal with one another that they constitute a fourth dimension worthy of analysis in its own right. It is a

---

[62] The three studies are:

a. "Equipped for the Future: Managing U.S. Foreign Affairs in the 21st Century," Frank Carlucci et al., The Henry L. Stimson Center, October 1998, at: http://www.stimson.org/pubs/ausia/#final.

b. "America's Overseas Presence in the 21st Century," Overseas Presence Advisory Panel, Lewis B. Kaden, Chairman, U.S. Department of State, November 1999.

c. "Reinventing Diplomacy in the Information Age," Project Co-Chairs Richard Burt and Olin Robinson, The Center for Strategic and International Studies, Washington, DC, October 1998, at: http://www.csis.org/ics/dia/final.html.

[63] For a descriptive view of an American Embassy in 2015, see: Charles A. Schmitz, "A Vision of an American Embassy in 2015: A Disquisition in Three Acts and Six and a Half Premises," *iMP: The Magazine on Information Impacts,* July 23, 2001.

dimension often overlooked by scholars of international relations and even by historians. Within it are phenomena such as the role of public and media opinion, the censorship and the propagandistic manipulation of the opinion for self-ending ends, the dissemination of messages to foreign governments and people by whatever communication technologies are available to serve national self-interests, public diplomacy, cultural affairs and psychological warfare.

The fourth dimension of international affairs, notes Taylor (1997, p. 21), was recognized as important by early scholars of political science and foreign policy in the 1950s. Reflecting the Cold War climate in which he was writing, Harold Lasswell saw *political warfare* central to inter-state activity, embracing more than the means of mass communication:

> Political warfare adds the important idea that all instruments of policy need to be properly correlated.... Diplomacy, for example, can be used to keep potential enemies neutral or to detach allies from the enemy.... When we speak of diplomacy, we have in mind the making of official comments. Whereas mass communications aims to large audiences, diplomacy proceeds by means of official negotiations.... Political warfare also includes the use of economic means. [64]

In an attempt to secure their national objectives, states accordingly deal with others in essentially four ways, or dimensions. The first dimension is diplomacy, the negotiation of contracts suitable to both sides (or to all sides in the case of multi-lateral diplomacy). The second is the economic dimension, concerning the exchange of resources. The third is the military dimension, the use or threatened use of military resources to achieve national, and now increasingly multi-national, objectives.

Referred to at times as the "hidden dimension," the fourth dimension is intelligence activity, namely the gathering of secret information to fuel the activities of the political and military establishments to assist their bargaining positions. This type of work feeds all the other dimensions and is generally covert. It is also what may be termed the psychological or informational dimension, which involves the gathering and communication of information, ideas, perceptions and messages. Naturally, this takes

---

[64] Harold Lasswell, "Political and Psychological Warfare," in W. Daugherty and M. Janowitz (eds.), *A Psychological Warfare Casebook,* Baltimore: John Hopkins Press, 1958, p. 24.

place within the other three dimensions, but "it has become a distinctive aspect of inter-state relations in its own right," asserts Taylor (1997, p. 21).

Respectively, gathering information on political, military and economic development and reporting it back home has long been recognized as one of the most important functions of the resident embassy. Immersed in the local scene and sharing information with other members of the diplomat corps, embassy personnel are ideally situated to provide information reports, as it seems quite difficult to see this assignment ever being efficiently performed in any other way.

A distinction, however, is often made between information and knowledge derived 'honestly,' although not necessarily openly, from publications and conversations with journalists, other diplomats, officials and politicians, and on the other hand, intelligence acquired by clandestine means, which might involve bribery, cryptoanalysis, and the engagement of secret agents and technical devices. The provision of the former is generally regarded as a 'legitimate' function of diplomacy, while the latter—in contrast— is better understood as espionage.[65]

Particularly impressive is the extent of reliance on embassies for knowledge of the mind and way of thinking of the local leadership. For instance, during the American-mediated negotiations between Israel and Egypt throughout the years 1977-1979, when correctly sensing the mood of Egyptian president Anwar Al-Sadat was a vital importance to the Carter administration, a great deal of reliance was placed on the reports of the U.S. ambassador in Cairo, Herman Eilts, who by November 28, 1978 had achieved more than 250 meetings with the Egyptian leader.[66]

---

[65] Keith Hamilton and Richard Langhorne, *The Practice of Diplomacy: its evolution, theory and administration,* London: Routledge, 1995, p. 189.

[66] J. Carter, *Keeping Faith: Memoirs of a President,* New York: Bantam, 1982, pp. 320-21. The Center for the Analysis of Personality and Political Behavior at the CIA has created hundreds of political profiles of American foes, and also of Anwar Al-Sadat and Menachem Begin for president Carter to use at the Camp David talks that led to peace between Egypt and Israel in 1979. The Center develops profiles from biographies, speeches and interviews with people who know the leaders. See: Elisabeth Bumiller, "Tracing Roots of Cruelty That Spawned a Tyrant", 'The New York Times' weekly supplement, page 3, in *Le Monde,* May 23-24, 2004.

Fast-flowing, multi-dimensional developments require specialist teams used to quick assembling, sharing expertise without much regard to rank, coordinating their efforts under facilitating leadership and overall supervision, and as fast disassembling before reassembling in a different outline to deal with another issue. The narrowly vertical hierarchy with its limited vision is simply too out-dated to be useful, if the ministry's objective is to be effective and in time.

Consider the following assimilation as a noteworthy illustration.

Take two Foreign Service officers of equal competence and experience and place them in two separate rooms for a certain period of time. Equip Officer A with computer and access to every classified network and database a ministry and an entire foreign affairs community can provide. Add a telephone and cable television. Give Officer B a computer and unrestricted Internet access. Nothing more. Both have a standard set of office applications on their desktop. Now, assign both officers the classic kinds of tasks any mid-level Foreign Service professional might be called upon to perform. For instance:

- Provide talking points for a briefing on bilateral relations between two countries;
- Compare U.S., European and Asian emissions of greenhouse gases in the past decade, per capita and total;
- Draft questions and answers explaining how the WTO deals with disputes;
- Find examples of public health programs that can serve as models for combating AIDS inside the country and abroad;
- Prepare a background profile and analysis of the anarchist groups mobilized against globalization.

The winner of the contest would obviously be Officer B: The Internet equipped officer. At first glance, the Internet simply offers access to unparalleled wealth of information; and open-source systems, here, will always triumph over closed systems (provided that this mass data can also prove impenetrable, and the hypothetical officer should certainly be adept at navigating these resources).

Yet, the less apparent reason is that the issues of 21st century diplomacy have shifted, from bilateral negotiations to global or transnational issues over which diplomats have neither special knowledge nor expertise found merely in closed or classified files.[67]

Radio and television broadcasts, together with official Web sites, can also be used for direct communication between states. State-supervised monitoring services pick up foreign broadcasts and then translate and summarize them with focus on the particular interests of their *customers* in government. They are significantly proficient at identifying important messages, despite the notion only a few states have established such services. According to Rawnsley,[68] the most proficient appear to be the Foreign Broadcast Information Service (FBIS) of the United States, and the BBC Monitoring Service. Varying in budget allocations, means and influence, other countries known to have developed systems for monitoring foreign broadcasts include France, Germany, Japan, Russia, and most recently Australia.

According to its official Web site, the BBC Monitoring Service operates "around the clock to monitor more than 3,000 radio, TV, press, internet and news agency sources, translating from up to 100 languages." Its subscribers include government departments, journalists and academics, as well as businesses with international interests.[69]

---

[67] The assimilation is enriched from: Howard Cincotta, "Post-Modern Diplomacy and the New Media," *iMP Magazine*, July 23, 2001.

[68] G.D. Rawnsley, "Monitored Broadcasts and Diplomacy," in J. Melissen (ed.), *Innovation in Diplomatic Practice,* Basingstoke: Macmillan, 1999, p. 135.

[69] The BBC Monitoring Service, at: http://www.monitor.bbc.co.uk.

II.II. Intelligence in the Information Age

Throughout the last two to three decades, intelligence has been regularly receiving much attention and interest of news media, and has also moved to a center position of significant academic research and writing. Moreover, open discussions of intelligence issues no longer constitute a taboo or scandal, as they become an increasing, normal part of the general public debate on government activities, whether of political, economic or technological in nature. This section seeks to address the essential concepts involved in the sphere of intelligence, and the evolving principles if its traditional guidelines in information-based societies. Although the presentation stems from the Anglo-American theoretical and practical conduct of intelligence activity, reference is also made (whenever possible and appropriate) to available information, understandings and comparisons in respect of other intelligence cultures.

II.II.I. Traditional vs. Modern View of Intelligence

Intelligence refers to *information* relevant to a government's policy formulation and implementation to further its national security interests and to deal with threats from actual or potential adversaries.[70] Since the term "national security" is itself vague, the scope of intelligence remains somewhat undefined.

The "traditional" view of intelligence (which emphasizes obtaining, protecting, and exploiting secret information relevant to the struggle among nations) is comparable to a newer, characteristically American view of intelligence that has evolved since World War II. Traced back to one of the oldest known thematic discussions of intelligence, the traditional view is cited in the Chinese classic *The Art of War*, attributed to the 6th century B.C. general and military thinker Sun Tzu. He illustrates the importance of intelligence as follow:

---

[70] The definition of intelligence is adopted from: Abram N. Shulsky and Gary J. Schmitt, *Silence Warfare: Understanding the World of Intelligence*, Virginia (U.S.A.): Brassey's, Inc., 2002, pp. 1, 3.

> Now the reason the enlightened prince and the wise general conquer the enemy whenever they move and their achievements surpass those of ordinary men is foreknowledge.
>
> What is called "foreknowledge" cannot be elicited from spirits, nor from the gods, nor by analogy with past events, nor from calculations. It must be obtained from men who know the enemy situation [directly–that is, men with access to the enemy camp].[71]

At the core of this understanding of intelligence lies espionage. Considering the close connection between learning the enemy's secrets and achieving victory, it would follow that the protection of one's own secrets (counterintelligence) is indeed as important as obtaining that of the adversary. The ultimate goal of such espionage is to understand the adversary's strategy well enough to devise means to circumvent and defeat it–at the least possible cost.

According to Sun Tzu, for whom defeating an enemy's strategy is more important than defeating its army, the intelligence component of international struggle is as vital as the armed component:

> Thus, what is of supreme important in war is to attack the enemy's strategy; Next best is to disrupt his alliances; The next best is to attack his army.[72]

The circumstances brought by the beginning of World War II and America's subsequent engagement made the United States devote massive increases in intelligence resources. That also led to a new bureaucratic development, the creation of a central intelligence service (first known as the Office of the Coordinator of Information, and then as the Office of Strategic Services, or the OSS) It duties included the collection, analysis, and correlation of national security information and data.

Despite the decision of U.S. president Franklin Roosevelt in July 1941 to create a central capability to correlate information, nothing was in place in December 1941,

---

[71] Sun Tzu, *The Art of War*, trans. by Samuel B. Griffith, Oxford: Oxford University Press, 1963, pp. 144-45 (chap. 13, pars. 3-4).

[72] Sun Tzu, *The Art of War*, 1963, p. 146 (chap. 13, pars. 9-10).

when the failure to foresee the Japanese attack on Pearl Harbor highlighted the lack of the intelligence correlation and analysis, though many relevant 'bits and pieces' of information had been available. Nevertheless, some historians and scholars have even raised the notion that Roosevelt was well-aware of the Japanese attack plans, yet had intentionally decided to neglect them as a prelude to U.S. engagement in World War II.

The OSS set up a research and analysis branch to analyze "all the relevant information, which was overtly available as well as that secretly obtained".[73] Though not fulfilled during World War II, this goal remained the ideal situation until being essentially materialized with the creation of the Central Intelligence Agency (CIA) in 1947.

As a result, this emphasis on intelligence analysis, the intellectual work of piecing together disparate bits of information to develop an accurate picture, suggests a view of intelligence different from the "traditional" one. The modern view pays less attention to secrecy and the means of overcoming it, and pays more attention to the analytic function, broadly perceived.

This vision was most influentially put forward immediately after World War II by Sherman Kent, former OSS officer and future head of the Office of National Estimates, the CIA office then in charge of producing overall assessments of the world situation. He argued the case for understanding intelligence as the scientific method (in its social science variant) applied to strategic matters. In *Strategic Intelligence for American World Policy,*[74] Kent provides in Table 2.3. the contents of a directory about a country of interest prepared in Germany and for use during World War II:

---

[73] William E. Colby, "Intelligence in the 1980s," *The Information Society*, no. 1, 1981, 54, New York: Taylor & Francis, Inc.

[74] Sherman Kent, *Strategic Intelligence for American World Policy,* Princeton, NJ: Princeton University Press, 1949 (reprint, 1966, pp. 12-3).

I	*General Background*	Location. Frontiers. Area. History. Governmental and Administrative Structure
II	*Character of the Country*	Surface Forms. Soils. Ground Cover. Climate. Water Supply.
III	*People*	Nationalities. Language. Attitudes. Population Distribution. Settlement. Health. Structure of Society.
IV	*Economic*	Agriculture. Industry. Trade and Commerce. Mining. Fisheries.
V	*Transportation*	Railroads. Roads. Ports. Airfields. Inland Waterways.
VI	*Military Geography*	[Detailed regional breakdown]
VII	*Military Establishment in Being*	- Army: Order of Battle, Fixed Defenses, Military Installations, Supply. - Navy: Order of Battle, the Fleet, Naval Shore Installations, Naval Air, Supply. - Air: Order of Battle. Military Aircraft, Air Installations, Lighter than Air, Supply.
VIII	*Special Appendixes*	Biographical data on key figures of government. Local geographical terminology. Description of rivers, lakes, canals. List and specifications of electric power plants. Description of roads. List of airdromes and most important landing grounds. List of main telephone and telegraph lines. Money, weights, and measures. Beaches [as for amphibious military operations].

Table 2. 3. Information directory of a country of interest (Source: Kent, 1966)

For the "traditional" view, the fact that an adversary is trying to keep vital information secret is the very essence of the matter. If an adversary was not trying to hide his intentions, there would be no need for complicated analyses of the situation in the first place.

These two varying stances towards the importance of secrecy reflect basic differences with respect to what intelligence is. If, according to the traditional view, intelligence is part of the real struggle with human adversaries, then in the modern view, intelligence–like science in general–is a process of discovering truths about the world or nature that can be thus called a struggle only metaphorically. That is, while there are secrets of nature, they are not pieces of information being jealously guarded from our attention; They are simply truths we have not yet discovered. The paradigmatic intelligence problem is not so much digging out the adversary's secret intention as it is of predicting his behavior through social sciences methodology. This is particularly true the more the emphasis in intelligence analysis shifts to research on long-term trends, often societal and economic in nature. With respect to future social or economic conditions, no real secrets can be obtained, because the adversary is uncertain what will happen or, accordingly, what choices will avail and under what circumstances.

The same perception noting that counterintelligence occupies a marginal place in intelligence also affects the importance accorded to deception and counter deception. By underlining intelligence as akin to a social science endeavor, the modern view ignores, or at least minimizes, the possibility of deception. "Nature, while it may hide its secrets from scientific investigators, does not actively try to deceive them," emphasize Shulsky and Schmitt (2002, p. 166).

Finally, the two views of intelligence also differ in respect of who the recipients of intelligence information, its consumers, are. The traditional view sees the head of state as the prime, and perhaps the only, recipient of intelligence. Such a view was reflected in the U.S. National Security Act of 1947, having established the CIA, which placed it under the authority of the National Security Council and the President rather than under the Department of State or Defense. The implication of this bureaucratic arrangement seemed to be that the CIA would remain close to high-level policy makers and would monitor and coordinate the work of the other departmental intelligence agencies on their behalf.

As the modern view tends to depreciate secrecy, it is no surprising that it also seeks to enlarge the audience for intelligence to the widest extent. In "Secrecy and Democracy: The CIA in Transition," Turner envisages the creation of an international satellite agency to conduct technical intelligence collection on behalf of the U.N., with the information being made available to the entire world.[75] Likewise, Colby (1981, p. 69) argues that we are, or should be, entering a period of 'free-trade' with respect to

---

[75] Stansfield Turner, *Secrecy and Democracy: The CIA in Transition*, New York: Harper and Row, 1986, pp. 279-85.

intelligence, in which the large volume of information available thanks to modern technology can be seen to provide mutual rather than one-sided benefits. This philosophy is remindful of the *win-win* concept in knowledge societies, as it insists on the recognition of mutual benefit from the free flow and exchange of information.

II.II.II. Attributing Information and Intelligence

The evolving progress in technologies related to telecommunications and data processing has led to widespread changes in the ways organizations deal with information. In addition to the broad use of the Internet, the collapse of the Soviet Union is also a principal cause of the explosion and increased availability of open-source information–when the demands to keep secret even the minor facts had vanished. More generally, globalization in all its forms has multiplied information flow across borders and has opened countless new information channels.

Even before the advent of the Information Age, a considerable volume of information reached policy makers from outside the realms of traditional intelligence channels. Developments in the international political environment and those associated with the Information Revolution, nevertheless, suggest more information generated outside of intelligence circles will be available in the future. As this assumption presents important opportunities for policy makers, it also creates concerns in:

- How to locate these sources;

- How to evaluate their availability;[76]

- How to analyze the information they provide and fuse it with information available via intelligence channels; and,

---

[76] On disinformation, Vladimir Volkoff writes: «Si la télévision est le paradis de la désinformation, la cybernétique en est devenue l'Olympe.... Internet est devenu le terrain par excellence où la guerre de l'information peut se donner libre cours... Les grandes sociétés utilisent bien entendu Internet pour se renseigner, mais aussi pour désinformer leurs concurrents». ('If television is the paradise of disinformation, the Net has become the champion....The Internet has by excellence become the free terrain of information war...Grand companies obviously use the Internet for information gathering, but also to disinform their competitors.') In: *Petite histoire de la désinformation: Du cheval de Troie à l'Internet,* ('Brief background of disinformation : from Trojan horse to the Internet'), Monaco: éditions du Rocher, 1999, pp. 248-49.

- How to preserve confidentiality with respect to the issues in which the policy maker is interested.

While the above concerns are not new, the question raised here is whether or not the changes brought about by the Information Age are of such magnitude that they require to be addressed more systematically than in the past. In other words, do policy makers, in particular, need "information specialists" to help them sort through the wealth of sources now available? At present, this information assignment is already being performed by three ranks concerned: by *the policy makers themselves*; by *their staffs*; and by *intelligence analysts*.

Each of these three has its proper set of advantages and disadvantages. In the forefront, policy makers are ultimately responsible for their actions/decisions, and therefore must have confidence that the relevant information has been received and properly understood. Eventually, this means at least some of the analysis has to be their own. Also, they may have access to information sources that others do not, such as high-level communications with other governments, and such as the thoughts and plans of high-level officials of their own government and certain key non-governmental actors. Some policy makers may as well enjoy more extensive experience in the given policy area than intelligence analysts or their staffs.

Yet, on the other hand, policy makers are just too busy to do much information gathering and analysis–other than reading newspapers, highly sensitive cables and material that have been sorted out and highlighted by their staffs. That being considered, most of the information forwarded to them is in excerpted or analyzed forms, in briefings or in written summaries. Varying in degrees and nature of their individual 'intelligence culture' (or, *la culture du renseignement*) as well as in their competence in the domain, some political leaders are particularly not even fond of relying on intelligence sources.

Unlike their superiors, staff members can afford the time to gather and analyze much of the necessary information. As they are also involved in the policy-making, they should be aware of the relevant issues and objectives sought. Apart from the most sensitive issues, they are involved in interactions with other governments or with the other organs of their own government. And though they generally enjoy the trust of their chiefs, there may be cases where superiors prefer to explore certain issues without engaging the staff.

Regardless of that, staff members are known to focus more on policy formation than on information gathering and analysis. As a result, they may not develop the necessary expertise in the information arena. For them, these information-related responsibilities draw a lower priority than those related to policy formations. In general, staffers do not have time to up-grade and up-date substantive knowledge beyond the *intellectual capital* they possessed when they assumed their positions. Even more, they (in common) have neither the access nor the expertise relevant to specialized intelligence sources and methods; and accordingly, they may not be able to fuse information with the other information that reaches them from intelligences agencies. Stating all that, staffers may be subject to pressure from their superiors to ensure that the analyses forwarded support policy preferences/decisions already adopted.

Last, intelligence analysts are entirely focused on the information tasks that are free from direct responsibility for policy choices. Their career paths remain within the information sphere, and hence, make it easier for policy makers to directly address them questions that imply policy choices too controversially to raise more openly within policy bureaucracies. Here, analysts enjoy access to and familiarity with specialized intelligence sources and methods. Eventually, they are more competent to fuse information with other information from such channels. More importantly, they are (or should be) experienced well enough to evaluate and distinguish between what is valid information and what might seem to be the product of an adversary's deception effort.

But even with all those advantages, intelligence analysts do as well have certain disadvantages. Lack of awareness of their own government's policy options/priorities may render their work useless both in terms of relevance and timing. Intelligence analysts may also tend to ignore information sources outside the usual intelligence channels, where the reliability of such sources may be more difficult to determine, and also because providers of information outside the government such as academics, specialists, businessmen) may be less willing to cooperate with an intelligence organization than with another government agency.

This assessment leads us to the various *products* designed by intelligence agencies to inform policy makers of remarkable new aspects that may affect policy. In this respect, agencies function in a similar way to that of the news media, where the range of information covered depends on the scope of the nation's intelligence interest. While a formal system of priorities may exist, it must be enriched by the intelligence producer's own judgments about what is important to their consumers. This outcome, essentially once again, relies not only on the intelligence analysts' common sense but also on the closeness of their contact with policy makers.

Noteworthy are a few examples of these products in the United States. Among the most known is the *President's Daily Brief (PDB)*, which is intended to include "intelligence items of the highest significance necessary for the President to perform the national security duties of his office" and "is distributed only to the President, the Vice President, and a select group of executive branch officials designated by the President."[77] A former career CIA official further illustrates the PDB:

> It is designed to be read in ten or fifteen minutes by the President at the beginning of each working day. It does not attempt to recapitulate what the news media have reported in the last twenty-four hour period, but rather to summarize the significance of what secret sources have reported that bears on current world developments.[78]

---

[77] CIA Directorate of Intelligence Web site at: *www.odci.gov/cia/di/work/daily.html.* The PDB replaced the first issue of a top-secret CIA publication called the 'Current Intelligence Bulletin' in 1951. That Bulletin, which was also a daily digest of intelligence for the president and his top advisors, included developments in the Korean War.

[78] Cord Meyer, *Facing Reality: From World Federalism to the CIA,* New York: Harper and Row, 1980, p. 352. See Appendix II for an example of one of the few declassified, yet much-debated and controversial PDBs.

Former DCI Robert Gates notions in 1989 that:

> The PDB has varied little from president to president: a few (three to six) DoS (Department of State) and CIA cables of special significance; occasionally a sensitive intelligence report from the CIA, the Defense Intelligence Agency, or the National Security Agency (NSA); selected wire service items; DoS or CIA situation reports (rarely both), if there is a crisis abroad; and often NSC and DoS morning cable summaries.[79]

There is also the *Senior Executive Intelligence Brief (SEIB)*, which is less restricted in circulation and has apparently replaced an older publication known as the *National Intelligence Daily (NID)*. The SEIB is "compiled in consultation with other intelligence agencies" and includes "key current intelligence items...tailored to the needs of senior officials throughout the United States Government responsible for national security."[80]

Stemming from the Clinton administration's emphasis on the economic aspects of international issues, a third daily publication called the *Economic Executives' Intelligence Brief (EEIB)* was initiated to cover "the issues on economic officials' agendas, including foreign trade practices, illicit finance, and international energy development."[81]

Issuing a version similar to the EEIB elsewhere, nevertheless, would depend on the nature of a government and its economic system. In a government-run economy, intelligence would be concerned with the economic aspects of the government's relations with foreign governments, such as international trade, in much the same way it would be with all other aspects of its international relations. Here, intelligence can be employed to enhance the state's economic well-being. For instance, the acquisition of advanced Western technology was a vital function of the former Soviet Union's

---

[79] Robert Gates, "An Opportunity Unfulfilled: The Use and Perceptions of Intelligence at the White House," *The Washington Quarterly*, 12, no. 1, Winter 1989, 37. Gates sees the creation of the White House Situation Room by the Kennedy administration in the early 1960s as the real turning point in current intelligence for the White House. A 1996 Study by the CIA's history offices states presidents sometimes complained the PDB contained too much material available in newspapers. See: John Diamond, "Few PDBs declassified for public," *USA Today*, online edition, April 11, 2004.

[80] CIA Directorate of Intelligence Web site.

[81] *Ibid.*

intelligence services, and it still remains an important objective for the Russian and Chinese services. This activity not only advances the technological level of these two countries but also saves them both the tremendous expenses and difficulties of developing technology on their own, whether for civilian or military purposes.

But in a market economy, it is much less obvious to determine which economic issues have national security dimensions that justify or demand the involvement of intelligence agencies. Specific areas, such as assessing the economic ability of a potential military adversary or such as following developments affecting the flow of vital strategic resources, may push governments for detailed information. In these cases, the engagement of intelligence agencies to obtain information of that nature would depend to a certain extent on whether or not other companies attempt to keep it secret. A nation's *lust* for economic intelligence on industrial, commercial and financial activity in other countries may also depend on the probable existence of an industrial policy bureaucracy that a government may make use of.

In addition to economics and business, overlapping issues in the global world have led to *non-traditional* concerns within the scope of intelligence. Environmental issues are one. Arguing that environmental problems can affect national security, the principle motivation arises from the fact that technical intelligence collection systems developed for other purposes may help track environmental changes over time and across vast territories.

A study conducted by RAND in this regard concluded "The United States has an impressive array of technical systems for monitoring large areas of the earth, oceans, and atmosphere for national security purposes. These systems have collected sophisticated datasets that span decades, and constitute a unique historical record. These systems could be used for environmental monitoring as well."[82]

Artificial Intelligence (AI) is another non-traditional domain is, related to the science and engineering of making intelligent machines, especially intelligent computer programs. AI is linked to the similar task of using computers to understand human

---

[82] Scott Pace, Kevin M. O'Connell and Beth E. Lachman, *Using Intelligence Data for Environmental Needs: Balancing National Interests,* MR-799-CMS, RAND Corporation, Santa Monica, CA, 1997, p. 2.

intelligence and behavior. Its branch of pattern recognition and its application in speech recognition, among others, are developing methods in systematic information gathering and analysis.[83]

With all the intelligence products mentioned above, there remains an ambitious product that not only describes the current situation but also attempts to predict how it will evolve. Referred to in the U.S. intelligence parlance as "estimates," the *National Intelligence Estimate (NIE)* represents the most authoritative statement on a subject by American intelligence agencies collectively. These estimates, which are produced by a special staff and with the support of analysts throughout the intelligence agencies, are supposed to take the broadest view of their subject and project the current situation in the future.

As a good deal of effort is devoted to finding a consensus position among the intelligence community,[84] NIEs on certain topics of major importance are produced annually (or at other fixed intervals); other topics are covered in response to specific requirements, either self-generated (i.e., the idea for the estimate arises within the intelligence community itself) or from elsewhere in the government, most often the National Security Council (NSC). Shorter, more topical estimates known as Special NIEs (SNIE) may be produced in response to more urgent requirements.

At the center of the political debate over the intelligence preceding the U.S. invasion in Iraq is the 100-page, top secret now-infamous October 2002 NIE that hurriedly pulled together judgments from across the American intelligence community about the threat posed by Saddam Hussein and the potential dangers involved in the invasion. NIE drafting guidelines are described in three rough timeframes: a 'fast track' of two to three weeks, a 'normal track' of four to eight weeks, and a 'long track' of two

---

[83] For a brief explanation of Artificial Intelligence, its branches and applications, read: John McCarthy, *What is Artificial Intelligence?,* Computer Science Department, Stanford University, Stanford, CA, September 28, 2001, at: http://www-formal.stamford.edu/jmc/whatisai/whatisai.html.

[84] The U.S. *intelligence community* includes the CIA, the National Security Agency, the Defense Intelligence Agency, offices within the Department of Defense for the collection of specialized national foreign intelligence through reconnaissance programs, the State Department's Bureau of Intelligence and Research, the intelligence elements of the armed services, the FBI, and the Departments of the Treasury and of Energy, (according to Executive Order 12333 of December 4, 1981, available at: www.nara.gov/fedreg/codific/eos/e12333.html).

months or more. A vice chairman of the NIC stated to Senate investigators that an NIE prepared in 60 days would be considered a very fast schedule, and that NIEs typically take three to six months to complete. That particular NIE on Iraq, stressed a senior intelligence officer, "was hastily done in three weeks" in what was a "cut-and-paste job, with agencies and officials given only one day to review the draft final product when they usually take months...Today they still disagree on the meaning of what came out."[85]

Several months after the release of that NIE, and in reference to his infamous U.N. presentation on February 5, 2003, former U.S. secretary of state Colin Powell declared:

> the sourcing [of the information] was inaccurate and wrong and in some cases, deliberately misleading. And for that, I am disappointed and I regret it.[86]

Finally, recent trends in intelligence practice have given birth to a number of terms and references, with some being replaced and others completely new. Some of them are illustrated in Table 2.4.

---

[85] See: Walter Pincus, "Intelligence Report for Iraq War Was Hastily Done," *The Washington Post*, October 24, 2003, A18; And: Dana Priest, "Inquiry Faults Intelligence on Iraq: Threat From Saddam Hussein Was Overstated, Senate Committee Report Finds," *The Washington Post,* October 24, 2003, A01. For more details on NIEs, refer to: Sharon Otterman, "National Intelligence Estimates," Council on Foreign Relations, at: http://www.cfr.org/background/intel_nie (updated on July 15, 2004).

[86] Douglas Jehl and David E. Sanger, "Powell Presses C.I.A. on Faulty Intelligence on Iraq Arms," *The New York Times,* online edition, June 2, 2004.

Term	In reference to
E-fraud	Electronic fraud
Netspionage	Internet espionage
Netquette	Internet étiquette
Netsploitation	Internet exploitation
Netspertise	Internet expertise
Spyware	Spy software
Elint	Electronic intelligence
Humint	Human intelligence
SCIF	Secret Compartmented Intelligence Facility: a room that has been secured and sealed under very tight regulations, where classified information can be safely discussed, read and handled (what used to be called a 'clean room')
Perception Management	Tricking an adversary into believing false information by persuading it that a source, actually under a given country, was selling secrets of another country
The Company	The CIA
Kontora	The Russian Sluzhba Vneshney Razvedki (SVR), or Foreign Intelligence Service, formerly the Komitet Gosudarstvennoi Bezopasnosti (KGB), or Committee for State Security, Yasenova
A Dead drop	often a tree in which secrets are left to be picked up by another agent, also 'dubok', or little oak
Sick think	a predisposition to believe one's own agents are controlled by the other side, usually accompanied by intimations of paranoia
Surreptitious	from Latin *surreptitious*, to mean taken by "stealth, unauthorized, clandestine"
Clandestine	from Latin *clandestinus*, to mean "secret, hidden"
Deer Park	a diplomatic area, like the U.N., in which headhunters recruit agents
Regime Lethal	a phrase to cover the idea of bombing the general area in which an unfriendly leader or terrorist is likely to be resident[87]

Table 2. 4. Some recent and coined terms associated with intelligence (Source: Safire, 2000)

II.II.III. <u>Causes of Failure in Intelligence and Information Analysis</u>

Other than instances where relevant information cannot be obtained at all, intelligence failure refers to a disorder of the analytical process that causes data to be ignored or misinterpreted. In other words, it is basically a misunderstanding of the

---

[87] William Safire, "Netspionage: Cyberspying and E-spookspeak," *IHT,* December 4, 2000, 7.

situation that leads a government or a party to take actions inappropriate and counterproductive to its own interests. Hence, intelligence failure is similar to a mistake or error in any other intellectual endeavor such as, for example, one committed by a historian in interpreting an ancient text–leading to an inaccurate description of some aspect of antiquity, or such as one made by a meteorologist in assessing the gravity of a low-pressure system–resulting to an incorrect prediction about the weather the next day.

Some peculiarities of the intelligence analysis process do, however, introduce further sources of errors. The nature of intelligence analysis as an intellectual activity takes place in an institutional setting and in accordance to standard procedures, where the outcome is more the product of a system than of an individual. That being stressed, it is vulnerable to certain pathologies that can be addressed in institutional or bureaucratic terms. The following causes of failures in information gathering and analysis (of intelligence nature) examine first those at the institutional level and then those related more directly to the intellectual content of the intelligence work.

*   *Subordination of Intelligence to Policy*

The possibility intelligence judgments are fabricated to produce results superiors wish/hope to hear instead of what the actual evidence indicates is among the most commonly discussed source of error or bias in intelligence gathering and analysis. It is, yet, contradictory to the intelligence analysis process itself, as the analyst realizes that the results forwarded do not follow his own conscious judgment.

The final Report presented to the President of the United States by "The Commission on the Intelligence Capabilities of the United States Regarding Weapons of Mass Destruction" draws clear attention to that dramatic intelligence failure. Concluding "the Intelligence Community was dead wrong in almost all of its pre-war judgments about Iraq's weapons of mass destruction," the Report states there was an "overemphasis on and underperformance in daily intelligence products." It stresses (emphasis in bold type added):[88]

> As problematic as the October 2002 NIE was, it was not the Community's biggest analytic failure on Iraq. Even more misleading was the river of intelligence that flowed from the CIA to top policymakers over long periods of time–in the President's Daily Brief (PDB) and in its more widely distributed companion, the Senior Executive Intelligence Brief (SEIB). These daily reports were, if anything, more alarmist and less nuanced than the NIE. It was not that the intelligence was markedly different. Rather, it was that the PDBs and SEIBs, **with their attention-grabbing headlines and drum-beat repetition**, left an impression of many corroborating reports where in fact there were very few sources. **And in other instances, intelligence suggesting the existence of weapons programs was conveyed to senior policy-makers, but later information casting doubt upon the validity of that intelligence was not.** In ways both subtle and not so subtle, **the daily reports seemed to be "selling" intelligence–in order to keep its customers, or at least the First Customer, interested.**

*   *Unavailability of Information when and where needed*

Considering the large structure of the organizations involved in collecting and analyzing intelligence, a *possible* source of problem is the unavailability of information in the system of those in need of it, when they need it. Various factors, among others, are behind this unavailability: security regulations that restrict the circulation of sensitive information, bureaucratic jealousies and power struggles where control over information becomes a weapon, or merely lack of awareness in the office possessing the data of the information needs of the office just next door.

Also, a problem can arise here if an office does not have the responsibility to conduct analysis in a given area nor access to all information relevant to it. While different offices work on different aspects of the problem, in this case, a key piece of information may become apparent only in the context of all the available data. To note last yet importantly, information sharing may remarkably depend on physical co-

---

[88] "The Commission on the Intelligence Capabilities of the United States Regarding Weapons of Mass Destruction," Report to the President of the United States, Washington, DC, March 31, 2005, p. 14.

location and personal relationships as opposed to integrated, community-wide information gathering and analysis networks.

Examine for instance Illustration 2.1., which demonstrates the significance of the problem of information sharing in respect of the numerous and various intelligence sectors of the U.S. intelligence community.

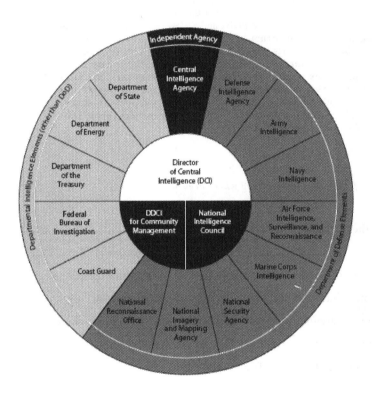

Illustration 2. 1. The U.S. Intelligence Community (RAND)

Several investigation reports and studies have outlined the U.S. intelligence deficiencies in this matter, especially after the September 11, 2001 attacks on the United States. For example, one report recommends ensuring adequate information sharing:

> [The] CIA should lead an effort to improve watch listing to ensure that all relevant agencies, including FBI, Homeland Security, and others, have access to a common database of up-to-date terrorist person–related data collected by US government agencies and other appropriate sources.[89]

Another review concludes:

> In a criminal investigation, rules restricting information are perceived as cumbersome, inefficient, and a bar to success. A law-enforcement culture grounded in shared information is radically different from an intelligence culture grounded in secrecy....
> Operational efficiency is important...and tightening controls on classified information will come with a cost efficiency and resources.[90]

In France, *les Renseignements Généraux (RG)* and *la Direction de la Surveillance du Territoire (DST)* were instructed to *mis en place* at the central and regional levels a "reinforced structure for operational cooperation," as they focus in priority on urban violence, underground economy practices, business intelligence, and antiterrorism.[91]

Nevertheless, this is not to suggest that the British, French, Canadian, and Australian models have not been without weaknesses in terms of information dissemination. The UK Security Services (M15) and the Canadian Security Intelligence Services (CSIS) "have been accused of failing to pass on intelligence to relevant authorities that could have prevented several high-profile terrorist incidents." Meanwhile, the Australian Security Intelligence Organization (ASIO) "has, on occasion, deliberately withheld information on the basis of its own idiosyncratic calculation of the national interest."[92] In France, where no independent system of legislative control exists, "coordination between the police and intelligence services has (at least historically)

---

[89] "Counterterrorism Intelligence Capabilities and Performance Prior to 9-11," Report of the Subcommittee on Terrorism and Homeland Security, the U.S. House Permanent Select Committee on Intelligence, July 17, 2002, Executive Summary, p. 5.

[90] "A Review of FBI Security Programs," Commission for Review of FBI Security Programs, U.S. Department of Justice, March 31, 2002, Executive Summary.

[91] Piotr Smolar, «Les renseignements généraux révisant leurs priorités», ('The General Intelligence revise their priorities'), *Le Monde*, Tuesday, May 26, 2004, 12.

[92] Peter Chalk and William Rosenau, *Confronting the "Enemy Within": Security Intelligence, the Police, and Counterterrorism in Four Democracies*, RAND Corporation, Santa Monica, CA, 2004, p. xiv.

been subject to chronic problems of mistrust, with agencies not only failing to collaborate but moreover occasionally working at complete cross purposes with one another."[93]

* *Received Opinion*

Also referred to as "conventional wisdom," received opinion is the case when an opinion about a subject is generally regarded, without sufficient investigation, as true. Relying on received opinion poses the danger of either misunderstanding or probably ignoring evidence that suggests the truth is otherwise.

Conventional wisdom, for instance, for Iraq in late 2002 and early 2003 was that the U.S. military build-up in the Gulf region was just another 'muscle-show', or to the most, a prelude to another cruise-missile strike 'for just a few days'.

* *Mirror-Imaging*

Mirror-imaging implies the judgment of unfamiliar situations on the basis of familiar ones. In intelligence, it commonly means assessing or predicting a foreign government's actions by analogy with the actions the analyst presumes he or his government would take were he or it in a similar position. This error in intelligence analysis reflects a more typical intellectual failure not associated to the setting in which the analysis is conducted.

Among the ideal institutional solutions to intelligence failure suggested by Shulsky and Schmitt (2002, p. 70) is *competitive analysis* and the establishment of a "devil's advocate." The former refers to the deliberate fostering of separate analytical centers within a government, where each one formulates and distributes its own intelligence assessments based on the comprehensive access to the overall raw data available. To avoid any conventional wisdom that may arise from influencing opinions by one part of

---

[93] *Confronting the "Enemy Within,"* 2004, p. xv.

the government or another, a devil's advocate may be created as an analytical entity to explicitly challenge accepted views.

Improving thought process (i.e., the intellectual aspect of intelligence) is not an aspect administrative means can treat directly. An attempt to define what the "improvement of thought processes," other than the general ideal of being 'smarter', does not lead far. Therefore, while it is much less obvious to prescribe guidelines to analyze information correctly, it is useful to identify intellectual errors or deficiencies that may be characteristic of the analytical process. These could be realized either in general terms or as they prevail at a certain time and place, and once being outlined, subsequently be corrected.

Since any intelligence analyst is vulnerable to the fault of mirror-imaging, cultural reasons may make it a specific problem for the American intelligence community. According to Shulsky and Schmitt (2002, p. 73), Americans are more open to belief in the basic similarity of people throughout the world, perhaps because of America's experience in absorbing and assimilating immigrants from diverse cultural and religious backgrounds. Eventually, U.S. intelligence analysts risk being more likely than other analysts to comprehend and predict the actions of others on the basis of what they would do under similar circumstances.

Therefore, an emphasis on knowledge of foreign societies and cultures is a substantial corrective to this error. Expertise can be up-graded by a study of the language and history of a nation, by an awareness of its religious and cultural traditions, among other significant aspects. Simply said, a serious attempt must be made to see the international situation from the other nation's perspectives, rather than that of oneself.

The U.S. report in July 2002 on Counterintelligence Intelligence Capabilities and Performance Prior to 9-11 (*op. cit.*) concluded the CIA, the FBI and the National Security Agency (NSA) share at least one common weakness: a shortage of linguists skilled in foreign languages.

For example:

> [The] CIA has paid insufficient attention to foreign language training and document exploitation efforts requiring linguists. In the most recent class of new case officers in training, less than one-third had any language expertise. CIA also needs to focus on finding ways to provide clearances for people with the right language skills in less commonly taught languages for document exploitation and other linguist needs. (p. 5)

> A January 2002 report noted that the FBI projected shortages of permanent translators and interpreters in FY 2002 and 2003, and reported backlogs of thousands of un-reviewed and untranslated materials. In key counterterrorism languages, FBI reported having in June 2001 a critical shortage of special agents with some proficiency, and FBI had very few translators and interpreters with native language skills in those languages. (p. 7)

> In April 2000, the GAO [General Accounting Office] reported a significant shortfall in linguists at NSA. After the 9-11 attacks, this shortfall actually increased slightly and was well below additional requirements identified since 9-11. A long-term linguist and analyst hiring strategy is required, as well as a methodical program to improve skills of non-native linguists. This solution should not be agency specific. (p. 7)

Respectively, after the September 11 events the FBI has cited a "critical need" for translators, as it pleaded for help from Americans fluent in some 30 different languages.[94] Around 2,000 of the 11,000 people who applied in January and February 2002 spoke a foreign language, and mostly appeared to be foreign born or first-generation Arab-Americans.[95] Yet, the newly recruited translators or contract linguists, who must undergo background checks, need more than language skills. They need law enforcement sensibilities and an ability to quickly decipher obscure information.

Likewise, three French security agencies (la Direction Générale de la Sécurité Extérieure, la Direction de la Surveillance du Territoire, et les Renseignements

---

[94] The languages cited on the FBI Web site, at: http://www.fbi.gov/page2/employ101403.htm (consulted on October 17, 2003) are: Albanian, Amharic, Arabic, Bulgarian, Burmese, Chinese (all dialects), French, German, Hebrew, Indonesian, Kazakh, Korean, Kurdish, Malay, Malayalam, Pashto, Serbo-Croatian, Somali, Swahili, Tajik, Thai, Tamil, Tigrinya, Turkish, Turkmen, Uigur, Urdu, Uzbek, and Vietnamese.

[95] Richard Willing, "Arab Speakers Answer to FBI Call for Translators," *USA Today*, online edition, April 24, 2002. Also: Joby Warrick et al., "FBI Agents Ill-Equipped to Predict Terror Acts," *The Washington Post*, September 24, 2001. *Time* magazine reported that the FBI had received 'some 40,000 applications for linguist jobs', while only 'about ten percent get hired'. See: Elaine Shannon, "Linguists: The Feds Want You," online edition, October 14, 2003.

Généraux) announced their need to recruit (in 2002) some 100 new agents, especially those who speak rare languages.[96]

Consider as well China, which in recent years has relied heavily on non-official cover to carry out its collection program in the United States. Though China's intelligence services do conduct some traditional recruitment and collection using official cover, Chinese HUMINT regularly employs a variety of non-official cover mechanisms, including front companies, scientific and student exchange programs, and commercial and scientific delegations. Chinese intelligence also deploy long-term *sleeper* agents who emigrate from China and establish themselves as residents for an extended period before being assigned intelligence-related activities in the countries to which they have emigrated. Shulsky and Schmitt (2002, p. 15) see that this extensive use of non-official covers follows from:

> the priority that the Chinese government has given to acquiring advanced American technology and related information, the relatively open nature of US Commercial markets, the ease of establishing residence in the US, and the existence of a substantial American-Chinese ethnic community into which recent immigrants can blend.

II.II.IV. <u>Secrecy in the Information Age</u>

Information is power, and thus governments have always safeguarded their own secrets and sought to uncover those of competing states. In the United States, for instance, the 1917 Espionage Act, the 1947 National Security Act, and numerous Executive Orders have tightened a secrecy regime inspired by the challenges of the two World Wars, the Cold War, and the nuclear arms race. The bureaucracy structures put in place to ensure high levels of official secrecy have also produced a government culture of excessive secrecy.

A classification system categorizes information according to its sensitivity, that is, the amount of damage its revelation to a hostile foreign power could cause, and hence,

---

[96] «Recherche espions», ('Looking for spies'), *L'express*, Paris, December 6, 2001, 168.

the importance of protecting it. The current American system of classifying information is governed by an Executive Order promulgated by former president Bill Clinton in 1995 that sets out definitions, rules, and procedures.[97]

The American classification system attempts to sort information according to the degree of harm to the national security its unauthorized release to an adversary would cause. The more sensitive the information, the more carefully it is to be protected and the fewer the people who are *cleared* (authorized) have access to it. Under the current system, the basic levels of classification are: *confidential, secret,* and *top secret*. All of the three are defined in view of the damage to national security their unauthorized disclosure could be expected to raise:

- Top secret: "exceptionally grave damage"
- Secret: "serious damage"
- Confidential: "damage."[98]

To a certain measure, secrecy is a natural characteristic of any government. With the openness of the American political system, the practice seems particularly anomalous and has evoked more objections in the United States than elsewhere. In recent years, the same issue has surfaced in other countries, notable in Great Britain, where the laws governing the release of government information are much stricter than in the United States.[99]

---

[97] Executive Order 12958, "Classified National Security Information," April 17, 1995. The Information Security Oversight Office (ISOO) is responsible for overseeing the government's security classification programs. The ISOO annual report in 2000 stated more than eight million decisions to classify documents were made during the previous year. Of these, the CIA counted for 44%, the Defense Department for 27%, the National Reconnaissance Office for 24%, the Justice Department for 2%, the State Department for 2% and all other agencies for 1%. Also, nearly 127 million pages of previous classified materials were declassified. Source: ISOO, *FY 1999 Report to the President*, August 15, 2000. ISOO annual reports are available at: www.fas.org/sgp/isoo/index.html. The ISOO was reported discovering more than 14 million new secrets in 2003, a 25% increase over the prior year 'in creating things that must be secret'. Before September 11, 2001, the rate was 8 million a year. See: Al Kamen, "Millions of Secrets," *The Washington Post*, May 3, 2004, A19.

[98] Executive Order 12958, Section 1.3.

[99] For example, see the text of the Great Britain Freedom of Information Act 2000, at: www.legislation.hmso.gov.uk/acts2000/20000036.htm.

The high levels of secrecy and *over classification* have become a national liability in the Information Age. With massive amounts of relevant information on most topics now available on the Internet and elsewhere, relevance does not come from reserving information. Instead, argues Metzl, "it comes from developing and identifying appropriate filters to sort through masses of data, and by building relationships with those, often outside of government, who have the most immediate access to relevant information."[100]

Though some extent of secrecy might be demanded to protect the sources of *important* bits of confidential information, the essential facts concerning the political, economic, social, technologies, and demographic trends that shape a country's behavior in the long run would not be secret. Respectively, Shulsky and Schmitt (2002, p. xii) agree with Metzl in that "not only could intelligence matters be discussed publicly without inherent difficulty but public discussion might, by demystifying intelligence and encouraging the flow of ideas between the intelligence communities, help intelligence progress even farther towards its proper goal of becoming more like a social science (and intelligence agencies more like *"think tanks"*).

The connection between intelligence and secrecy in turn reflects the fundamental issues of relationship, once again, between intelligence and science. At a time when science is knowledge either for its own sake or to further the conquest of nature, intelligence on the other hand involves a real struggle with human opponents, carried on only to gain advantage over them. Therefore, it is neither surprising nor incidental that those opponents continuously try not only to obstruct one's efforts to learn about them but also to mislead and deceive them. Simply said, one side's intelligence failure is likely to be another side's counterintelligence success. Reversibly, an intelligence *coup* by one country implies a counterintelligence or security failure on the part of its opponents.

---

[100] Jamie F. Metzl, "The Perils of Secrecy in an Information Age," *iMP Magazine,* July 23, 2001.

A succession of espionage cases has involved employees of U.S. government agencies, or contractors, since the mid 1970s.[101] In these cases, the motivation has been primarily financial, occasionally with emotional instability. One of the storming cases in this regard is that of Robert Philip Hanssen, an FBI Supervisory Special Agent, "who over twenty-two years gave the Soviet Union and Russia vast quantities of documents and computer diskettes filled with national security information of incalculable value."[102] Hanssen was arrested in 2001.

That case differed from the common American and British espionage cases of the 1940s and 1950s, when the motivation at that time was primarily ideological. These unaffordable incidents call for measures to improve personal security, such as developing detailed psychological profiles and instituting a system for alerting security officials when individuals with access to classified information either face financial difficulties (as was the case of Hanssen), or appear to be living beyond their means of support.

The CIA, for example, began to focus on its officer Aldrich Ames, who spied for the Soviet Union and Russia as well–from 1985 to 1994 (almost nine years), not as a result of a counterintelligence analysis of the losses suffered but simply because a fellow employee noticed and reported that Ames was indeed living beyond his means.[103]

Once these cases and their reasons are better perceived, it becomes easier to understand why counterintelligence is not merely an afterthought but is rather an integral part of the struggle. Important as it may be to limit or distort what one's adversary can learn about the other, one cannot even be absolute of what one knows about an adversary without the counterintelligence capability to detect any deception effort perhaps undertaken.

---

[101] A listing of espionage cases are included in: *"Recent Espionage Cases, 1975-1999: Summaries and Sources,"* U.S. Defense Security Service, Security Research Center, September 1999, available at: www.dss.mil/training/pub.htm.

[102] "A Review of FBI Security Programs," March 31, 2002, Executive Summary, p. 1.

[103] "An Assessment of the Aldrich H. Ames Espionage Case and Its Implications for U.S. Intelligence," U.S. Senate Select Committee on Intelligence, November 1, 1994, pp. 64-66.

One objection commonly made to this approach is that it ignores the key role that *open-source information* can play in the intelligence process. Yet, this objection is in fact based on a misunderstanding. Open-source information is vital for both intelligence and social science; the principle distinction is that for the traditional understanding of intelligence, open-source is primarily a means to get around the barriers obstructing direct access to the information being sought. In other words, in the absence of direct access, it may be possible to deduce deniable information from the analysis of other data, whether from open-source and /or data available.

Accordingly, it is necessary policy makers be able to exploit these information sources effectively, with attention devoted so that they do not become additional channels for the propagation of disinformation. Certainly, one could argue the likelihood of being misled or deceived increases as policy makers become accustomed to getting up-to-the minute information from Internet (and other open-source material) whose reliability is unknown or unverified, and to getting such information directly, unfiltered by specialists and analysts..

But then, what are "open-sources"? Broadly speaking, open-sources extend far beyond the information available on the Internet and premium online services (several more times than that of the Internet, with value-added) to include *gray literature* (limited edition publications including dissertations and local directories from all over the world), specialized market research, private surveys and investigations along with other information-nature services, and geo-spatial information services including commercial imagery and Russian military maps around the globe. Open-sources, and respectively, Open Source Intelligence (OSINT), embodies experts on any subject and in any language of concern–from terrorism to the environment to human trafficking to corruption to disease and public health–all that and much more of a fortune to create a new craft of intelligence.[104]

In an article titled "Smarter Intelligence," Deutch and Smith emphasis the importance of open-sources in confronting terrorism. They state:

---

[104] In "The New Craft of Intelligence: Making the Most of Open Private Sector Knowledge," U.S. national security community veteran Robert David Steele lists a number of open-source initiatives. *Time,* online edition, March 3, 2002.

A prerequisite for good human intelligence is a thorough understanding of the sources of terrorism, and much of this kind of information can be obtained from open sources such as local newspapers in the communities that spawn and protect terrorist organizations. Such analytic information is essential for planning collection strategies, successfully penetrating terrorist groups, and mounting covert operations to disrupt terrorist activities and facilities.[105]

II.II.V. <u>An Increasing Encircled Surveillance Society</u>

Reference to "tracking" implies the ability to monitor an individual's actions in real time or over a period of time. In its most extreme incarnation, tracking may become a kind of *super surveillance* that enables the trackers to both follow a person today as well as search databases to learn where he/she was at a previous given time. The possibility a government could compile such massive databases, and that such databases could be used by law enforcement, raises the specter of "Big Brother" tracking its citizens every move.[106]

Computer databases have already recorded a lot on each individual: credit cards keep track of airline ticket purchases and car rentals, supermarket discount programs know our eating habits, libraries track books checked out, schools record grades and enrollment, Internet usage logs and computerized records of books currently checked out may infer (thought not always correctly) one's political beliefs based on what one reads, and above all that, government agencies generate a mass of information on large cash transfers, taxes, employment record, driving history, and visas.

So what if computers become intelligent enough to link all those government and commercial resources and eventually discern patterns from people's electronic traces? Could they help predict behavior? With all the suspects dead and no conclusive evidence, as yet, of any accomplices, American investigators were left trying to recreate the architecture and orchestration of the September 11, 2001 plot largely from the

---

[105] John Deutch and Jeffrey K. Smith, "Smarter Intelligence," *Foreign Policy*, online edition, January-February 2002.

[106] This working definition of "tracking" is adopted from John D. Woodward, Jr., Esq., *Privacy vs. Security: Electronic Surveillance in the Nation's Capital,* RAND Corporation, Santa Monica, CA, March 2002, p. 1.

registered minutiae of the hijackers' brief American lives (particularly their cell phone calls, credit card charges, Internet communications, and automated teller machine withdrawals).[107] In brief, as new technology projects are intended to make us feel safer and more secure, they also stir concern that we are unwittingly building a surveillance society.

In a series of wartime counterterrorism measures, especially in the United States, security agents are being granted increasing surveillance powers to collect information that *might* lead to terrorism investigations. In the 1960s and 1970s, such monitoring was not allowed by the Department of Justice unless it was conducted during an active investigation in which the surveillance target was clearly defined, or unless there was 'probably cause' to believe a crime was being committed.[108]

In the early years of Internet use, *American Online*, one of the world's largest Internet providers, recruited nearly fourteen thousand volunteers to *patrol* over a hundred and eighty thousand continuing conversation groups to ensure people do not harass, threaten, or deliberately embarrass others, a code of conduct accepted by subscribers when they sign up for the services. A further group of about a hundred, known as the Community Action Team, help determine when a comment crosses the line.[109]

A sophisticated eavesdropping technology developed by the FBI afterwards is a system code-named "Carnivore." It can be installed on the network of an Internet service provider such as American Online or Earthlink to capture e-mail messages to and from a specific account or simply capture routing information on whom a specific user corresponds with. In other words, Carnivore is the electronic e-mail equivalent of a telephone wire tap that traces calls or eavesdrops on conversations.[110]

---

[107] See: Don Van Natta Jr. and Kate Zernike, "Hijackers' Meticulous Strategy of Brains, Muscle and Practice," *The New York Times,* online edition, November 4, 2001

[108] Kevin Johnson, "Justice Dept. eases restrictions on domestic spying," *USA Today*, online edition, May 30, 2002.

[109] William Ury, *Getting to Peace*, 1999, p. 179.

[110] For more about 'Carnivore', see: Guy Gugliotta and Jonathan Krim, "Push for Increased Surveillance Powers Worries Some," *The Washington Post*, September 25, 2001, A04.

Liberty advocates criticize harshly measures such as monitoring Internet sites, public meetings and religions congregation. An activist for the American Civil Liberties Union comments that when the government fails, as it increasingly appears to have done before the September 11 events, the Bush administration's response is to give itself new power, rather than seriously investigate why the failure occurred," adding the new practices "will do little to make us safer but will inevitably make us less free."[111]

Following are a number of surveillance means and techniques driven by technology in an increasing encircled society.

II.II.V.I. Electronic Mail (e-mail)

With software developed by a South Korean company, it is now possible to learn, undetected, whether or not a person did open a message, and even more, tell precisely when recipients read e-mails, and if they were sent on to anyone else–certainly making monitoring easy and nearly imperceptible. While many Internet users have come to odds with advertisers tracking their anonymous trail of clicks across the World Wide Web, the limits of the electronic privacy wars are shifting to the more personal realm of the e-mail *in box*. For instance, marketing companies now regularly keep eyes on which prospective customers open their e-mail solicitations, and at what time of day, arguing "consumers benefit because the information is used to devise more personalized promotions."[112]

Also, by monitoring the flashes of light-emitting diodes (LED) lights on electronics equipment and the indirect glow from monitors, scientists have discovered ways to remotely eavesdrop on computer data. Optical signals from the flashing LEDs, usually red and dotting everything from modems to keyboards and routers, can be captured with a telescope and processed to reveal all the data passing through the

---

[111] Guy Gugliotta and Jonathan Krim, "Push for Increased Surveillance Powers Worries Some."

[112] Amy Harmon, "E-mail: Your Eyes Only?: Improving Software Makes Privacy an Issue," *IHT*, November 23, 2000, 1.

device. All that just "requires little apparatus, can be done at a considerable distance, and is completely undetectable."[113]

Last, amazingly but unexpectedly, it only costs a hundred dollars to trace your movement all month long, with dozens of Web sites offering to sell a copy of anyone's cell phone or long distance calling bill. Armed with such evidence, a stalker could observe your traveling patterns, a business competitor could contact all your customers, and anyone could easily find out who your friends are, where they are, and when you call them.

Furthermore, Web sites like *registeredtovoteornot.com* and *voterlistsonline.com*, allow U.S. residents to check their voter registration status online, providing database including name, address, birth date and party affiliation of any particular person (noting that Web sites like those were initially created to encourage more people to vote). Another Web site, *anybirthday.com*, gives the birth date of almost any adult living in the States, simply by providing their first and last names.[114] While birth dates are free, addresses are charged.

There is also the "Wayback Machine," a free service founded in 1996, which makes old Internet pages (of more than 6 months) available to anyone who gets connected to the World Wide Web, at *web.archive.org*. The archive computers were reported in November 2001 to hold some 100 terabytes of data–compared with an estimated 20 terabytes of information in the entire U.S. Library of Congress. The Internet archive was then growing by 10 terabytes a month.[115]

---

[113] "New security threat: LED lights?" *Reuters*, March 7, 2002.

[114] Refer to: Richard M. Smith, "Revealing information online," *MSNBC* online news, August 28, 2001, at: http://www.msnbc.com/news/620856.asp; and also: Bob Sullivan, "I know who you called last month," *MSNBC* online news, October 16, 2001, at: http://www.msnbc.com/news/643573.asp.

[115] The Web site of the Wayback Machine, at: www.archive.org, stated that the Internet Archive had included approximately 1 petabyte of data (some 30 billion Web pages), and was growing at a rate of 20 terabytes a month (data up-date retrieved on March 4, 2005). The Archive does not collect chat systems or personal e-mail messages that are not publicly accessible.

II.II.V.II. Biometrics

Biometric surveillance makes use of a person's physical characteristics or personal traits for human recognition. Examples of this technology include digitized fingerprints, voiceprints, iris and retinal scans, hand geometry, and keystroke dynamics. Biometric technologies may seem exotic, but their use is becoming increasingly common, recalling that the 2001 MIT Technology Review named biometrics as one of the "top ten emerging technologies that will change the world."

Although it is far from perfection, biometric facial recognition is being used in a wide array of applications. It is being used, for instance, to control access to computers and facilities, replacing badges and passwords. The British use it to combat hooliganism at football matches. Also the Israeli government uses facial recognition to automate the border-crossing process for workers entering Israel from Palestine. In 1999, the Mexican government employed a facial recognition system to eliminate duplicate voter registration in the presidential elections.[116] With technology improving and becoming more cost-effective, its uses expand. A French magazine has even pointed to the fact considerable studies are undergoing to identify people with reference to their unique odor (body smell) and walking styles.[117]

II.II.V.III. Satellite-driven technology

A new generation of American spy satellites is expected to go into orbit in 2005, and with an estimated 20-year price tag of $25 billion, this program is the most expensive venture ever mounted by U.S. intelligence services.[118] In return for that sum of money, Washington seeks to receive a new system of cameras that can focus on

---

[116] For a review of the use of biometrics and facial recognition in surveillance, see: John. D. Woodward, Jr., *Super Bowl Surveillance: Facing Up to Biometrics*, RAND Corporation, Santa Monica, CA, May 2001.

[117] Stéphane Barge, «La folié de la techno-surveillance», ('The craze of techno-surveillance'), *NewBiz*, November 2001, no. 15, 14.

[118] In comparison, the Manhattan Project, the World War II crash project to build the atomic bomb, cost $20 billion in inflation-adjusted dollars.

potential trouble spots all over the planet on a couple of hours' notice or less, being potentially capable of tracking objects as small as a baseball anywhere, anytime.

Initiated during the Clinton administration, the "Future Imagery Architecture" program envisions having five to six optical satellites and radar satellites in orbit each expected to function for 20 to 30 years as of 2005. Meanwhile, France has taken the lead in arguing that EU governments should invest in spy satellites since they (the Europeans) cannot rely entirely on Washington. Germany has supported that view after its Defense Ministry complained its troops on the ground during the 1999 Kosovo Conflict were exposed to needless risk because the allies had inadequate access to U.S. satellites.[119]

The race to acquire and launch satellites draws attention to the fact there are no universal agreements or international law provisions that permit satellite reconnaissance. The Outer Space Treaty of 1967, as an example, does not directly address the issue of space reconnaissance. Arms control treaties make reference to "national technical means of verification" but do not define those terms. And Article IX of the 1991 Strategic Arms Reduction Treaty concluded between the United States and the former Soviet Union only states "national technical means of verification [be used]...in a manner consistent with generally recognized principles of international law."

The American position has been that a nation's sovereignty does not extend into outer space (i.e., beyond the earth's atmosphere), and accordingly a nation is free to conduct reconnaissance activities from outer space as it is on high seas. At the start of the space race, the Soviet Union's view was that reconnaissance from space was just as illegal as aerial reconnaissance involving the unsanctioned overflight of another nation's territory. Yet for all practical purposes, the current and actual use of space for reconnaissance by a number of states, including the former Soviet Union, has rendered controversial the question of its legality under international law.

---

[119] On the "Future Imagery Architecture" program and the position of France and Germany, see: Joseph Fitchett, "Spying From Space: U.S. to Sharpen the Focus," *IHT,* April 10, 2001, 1.

Another means of surveillance involves satellite-based Global Positioning System (GPS) technology, which is commercially available for airplanes, boats, cars and hikers, and more recently, in wireless communications devices. This technology uses satellite signals to determine geographic coordinates that locate where the person with the receiving device is situated. Now, a chip has been developed that can be implanted beneath human skin to enable a tracer to track the location of a person almost anywhere using a combination of satellites and radio technology. The technology is already being used by the military, firemen, people making emergency calls, and by parents to keep an eye on their children. Wireless location systems can also send update alerts to mobile phone users and travelers when they approach a nearby restaurant or find hotel vacancies.[120]

Reference is also made here to "Galileo," a joint initiative by the European Union and the intergovernmental European Space Agency (ESA). Expected to be operational in 2008, Galileo is to be the first satellite positioning and navigation system specifically for civil purposes, open to international cooperation and operated commercially. The technology promises to considerably improve guidance systems, accident prevention, the efficiency of civil protection (such as emergency or distress calls), and environmental protection.

Comprising a constellation of 30 satellites orbiting at an altitude of nearly 24,000 kilometers (14,900 miles), Galileo is expected to offer Europe with a choice both strategic and independent of the current American GPS, and with greater accuracy.[121] However, two essential questions and perhaps concerns, among others, are recalled here.

First, when and to what extent may Galileo be employed for military purposes in development and in operational theaters, whether by a member country individually, by

---

[120] Read: Simon Romero, "As Wireless Tracking Is Born, Does Privacy Die?," *IHT*, March 5, 2001, 1. Also watch the film "The Enemy of the State," by Tony Scott, which illustrates, though partly dramatized, the use of surveillance technology to trace people. And to view the extent of cooperation between the CIA, the Pentagon and Hollywood, read: Samuel Blumenfeld, «Le Pentagone et la CIA enrôlent Hollywood», ('The Pentagon and the CIA enlist Hollywood'), *Le Monde*, Wednesday, July 24, 2002, 19.

[121] For a concise presentation, along with questions and concerns, on the development of the American GPS and the European Galileo projects, refer to: Thierry GARCIN, in *Les enjeux stratégiques de l'espace*, 2001, pp. 151-55.

a certain number of countries, or collectively? Second, with a growing number of members in the ESA, how is the project expected to assure policy harmony in terms of objectives and management, both in the short and long terms?

Last, and in what may be considered as the greatest surveillance effort ever established, the U.S. National Security Agency is highly believed to have created a global spy system, codename ECHELON, capturing and analyzing virtually every phone call, fax, email and telex message sent anywhere in the world. The ECHELON system includes position intercept stations all over the world to intercept all satellite, microwave, cellular and fiber-optic communications traffic, and then processes the information thanks to computer capabilities, advanced voice recognition, and optical character recognition programs. Detected code words or phrases, known as the 'ECHELON Dictionary' are signaled out and forwarded for further analysis by intelligence specialists.

ECHELON was structured under a 1948 agreement, the 'UKUSA,' where the program is to be controlled by the NSA (deemed as the First Party), and to be operated in conjunction with the General Communications Head Quarters (GCHQ) of England, along with the agencies of its Commonwealth partners the Communications Security Establishment (CSE) of Canada, the Defense Security Directorate (DSD) of Australia, and the General Communications Security Bureau (GCSB) of New Zealand (all referred to as the Second Party). Third Party members later joining the UKUSA agreement include Germany, Japan, Norway, South Korea, and Turkey–not excluding perhaps other members (such as Ireland, and China with limited involvement?).

The project was initially created as a channel for political spying to contain the Soviet Empire, target 'unpopular' political groups, and reportedly peaceful groups such as Amnesty International, Greenpeace, and Christian ministries. Once communism diminished in Eastern Europe, the system redefined national security to incorporate economic and commercial concerns, and eventually espionage.

According to very limited open information on ECHELON, the program is said to be able to process some 1 million message inputs every 30 minutes, with only 10 of those inputs passed for detailed analysis. Searching for words as *militia, gun, bomb,*

Delta Force, explosive, the program intercepts the following: Internet traffic, including e-mail and chat-rooms, most (if not all) long-distance telephone conversations, any electronic signals transmitted by communications satellites, pager signals, and fax transmissions.[122]

NSA facilities in the United States cover the communications signals of both American continents; the GCHG (Britain) is responsible for Europe, Africa and Russia west of the Ural Mountains; the DSD (Australia) provides assistance in signal intelligence (SIGINT) collection in Southeastern Asia and the areas around the Southwest Pacific and Eastern Indian Ocean; the GSCB (New Zealand) covers collections in the Southern Pacific Ocean; and the CSE (Canada) handles additional communications interceptions in northern Russia and northern Europe.

Concerns among the European countries neither involved in nor aware of the project questioned to what extent ECHELON communication interceptions (if the system did indeed exist) violate the sovereignty and privacy of citizens in other countries. Such increasing concerns, along with reported assumptions of real espionage incidents (particularly of commercial nature affecting European companies, and intrusions to individual privacy), led the Civil Liberties Committee of the European Parliament to set up a "Temporary Committee on the ECHELON Interception System" on July 5, 2000.

On July 11, 2001, the Parliamentarian Committee presented its final report, and concluded among other points the following:

> That a global system for intercepting communications exists, operating by means of cooperation proportionate to their capabilities among the USA, the UK, Canada, Australia and New Zealand under the UKUSA Agreement, is no longer in doubt. It may be assumed, in view of the evidence and the consistent pattern of statements from a wide range of individuals and organizations, including American sources, that the

---

[122] For more information on ECHELON, read: Patrick S. Poole, ECHELON: "America's Secret Global Surveillance Network," Washington, DC: Free Congress Research and Education Foundation, undated document retrieved on March 22, 2005, at: http://www.shire.net/big.brother/echelon.htm; and also: Bill Wallace, "Feds may be reading your mail," *CNN*, online edition, April 26, 2000; and: "E-mail users warned over spy network," *BBC News*, online edition, May 29, 2001. The United States denies the system exists, while the United Kingdom refuses to give details about it.

system or parts of it were, at least for some time, code-named ECHELON. What is important is that its purpose is to intercept private and commercial communications, and not military communications.

Analysis has revealed that the technical capabilities of the system are probably not nearly as extensive as some sections of the media had assumed. Nevertheless, it is worrying that many senior Community figures, in particular European Commissioners, who gave evidence to the Temporary Committee, claimed to be unaware of this phenomenon.[123]

In respect of ECHELON's compatibility with the law provisions of the European Union, the Report adds (pp. 133-34):

If a system is used purely for intelligence purposes, there is no violation of EU law, since operations in the interests of state security are not subject to the EC Treaty.... If, on the other hand, the system is misused for the purpose of gathering competitive intelligence, such action is at odds with the Member States' duty of loyalty and with the concept of a common market based on free competition. If a Member State participates in such a system, it violates EC law.

Nevertheless, a number of questions concerning the system are raised here. For instance, how have the parties involved in the UKUSA Agreement been able to ensure the absolute secrecy of such an enormous, ambitious program throughout nearly six decades? Also, if the interception capability is reportedly to be efficient, how were the intelligence agencies concerned not aware of the September 11, 2001 attacks (or were they)? Will other non-member states of the UKUSA Agreement–particularly European countries–be encouraged to conduct similar intelligence activities and programs directed at the cultural civil liberties of their citizens? And last, how does the program distinguish between a youngster jokingly using words from the ECHELON dictionary to those individuals or groups that really intend to do so?

To sum up the overall presentation on surveillance, both the public and private sectors are making growing use of electronic surveillance technologies as well as other emerging technologies that can gather information about individuals. More than ever

---

[123] "Report on the Existence of a Global System for the Interception of Private and Commercial Communications (ECHELON interception system)," Temporary Committee on the ECHELON Interception System, European Parliament, July 11, 2001.

before, we are witnessing increasing interlinkages among these various information-gathering technologies, as demonstrated in Illustration 2.2.

The center of the design depicts average citizens, all of whom have different types of personal information associated with them (e.g., biographical, consumer, biometric, medical, financial, and behavioral). Surrounding the information are various technologies that can obtain such personal information (e.g., overhead imaging, genomic, biometrics, thermal imaging, computer monitoring, data mining, micro sensors, global positioning systems, geographical information systems, surveillance cameras, and bio-nano-materials technology). When these technologies are interlinked, the ability to collect information–along with the volume of information collected–increase significantly, thereby remarkably mounting the potential privacy invasions.

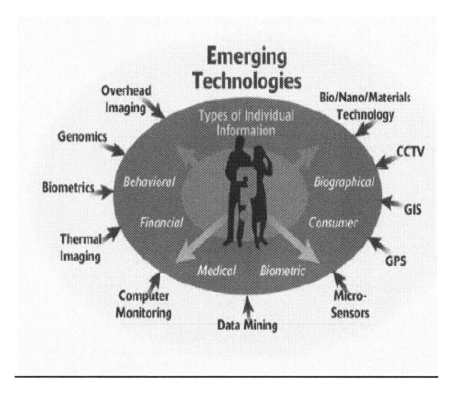

Illustration 2. 2. Emerging technologies that may gather personal information
(Source: Woodward, *Privacy vs. Security*, 2002: 6)

CCTV: Closed circuit television (a system in which the circuit is closed and all the elements are directly connected). Open circuit television (OCTV) transmits video images over wireless networks to portable devices. Cameras are used for both systems. "Video surveillance" is the use of CCTV to conduct a visual surveillance of a person or a place.
The United Kingdom, for instance, has an estimated one million CCTV cameras in operation.

GIS: Geographical Information Systems   GPS: Global Positioning Systems

II.II.VI. Operations Against Leaders

Operations that threaten the person and power of senior *enemy* decision makers have long been considered throughout history to have a high payoff potential. They target a key enemy center of gravity and place at risk the individuals considered responsible for initiating and substaining assaults on the interests of a given state. Documented accounts on such operations in history speak for themselves. The first *coup d'état* known in history was by the officer Sargon (born in the 24th century B.C.) over the King of Kish in Mesopotamia.[124] And in China:

> For several centuries after the fall of the Han Dynasty (A.D. 222), Chinese history followed the same pattern of violent and bloody coups, one after the other. Army men would plot to kill a weak emperor, then would replace him on the Dragon Throne with a strong general. The general would start a new dynasty and crown himself emperor; to ensure his own survival he would kill off his fellow generals. A few years later, however, the pattern would resume: New generals would rise up and assassinate him or his sons in their turn. To be emperor of China was to be alone, surrounded by a pack of enemies–it was the least powerful, least secure position in the realm.
>
> In A.D. 959, General Chao K'uang-yin became Emperor Sung. He knew the odds, the probability that within a year or two he would be murdered; how could he break the pattern? Soon after becoming emperor, Sung ordered a banquet to celebrate the new dynasty, and invited the most powerful commanders in the army. After they had drunk much wine, he dismissed the guards and everybody else except the generals, who now feared he would murder them in one full swoop. Instead, he addressed them: "The whole day is spent in fear, and I am unhappy both at the table and in my bed. For which one of you does not dream of ascending the throne? I do not doubt your allegiance, but if by some chance your subordinates, seeking wealth and position, were to force the emperor's yellow robe upon you in the turn, how could you refuse it?"
>
> Drunk and fearing for their lives, the generals proclaimed their innocence and their loyalty. But Sung had other ideas: "The best way to pass one's day is in peaceful enjoyment of riches and honor. If you are willing to give up your commands, I am ready to provide you with fine estates and beautiful dwellings where you may take your pleasure with singers and girls as your companions."
>
> The astonished generals realized that instead of a life of anxiety and struggle, Sung was offering them riches and security. The next day, all the generals tendered their resignations, and they retired as nobles to the estates that Sung bestowed on them.
>
> In one stroke, Sung turned a pack of "friendly" wolves, who would likely have betrayed him, into a group of docile lamps, far from all power.[125]

---

[124] Christophe Courau, «De Babylone à Bagdad: L'Irak terre de conflits», ('From Babylon to Baghdad: Iraq the land of conflicts'), *Historia*, no. 670, October 2002, 14. Also refer to: "The Top 10 Battles for the Control of Iraq," at: http://www.livescience.com/history/top10_iraq_battles.html.

[125] Eventually, the Sung Dynasty ruled China for more than three hundred years. Greene & Elffers, *The 48 Laws of Power*, 1998, pp. 10-11.

In modern history, the United States has long attempted to use leadership attacks to shape the policy and behavior of enemy states and other hostile actors. Over the years, both overt and covert operations[126] have been mounted in attempts to:

- compel enemy states to abandon policies and behavior injurious to American interests;
- deter adversaries from making future assaults on those interests;
- depose potentially dangerous regimes; and,
- degrade enemy capabilities to wage war and engage in terrorism.[127]

The promise of such benefits has, thus, led American civilian and military officials to propose sanctions and order attacks against senior enemy leaders. The forms of attacks that have been used can be summarized by:

- direct attacks on the leader's person by U.S. forces or agents;
- coups and rebellions fomented and supported by the United States;
- takedown operations conducted by U.S. invasion and occupation forces.[128]

With the exception of the shoot down of Japanese Admiral Isoroku Yamamoto's aircraft in World War II in 1943 (based on predictive intelligence by the decryption of messages concerning the admiral's itinerary), all U.S. efforts to directly attack senior enemy leaders–from Fidel Castro of Cuba to Muammar Al-Qaddafi of Libya to Saddam Hussein of Iraq and to Slobodan Milosevic of the F.R. of Yugoslavia–have failed.

---

[126] "Covert," from the Latin *cooperire* (to cover), means "concealed, hidden, under cover, not avowed." A National Security Council directive in 1948 defined covert operations as actions by the United States against foreign states "which are so planned and executed that any U.S. Government responsibility for them is not evident to unauthorized persons and that if uncovered the U.S. Government can plausibly disclaim any responsibility for them." More recently, Title 50 Section 413b of the U.S. Code defines "covert action" as activity "to influence political, economic, or military conditions abroad, where it is intended that the role of the United States Government will not be apparent or acknowledged publicly." The American Congress in 1991 passed a law requiring the U.S. President to sign a secret "finding" authorizing the CIA to conduct a "covert action" and to inform intelligence committee leaders. A *clandestine* operation differs from a covert operation in that emphasis is placed on the concealment of the operation rather than on the concealment of the identity of the sponsor. See: William Safire, "Spookspeak," *The New York Times*, online edition, February 13, 2005.

[127] Stephen T. Hosmer, *Operations Against Enemy Leaders,* RAND Corporation, Santa Monica, CA, 2001, p. 1.

[128] Stephen T. Hosmer, *Operations Against Enemy Leaders,* 2001, p. xi.

The only coups d'état explicitly sponsored or sanctioned by the United States that have succeeded have been those against leaders who had lost the support of significant elements of their own military. Among them are:

- In 1953, against Iranian prime minister Mohammed Mossadeq, whom the United States saw as becoming increasingly alienated from the West and more closely allied with Iran's Soviet-dominated Tudeh Party; and,

- In 1963, senior officials in the Kennedy administration concluded that South Vietnamese president Ngo Dinh Diem was hindering the successful prosecution of the counterinsurgency war in South Vietnam and that he had to be replaced (Hosmer, pp. 50, 54).

The one successful ouster of a leader by a rebellion organized by the United States was when the CIA orchestrated and launched from neighboring Honduras a combination of military and psychological pressures to drive the leftist Guatemalan president Jacobo Arbenz from office in 1954. This was accomplished by limited air attacks and ground force demonstrations against a government that was once again denied backing from its own armed forces.

A last resort to remove a hostile government it to overthrow it with external military force. In this case, the target country would be invaded and occupied, the old *regime* and its security structure would be eradicated, and a new pro-U.S. government would be set in place. The ground force component of such an external invasion could be assured by troops from a neighboring country, by American ground forces, or by a coalition of American and allied forces. During World War II, U.S. forces helped bring down the Axis regimes in Germany, Italy, and Japan. More recently, the United States employed its armed forces to remove *hostile* regimes in Grenada (1983), Panama (1989), to force the abdication of the ruling military junta in Haiti (1994), and even more recently, to dislocate the Taliban regime in Afghanistan (2001), and disperse the ruling Arab Ba'ath Socialist Party of Iraq and Saddam Hussein (2003). All the above post World War II operations were conducted against relatively weak opposing military and security forces, and were all accomplished in considerable short periods of time.[129]

---

[129] Bob Woodward outlines in "President Broadens Anti-Hussein Order," *The Washington Post*, (June 16, 2002, A01) the intelligence order directing the CIA to undertake a comprehensive, covert program to topple Saddam Hussein, including authority to use lethal force to capture the Iraqi president.

II.III. Contemporary Traditional and Non-Traditional Conflicts in the Information Age

The relevance and significance of treating issues pertaining to the reasons behind and means of waging conflicts arises from the fact that such patterns and objectives are constantly evolving in today's world. In addition to the still-present classic norms of conflictual disputes and direct military involvement, emerging non-state actors and agents are initiating non-conventional approaches in the designated battlefield. Despite hopes that the Information Age and an interdependent globe may all together eliminate conflicts, the world has not yet reached an idealistic stage of universal peace. Accordingly, this section examines some of those traditional and non-traditional developments of conflicts.

II.III.I. Defining and Tracing Areas of Conflict

Long throughout history, as the pyramids of power controlled conflict by suppressing it, they also bred new conflicts. Almost every hierarchy and state was established out of a struggle for power, and once gained, was always open to challenge. Different factions and individuals competed for position inside the hierarchy, and so outsiders regularly threatened the state. The state was a valuable prize, a treasure of wealth and power. The continuous struggle for control easily and frequently escalated into violence[130] and war.

Hence began a history-making process of violent coups d'état and conquests by war. A strong city-state conquered other city-states around it and grew into an empire. The Sumerian Empire, the Babylonian Empire, the Assyrian Empire, the Egyptian Empire all rose through conquest and fell through conquest. Dynasties were born out of violence, empires out of war. Remember how Emperor Sung was finally able to break

---

[130] Acts of violence can be classified according to their degree of intensity into: psychological violence, sporadic violence, targeted violence, blind violence, legitimated violence, and generalized violence. See: Loup Francart and Jean-Jacques Patry, *Mastering Violence: An Option for Operational Military Strategy,* Commandement de la doctrine et de l'enseignement militaire supérieur de l'armée de terre, Centre de recherche, Paris, November 24, 1998, pp. 10-11.

the pattern of coups, violence, and civil war–as the Sung Dynasty ruled China for more than three hundred years.

The state and war, and domination and violence, became inseparable. Eventually, the state took on the characteristics of a military organization. As the periods of peace and truce shortened and the frequency of war increased, states became garrisons, machines dedicated to raising tribute and soldiers from the people in order to sustain the capacity to wage war. Thus war became the chief preoccupation of the nobility, who served as warriors and military officers, and of the king, who was commander-in-chief. Temporary armies, drafted from the peasantry, gave way to professional standing armies. Those standing armies created the temptation to use them against neighbors to acquire their lands and power, win prestige and glory, or to preempt another attack. In societies dedicated to the acquisition and maintenance of power, *brutal force* became the ultimate arbiter. It simply made kings and unmade them, raised groups up and cast them down, created states and empires and destroyed them. In other words, it became the driving thrust of history.

Around some three thousand years after Ashurbanipal, war has not changed much. Adolph Hitler went to war for much the same reasons Ashurbanipal did: for land and power. That said, living in the 20th century may have given the impression of co-existing in the most advanced, most civilized, and most humane societies the world has ever seen. Yet, the irony is that the past century has been the bloodiest century the human race has ever known. Statistics reveal that over a hundred million people have perished in warfare, along with another hundred and seventy million dying through political violence.[131]

"From center stage in human politics, war has moved to center stage in human evolution," writes William Ury (1999). The know-how of making nuclear, chemical and biological weapons continues to spread slowly but relentlessly. So too does the technology of rockets and missiles to carry these weapons, any spot on earth can now be reached and destroyed within thirty minutes. While the treat of global nuclear destruction appears to have faded with the end of the Cold War, nuclear weapons still

---

[131] For casualty statistics, see: Ruth Leger Sivard, *World Military and Social Expenditures 1996*, Washington, DC: World Priorities, 1996, pp. 18-19.

remain in place, armed and ready for instant use. Consequently, no one can expect the technological drive to stop with the atomic bomb. With advances in genetic research and artificial intelligence, human ingenuity is likely to devise even more destructive weapons.

Despite the great hopes for peace after the end of the Cold War in the late 1980s, *hot conflicts* range in more than thirty countries and regions with the turn of the millennium. Although armed conflict is a worldwide phenomenon, certain regions are more affected than others.[132] In 2003, the number of armed conflicts totaled to 36 in 28 countries, a figure that reflects the fewest number of states hosting wars since at least 1987. Africa and Asia were the most war-torn continents, with around 28% and 19% of the countries in each of these two regions respectively hosting armed conflicts on their territory. In Europe and the Americas, only 5% and 2% of the countries respectively were the scene of conflict. The instability in Colombia was the Western Hemisphere's singly armed dispute, rendering the Americas, and particularly, North America, the region least affected by war.

In 2003, the U.S. invasion in Iraq was the sole international war. Despite the fact it was fought on the territory of a single state, it is considered a war between states (Iraq

---

[132] The working definition of an "armed conflict" here is a political conflict in which armed combat involves the armed forces of at least one state (or one or more armed factions seeking to gain control of all or part of the state), and in which at least 1,000 people have been killed by the fighting during the course of the conflict. An armed conflict is added to the annual list of current armed conflicts in the year in which the death toll reaches that figure.

It is important to note that the definition of 'political conflict' becomes even more difficult as the trend in current intrastate armed conflicts increasingly obscures the distinction between political and criminal violence. That is, in a growing number of armed conflicts, armed bands, militia, or factions engage in activity of criminal nature (e.g., theft, looting, extortion) so as to fund their political/military campaigns, as well as for the personal enrichment of the leadership and the general livelihood of the fighting forces. In some circumstances, therefore, while the disintegrating order reflects the social chaos resulting from state failure, the erupting violence or armed confrontation is not necessarily guided by a political program or a series of politically motivated or defined military objectives. Nevertheless, such trends are part of the evolving character of war, and conflicts characterized more by social chaos than political/military disputes may hence be included when referring to current armed conflicts.

To conclude, an armed conflict is deemed to have ended if there has been a formal ceasefire or peace agreement and, after then, there are no longer combat deaths (or fewer than 25 per year). In the absence of a formal cease fire, a conflict is deemed to have ended after two years of dormancy (with fewer than 25 deaths per year). Source: "The Armed Conflicts Report 2004," Project Ploughshares, Institute of Peace and Conflict Studies, Conrad Grebel College, Waterloo, Ontario, Canada, 2004. Also refer to: *Manière de voir,* 55, «Atlas 2001 des Conflits», ('2001 Conflict Atlas'), January-February 2001, Paris: le Monde Diplomatique; and also to: Jean-Louis Dufour and Maurice Vaisse, «*La guerre au XXe siecle*», ('War in the 20th century'), Paris: Hachette, 1993.

against the United States and its coalition partners). During that year all the rest of the conflicts were internal disputes.

Except for five, all of the 36 armed conflicts are more than two years old. Some 23 conflicts (two-thirds) have been going on for more than 10 years, and another eight of the current armed conflicts have endured for over 25 years. In Iraq and in Angola, the year 2003 witnessed both the end of one armed conflict and the beginning of another. Conflicts, elsewhere, ended in Guinea and Rwanda. The number of disputes within the country of Indonesia declined from five to four. The conflict involving Iran also ended when U.S. forces disarmed and dispersed the headquarters and bases of the Mujahedeen Khalq Organization in Iraq (that is opposed to the Iranian government).

In 2003, three additional conflicts emerged in Africa. An outbreak of armed violence in Côte d'Ivoire in 2002 caused more than 1,000 deaths by early 2003. Ethnic groups in Ethiopia clashed with each other in the Gambella region. In the Horn of Africa, a crisis broke out as a result of the conflict in the Darfur region of Sudan. See Figure 2.2.

The coming years, as well, do not seem to be so peaceful. In projecting future conflicts, *Global Trends 2015* states:

> The risk of war among developed countries will be low. The international community will continue, however, to face conflicts around the world, ranging from relatively frequent small-scale internal upheavals to less frequent regional interstate wars. The potential for conflict will arise from rivalries in Asia, ranging from India-Pakistan to China-Taiwan, as well as among the antagonists in the Middle East. Their potential lethality will grow, driven by the availability of WMD, longer-range missile delivery systems and other technologies.
>
> Internal conflicts stemming from religious, ethnic, economic or political disputes will remain at current levels or even increase in number. The United Nations and regional organizations will be called upon to manage such conflicts because major states–stressed by domestic concerns, perceived risk of failure, lack of political will, or tight resources–will minimize their direct involvement.[133]

---

[133] *Global Trends 2015*, NIC, December 2000, p. 12.

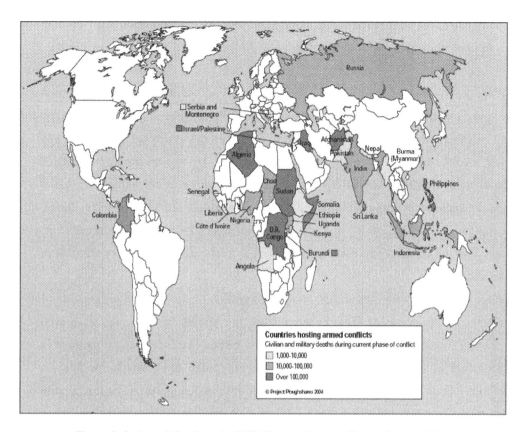

Figure 2. 2. Armed Conflicts in 2003 (Source: Project Ploughshares, 2004)

The following section takes a deeper insight at conflicts evoked by claims and needs over resources and land. Some of those conflicts date back to several years, while certain others are yet to come. Before moving on, it is noteworthy to point out that two former Clinton administration officials laid out a scheme to evaluate risks to U.S. security and to help reassert national priorities in cases that might involve the use of force. At the top of their hierarchy, enlist William Perry and Ashton Carter[134] is so-called *A-list* threats, of the scale that the Soviet Union presented to America's survival. A threatening China, or spread of nuclear materials would also fit in that category. The *B-list* of imminent threats to its interests (but not to its survival) would include situations such as those in the Korean Peninsula and in the Arab Gulf. Their *C-list* of

---

[134] Ashton B. Carter and William. J. Perry, *Preventive Defense: A New Security Strategy for America,* Washington, DC: Brookings Institution Press, 1999, pp. 11-15.

important contingencies that indirectly affect U.S. security but do not directly threaten American interests would include that of Kosovo, Bosnia, Somalia, Rwanda, and Haiti.

Remarkably, the C-list of humanitarian interventions often dominates the foreign policy agenda. While this may partly be attributed to the absence of A-list threats after the end of the Cold War, another reason beyond that is the ability of C-list issues to dominate media attention in the global Information Age. Dramatic visual portrayals of immediate human conflict and suffering are far easier to convey to the public than A-list abstractions such as the importance of the American alliance with, just to name, Japan, or the potential collapse of the international system of trade and investment. Yet, apparently simple cases can turn out to be extremely difficult from the very start, as in Somalia and Kosovo.

Ever since the events of September 11, 2001, the Middle East has played an even more prominent role in U.S. policy than before. The United States relies on it partners in the region such as Israel, Saudi Arabia, Qatar, Egypt, Jordan and others in its "War on Terror" and to halt the proliferation of WMD. The loss of key partners due to "hostile regime" changes or increasing anti-Americanism may limit the United States' ability in the region. Also, the United States has an interest in maintaining stable energy prices and reliable supplies. In view of the West's dependence on oil from the Middle East, political instability in the region could hurt economies around the world. Key findings of a recent report examined current political, economic, and social trends in the Middle East to forecast future threats to regional security and their potential impact on the United States.[135] Among them are:

- Liberalization will advance slowly and democratization will be even more limited. Middle East states are typically controlled by authoritarian powers;

- Declining economies will likely increase popular dissatisfaction with governments. Recent economic reform efforts have failed to create jobs or to attract foreign investment to the regions;

---

[135] Nora Bensahel and Daniel L. Byman, *The Future Security Environment in the Middle East: Conflict, Stability, and Political Change,* RAND Corporation, Santa Monica, CA, 2004, pp. xiv-xvii.

- Militaries will be more devoted to internal control than to external defense. Many Middle East states have *dual mandate* militaries responsible for protecting their regimes from internal challenges as well as defending their countries from external dangers;

- New leaders may be weaker and less likely to cooperate with the United States. Since 1997, new leaders have come to power in Iran, Algeria, Bahrain, Jordan, Morocco, Syria and Palestine. Further leadership changes are expected in Saudi Arabia, Kuwait, Egypt and Libya in the near future;

- Changing patterns in the energy market will strengthen Middle East ties to Asia. The Middle East dominates the global energy market with roughly 70% of the world's proven oil reserves. As Asian energy demands increase, the defense trade between Asia and the Middle East is likely to grow. Consequently, the United States will find it more difficult to pressure Asian governments not to export arms to its hostile Middle East governments;

- Communications technologies may increase the demand for public participation in government. Advance technologies such as the Internet are primarily limited to the wealthier and more educated echelons of Middle Eastern society. Yet, mid-level technologies like satellite television, videocassettes, facsimile machines, and photocopiers have become widespread among the general population (permitting quick and inexpensive circulation of materials that are beyond the control of government media and publishing monopolies); and,

- Middle East states will continue to develop and acquire WMD (as long as Israel does). Many states seek to develop or acquire chemical, biological, radiological, or nuclear weapons and advanced delivery systems, noting that the geographical distance between adversaries in the Middle East is very short.

II.III.II. Conflicts over Resources

The areas of greatest concern to strategic and military planners during the Cold War were those of confrontation between the United States and the Soviet blocs: central and southeastern Europe and the Far East. Since the end of the Cold War, nevertheless, these areas have lost much strategic significance for the United States, while other regions, such as the Arabian Gulf, the Caspian Sea basin and the South China Sea, are receiving increased attention from the Pentagon.

Behind the shift in strategic geography lies a new emphasis on the protection of supplies of vital resources, especially oil and natural gas. In other words, while Cold War-era divisions were created and alliances formed along ideological lines, economic competition now drives international relations. Competition over access to these vital economic assets has intensified accordingly. Because an interruption in the supply of nature resources would portend severe economic consequences, the major importing countries now consider the protection of this flow an essential national concern. With global energy consumption rising annually, competition for access to large energy reserves will only grow more intense in the years to come.

A common focus on the acquisition or protection of energy supplies is evident in the strategic thinking of powers other than the American heavy energy importers, like China, Japan, and other major European states, who have made the issue of ensuring the stability of their supplies a top priority. Russia is placing greater foreign emphasis on energy-producing areas of Central Asia. Although Moscow continues to worry about developments along its western frontiers in the areas facing NATO, it has devoted considerable resources to strengthen its military presence in the South, in the Caucasus (including Chechnya and Dagestan), and among the former Soviet Central Asian republics. Similarly, the Chinese military has shifted its concentration from the northern border with Russia to Xinjiang in the west (a potential oil source) and to offshore areas of East and South China Seas. Japan has followed China to these Seas and boosted its own ability to operate there, procuring and developing new warships and a fleet of missile-armed patrol planes. Securing access to sufficient oil and gas supplies is also a great concern of the more recent industrializing nations of the developing world, such as Brazil, Israel, Malaysia, Thailand and Turkey–particularly in view of their anticipated increase in energy consumption rates over the next 20 years.

Though obtaining sufficient energy supplies is becoming the foremost resource priority for some states, the pursuit of adequate water has become the central focus for others. Water supplies are already insufficient in many parts of the Middle East and Southwest Asia. Also, continued population growth and the increased likelihood of drought from global warming will most probably create similar scarcities elsewhere. A more complicated issue, water supplies are not restricted to political boundaries, and thus many countries in these regions concerned must share a limited number of major water sources. With all these countries seeking to increase their allotted *flow*, the danger of conflict over competition for these shared supplies inevitably grows.

Other parts of the globe have witnessed localized conflicts breaking out for control of valuable timbers and minerals. Typically, such conflicts entail a struggle between competitive elites or tribes over the income derived from commodity exports. In Angola and Sierra Leone, for instance, rival groups battle for control over lucrative diamond fields; in the Democratic Republic of Congo, the conflict concerns copper as well as diamonds; and various groups in parts of Southeast Asia fight over valuable stands of timber. These conflicts, which may not constitute a direct threat to the security of the major powers, can lead to the deployment of UN peacekeeping forces–as in Sierra Leone–and therefore impose significant demands on the world's capacity to manage ethnic and regional violence.

The entire scope of these phenomena, where increased competition over access to major oil and gas sources, growing friction over the allocation of shared water supplies, and internal warfare over valuable export commodities, have generated a new geography of conflict. That geography is more of a reconfigured cartography in which resource flows rather than political and ideological division constitute the major fault lines. Referred to as current (and potential) traditional conflict zones in the 21st century, the following is a brief look at some of the *unsettled* resource deposits in terms of contested oil and gas fields, shared water systems, and embattled diamond and mineral mines.

II.III.II.I. Energy and Oil

Identifying areas of potential conflict over natural resources is becoming increasingly important as the pressure on these fault lines grows. According to Klare, the pressure derives from a number of sources–starting with the basic mechanism of supply and demand.[136] As populations grow in numbers and economic activity expands in many parts of the world, the appetite for vital materials swell more quickly than nature (and the world's resource firms) can accommodate. The result will be recurring

---

[136] Michael T. Klare, "The New Geography of Conflict," *Foreign Affairs*, May/June 2001, Vol. 80, no. 3, 56, New York: Council on Foreign Affairs.

shortages of key materials, becoming chronic in some cases. Technologies that introduce alternative materials and production techniques will help overcome some of these scarcities but can also present problems of their own, as realized, for example, by the mounting demand for electricity in Silicon Valley and other centers of digital technology. While shortages of critical materials arise in frequency and severity, the competition for access to the remaining supplies of these commodities grows more intense.

The pressure on global petroleum supplies is likely to prove especially severe. The U.S. Department of Energy foresees global oil consumption to rise from around 77 million barrels per day in 2000 to some 110 million barrels in 2020 (an increase of 43%).[137] If these estimates turn out to be accurate, the world would have had consumed approximately 670 billion barrels of oil until 2020, or about two-thirds of the world's known petroleum reserves. Certainly (and hopefully), new reserves will be discovered during this period, and emerging technologies will allow us to tap into supplies previously considered inaccessible, such as those in remote northern Siberian, and beneath the deep Atlantic. Yet the production of petroleum products is still not likely to keep pace with rising demand.[138]

These current or potential trouble zones include the Arabian Gulf, the Caspian Sea basin, and the South China Sea, along with Algeria, Angola, Chad, Colombia, Indonesia, Nigeria, Sudan, and Venezuela—areas and countries that together embody about four-fifths of the world's known petroleum reserves. Not to forget the pipelines and tanker routes used to carry oil and natural gas from their supply points to markets in the West, reminding as well many of these routes pass through areas subject to periodic violence. For instance, the energy supplies of the Caspian region must cross the troubled Caucasus (encompassing Armenia, Azerbaijan, Georgia, and parts of southern Russia) before reaching a secure outlet to the sea. In addition, the five costal countries of the

---

[137] Michael T. Klare, "The New Geography of Conflict," 2001.

[138] That is, periodic shortages of the kind experienced in summer and fall of 2000 are likely to reoccur more often. At that time, former U.S. president Bill Clinton flew to Africa in August 2000 with the hope of obtaining additional oil from Nigeria, and also pushed the Caspian states to accelerate the construction of new pipelines to Europe and to the Mediterranean. Likewise, and once he was elected, President George W. Bush met with President Vincent Fox of Mexico to discuss proposals for increasing the flow of energy from Mexico to the United States.

Caspian Sea have yet to agree on a plan to divide their offshore resource zones. The situation in the South China Sea is even more problematic, with seven countries claiming all or part of the region. Furthermore, major disagreements over the ownership of oil-bearing border regions and offshore fields also prevail in the regions of the Arabian Gulf, the Red Sea, and Timor Sea, and the Gulf of Guinea.

But even when the ownership of particular reserves is not subject to dispute, as in the major fields of Colombia, Iran, Saudi Arabia, and Venezuela, the future availability of these supplies cannot be taken for grant. This is because of political and social unrest that may be completely unrelated to resource issues and which could eventually endanger the supplies. For instance, consider the frequent disturbance of Iraqi oil flow after the U.S. invasion in Iraq in March 2003. The opponents to the Saudi monarchy appear to be growing, and there is no guarantee that they can be contained *forever*.[139] The internal strains in Iran are also evident, with tensions far from diminishing. Across the globe, we see Colombia in the midst of a civil war, and political conditions in Venezuela have become highly volatile. Further prone to political and social disorder are countries such as Algeria, Angola, Indonesia, Nigeria, and Sudan–all which house considerable oil and gas supplies.

II.III.II.II Water Flows

An illustration of worrisome resource zones would show all major water systems shared by two or more countries in droughty or semi-droughty areas. That would include large river systems such as the Nile (shared by among others, Egypt, Ethiopia, and Sudan), the Jordan (by Jordan, Israel, Lebanon, and Syria) the Tigris and Euphrates (by Iraq, Syria, and Turkey), the Indus (by India, and Pakistan), and the Amu Darya (shared by Tajikistan, Turkmenistan, and Uzbekistan). Also implied would be underground aquifers that similarly cross borders, such as the Mountain Aquifer lying beneath the West Bank and Israel.

---

[139] For further reading on the contest for energy dominance between two principal oil exporters, Saudi Arabia and Russia, see: Edward L. Morse and James Richard, "The Battle for Energy Dominance," *Foreign Affairs,* March/April 2002.

Thanks to regular fresh supplies from rains and snowfalls, water is considered a renewable resource. However, the amount of replaceable water that is available for human use in any given year is actually quite limited (as is the case with oil supplies). Many areas of the Middle East and Asia already suffer from persistent water scarcity, with the number of countries experiencing such conditions expected to double over the next 25 years as the world population rises and more people settle in urban areas. By the year 2050, the demand for water could approach 100% of the available supply, evoking intense competition for this essential substance in all but a few well-watered areas of the planet.

Two prominent report conclusions highlight the concern over water scarcity:

> In contrast to food and energy, water scarcities and allocation will pose significant challenges to governments in the Middle East, Sub-Saharan Africa, South Asia, and Northern China. Regional tensions over water will be heightened by 2015.[140]

And:

> A constraint to development that demands investment and planning is the shortage of water throughout the region, which is characteristic of almost all Arab States. In fact, Arabs account for 15 of the 22 countries that the World Bank identifies as below the water poverty line of less than 1,000 cubic metres per person per year.[141]

Environment trends such as global warming, furthermore, affect the worldwide availability of many resources, including water and arable land. Though higher temperatures do produce increased rainfall in areas located near oceans and other large waters, inland regions will generally experience drier conditions, with prolonged drought turning into a recurring phenomenon. Higher temperatures will as well increase evaporation rates from rivers, lakes, and reservoirs. As a consequence, it is likely that many farming areas will be lost, either to drought and encroaching desert inland, or to coastal flooding and the rise of global sea levels in maritime regions.

---

[140] *Global Trends 2015*, 2000, p. 9.

[141] "Arab Economies Need Rapid Growth–From a Strategy Knowledge Base," *Arab Human Development Report 2002: Creating Opportunities for Future Generations,* United Nations Development Programme, Press Kit, p. 3.

With the above threats and potential concerns in mind, it is essential that the countries involved reach mutually acceptable agreements for the allocation of available water supplies. Not surprisingly, few governments have chosen to do so. In 1959, Egypt and Sudan agreed to divide up the Nile's flow, but provide no supplies for Ethiopia and for the other countries that depend on the river's water–constituting an obviously *unstable* arrangement. Iraq and Syria concluded an agreement on their respective appropriations from the Euphrates, but the river itself arises in Turkey, which has declined to sign a water-sharing agreement. Israel has yet to reach an agreement with Syria over the Jordan River's headwaters, and has not carried through with promises made to Jordan in 1994 regarding cooperative water projects in the Jordan River Valley.[142]

The only major water-sharing arrangement that has demonstrated (to a certain extent) any degree of durability is the Indus Waters Treaty of 1960 between India and Pakistan, though even this pioneering agreement remains hostage to the future stability of these two countries' relations. "There and elsewhere," foresees Klare (2001, p. 59), "international disputes over the allocation of existing supplies will grow more intense as populations increase and the greenhouse process accelerates global warming."

II.III.II.III. Precious Minerals

Last, this chart points out major concentrations of gems, minerals, and old-growth timber in the developing world. Included in these precious assets would be the diamond fields of Angola, the Democratic Republic of Congo and Sierra Leone, the emerald mines of Colombia, the copper and gold mines of Congo, Indonesia, and Papua New Guinea, in addition to the forests of Brazil, Cambodia, Congo, Fiji, Liberia, Mexico, the Philippines, the Brunei, Indonesia, and the Malaysian Island of Borneo.

---

[142] On the importance of water settlements between rival countries, for example, Article 6 (para. 2) of the comprehensive Peace Agreement between Israel and Jordan concluded on October 26, 1994 states: "The Parties, recognizing the necessity to find a practical, just and agreed solution to their water problems and with the view that the subject of water can form the basis for the advancement of cooperation between them, jointly undertake to ensure that the management and development of their water resources do not, in any way, harm the water resources of the other Party."

Protecting–and even *conquering*–these valuable mines and terrains has evolved into a matter of vital interest to particularly poor countries that have few other wealth sources. The governments of Angola and Sierra Leone, for example, have devoted much of their national incomes to protracted efforts to reassert control over diamond fields occupied by rebel organizations. Likewise, the government of Papua New Guinea has launched several campaigns to *reconquer* the island of Bougainville–a troublesome territory housing the world's largest copper mine. Obviously, duels of this sort will continue to arise as long as warlords and other local factions in these countries perceive a potential benefit from seizing and exploiting major deposits of valuable materials.

Market mechanisms can perhaps alleviate most of the increased pressures on the world's existing supply of vital resources and minerals. Rising demands, along with higher prices, do stimulate the development of new materials and processes that allow resource firms to search for new deposits and bring those that were once inaccessible within reach. Yet, technology cannot completely reverse demographic and environmental pressures (as well as continuing political and social instability). Some countries and regions will also be unable to afford higher costs of alternative technologies, and thus in such circumstances, the basic notion of global supply and demand becomes increasingly unbalanced.

II.III.III. Non-Traditional Warfare and Networks

Two particular developments are altering the conflict spectrum in the Information Age. According to Arquilla and Ronfeldt,[143] the first is that the current revolution is favoring and strengthening network forms of organization, often entitling them to an advantage over hierarchical forms. The rise of networks means that power is migrating to non-state actors, because they are able to organize into sprawling multiorganizational networks more readily than can traditional, hierarchical, state actors. In other words, *networks* may increasingly wage conflicts, perhaps more than *hierarchies*. Also, this notion implies that whoever masters the network form stands to gain the advantage.

---

[143] John Arquilla and David Ronfeldt, *Networks and Netwars: The Future of Terror, Crime and Militancy,* RAND Corporation, Santa Monica, CA, 2001, p. 1.

As for the second development, the more the Information Revolution deepens, the more the conduct and outcome of conflicts increasingly depend on information and communications. Conflicts, more than ever before, revolve around *knowledge* and the proper employment of *soft power*. Opponents are learning to emphasize *information operations* and *perception management*. That is, media-oriented measures aim to attract or disorient rather than coerce, and eventually affect how secure a society, a military, or other actors feel about its knowledge of itself and of its adversaries. Here, psychological disruption may turn out to be as important a goal as physical destruction. Major transformations are thus coming in the nature of adversaries, in the form of threats they may pose, and how conflicts can be waged. Information Age threats are likely to be more diffuse, dispersed, multi-dimensional nonlinear, and ambiguous than were Industrial Age threats.

In 1996, the two authors John Arquilla and David Ronfeldt also coined and fully exposed the term *netwar*.[144] They referred to it as an emerging mode of conflict (and crime) at social levels, short of traditional military warfare, in which protagonists use network forms of organization and doctrines, strategies, and technologies attuned to the Information Age. Such protagonists are likely to consist of dispersed organizations, small groups, and individuals who communicate, coordinate and conduct their campaigns in an *internetted* manner, often without precise central command. Therefore, netwar differs from modes of conflict and crime in which the protagonists prefer to develop formal, stand-alone, hierarchical organizations, doctrines, and strategies as in past efforts, for instance, to build centralized movements along Leninist lines. Hence for example, netwar is about Zapatistas more than the Fidelistas, Hamas more than the Palestine Liberation Organization (PLO), and about the Asian Triads more than the Cosa Nostra.

Reference to *netwar* is meant to call attention to the prospect that network-based conflict and crime have now already become a major phenomenon–and will continue to be in the decades ahead. Various actors across the conflict and crime spectrum already evolve in this direction. This includes familiar adversaries who are modifying their

---

[144] John Arquilla, and David Ronfeldt, *The Advert of Netwar*, RAND, MR-789-OSD, Santa Monica, CA, 1996. The netwar concept treated here should not be confused with the U.S. military's network warfare simulation (NETWARS) system.

structures and strategies to take advantage of networked designs such as transnational "terrorist" groups, black-market proliferators of weapons of mass destruction, drug and other crime syndicates, fundamentalist and ethno-nationalist movements, intellectual-property pirates, and immigration and refugee smugglers. Some urban gangs, backcountry militias, as well as militant single-issues groups in the United States have also been developing netwar-like attributes.[145] The netwar spectrum, moreover, covers a new generation of revolutionaries, radicals, and activists that are beginning to create Information Age-ideologies, where identities and loyalties may shift from the nation state to the transnational level of *global civil society*. New actors, such as anarchistic and nihilistic leagues of computer-hacking *cyboteurs*, may also engage in netwar.

A grand majority of netwar actors will be nonstate, and perhaps even stateless. While some may be state agents, other may try to turn states into *their* agents. A netwar actor may also be both subnational and transnational in scope. Certain actors may threaten or target the interest of a given country, while certain others may address a completely different sort of targets. Some may aim at destruction; others may aim mainly at disruption and disorientation. In brief, many variations are possible.

In an archetypal netwar, the protagonists are likely to amount to a set of diverse, dispersed "modes" that share a set of ideas and interests and array to act in a fully internetted "all-channel" manner. Networks, as pointed out by Evan,[146] come in basically three types or topologies:

---

[145] *Networks and Netwars: The Future of Terror, Crime and Militancy*, 2001, p. 6.

[146] William M. Evan, "An Organization-Set Model of Interorganizational Relations," in Matthew Tuite, Roger Chisholm, and Michael Radnor (eds.), *Interorganizational Decision Making,* Chicago: Aldine Publishing Company, 1972, pp. 181-200.

- The *Chain* or line network (Illustration 2.4.), as in a smuggling chain where people, goods, or information move along a line of separated contacts, and where end-to-end communication must travel through the intermediate nodes.

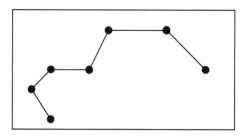

Illustration 2. 3. Chain network

- The *Hub*, star, or wheel network (Illustration 2.5.), as in a franchise of a cartel where a set of actors are tied to a central (but not hierarchical) node or actor, and must go through that node to communicate and coordinate with each other.

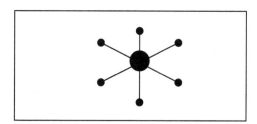

Illustration 2. 4. Hub network

- The *All-channel* or full-matrix network (Illustration 2.6.), as in a collaborative network of militant peace groups where everybody else connects everybody.

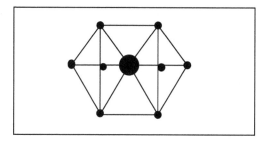

Illustration 2. 5. All-Channel network

In the diagrams, each node may refer to an individual, a group, an organization, part of a group organization, or even a state. The nodes may be large or small, tightly or loosely coupled, inclusive or exclusive in membership. They may be segmented or specialized, that is, they may look alike and engage in similar activities, or they may undertake a division of labor based on specialization. The network boundaries, or that of any node included in it, may be well defined, or simply blurred in relation to the outside environment. Once again, may variations prevail.

Furthermore, each type may be suited to different conditions and purposes, and all three may be found among netwar-related adversaries. For instance, consider the chain in smuggling operations, the hub at the core of "terrorist" and criminal syndicates, and the all-channel type among militant groups that are highly internetted and decentralized. Hybrids of the three various types may also exist, with different tasks being organized around different network types. A netwar actor may, for example, have an all-channel council or directorate at its core but uses hubs and chains for tactical operations.

Of the three network types, the all-channel has been the most difficult to organize and sustain, partly because it may demand dense communications. Yet, it is the type that gives the network form its new, high potential for collaborative undertakings and is quickly gaining new strength from the Information Revolution. The network as a whole (and not necessarily each individual node) has little to no hierarchy. In other words, there may be multiple leaders, as decision-making and operations are decentralized–allowing for local initiatives and autonomy.

Accordingly, the capacity of any activism to ensure effective performance may depend *over time* on the existence of shared principles, interests, and goals (even doctrine or ideology), which span all nodes and to which the members involved subscribe profoundly. Such a set of principles, framed through mutual consultation and consensus building, enables member to be 'all of one common mind' even if they are dispersed and devoted to different tasks. Providing a basis for operational coherence that allows for tactical decentralization, the all-channel network may as well outline boundaries and set guidelines for decisions and actions so that the members do not have (or need) to resort to a hierarchy since "they know what they have to do."

In an attempt to develop a matrix that helps policymakers identify the threat militant (or "terrorist") groups may pose, to assess how they adapt and change, as well as to identify such groups' vulnerabilities, Cragin and Daly[147] outline in Table 2.5. a number of factors that influence such groups' capabilities:

Organizational Tools	Operational Tools
Ideology	Command and Control
Leadership	Weapons
Recruitment Tools	Operational Space
Publicity	Training
	Intelligence
	Technical expertise and specialists
	External weapons sources
	Sanctuary
	Money
	Deception Skills

Table 2. 5. Capabilities influencing militant groups (Source: Cragin & Daly, 2004)

In another important feature, the network design may depend on having an infrastructure for the dense communication of functional information. This notion does not imply that all nodes must be in constant communication–since it would make no sense for safeguarding secrecy. But when communication is indeed needed, the members of the network should be able to disseminate information promptly and as broadly as desired, both within the network and to outside audiences.

Finally, it is essential to remind that netwar is a result of the rise of network organization forms, which in turn is partly a result of the computerized Information Revolution. To realize potential effectiveness, a fully interconnected network requires a capacity for constant, dense information and communication flows (much more than does other forms of organization, such as hierarchies). This capacity is facilitated by the

---

[147] Kim Cragin and Sara A. Daly, *The Dynamic Terrorist Threat: An Assessment of Group Motivations and Capabilities in a Changing World,* RAND, Santa Monica, CA, 2004, p. xiv.

availability of the latest ICTs–cellular telephones, facsimile machines, electronic mail, Web sites, computer conferencing, and Internet chatting platforms. Quite obviously, such technologies are highly advantageous for netwar actors whose constituents are geographically dispersed.

Despite that, two concluding observations remain in order. First of all, the new technologies, however empowering they may be for organizational networking, are not absolutely necessary for a netwar actor. Older technologies and means, like human couriers, and mixes of old and new systems may do the job in certain situations. Consider, for example, how the late Somali warlord Mohammed Farah Aidid proved adept at eluding those seeking to capture him while at the same time retaining full command and control over his forces by means of runners and drum codes.[148] Similarly, the first Chechen War of 1994-1996 had the Islamic forces make wide use of runners and old communications technologies such as ham radios for battle management along with other command and control functions.[149] Osama Bin Laden is on the run–avoiding all interceptable means of communications. Hence, netwar may be waged in *high-tech, low-tech,* or *no-tech* fashion.

Second of all, netwar is not simply a function of "the Net" (the Internet). It does not take place only in the realm of "cyberspace" or in the "infosphere." While some battles may occur there, a war's overall conduct and outcome will normally depend to a greater extent on what happens on ground, that is, in "the real world." Just as cyberwar is not merely about "strategic information warfare," netwar is not solely about Internet war. The Americans have a tendency to view modern conflict as being more about technology than organization and doctrine. This assumption, emphasize Arquilla and Ronfeldt, is "a misleading tendency."[150]

---

[148] Read: Mark Bowden, *Blackhawk Down: A Story of Modern War*, New York Atlantic Monthly Press, 1999.

[149] John Arquilla and Theodore Karasik, "Chechnya: A Glimpse of Future Conflict?" *Studies in Conflict and Terrorism,* Vol. 22, no.3, July–September 1999, pp. 207-30.

[150] *Networks and Netwars: The Future of Terror, Crime and Militancy,* 2001, p. 11.

II.III.III.I. Challenges for Counternetwar in the Information Age

The following observations and examples aim to outline implications for netwar and counternetwar as the Information Revolution goes on, and as the scope and volume of networks and netwars expand.

- *Hierarchies have a difficult time combating networks:* Examples to this observation prevail across the conflict spectrum. Consider the failings of many governments to defeat transnational criminal cartels engaged in drug smuggling, like in Colombia. In Algeria, the persistence of religious revivalist movements in the face of unremitting state opposition shows both the defensive and offensive robustness of the network form. In Mexico, the Zapatista movement, along with its supporters and sympathizers among local and transnational NGOs, illustrate how "social network can put a democratizing autocracy on the defensive and pressure it to continue adopting reforms."[151]

- *It takes networks to combat networks:* Governments seeking to defend themselves against netwars may have to adopt organizational designs and strategies similar to those of their adversaries. This does not mean, in fact, mirroring the adversary, but rather learning how to draw on the same design principles that the adversary has already acquired about the rise of network forms in the Information Age. While such principles depend to a certain extent on technological innovation, they also essentially depend on a willingness to innovate organizationally and doctrinally, and even perhaps by structuring new mechanisms for interagency and multi-jurisdictional cooperation.

- *Whoever masters the network form first and best gains major advantages:* In the early stages of the Information Age, adversaries who are advanced at networking (whether they are criminal, peaceful, social activists, or even those acting in concert with states) enjoy an increase in their power relative to state agencies. At a time networking once allowed them to simply keep away from being suppressed, it now allows them to compete on more nearly equal terms with states and other hierarchically-oriented actors. The histories of Hamas and of the Cali cartel illustrate this, as does the Zapatista movement in Mexico.

Counternetwar may therefore require effective interagency approaches, which by nature involve networked structures. Obviously, it is not necessary, desirable, or even

---

[151] *Networks and Netwars: The Future of Terror, Crime and Militancy,* 2001, p. 15.

possible to replace all hierarchies with networks in governments. Even better would be to blend these two forms skillfully, while retaining enough core authority to encourage and enforce adherence to networked processes. With the creation of effective hybrids, governments may become better prepared to confront the new threats and present emerging challenges, whether generated by ethno-nationalists, militias, criminals, or other actors.

Yet, Arquilla and Ronfeldt conclude governments tend to be so constrained by hierarchical habits and institutional interests that it may take some sharp reverses before a willingness to experiment more seriously with networking emerges. "The costs and risks associated with failing to engage in institutional redesign are likely to be high–and may grow even higher over time."[152] Although steps to improve intra- and international networking are being achieved, far more remains to be done, as acting networks continuously reshape themselves into more difficult targets.

In line with counternetwar initiatives at the state level, reference is here made to the Wassenaar Arrangement (WA), considered as the first global multilateral arrangement on export controls for conventional weapons and sensitive dual-use goods and technologies. With its headquarters and secretariat in Vienna, the WA received final approval by 33 co-founding countries in July 1996 and began functions in September that year.

The WA is designed to promote transparency, exchange views and information and greater responsibility in transfers of conventional arms and dual-use goods and technologies, and hence, prevent destabilizing accumulations. It intends to complement and reinforce, without duplication, the existing regimes for non-proliferation of weapons of mass destruction and their delivery systems. It does so by focusing on the threats to international and regional peace and security, which may eventually arise from transfers of armaments and sensitive dual-use goods and technologies where the risks are judged greatest. This arrangement also seeks to enhance cooperation to prevent the acquisition of armaments and sensitive dual-use items for military end-users, if the

---

[152] *Networks and Netwars: The Future of Terror, Crime and Militancy,* 2001, p. 16.

situation in a region or the behavior of a state is, or becomes, a cause for serious concern to the participating states.

II.III.III.II. Intellectual Wars

With *information* emerging as the world's most valuable currency, owners are asserting, and winning more control than ever before over how *ideas* are used, sold and consumed–in what may be referred to as *idea wars*.

Proponents acknowledge the rise of an era of "intellectual capitalism," regarded as the latest phase in the evolution of the post-industrial economy. Here, in the "knowledge economy," ideas become "the product." Yet critics warn that, far from promoting innovation, the United States "is in the midst of an information-age enclosure movement comparable to the fencing off of public grazing lands at the dawn of the Industrial Revolution."[153] Building on the ideas of others, a fundamental part of creativity, is much harder when a license must be negotiated to use any existing sliver of innovation. Critics complain "intellectual property rights are regularly trumping social values like free speech or public health."

Developing countries such as Brazil and India argue that America's devotion to the sanctity of patents puts drugs for AIDS and other diseases beyond the reach of the poor and costs millions of lives. They point to Washington's hypocrisy in October 2001 when it considered revoking Bayer's patent on the anthrax-fighting drug "Cipro" because the American's themselves seemed at risk. All of a sudden, the American stance that without patent protection there would be no drugs seemed hollow.

Several questions and concerns over innovation and idea property (ranging from Internet services to scientific research to movie characters) are raised. For instance, whether or not *one* corporation should have control over a lifesaving innovation; if anyone would develop new products and technologies without being guaranteed a

---

[153] Amy Harmon, "Suddenly, 'Idea Wars' Take On a New Global Urgency," *The New York Times*, online edition, November 11, 2001.

temporary monopoly on their use; and to what extent can strong protection impede innovation?

During the 1990s, the drug, entertainment and technology industries lobbied hard to erect the strictest protections for intellectual property rights in American history. The effective duration of patents for drugs, for example, has in some cases almost doubled to 16 years. Copyrights on creative works can as well now stretch 95 years–*thanks to* or *because of* the lobbying by companies like Walt Disney, which strived to keep the legend-old Mickey Mouse from slipping into public domain alongside the works of Shakespeare and Victor Hugo.

While patents and copyrights are indeed booming, consulting companies like InteCap Inc., which help corporations develop intellectual property strategies, are also in high demand. Entertainment companies hire technology firms to track people who are illegally trading copyrighted music and movies over the Internet. In counterattack, "Bounty quest," based in Boston, lets a customer offer a reward on its Web site in exchange for proof that an invention was publicly available before a patent was issued. In return, such information can be used to invalidate a patent in court. The company collects commissions for its services.

Established in 1790, the U.S. Patent and Trademark Office is tailored to the industry needs of products requiring years of work and large capital investment-manufacturing in the 19th and 20th centuries, or in the pharmaceutical industry today. Though proponents claim tighter protections on intellectual property stimulate creativity and innovation, Harmon (2001) reports that in a study of 150 years of patent policies in 60 countries "no evidence was found proving that increased patent protection in developing countries led to increased innovation among domestic companies."

II.III.IV. <u>Conflict Resolution in the Information Age</u>

The Information Age sharpens the "lose-lose" logic of conflict. As the spread of knowledge tends to equalize power, on the one hand, and with destructive weaponry becoming increasingly accessible, on the other, it is now therefore harder to win a dispute in a decisive and enduring fashion.

The logic of "no-one wins" was clearest during the Cold War. The United States and the Soviet Union spent billions and billions of dollars trying to find a way to make a nuclear war winnable, as they came up with weapon system after weapon system, doctrine after doctrine, and from decapitation to first strike. Each weapon and doctrine was designed to make it credible that nuclear weapons could be used to win a war. Some of the best scientific minds of a generation tried to solve this puzzle–to no avail. Over time, what did become clearer was that a nuclear war would bring only losers.

Even smaller wars have proven hard to win for the mighty nations on earth. The Vietnam War became a tough lesson for the United States (as does the American invasion in Iraq–up to this writing), and so did the war in Afghanistan for the Soviet Union. The spread of advanced weaponry, and new ideas of freedom and self-determination, both fruits of the Information Age, have made it more costly to impose control over others. Statistically speaking, the ratio of civilian to military casualties in war in 1900 ranged from 10 to 50%. The current average figure is over 90%.[154] As seen on television, they are mostly the innocent who die–elderly shoppers in the marketplace, young children playing in the streets, and women squeezed in corners in their houses with their babies. Delpech notions that the major countries are, for various reasons, too occupied themselves to look after world security.[155] Everyone in the world is therefore vulnerable. Where the old law of "An eye for an eye" is now out of place, the present realization is, as voiced by Mahatma Gandhi, "An eye for an eye and we all go blind."

Nevertheless, despite all the signs of insecurity all over the globe and though conflict is as old as mankind and civilization, there are still rays of hope for peace. First, in contrast to widely shared expectation during the forty years of the Cold War, the conflict between the United States and the Soviet Union never did erupt into a thermonuclear catastrophe. Although the superpowers went to the brink of war with each other on more than one occasion (such as during the Cuban missile crisis), they

---

[154] William Ury, *Getting to Peace,* 1999, p. 88.

[155] Thérèse Delpech, *Politique du chaos: l'autre face de la mondialisation,* ('The Politics of Chaos: The Other Side of Globalization'), Paris: édition du Seuil, 2002, p. 56.

both wisely refrained from using the ultimate weapon. In fact, not one of the tens of thousands of atomic weapons deployed around the world has been used in war ever since Hiroshima. Interestingly, wherever nations in conflict have developed nuclear weapons, their tendency to go to war has diminished rather than increased. Consider, for instance, the standoff between China and the Soviet Union, between China and India, between India and Pakistan, and between the countries in dispute in the Middle East.

Second, since 1945 there has been no war among the major powers. They have fought wars and proxy wars, but not directly with one another. Accordingly, the current period of peace among the world's major powers is the longest known in recorded history. The *state* and *war* are no longer synonymous. Nearly all current conflicts are taking place within states or former states that have recently broken up, or are either internal or civil wars among the poorer states of the Third World. Finally, war is eventually losing its legitimacy. Among the impacts of globalization on conflicts is "the internationalization of conflict resolution. Military interventions are now authorized by international organizations rather than by a unilateral decision. Even major powers that used to intervene unilaterally in their sphere of influence seek for a formal legitimacy."[156] The larger international community is now beginning to see *aggression* as what it has always been: acts of murder, rape, and theft. Expressed by an old French Legionnaire, a veteran of the Dien Bein Phu battle, "There is no such thing as a war crime. War itself is a crime."[157]

On what the Bush administration should do to prevent attacks like the ones that struck New York and Washington on September 11, Noam Chomsky writes:[158]

> ...We know quite well how the problem should be addressed, if we want to reduce the threat rather than escalate it. When IRA bombs were set off in London, there was no call to bomb West Belfast, or Boston, the source of much of the financial support for the IRA. Rather, steps were taken to apprehend the criminals, and efforts were made to deal with what lay behind the resort to terror. When a federal building was blown up in Oklahoma City, there were calls for bombing the Middle East, and it probably would have happened if the source turned out to be there. When

---

[156] *Mastering Violence: An Option for Operational Military Strategy,* (*op. cit.*, 1998), p. 8.

[157] Quoted in Bruce Chatwin, *The Songlines,* New York: Penguin Books, 1988.

[158] Noam Chomsky, *9-11*, New York: Seven Stories Press, 2001, pp. 23-24.

it was found to be domestic, with links to the ultra-right militias, there was no call to obliterate Montana and Idaho. Rather there was a search for the perpetrator, who was found, brought to court, and sentenced, and there were efforts to understand the grievances that lie behind such crimes and to address the problems. Just about every crime–whether a robbery in the streets or colossal atrocities–has reasons, and commonly we find that some of them are serious and should be addressed.

There are proper and lawful ways to proceed in the case of crimes, whatever their scale.

Peace does not require great prosperity. The little country of Costa Rica (not rich despite its name), to illustrate, enjoys a record of both internal and external peace during the last half of the 20th century that any of the rich nations may envy. The Costa Ricans achieved such a record by eliminating their army and using their resources instead for health, education, and development. In terms of mediation–though not everyone concludes successfully–statistics reveal roughly three-quarters of all *civil cases* that go through mediation end up with a settlement. As for *international disputes*, the proportion of successful attempts is lower but still substantial–with more then four out of ten.[159] While parties going into mediation are more open to agreement than those who refuse it altogether, the success rate is indeed encouraging.

It is worth recalling that peacekeeping operations were not provided for by the Charter of the United Nations, but rather emerged and developed over time in response to specific conflict situations. Initially considered as crisis control mechanisms, the early rationale of peacekeeping operations was that they would prevent escalation from regional conflict to super-power confrontation during the Cold War era. It was, thus, accordingly possible to assure Security Council consensus for activating Chapter VII enforcement measures. The end of the Cold War led to the emergence of a complex, multidimensional peacekeeping concept, which has eventually become characteristic as of the 1990s.[160]

---

[159] William Ury, *Getting to Peace*, 1999, p. 145. Statistics on the success rate of mediation of civil cases are available in: Jeanne M. Brett, Zoe. I. Barsness, and Stephen B. Goldberg, "The Effectiveness of Mediation: An Independent Analysis of Cases Handled by Four Major Service Providers," *Negotiation Journal,* 12:3, July 1996, Blackwell Publishing, 259-70.

[160] Refer to: Judith Large, "The evolution of peacekeeping," International Relations and Security Network (ISN), Center for Security Studies (CSS), Swiss Federal Institute of Technology, Zurich, at: http://www.isn.ch/news/dossier/peace_ops/editorial.

Nevertheless, there avails a contested debate about intervention for 'humanitarian' or for 'human protection' purposes. Throughout the 1990s, the concern for local security conditions became significant, as the role of regional actors and organs turned to be increasingly prominent. Furthermore, leading humanitarian actors face risks when intervening, as both aid and relief are politicized. The absence of clear, proportional, and accepted peacekeeping arrangements renders the perception of restabilization and reconstruction efforts a political exercise merely satisfying external interests, instead of actually addressing and responding to local necessities.

Proved in the Iraq case after the U.S. invasion in March 2003, prominent humanitarian organizations, such as the ICRC and MSF, face uneasy compromised positions that affect further engagements. In addition, resorting to private security forces and sub-contracting protection elements are even more complicated factors when addressing security demands. This has drawn back the debate on the merits and desirability of coordinated links and cooperation between the humanitarian and development communities, military forces, and peacekeeping actors.

To conclude, William Ury illustrates an interesting and useful guide to any conflict resolution. The strategy is to catch conflict as early as possible before it escalates. After all, conflict does not come out of nowhere but typically proceeds from latent tension, develops into an overt conflict, erupts into a power struggle, and then from there crosses the threshold of destructive conflict and violence. The aim, as third siders, is not to suppress conflict altogether but simply to keep the trajectory of escalation below the threshold.

Respectively, there are at least three major opportunities to channel the conflict's vertical momentum, leading destructive struggle to horizontal impulse, then to constructive change. The first is to 'prevent' destructive conflict from emerging in the first place by addressing latent tensions. The second is to 'resolve' any overt conflicts that do emerge. The third is to 'contain' any escalating power struggles that temporarily escape resolution. What is not prevented is resolved; and what is not resolved is contained. That is: *Contain if necessary, resolve if possible, best of all prevent* (Ury, 1999, p. 113).

II.IV. Implications of U.S. Unilateralism in Global Affairs

With increasing concerns on the role of the United States in contemporary global affairs, perceived with differing views, the following analysis seeks to point out the approach by which that country is conducting itself as it enters the 21st century. The presentation also intends to determine whether or not the United States is, at the current stage, in a position to lead other countries, not by force–but rather through the concept of soft power.

II.IV.I. Signaling the U.S. Unilateral Approach

Power, recalled once again here, is the ability to effect the outcomes desired, and if necessary, to change the behavior of others to make that happen. This ability is often associated with the possession of certain factors such as population, territory, natural resources, economic strength, military force, and political stability.

Traditionally, the test of a great power was "strength for war,"[161] when war determined the course of international politics. As technologies evolved over the centuries, the sources of power also changed. During the 17th and 18th century agrarian economies of Europe, populations proved vital power resources since they provided bases for taxes and for the infantry recruitment (mostly mercenaries). This combination of *men* and *money* accordingly gave France the lead. In the 19th century, however, the growing importance of industry benefited first Britain (with its unbeatable navy), and then Germany (with its efficient administration and railways to move armies for rapid victories). In the mid 20th century, with the rise of the nuclear age the United States and the Soviet Union possessed both industrial might and nuclear arsenals of intercontinental reach.

---

[161] A.J. Taylor, *The Struggle for Mastery in Europe, 1848-1918*, Oxford: Oxford University Press, 1954, p. xxix.

The foundations of power today, stresses Joseph S. Nye,[162] "have been moving away from the emphasis on military force and conquest." Paradoxically, one of the causes (as mentioned earlier) was nuclear weapon because of its too-destructive potential. Another considerable development is the rise of nationalism, which makes it even more difficult for empires to rule over weakened nations. For example in the 19th century, most of Africa was conquered with a handful of soldiers, while Britain ruled whole India with a colonial force that was a tiny fraction of the indigenous population. As the Cold War rivals discovered in Vietnam, Afghanistan and more recently in Iraq, colonial rule is not only widely condemned but also tremendously too costly. A third significant cause has been societal change within great powers, deriving the notion that post-industrial societies are focused on welfare rather than on glory. In other words, such societies detest high casualties–unless survival is in the question, and where the use of force requires an elaborate moral justification to ensure popular support above all.

In the Information Age, the relative importance of soft power is increasing, partly because it stems from credibility. Countries that are likely to gain soft power are those whose culture concepts and ideas are closer to prevailing global norms (that now focus on liberalism, pluralism, and autonomy). Others that may also gain are those with the utmost access to communication channels (and hence exercise more influence over how issues are framed), as well as those whose credibility is enhanced by domestic and international performance.[163]

Back in history, among the practices of soft power was the creation of *l'Alliance Française* in 1883, when the French government sought to promote its language and literature after the Franco-Prussian War. Eventually, the projection of French culture aboard has become a significant component of French diplomacy. Italy, Germany, and later the United States followed suit, as the advent of radio in the 1920s drove many governments to the scope of foreign language broadcasting.

---

[162] Joseph S. Nye, *The Paradox of American Power*, 2002, p. 5.

[163] Joseph S. Nye, *The Paradox of American Power*, 2002, p. 69.

Concerning American soft power, tensions prevail even within other Western secular cultures. In the mid-1990s, to note, 61% of French surveyed, 45% of Germans, and 32% of Italians perceived American culture as a threat to their own. Majorities in Spain, France, German, and Italy also pointed to too many American-made films and television programs on national television.[164] Not to forget Canada and the European Union (among others) place restrictions on the volume of American content that can be shown. Government policies at home as well as foreign policies that appear arrogant and unilateral in the eyes of others both diminish soft power.

In terms of international affairs,

> The US government has [since 2001] torn up more international treaties and disregarded more UN conventions than the rest of the world has done in 20 years.
>
> It has supported the biological weapons convention while experimenting, illegally, with biological weapons of its own. It has refused to grant chemical weapons inspectors full access to its laboratories, and has destroyed attempts to launch chemical inspections in Iraq. It has ripped up the anti-ballistic missile treaty, and appears to be ready to violate the nuclear test ban treaty. It has permitted CIA hit squads to recommence covert operations of the kind that included, in the past, the assassinations of foreign heads of state. It has sabotaged the small arms treaty, undermined the international criminal court, refused to sign the climate change protocol and, last month, sought to immobilise the UN convention against torture, so that it could keep foreign observers out of its prison camp in Guantanamo Bay. Even its preparedness to go to war with Iraq without a mandate from the UN Security Council is a defiance of international law far graver than Saddam Hussein's non-compliance with UN weapons inspections.[165]

American conservative lawmakers threatened the White House to hold the release of $582 million in back dues to the United Nations (as part of the roughly $1 billion in U.S. arrears) unless it is approved together with the American Service Member's Protection Act. At a time the American administration was trying to convince the world it is not pursuing a unilateral or isolationist approach to foreign affairs, that legislation

---

[164] United States Information Agency Office of Research, "European Opinion Alert," March 16, 1994, and May 27, 1994.

[165] George Monboit, "America's doormat," *The Guardian*, August 6, 2002, 7.

aimed at exempting Americans from the International Criminal Court (ICC). The legislation would:

> cut off U.S. military assistance to any non-NATO country that ratified the international-court treaty. It would also prohibit U.S. troops from serving in any UN peacekeeping forces unless the Security Council gives American soldiers immunity from the international court's jurisdiction. And it would authorize the president to use military force to free U.S. or allied service members held for prosecution by the court.[166]

Furthermore, in November 2001 U.S. President George W. Bush signed the military order that would allow for the trial of *non-U.S. citizens* accused of terrorism by a special military commission instead of civilian courts. Military commissions are supposed to be easier in protecting the sources and methods of investigators in military proceedings. A military trial can also be held overseas, and can sit at any time and at any place. Conviction would simply require agreement by two-thirds of the panel members.[167]

In respect of that military order, Barbara Olshansky of the Center for Constitutional Rights (in New York) states the following:

> With a single swipe of his pen, President Bush replaced the democratic pillars of our legal system with that of a military commission system in which he, or his designee, is rule-maker, investigator, accuser, prosecutor, judge, jury, sentencing court, reviewing court, and jailer or executioner. This new system radically abandons the core constitutional guarantees at the heart of American democracy: the right to an independent judiciary, trial by jury, public proceedings, due process, and appeals to higher courts. In the newly authorized military tribunal system, all of these safeguards against injustice are gone.[168]

---

[166] Steven Mufson and Alian Sipress, "U.S. Foes of World Court Play Tough," *IHT*, August 17, 2001, 1.

[167] "Military Order: Detention, Treatment, and Trial of Certain Non-Citizens in the War Against Terrorism," the White House, Office of the Press Secretary, November 13, 2001.

[168] Barbara Olshansky, *Secret Trials and Executions: Military Tribunals and the Threat to Democracy*, New York: Seven Stories Press, 2002, pp. 7-8.

In addition, Amnesty International stated that the operating guidelines for trials by an executive military commission, issued by the U.S. Secretary of Defense in March 2002, "have thrown into stark relief the fundamental defects of the Military orders." It outlined the following fundamental flaws included:

- The Military Order is *discriminatory*. American nationals will not be tried by military commission, even if accused of the same offence as a foreign national, but rather tried by ordinary civilian courts with a broad range of fair trial protections.

- The commissions would allow a *lower standard of evidence* than is admissible in ordinary courts, including hearsay evidence. Such a deficiency is particularly troubling given the lack of due safeguards during interrogation and the fact that the commissions will have the power to hand down death sentences.

- In violation of international law, there will be *no right of appeal* to an independent and impartial court established by law. Instead, there would be a review by a three-member panel appointed by the Secretary of Defense.

- The military commissions would entirely *lack independence* from the executive. The President has given himself or the Secretary of Defense the power to name who will be tried by the commissions, to appoint or to remove the members of those commissions, to select the panel that will review convictions and sentences, and to make the final decisions in any case.[169]

Last, some American writers do praise this U.S. *imperialist* role in the form of "an empire of democracy and liberty" arguing that "it is not conquering land or establishing colonies, but it has a dominating global presence militarily, economically and culturally."[170] While people label the reference *imperialist* as an insult, such supporters of current American policies in fact encourage the United States to embrace that role even more.

---

[169] Amnesty International, "USA-Military Commissions: Second-class justice," AMR 51/049/2002, March 22, 2002. Amnesty International noted that by the end of the year 2004, a number of 15 detainees were subject to that 2001 Military Order. "Amnesty International Report 2005: the state of the world's human rights," Amnesty International, London, May 25, 2005, p. 269.

[170] Thomas E. Ricks, "U.S. Urged to Embrace An 'Imperialist' Role," *IHT*, August 22, 2001, 1.

Ironically, and before moving on to the wave of anti-Americanism, it is worth reminding that the U.S. government by the end of May 2002 issued new restrictions that bar thousands of blood donors who have lived in or traveled to Britain and Europe. In a move to protect American blood supply from the mad cow disease, and according to the decision, blood banks have to bar donors who:

- have spent 3 or more cumulative months in Britain from 1980 through 1996;
- have spent five cumulative years or more in France from 1980 to the present;
- have received a blood transfusion in Britain since 1980; and,
- as American military personnel or dependents, spent 6 months or more on a base in Northern Europe from 1980 through 1990, and elsewhere in Europe from 1980 through 1996.[171]

II.IV.II. The Wave of Anti-Americanism

In order to identify and better understand the various, and open-ended, aspects of anti-Americanism, five different but major features will be treated: political, economic, religious/historical, cultural, and psychological.[172]

II.IV.II.I. Political

Quite obviously, anti-Americanism represents a reaction to both recent and current U.S. foreign policies. To name some, in 2001 the United State was imposing unilaterally arms trade embargoes on 26 countries.[173] The United States still refuses to support and endorse the Kyoto Protocol on climate change, disputing the scientific evidence and

---

[171] "U.S. Issues Blood Donor Rules," *IHT*, August 28, 2001, 3.

[172] Moisés Naim, editor of *Foreign Policy* magazine, outlines anti-Americanism into five similar 'pure' types. "Anti-Americanism: A Guide to hating Uncle Sam," *Foreign Policy*, online edition, January-February 2002.

[173] List of countries concerned available at: U.S. State Department Office of Defense Trade Controls, Embargo Reference Chart, consulted on October 22, 2001. The list, again consulted in mid August 2004, had then included 21 countries.

insisting the treaty was intolerable because of the damage it would inflict on the American economy. This stance:

> Only compounded world outrage over what is perceived by many as an arrogant superpower that represents only 4 percent of the world's population yet produces about 25 percent of the greenhouse gases, such as carbondioxide, that are raising world temperatures and causing oceans to rise to levels that may inundate many islands within this century. [174]

The United States, as well, has voiced opposition to ratify the International Criminal Court (though the Treaty was initially signed by the Clinton administration). It has opposed the Ottawa Treaty on land mines, already abrogated the Anti-Ballistic Missile Treaty, and has begun constructing a missile defense shield–despite widespread disagreement.

In the Middle East, the country continues to support Israel in an isolated manner on certain issues. Consider, for instance, the "World Conference Against Racism, Racial Discrimination, Xenophobia and Related Tolerance" held in Durban in August 2001 where the United States announced withdrawing from it as a result of the Conference's treatment of Israel. It is recalled here that the United States had not participated in the first two World Racism Conferences in 1978 and in 1983, ostensibly because the Zionism issue had been on the agenda.

One article wrote "there must be a better way to win friends and influence nations than walking out of conferences, denouncing treaties or sitting on your hands while the Middle East burns."[175] Another article concluded:

> at the very least, the Durban walkout shows failures in preparation, negotiation skills, vision and leadership on the part of the Bush administration. At worst, the administration risks lasting damage to

---

[174] William Drozdiak, "President Faces Fury on his Trip to Europe," *IHT*, June 12, 2001, 1.

[175] Jim Hoagland, "Is Bush's America to Be Absent in World Affairs?" *IHT*, September 6, 2001. The walkout decision was said to be the continued presence in the conference documents of language singling out Israel for racist violations of the rights of Palestinians.

international relations during a period when good relations will be more important than ever.[176]

Concerned by the perceived hand-off approach to the mounting Israeli-Palestinian conflict, in August 2001 European governments started initiatives to try to arrange lasting cease-fires in the region (as a shift from U.S. monopoly in peace-making diplomacy). European leaders have also begun publicly complaining Washington needs to do more to tackle the problem, as former foreign minister of France Hubert Védrine accused the American administration of acting like "Pontius Pilate" in seeking to remain aloof from the crisis. France and other European countries, Mr. Védrine said, expected Washington to move away from a "wait and see" attitude and play a leading role in resolving a crisis with global implications.

As a consequence of some of the above American practices along with others in respect of human rights (such as rendering AIDS drug available to all in need), the United States suffered a highly publicized defeat when it failed in May 2001 to win one of the three seats allocated to Western countries on the UN Human Rights Commission for the first time since it was established in 1947. The seats went instead to three members of the European Union: France, Austria and Sweden. The defeat also came during the same week the American candidate was defeated in his effort to win re-election to a seat on the International Narcotics Control Board. There once again, three EU members were elected: France, Austria and the Netherlands. "There is little question that the distance between the United States and its NATO allies has grown in the last decade. The European press shows its displeasure in a steady stream of articles highly critical of the United States and the *American way.*"[177] Illustration 2.6. is one example.

---

[176] Chip Pitts, "Walking Out of an Ambitions Conference Like Spoiled Children," *IHT*, September 6, 2001, 6.

[177] Jeane Kirkpartick, "European Allies Are Behind US Defeat at the United Nations," *IHT*, May 9, 2001, 8.

Illustration 2. 6. Bush's Wild Wild West Rhetoric

Immediately after the September 11 attacks, the world watched President Bush move from the quiet language of grief to the rowdy colloquialisms of the *Old West*: The United States wants Osama Bin Laden *dead or alive.* The country will go after those *folks* if it has to *smoke them out and get them running.* And they are *evil-doers, those barbaric people.* (See: Elizabeth Bumiller and Frank Bruni, "Unscripted, Bush Shoots From the Lip," *IHT*, September 20, 2001, 1.)

Still in politics, America's public embrace of internationalism has not translated into greater support in Washington for American engagement abroad. This is because what counts most is not how many people stand on each side of an issue but rather how intensely each side holds its position. With the public's commitment to internationalism having ebbed over the past decade, intensity is now crucial to the politics of foreign policy. In "The New Apathy: How an Uninterested Public Is Reshaping Foreign Policy," James Lindsay writes the following on the scope of awareness reflected by the American public in foreign affairs:

> During the Cold War, foreign affairs almost always topped the country's political agenda. Gallup regularly found that 10 to 20 percent– and sometimes even more–of those polled named a foreign policy issue as the most important problem facing the United States. But today most Americans dismiss foreign policy as relatively unimportant. Only two to three percent name foreign policy concerns as the most important problem facing the country, and Americans have trouble identifying foreign issues that concern them. When the Chicago Council on Foreign Relations asked people in 1998 to name the "two or three biggest foreign policy problems facing the United States today," the most common response by far, at 21 percent, was "don't know."
>
> The "don't know"s predominate because fewer Americans follow foreign affairs. In February 1999, as the Rambouillet summit convened, Pew [Research Center] found that only one in nine Americans said they followed news about Kosovo "very closely."
>
> Americans ignore much of what happens overseas because they see little at stake. In September 1997, Pew asked 2,000 Americans how much impact other parts of the world had on the United States. Solid majorities answered "very little," even when asked about America's allies. (About 60 percent said that western Europe had little or no impact on their lives).
>
> These polls numbers all jibe with what people at both ends of Pennsylvania Avenue know firsthand: Americans endorse internationalism in theory but seldom do anything about it in practice. Americans approach foreign policy the way they approach physical fitness–they understand the benefits of being in good shape, but they still avoid exercise.[178]

The idea Americans were less and less interested in global news took hold for several years and had resulted in reduced levels of international news in and on American media. With the exception of perhaps CNN, American television networks had essentially abandoned such coverage. Readers of *The New York Times*, *The Washington Post*, *Los Angeles Times*, *USA Today*, *The Wall Street Journal*, along with a handful of smaller newspapers are fortunate these publications bear the high costs of maintaining large staffs of correspondents abroad who are able to bring sophisticated and in-depth reporting of global events to their readers. With that said, it is still too

---

[178] James M. Lindsay, "The New Apathy: How an Uninterested Public Is Reshaping Foreign Policy," *Foreign Affairs*, Vol. 79, no. 5, September-October 2000, 3-4 (New York: Council on Foreign Relations).

early to assess how the September 11 events, the war on Afghanistan, and the invasion in Iraq have influenced the American public in terms of foreign policy.

One last remark is worth emphasizing, which has evoked increasing anti-Americanism all over the world. In selecting Iraq as the next target in its "War on Terror," the Bush administration *sought* to redefine the war in more conventional terms–as a confrontation between nation-states–as it buys more time for a covert war it must wage.

The fundamental problem with the war on Al Qaida is that it is invisible. It is a covert war against, at most, a few thousand individuals who are both scattered throughout the world and highly mobile. It is also a war of inferences, lies and, ultimately, confusion. It is also a war of contemplation rather than a war of action, where intelligence analysts on both sides try to determine what the other side knows and when it knew it. In a war of sudden, unpredictable actions often undetectable by the other side, it is also a war invisible to the media and, thus, to the public at large.

Furthermore, in selecting Iraq as the second phase,[179] the Bush administration *sought* to keep united and shape the vague alliances into a war-fighting coalition instead of a debating society. The United States' allies, particularly in Europe, do not understand nor accept American thinking in this respect.[180] They see the September 11 attacks, the threat of future attacks and the strange war upon which the United States has embarked are merely one strand in the course of international relations. Life goes on, with the normal protocols of a peacetime relationship in place. Yet, the United States sees an existing extraordinary and unprecedented state of emergence where the most fundamental American interests are at stake. For the Americans, the normal state of affairs has been suspended.

---

[179] It is also recalled here that the second Bush administration had unfinished business to settle in Iraq, namely, to topple Saddam Hussein; Noting that 79 of George W. Bush's initial 189 appointees had also served in his father's administration. Refer to: Graydom Carter, "Bush by numbers: Four years of double standards," *The Independent*, online edition, September 3, 2004.

[180] Compare in this regard, for example, the number of countries and the nature of their contribution in the U.S.-led war on Afghanistan in 'Operation Enduring Freedom' (in late 2001), with those which took part in the 'Coalition of the Willing' against Iraq (in 2003).

Accordingly, while the Europeans stress saying: "Surely you don't expect us to simply rubber-stamp your decisions and actions?", the Americans answer by saying: "Surely you don't expect us to spend our time trying to convince you to stand by us?"

II.IV.II.II. Economic

U.S. international economic policies are also being unappreciated, whether in concern of trade policies that limit imports from poor countries, or the *exploitation* of the international institutions such as the IMF and the World Bank to advance American interests. For example, recall when the United States threatened not to release foreign aid to Yugoslavia unless former president Slobodan Milosevic was handed over. In addition, the United States imposes unilateral economic sanctions on Cuba, Libya, Iran, Syria, and other *states of concern.*

The economies of the United States and Europe may seem to be "so deeply intertwined." According to co-chairman of the Trans-Atlantic Business Dialogue,[181] "nearly 60 percent of all American foreign corporate assets are located in Europe, while Europe provides nearly 75 percent of all foreign investment in the United States." Moreover, "Americans consume a quarter of total EU exports, while the United States sends a third of its total exports to Europe. More than 13 million Americans and Europeans are employed by local affiliates of EU and U.S. parent companies."

However, interdependence does not mean the United States and Europe are enjoying a long-lasting honeymoon when it comes to trade policies. Several issues of disputes prevail which rage concern by both sides. Among the standing issues included the banana dispute (since 1993 and resolved in April 2001) where the European Union's import quota system favored to benefit growers in former European colonies. Concerning food production, the European Union has set new standards requiring American companies to put on all products made from engineered material a label noting 'genetically modified organisms,' and to document all their ingredient sources. Since the American crop-handling system generally does not separate modified and

---

[181] Niall Fitzgerald, Co-Chairman of the Trans-Atlantic Business Dialogue, "U.S.-EU trade: Dismantling barriers across the Atlantic," *IHT*, online edition, July 8, 2004.

conventional crops, the new requirements could cost American companies up to $4 billion a year. This step stems from European anxiety about food safety that is far more profound than in the United States, the world leader in agricultural biotechnology. That particular issue is not limited only to the European Union, as the governments of Saudi Arabia and Sri Lanka have also proposed bans on importing genetically modified foods, at a time Mexican legislators discuss tough labeling laws.[182] Furthermore, the European Union continues to ban the use of growth promoting hormones for meat production.

On foreign sales corporation, the WTO ruled in August 2002 that the European Union could impose $4 billion worth of sanctions as counter measures against U.S. tax breaks for its exporters that are deemed to constitute an illegal export subsidy. WTO panels have repeatedly ruled that the U.S. tax breaks for exporters contravene international trade rules. Regarding online taxation, and under current EU rules, companies based outside the European Union do not have to charge European customers value added tax (VAT) on services supplied by electronic means, whilst companies based within the EU do have to. In the Internet Age, this arrangement has become a competitive disadvantage for EU companies. The EU position stems from addressing this competitive disadvantage. As the EU position has consequences for non-EU (such as U.S.) companies, the EU online taxation issue has taken an international dimension.[183]

Another problem is the steel industry. The European Union believes the United States is trying to shift the cost of restructuring its steel industry onto the rest of the world by introducing restrictions on steel imports. The American steel industry, itself backed by the U.S. government and congress, sees its current problem as being the result of cheap imports that are themselves a product of unfair trade practices.

Last, in aircraft production, the European Union has threatened to block U.S. airlines from flying to Europe with hush kits fitted on their engines, claiming they do not meet new environmental standards on noise reduction (the United States sees these measures as discriminating). Both the European Union and the United States are also

---

[182] Alan Sipress and Mare Kaufmang "U.S. Presses EU to Drop Restrictions on Genetically Modified Foods," *IHT*, August 27, 2001, 5.

[183] The United States is opposed to EU proposals for VAT on electronically delivered services, stating this means EU rules would have effects in American jurisdiction.

being accused (by each other) of providing financial government support and subsidies–contrary to trade and commercial terms–to Airbus and Boeing respectively.

II.IV.II.III. Religious/Historical

In the past few years anti-Americanism has increased steeply, in a wave most virulently expressed by Muslims all over the globe.

Muslims were outraged when President George W. Bush on September 15, 2001 declared "this crusade, this war on terrorism is going to take a while." The President was using–*intentionally or not*–"crusade" in its Western sense of "any vigorous action on behalf of a cause". Yet, Muslims, and particularly Arabs, recognize no such usage. To them, "crusade," even uncapitalized, is a profoundly loaded term. It evokes not just a war against their people, who were hacked apart, man and child, 1000 years ago, until the streets of Al Quds and other cities ran deep in blood. "It evokes an unprovoked war against their religion and their every way of life–a war they see mirrored today in the steady corrosion of Islamic values by a globalizing Western culture they believe undermines their families, trivializes learning and profanes [Allah]."[184] The rhetoric was therefore shifted sharply to "War on Terrorism" (though there is no precise definition of "war," as people speak of *war on poverty, the drug war*, etc).[185]

However, religious anti-Americanism is by no means exclusively Muslim. Moisés Naim notes that Roman Catholic liberation theologists, Greek Orthodox prelates, fundamentalist Jewish rabbis, and U.S. televangelists also deliver scathing condemnations of American society's corrupting immorality–never mind the United States is actually among the more religiously observant of the Western democracies, at least in terms of church attendance and public self-perception.[186]

---

[184] Ken Ringle, "The Crusaders' Giant Footprints: After a Millennium, Their Mark Remains," *The Washington Post*, October 23, 2001, C01.

[185] On coining the expression, 'War on Terrorism,' see: Noam Chomsky, *9-11*, 2001, pp. 14-16.

[186] Moisés Naim, "Anti-Americanism: A Guide to hating Uncle Sam," *Foreign Policy,* Jan.-Feb. 2002.

Historically, anti-Americanism has its roots in past American behavior. Around 50 years of anti-communist struggle created memories and instincts that continue to inspire anti-American feelings in former communist countries, and in France and Italy as well, which together hosted millions of communist party members.

In France, anti-Americanism moved in waves throughout the last century, intensifying politically in the 1950s under the twin influences of the French Communist Party and General Charles de Gaulle. Reflecting France's universalistic ambition, De Gaulle had stated that his country would show the world how to "build an industrial civilization which is not derived from the American model and in which man will serve as an end, not a means."[187] That is, the French regard America as the epitome of liberal *Anglo-Saxon* capitalism; and what sets their model apart from the individualist American one, according to them, are the values of equality, community and solidarity.

Moreover, politicians and intellectuals in developing countries have blamed the economic underdevelopment of their countries on the exploitation by rich ones, with particular reference to the United States. One French commented the September 11 attacks were "the revenge of the poor on the rich."[188]

II.IV.II.IV. Cultural

Anti-Americanism is counter-generated by the ability of American culture forces, especially in the Information Age, to influence and often displace local cultures. As mentioned earlier, satellites and media channels that beam American television and concepts overseas wake anxiety and anger about cultural invasion. This seems to run counter to many European domestic policies that appeal to young populations in modern democracies.

In depicting moral decay in the country as a whole, conservative historian Gertrude Himmelfarb points the United States is currently confronting "the collapse of

---

[187] "The grand illusion," Survey: France, *The Economist*, online edition, June 3, 1999.

[188] *'C'est la revanche des pauvres contre les riches,'* in *Marianne*, October 1-7, 2001, no. 232, «De l'anti-américanisme des Français», ('From the French anti-Americanism').

ethical principles and habits, the loss of respect for authorities and institutions, the breakdown of the family, the decline of civility, the vulgarization of high culture, and the degradation of popular culture."[189]

According to official figures, the American prison population is the highest rate in the world, increasing between midyear 2003 to midyear 2004 by 932 inmates each week. As of June 30, 2004, the U.S. prison population reached a record of 726 people per 100,000 residents (1 in every 138 people). That figure is compared to incarceration rates in the United Kingdom with 142 people (per 100,000 citizens), China 118, France 91, Japan 58, and Nigeria 31.[190]

Also take, for instance, European policies on capital punishment, gun ownership and control,[191] the right of homosexuals, women's rights, drug use, racism, and among several others, the tendency for fast food restaurants.[192] These policies are probably closer to the views of many people in rich countries around the world than are American government policies.

In respect of human rights, and in response to the U.S. State Department's annual Human Rights Report issued in late February 2004, Amnesty International USA noted "the Bush administration's *erratic and inconsistent* behavior on human rights. The content of this report has little correspondence with the administration's foreign policy. Indeed, the U.S. is increasingly guilty of *sincerity gap*."[193]

Likewise, human rights groups also charged the United States for becoming a major violator of international standards because of its own conduct in the war on

---

[189] Gertrude Himmelfarb, *One Nation, Two Cultures*, New York: Knopf, 1999, p. 20.

[190] "Nation's Prison and Jail Population Grew by 932 Inmates per Week," U.S. Department of Justice, Office of Justice Programs, Bureau of Justice Statistics, Washington, DC, April 24, 2005. And also: "Nearly 1,000 new individuals incarcerated each week in US," Justice Policy Institute, Washington, DC, April 25, 2005, at: www.justicepolicy.org.

[191] On gun ownership and control, noteworthy here is the American Oscar-Award winning documentary film *Bowling for Columbine*, directed by Michael Moore, 2002.

[192] Consider also the increasing volume of alternatives to American brands, such as 'Mecca Cola' and 'Paris Fried Chicken.'

[193] Robin Wright, "U.S. Report Criticizes Russia on Human Rights," *The Washington Post*, February 26, 2004, A02.

terrorism. The U.S. Human Rights Network (a new coalition of more than 100 legal and human rights groups) stated the "United States has now *lost the moral authority* to evaluate human rights worldwide while it detains both Americans and foreign nationals indefinitely, without charges or recourse to a speedy trial, in the name of national security. These dramatic and flagrant violations are occurring in the context of sustained general attacks on privacy, freedom of information and expression, due process, and economic social rights, among others" (Wright). More recently, in launching its 2005 report on the status of human rights worldwide, Amnesty International outlined:

> Despite the US administration's repeated use of the language of justice and freedom there was a huge gap between rhetoric and reality. This was starkly illustrated by the failure to conduct a full and independent investigation into the appalling torture and ill-treatment of detainees by US soldiers in Iraq's Abu Ghraib prison and the failure to hold senior individuals to account.[194]

In terms of Europe's potential soft power resources, Joseph S. Nye draws attention to the fact France ranks first in Nobel Prizes for literature, with Britain, Germany and Spain third, fourth and fifth. In Noble Prizes in physics and chemistry, Britain, Germany and France are second, third, and fourth. France ranks ahead of the United States in attracting tourists. Life expectancy at birth prevails higher in France, Germany, Italy and Britain than in the Untied States. And according to UNICEF, the United States has one of the highest rates of relative child poverty among the world's wealthiest countries (second only to Mexico, see Figure 2.3.).[195] Not to forget football (soccer)–Europe's primary sport–is far still more popular globally than American's football or baseball.[196]

---

[194] "Report 2005: A dangerous new agenda," Amnesty International, London, Press Release, May 25, 2005.

[195] Based on UNICEF figures of those under 18 years of age, and derived from 24 of the 30 states of the Organization for Economic Cooperation and Development (OECD). "US high in UN child poverty table," *BBC News*, online edition, March 1, 2005.

[196] Joseph S. Nye, *Europe's Soft Power*, May 3, 2004, at: http://www.globalpolicy.org/empire/analysis/2004/0503softpower.htm.

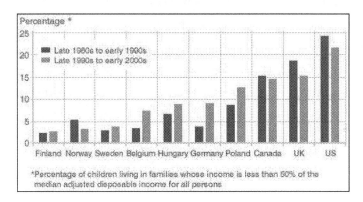

Figure 2. 3. Child Poverty in Selected Industrialized Countries (Source: UNICEF, 2005)

In another separate article, Joseph S. Nye writes:

> Anti-Americanism has increased sharply in the past two years. In addition to the polls, we see it in hockey fans in Montreal who boo the American national anthem, in high school students in Switzerland who do not want to go to the United States as exchange students, and in increased terrorist recruitment in the Islamic world. We are losing our soft power, our ability to attract others...
>
> When we discount the importance of our attractiveness to other countries, we pay a price...
>
> And when American policies lose their legitimacy and credibility in the eyes of others, attitudes of distrust tend to fester and further reduce our [American] leverage. For example, after Sept. 11, there was an outpouring of sympathy in Germany for the United States. But Germans expressed widespread disbelief about the reasons the U.S. gave for going to war such as the alleged connection of Iraq to Sept. 11 and the immense of the threat of weapons of mass destruction. The confirmation of those suspicions fostered a climate in which conspiracy theories flourished. By July 2003, one-third of young Germans under the age of 30 said that they thought the American government might even have staged the original Sept. 11 attacks.[197]

In an attempt to distinguish between the features of the American and French cultures, one French woman commented:

---

[197] Joseph S. Nye, "Ignoring Soft Power Carries a High Cost," May 16, 2004, at: http://www.ksg.harvard.edu/news/opeds/2004/nye_softpower_chitrib_051604.htm, (reprinted from *The Chicago Tribune).*

Les Américains...se veulent "la" civilisation contre les ténèbres extérieures. Rien n'est plus étranger à l'idée française qui va chercher, au contraire, dans toutes les civilisations un peu de miel. Nous ne découpons pas l'univers en blocs distincts: chaque monde a son excellence et sa culture. Dès 1527, François Ier nouait une alliance avec Soliman le Magnifique. Louis XIV créa une école des langues orientales. Notre universalisme chérit la diversité. Leur mondialisation est uniformisante. Leur logiciel, c'est Dieu et le dollar. Le nôtre, c'est l'homme dans l'histoire."[198]

II.IV.II.V. <u>Psychological</u>

Anti-Americanism is fueled by jealousy, resentment and ambivalence. "The seductive allure of American capitalism, freedoms, products, and culture often coexist with ambivalence about them as economically or politically unattainable," writes Moisès Naim.[199] This love-hate relationship can fume intense hatred. In the early 1990s, millions around the world believed it was just a matter of time before economic liberalization, political reforms, and globalization would raise their standards of living closer to those enjoyed by Americans. Yet, most transition economies and emerging markets still struggle–as they continue to watch how much better Americans live. Unilateral actions taken by the United States and addressed to the core issue of civil liberties and personal data of non-U.S. citizens also fuel anti-Americanism. Consider here, for instance, the 34 points of personal information that *must* be forwarded to the American authorities for any European citizen intending to travel to the States.[200]

One European citizen commented on the love-hate relationship, saying:

---

[198] ('The Americans...want the civilization against outside darkness. Nothing is more odd to the French idea, which in contrast tries to find in all civilizations a little bit of honey. We do not cut the world in distinct blocs: each world has its own excellence and culture. Since 1527, François I formed an alliance with Suleiman the Magnificent. Louis XIV created a school for oriental languages. Our universalism seeks for diversity. Their globalization is uniformist. Their logic is God and the dollar. Ours is man throughout history.'), «Anti-Américanisme: Pourquoi cette haine», ('Anti-Americanism: Why to such a hatred'), *Marianne*, no. 232, October 1-7, 2001, 38.

[199] Moisés Naim, "Anti-Americanism: A Guide to hating Uncle Sam," *Foreign Policy,* Jan.-Feb. 2002.

[200] «L'Amérique dicte sa loi antiterroriste au trafic aérien avec l'Europe», ('America imposes its anti-terrorist law on air traffic with Europe'), *Le Monde*, June 22, 2004. Noting here that the U.S. President signed on November 19, 2001 an aviation security law demanding some 58 carriers to begin the electronic transmission of passenger and crew lists for all flights to the United States. Among the carriers concerned are Saudi Arabia Airlines, Royal Jordanian Airlines, Pakistan International Airlines, Ethiopian Airlines, Aeroflot, Air China, China Eastern and China Southern. See: Robert Pear, "U.S. Pressures Foreign Airlines Over Manifests," *The New York Times*, online edition, November 27, 2001.

> Nous avons des raisons d'aimer les Américains–parce qu'ils nous ont
> soutenus lors des deux guerres mondiales, parce que nous aimons leur
> culture... et, dans le même temps, nous détestons leur politique, leur
> arrogance....[201]

To end with this noteworthy incident, and perhaps coincidentally, U.S. consular officials confirmed the number of Americans reporting missing passports in Paris in summer 2001 had soared around 30% compared to summer 2000. "Americans are among the pickpockets' favorite targets, because they are known for carrying cash and credit cards," stated USA Today.[202]

II.IV.III. The Potential Power of Russia, China and the European Union in the face of U.S. Unilateralism

Russia may still pose a threat to the United States, mainly because it is the sole country with enough missiles and nuclear warheads to destroy the United States. Its relative decline in current world affairs has made it more reluctant to renounce and provide further concessions in terms of its nuclear status. In addition, Russia possesses other significant and vital resources: vast territory, an educated population, skilled scientists and engineers, and enormous natural resources. Yet despite all that, Russia does not seem, for the meantime, to constitute the same sort of challenge to American power and unilateralism that the Soviet Union had presented during the four decades after World War II.

Delpech underlines the main reason for that position, namely for economic aid. She states Moscow seems to have decided to protest to the minimum–with the hopes of obtaining compensations in the form of economic assistance, its immediate needs. She

---

[201] 'We have reasons to like the Americans–because they supported us during the two world wars, because we like their culture...and, at the same time, we hate their politics, their arrogance.' «L'Amérique, cet idéal déteste», ('America: this ideal dislike'), *Marianne,* no. 232, October 1-7, 2001, 48.

[202] Vivienne Walt, "French thieves target Americans", *USA Today,* August 17, 2001, 11B.

adds even NATO's enlargement towards the Baltic states, and an eventual U.S. military action on Iraq, may all be tolerated by Moscow.[203]

With China emerging as an economic and military force in Asia, government officials and policy analysts in Washington and Beijing are increasingly concerned the two countries are heading towards confrontation. The two also seem to have lost confidence and patience in a constructive relationship based on common interests. Therefore, and instead of predicting a new Cold War, U.S.-China ties (at present) could be characterized by *hot peace*, where intensive competition and heated rhetoric stop short of military conflict.

China's present concerns are threefold: securing its borders, meeting massive demands for food, oil, wood and other natural resources, and uniting the mainland with Taiwan—a task Mao Zedong left unfinished ever since the island was separated from its mainland in 1949.

With the peaceful return of Hong Kong in 1997, and Macao in 1999, Taiwan still remains the outstanding piece of territory claimed as part of China. However, now that China's historic land borders are largely intact and unthreatened, the government and its military are increasingly turning their attention to reclaiming and safeguarding what they assert are the country's rightful maritime frontiers. While China is in dispute with Japan and Korea over sea borders and small islands in the East China Sea and the Yellow Sea, a number of strategically sensitive Chinese maritime claims have surfaced, specifically the assertion of sovereignty over all disputed islands and reefs in the South China Sea.

By referring to the territorial claim line covering virtually the entire South China Sea that is marked on official Chinese maps, Beijing regards the South China Sea historic waters. After its forces seized the Paracel Islands from Vietnam in 1974, China has been pursuing what may be called a "step-by-step" or "creeping" recovery of the Sea. Since then, Beijing has fortified the islands, some 650 kilometers southeast of China's Hainan Island, and eventually turned them into an air and naval base.

---

[203] Thérèse Delpech, *Politique du chaos: l'autre face de la mondialisation*, 2002, pp. 50-51.

Furthermore, as rapid economic growth in the 1980s and 1990s strengthened its armed forces and extended its reach, China took control of some of the Spratly Islands, which are widely scattered over the central and southern sectors of the South China Sea (noting that the Sea is named differently by the countries neighboring it). Taiwan, Vietnam, the Philippines, Malaysia and Brunei also claim the islands–in whole or part. Beijing regards control over Spratly archipelago the key to enforcing its wider territorial claims and to its oil, natural gas and fishing resources–all vital components of security and survival.

Reminding the country shares frontiers with 14 neighbors, in 1992 China's National People's Congress issued the "Law on the Territorial Waters and Their Contiguous Areas," which claimed 80% of the South China Sea in a horse-shaped arc along the length of Vietnam's coastline. Although no other country recognized the law, the stakes of such a move are high with 70% of Japan's crude oil moving through the sea, which contains huge fishing resources and possible gas and oil deposits.

Economically, China is manufacturing a sophisticated variety of goods at costs significantly below those in South Korea, Taiwan or competing Southeast Asian countries. China's low labor wages have contributed to a worldwide drop in clothing prices. Next to come will be prices for electronic appliances and computers.[204]

Since assuming power in 2001, the Bush administration has adopted a more assertive policy towards Beijing. Bush's comments in April 2001 that the United States would defend Taiwan in case of a mainland attack were interpreted by China as "basically an end to the long-time American policy of strategic ambiguity."[205] The United States backed a national missile defense system, which China fears will negate its nuclear deterrent. Washington permitted President Chen Shui-bian of Taiwan unprecedented access to the United States, even allowing him to meet lawmakers. Furthermore, President Bush hosted at the White House the Tibetan spiritual leader, the Dalai Lama. He also approved a multi-billion dollar weapons package for Taiwan, including for the first time submarines. Backed by the United States, and following

---

[204] John Pomfret, "In Its Own Neighborhood, China Emerges as a Leader," *The Washington Post*, October 18, 2001, A01.

[205] John Pomfret, "China Fearful of a 'Hot Peace'," *IHT*, June 23-24, 2001, 1.

China by one day, in September 2001 Taiwan won formal clearance to join the World Trade Organization (though formally named as *Chinese Taipei* at the WTO).[206]

In addition, the United States was reported to have virtually cut off all Pentagon contacts with the Chinese armed forces, while it conducts a case-by-case review of seminars, visits and other contacts with China. Pentagon contacts with the Chinese go back to the years of the Reagan administration when Washington's goal was to contain Soviet power. The United States sold arms to China and provided it with advice on logistics and personnel. As the Cold War came to an end, that policy gradually faded away. The United States suspended contacts with the Chinese military after the Tiananmen Square events in June 1989.[207]

European Union moves to put an end to the non-binding arms embargo against China (imposed since 1989) have strained relations with the United States. Since a number of EU governments consider the embargo to be outdated and a barrier to improving relations with the European Union, several European countries were not stopped from supplying military technology to China. European Union members argue that lifting the embargo does not systematically imply an increase in arms sales.[208]

In terms of arms imports, China is almost completely dependent on Russia, although its relationship is shifting from a recipient of complete weapons to a recipient of components and technology sought to be later employed in Chinese weapon platforms. However, and partly because Russian technology is becoming outdated, China has shown increasing anxiety to gain technology access from elsewhere.[209]

---

[206] Taiwan's allies (among others, El Salvador, Senegal, The Dominican Republic, Gambia, Chad, Burkina Faso, Nicaragua, Tuvalu, Palou, and Belize) have for several years unsuccessfully applied to get the steering committee of the UN General Assembly to include the status of Taiwan on the assembly's agenda to join the United Nations. Source: "10 Allies Promote Taiwan for the UN," *IHT*, August 10, 2001, 9.

[207] Michael R. Gordon, "As Pentagon Cuts Most China Ties, Some Experts Call It a Mistake," *IHT*, June 5, 2001, 4.

[208] "SIPRI Yearbook 2005: Armaments, Disarmament and International Security," Stockholm International Peace Research Institute, Solna, Sweden, Press Release, June 7, 2005, p. 15.

[209] "SIPRI Yearbook 2005: Armaments, Disarmament and International Security," Press Release, p. 15.

Voicing "strong opposition" to the government of the Taiwanese leader and what it claimed was his failure to improve ties on the basis of "one-China principle" with mainland, *Beijingnews.com* (Chinese official news Web site) reported on May 31, 2001 that the biggest military exercises in years (in June 2001) were to practice "attacking and occupying an outlying Taiwanese island and fighting off an aircraft carrier," an obvious reference to the American navy.

Even more recently in respect of Taiwan, in March 2005 the Chinese National People's Congress (Parliament) adopted a law that would effectively pre-authorize military action if Taiwan took concrete steps towards formal independence. The law specifies that any changes in Taiwan's Constitution intended to legalize the *de facto* independent status of the island could be a trigger for military action:

> In the event that the 'Taiwan independence' forces should act under any name or by any means to cause the fact of Taiwan's secession from China, or that major incidents entailing Taiwan's secession from China should occur, or that possibilities for a peaceful reunification should be completely exhausted, that state shall employ nonpeaceful means and other necessary measures to protect China's sovereignty and territorial integrity.[210]

Along the U.S.-China human rights dispute, the Chinese State Council released a report titled "Human Right Record of the United States in 2001," covering topics such as personal safety, law enforcement, racial discrimination and the infringement on the human rights of other countries. The 10,000-word account critical of the United States' human rights record cites American government statistics and international media reports to build a case-by-case indictment of human rights practices in the United States.[211] The March 2002 paper was a response to Washington's annual human rights report on China, as Chinese leaders feel increasingly constrained by Washington's global war against terrorism and its emerging foreign policy.

---

[210] Joseph Kahn, "Beijing Leaders Speak of Force to Keep Taiwan 'Chinese'," *The New York Times*, online edition, March 8, 2005. The United States criticized the legislation in advance of its presentation as a 'hardening of positions'. China's emphasis on 'nonpeaceful' means appear to designate alternatives to military force, such as sanctions.

[211] "China Strikes Back at U.S. Through Human Rights Report," *www.stratfor.com*, March 11, 2002.

To conclude this analysis on the U.S.-China *hot-peace* relations, it is important to refer to the crisis evoked by the collision between an American navy surveillance plane and a Chinese jet fighter on April 1, 2001. The crisis erupted as a result of the navy plane's subsequent violation of Chinese airspace when it made an emergency landing (carrying 24 U.S. servicemen and women) and the loss of the Chinese pilot (Wang Wei, who was designated a national hero). The resolution of the crisis revealed a tangled web of historical, cultural, linguistic, political, and security issues.

From the start, China set several conditions for returning the crew and plane. That included a U.S. apology, an explanation of what happened, compensation, and suspension of future espionage flights. Diplomacy wore these down to two primary requirements: an apology and a joint investigation.

Not yielding to President George W. Bush's warning that relations with Beijing could suffer unless the Chinese quickly release the plane and its crew, president Jiang Zemin instead stated:

> The U.S. side should apologize to the Chinese people. The United States should do something favorable to the smooth development of China-U.S. relations, rather than make remarks that confuse right and wrong and are harmful to the relations.[212]

In Chinese culture, apologies are complicated matters, weighty acts that are rarely offered or accepted. To the Chinese, apologies require a great loss of face, where the offhand American "sorry about that" or "excuse me" have neither significance nor meaning. In 1999, most Chinese were outraged at former president Bill Clinton's first apology after the bombing of the Chinese Embassy in Belgrade during the Kosovo Conflict because it was considered to be 'too causal'–delivered while Clinton was outdoors and wearing a polo shirt.[213]

---

[212] David Stout, "U.S. Regret, but No Apology," *IHT,* April 5, 2001, 1.

[213] In 1998, the two sides established a 'hotline' between the White House and Zhongnanhai (the house of the Communist Party in Beijing). Yet at key moments, such as the bombing of the Chinese Embassy in Belgrade in May 1999, Chinese leaders have chosen not to answer U.S. phone calls.

The United States, this time, expressed *regret* over the death of the Chinese pilot, but that regret did not include a formal apology. Secretary of state Colin Powell voiced the American response:

> We regret the loss of life of that Chinese pilot. Now we need to move on. We need to bring this to a resolution, and we're using every avenue available to us to talk to the Chinese side to exchange explanations.[214]

The American ambassador to China handed the Chinese Foreign Ministry a letter asking the Minister to "covey to the Chinese people and the family of the pilot Wang Wei that we are very sorry for their loss," and stated "we are very sorry the entering of China's airspace and the landing did not have verbal clearance." In announcing this American move, China chose to translate "very sorry" as *shenbiao qianyi*, which means " a deep expression of apology or regret." Yet the English (and American) translation into Chinese chose an even more vague term. The phrase "very sorry" in English does not necessarily imply an acknowledgement of error or an acceptance of responsibility– although the Chinese translation used by the Foreign Ministry certainly involves both. In other words, this creative mistranslation gave the two countries maneuverability (refer to the text of letter in Appendix III).

Language games between the United States and China are not new. In the 1970s, national security advisor Henry Kissinger and prime minister Zhou Enlai used the words "acknowledge" and its sometimes Chinese equivalent *chengren* interchangeably when they described the American attitude towards the one-China policy. The United States said it 'acknowledged' Beijing's one-China policy, a notion that did not necessarily imply acceptance. Beijing, on the other hand, translated 'acknowledged' as *chengren*, implying acceptance and support.[215]

---

[214] David Stout, "U.S. Regret, but No Apology," 2001.

[215] Back "On September 14, 1793, Lord George Macartney had an audience with Emperor Qianlong in the first contact between a representative of the British crown and the leader of one of the mightiest empires in the world. For weeks before the audience, Lord Macartney, seeking to be the first foreign envoy to be accredited as a permanent representative to the Son of Heaven, haggled with his Chinese escorts over a key element. Would he kowtow to the emperor, his forehead knocking the ground nine times in all? He rejected the Chinese demand, only offered to bend on one knee and never actually knocked his head at the emperor's feet...

With Russia busy striving to regain economic power, and China in a tug-of-war relation with the United States, there then remains the European Union as a potential force in the face of American unilaterlism at the present stage.

The key question in assessing the challenge presented by the European Union is whether it will develop enough political and social-cultural cohesion to act as one unit on a wide range of international issues, or whether it will remain as a limited grouping of countries with strongly different nationalisms and foreign policies. Huntington argues that a cohesive Europe would have the population resources, economic strength, technology, and actual and potential military strength to be the pre-eminent power of the 21st century.[216]

In opening the way for the European Union's enlargement into Eastern Europe, its leaders came up in their Summit Meeting in Nice (December 2000) with a treaty that rearranged details of its organization yet failed once again to bring to the European Union a sense of unified power or direction. The aim of the Summit was to adjust the institutions created in the 1950s (initially set for a community of six countries) to ones that were expected to deal with 28 members or more, and follow the course of transformations of the Maastricht Treaty (1992) and the Amsterdam Treaty (1997). Contradictory, the agreement on EU reforms assured instead the perpetuations of a picture of a complicated Europe too self-absorbed to re-create itself as a more coherent whole before it took in applications from the former Soviet orbit. Delegates had attended the Summit armed with calculators and computers to track the benefits and costs of every move in the bid of strategic trade-offs.

The dispute among the then 15 members states trying to rationalize the functioning of the European Union led to long-term certainty: that a European Union with eventual 28 members means an increasing focus on a Europe that could subdivide into a system

His audience with the emperor failed to open up China to the Western world. The British envoy was sent packing. Fifty years later, British warships did the job, blasting open China's treaty ports...

Again, Lord Macartney's case comes to mind. Accounts of British witnesses and histories say that he never kowtowed. But even today, Chinese historians, referring to documents in China's imperial archives, insist that he did." John Pomfret, "China-U.S. Word Game Again Helps to Salve Historic Wounds," *IHT,* April 12, 2001, 1.

[216] Samuel Huntington, "The U.S.–Decline or Renewal?," *Foreign Affairs,* Winter 1988-1989, 93.

of hard-core task forces created among countries wanting to move ahead in defined areas like the common currency. The Treaty dealt partially with this idea by making it easier for such groups to form.

Another issue of concern was to increase the number of questions settled by a majority vote rather than by a unanimous one, to prevent one country from holding up the group by issuing a veto. But members made certain they kept their own veto items firmly in place. That is, the Treaty effectively widened the areas where countries had to abide by majority decisions and could not use their veto power. In the areas of jurisdiction there was no profound step forward, however, where the issue matters in terms of ideology, domestic policies and national self-esteem–the zones for testing Europe's willingness to render real concessions to unity.

For example, France continues to protect its culture and audiovisual industry against Hollywood. Britain keeps joint actions on taxes off the agenda for the indefinite future. Though Germany did increase its seats in the European Parliament, it failed to obtain more votes than France in the Council of Ministers–to reflect is population greater by millions than any of the rest of the then EU members–hence binding to an arrangement that is more of a historic symbol of post-war reconciliation to heal the divisions of World War II. Germany was also able to maintain firmly its asylum and immigration policy, and eventually succeeded in freeing itself from reliance on France in future ministerial meetings. The new voting system means any three of the big powers can block an initiative. Germany, in theory, could team up with Italy and Britain to overrule France. Belgium, as well, was reported to be 'unhappy' with a proposal to give the Netherlands greater voting weight. The three Benelux countries (Belgium, the Netherlands and Luxembourg) achieved a concession where together they would have the same voting weight as one of the major powers. Spain's relative weight over Portugal was reported to be substantially augmented–raising fears and warnings about the dangers of *humiliating* the smaller members. Like France, which kept its audiovisual industry out of the world trade talks to protect its cultural identity, and Britain's position on taxation and social affairs, Spain held control over regional aid fund–which particularly benefits the country.[217]

In a test once more on its unity, European policymakers wanted to avoid any Gallic chauvinism in designing the banknotes for the common European currency. Hoping to unite the Continent without inflaming old national loyalties, they stressed the bills introduced "should not be attributed to any particular monument in any single country." Therefore, the European Central Bank chose bridges, a metaphor for "communication among the people of Europe." The designed bridges were supposed to be anonymous structures that did not resemble any actual bridges claimed by one country or another. The issue of sufficient importance here is that the artist who designed the banknotes, Robert Kalina of the Austrian Central Bank, already did have to withdraw some of the initial designs in 1997 to strip out features reminiscent of specific bridges. On the initial designs, Europeans began noticing the Rialto Bridge in Venice on the €50 bill, the €100 bill was suggestive of the Pont de Neuilly near Paris, and the €500 bill showed a barely disguised Pont de Normandie. Meanwhile, locals in a southern France spot embrace the present €5 bill as the 2000-year-old Pont du Gard.[218]

One last point on Europe's potential coherence needs to be outlined, namely, the gap between elite and mass opinion on its enlargement and support. A EU barometer poll released in mid July 2001 reported only 45% of the people living in the European Union trust the European Commission in Brussels, and only 48% believe the EU membership is a good thing for their country. Even in Germany and France, the two pillars of the Union, less than half of the public voiced support to the Union with 45% and 49% respectively. In Britain, just 29% of the public believed EU membership is a good thing.[219]

---

[217] For a look at the diverse political structure of Europe, ranging from the Socialists, Democrats, Populars, Liberals, Greens, Conservatives, and among others, the Social Christians, also see: Rafaële Rivais, «Stratégies variables au Parlement européen», ('Differing strategies at the European Parliament'), *Le Monde,* Sunday 26-Monday 27 May, 2002, 19.

[218] John Schmid, "Euro Bill Hits a High Note With Folks in Small French Town," *IHT,* August 22, 2001, 1.

[219] David Ignatius, "Don't Try to Expand Europe Without Consulting the People," *IHT,* July 23, 2001, 6.

Only one country, Ireland, actually held a referendum to test whether the public supports the Treaty of Nice. The result of its June 7, 2001 vote was a clear *No* with 54% opposing the Treaty–winning with a simple poster: *You Will Lose Power Money Freedom*. Patricia McKenna of the Irish Green Party, who led the vote against Nice, commented the "people elect the government to run their economy, and if they don't like how it's run, they can vote it out. But the European economy is run by the EU central bank, which is unaccountable."[220] Considered the worst street violence in recent memory of Sweden, demonstrators in Gothenburg during the EU Summit in June 2001 also dramatized a problem of increasing urgency for the Union's leaders: "what may observers, including some of the leaders themselves, see as their remoteness and their inability to explain the benefits of European integration in terms that ordinary people can understand."[221]

Even more recent setbacks in harmony among European governments and societies, such as the 'No' votes to the referendum on the drafted European Constitution by some countries of the Union while others voted 'Yes' (in 2005), are not encouraging signs of a strong European Union in the face of American unilateralism in world affairs (although the process of ratifying the Constitution is still in process at the time of this writing). How members of the European Union are going to manage these tensions, politically–socially–culturally–economically, seems to be one of the major dramas of the early 21st century.

---

[220] Thomas L. Friedman, "Joining the World, but Staying Ireland," *IHT,* August 4-5, 2001, 6.

[221] Barry James, "After Summit, EU Enlargement Is 'Irreversible'," *IHT*, June 18, 2001, 6.

III. CHAPTER THREE:

CULTURAL MATTERS IN THE INFORMATION AGE

III.I. The Implications of Cultural Awareness in the Information Age

The following assessment stems from the growing significance of a current tendency where people attribute themselves to their cultural and national identities, and have come to think of common and distinctive features as they look to others. It also examines and foresees the future of cultural co-existence in an era of increasing social interdependence.

III.I.I. The Rise of Cultural Identity

In addition to grouping countries in terms of their political or economic systems, or in terms of their level of economic development (as was the case during the Cold War), it is also relevant to consider countries in respect of their culture and civilization.

A civilization is a cultural entity.[1] Villages, regions, ethnic groups, nationalists, religious groups, all enjoy distinct cultures with different levels of cultural heterogeneity. The culture of a village in northern Italy may be different from that of a village in southern Italy, yet both share in common Italian culture that distinguishes them both from, to say, German villages. European communities, in turn, share cultural features that distinguish them from Arab or Chinese communities. Arabs, Chinese, and Westerners, however, are not part of any broader cultural entity. They constitute civilizations. Hence, a civilization is the highest cultural grouping of people and the broadest level of cultural identity that distinguishes humans from other species. It is defined both by common objective elements, such as history, religion, language, traditions, institutions, and by the subjective self-identification of people.

Accordingly, people have several levels of identity: a resident of Rome may define oneself with varying degrees of intensity as a Roman, an Italian, a Catholic,

---

[1] The following presentation on culture and civilization is summarized from: Samuel P. Huntington, "The Clash of Civilizations?" in *The Clash of Civilizations? The Debate*, New York: Council on Foreign Relations, 1996.

a Christian, a European, and finally, as a Westerner. With civilization being presented as the broadest identification level, people can and do redefine their identities–leading to an eventual change in the composition and boundaries of civilizations. A civilization may involve a large number of people (as China), or a very small number of people (as the Anglophone Caribbean). It may embody several nation states (as with Western, Latin American, and Arab civilizations), or only one (as with the Japanese Civilization). Obviously, civilizations may blend, overlap, and include subcivilizations. Take, for example, the Western Civilization with its two major variants, European and North American, and also Islam with its Arab, Turkish and Malay subdivisions. Finally, civilizations are dynamic; they rise and fall, divide and merge, emerge or simply vanish along with time.

As people, in the future, are differentiated by civilization, countries with large numbers of peoples of different civilizations are subject for dismemberment. Other countries may have a fair degree of cultural homogeneity but are divided over whether their society belongs to one particular civilization or another. These are so-called *torn countries*. At times, their leaders typically wish to pursue a band-wagoning strategy and to make their countries members of the West, though the history, culture, and traditions of their countries and people are non-Western. The most obvious and prototypical torn country is Turkey. The late 20th century leaders of Turkey have followed in the Attatürk tradition and have outlined Turkey as a modern, secular, Western nation state. Thus, they allied Turkey with the West in NATO, and during the two conflicts in the Arab Gulf in 1991 and 2003. Furthermore, they have applied for membership in the European Community. Yet, elements in the Turkish society have supported an Islamic revival and have argued that Turkey is basically a Middle Eastern Muslim nation. In addition, while the elite of Turkey have defined Turkey as a Western-society, the elite of the West refuse to accept Turkey as such. After already distancing from Mecca, and still rejected by Brussels, the question remains on where Turkey now stands.

Mexico in recent years has assumed a position somewhat similar to that of Turkey. Mexico has stopped defining itself by its opposition to the United States and is instead attempting to imitate the United States and associate itself closer to it. Mexican leaders are engaged in the great task of redefining Mexican identity, and have introduced fundamental economic reforms that eventually seek to lead to fundamental political change. As in Turkey, significant elements in Mexico's society resist the redefinition of their nation's identity. European-oriented leaders in Turkey need to make gestures to Islam, as do North American-oriented leaders in Mexico who maintain Mexico a Latin American country.

Historically, the most profoundly torn country is Turkey. For the United States, the most immediate torn country is Mexico. Globally, the most important torn country is Russia. Whether Russia is part of the West or the leader of a distinct Slavic-Orthodox civilization is a question that has been resurfacing throughout Russian history. That issue was gradually obscured by the victory of the communists in Russia, which imported a Western ideology, framed it to Russian conditions, and then challenged the West in the name of ideology. While the dominance of communism *suspended* the historic debate over *Westernization* versus *Russification,* Russians–with communism discredited–once again argue that issue.

A torn country seeking to redefine its civilization identity must meet three essential requirements. First of all, its political and economic elite have to be generally supportive of and enthusiastic about such a move. Its public, second of all, has to be willing to acquiesce in the redefinition. And third of all, the dominant groups in the recipient civilization have to be willing to embrace the convert. All three requirements in large part exist with respect to Mexico. The first two in large part exist with respect to Turkey. It is not clear that any of the three requirements exist concerning Russia joining the West, concludes Huntington (1996, p. 21).

Civilization identity is becoming increasingly important, as the world is being shaped to a certain extent by the interactions among seven or eight major civilizations. These include the Western, Confucian, Japanese, Islamic, Hindu, Slavic-Orthodox, Latin American, and possibly African civilization. *Mapping the Global Future* foresees that:

Part of the pressure on governance will come from new forms of identity politics centered on religious convictions and ethnic affiliation. Over the next 15 years, religious identity is likely to become an increasingly factor in how people define themselves. The trend toward identity politics is linked to increased mobility, growing diversity of hostile groups within states, and the diffusion of modern communications technologies.[2]

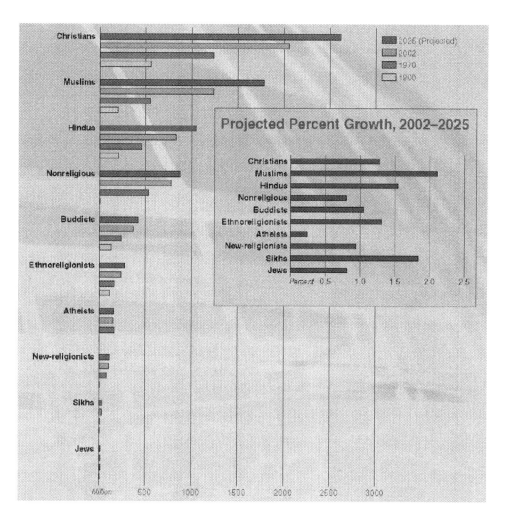

Figure 3. 1. Number of Religious Adherents, 1900-2025
(Source: World Evangelization Research Center, cited in *Mapping the Global Future*, 2004, p. 80)

[2] *Mapping the Global Future: Report of the National Intelligence Council's 2020 Project*, December 2004, p. 79. See projections on the number of religious adherents in Figure 3.1.

As the growing connectivity in the Information Age is also accompanied by the proliferation of transnational virtual communities of interest, several essential notions regarding the major civilizations are outlined below.

- *Differences among civilizations are not only real; they are basic.* Civilizations differ from each other in terms of history, language, culture, tradition, and religion. Civilizations have varying views on the relations between God and man, the individual and the group, the citizen and the state, parents and children, husband and wife, on the relative significance of rights and responsibilities, liberty and authority, equality and hierarchy. Prevailing throughout centuries, these differences are more fundamental than differences among political ideologies and government politics.[3]

- *The interactions between the peoples of different civilizations are increasing.* These interactions gradually intensify civilization consciousness and awareness of the differences between them. For example, Americans react far more negatively to Japanese investment than to larger investments from Canada or European countries. In one British view "globalization is the reason for the revival of local culture in different parts of the world.... Globalization not only pulls upwards, but also pushes downwards, creating new pressures for local autonomy."[4]

- *Economic modernization and social change around the world are separating people from longstanding local identities, and also weaken the nation states as reference for identity.* Eventually, religion (in much of the world) has moved in to fill such a gap, often in the form

---

[3] For a review on how Islam, for example, is perceived by the West, see: Paul Balta, *Idées reçues: L'Islam*, ('Ideas Perceived: Islam'), Paris: Le Cavalier Bleu, November 2001. The book divides the debate into three sections: History and Civilization, Religion and Society, and Islam and the Modern World.

[4] Anthony Giddens, *Runaway World: How Globalization Is Reshaping Our Lives*, New York: Routledge, 2000, p. 31.

of movements labeled *fundamentalists.* Those active in most of such fundamentalist movements are young, college-educated, middle-class technicians, professionals, and business people. The revival of religion, thus, provides a basis for identity and commitment that transcends national boundaries and unites civilizations.

- *Cultural characteristics and differences are less easily compromised and resolved than are political and economic ones.* Communists can become democrats, the rich can become poor, yet, Russians cannot become Estonians and Azeris cannot become Armenians.[5] In class and ideology, the key question is *which side are you on?* In this regard, people could (as they did) choose sides and change sides. However, the main question pertaining to civilization and culture is *What are you?* This is a given that cannot be changed. Even more, religion discriminates sharply and exclusively among people. A person can be half-French and half-Arab and furthermore a citizen of two countries. It is, however, more difficult to be half-Catholic and half-Muslim, or more profoundly, half-Sunni and half-Shiite.

- *Economic regionalism and blocs are increasing.* The European Community rests, in large, on the shared foundation of European culture and Western Christianity. Meanwhile, the Economic Cooperation Organization, founded originally in the 1960s, brings together ten non-Arab Muslim countries: Iran, Pakistan, Turkey, Azerbaijan, Kazakhstan, Kyrgyzstan, Turkmenistan, Tadjikistan, Uzbekistan, and Afghanistan. One impetus to the revival and expansion of this Organization, initiated by Turkey, Pakistan and Iran, is the realization by the leaders of several of these countries that they had no chance of admission to the European Community. In contrast, a country such as Japan faces difficulties in creating a comparable economic entity in East Asia because Japan is a society and

---

[5] In reference to the war that has been waged off and on since 1988 between Armenia and Azerbaijan over Nagorno-Karabakh, a mountain enclave of spectacular beauty whose population has been heavily Armenian for the past century but which lies within the territory of rival Azerbaijan.

civilization unique to itself. However strong trade and investment links Japan may develop with other East Asian countries, its cultural differences with those countries may hinder its efforts in promoting regional economic integration.

Accordingly, and as people define their identity in ethnic and religious terms, they are likely to see an *us* versus *them* relation existing between themselves and people of different ethnicity or religion. Differences in culture and religion lead to differences over policy issues, ranging from human rights to immigration to trade to the environment. The efforts of the West, with particular reference to the United States, to promote its values of democracy and liberalism as universal values, to maintain its military predominance and to advance its economic interests engender various countering responses from other civilizations. Decreasingly able to mobilize support and form alliances on the basis of ideology, governments and groups increasingly attempt to gather support by appealing to common religion and civilization identity.

Based on the above features and notions, Huntington (1996, p.1) outlines his hypothesis that "the most important conflicts of the future will occur along the cultural fault lines separating these civilizations from one another."

He writes that:

> The fundamental source of conflict in this new world will not be primarily ideological or primarily economic. The great divisions among humankind and the dominating source of conflict will be cultural. Nation's states will remain the most powerful actors in world affairs, but the principal conflicts of global politics will occur between nations and groups of different civilizations. The clash of civilizations will dominate global politics....
>
> Conflict between civilizations will be the latest phase in the evolution of conflicts in the modern world.

A civilization clash may occur at two levels. At the micro-level, states and groups within the same civilization struggle–often violently–over the control of territory and influence (as the case with rival Shiites in Iraq after the vacuum of power in 2003). Such conflicts, however, are likely to be less intense and less likely to expand than conflicts between two different civilizations.

At the macro-level, states from different civilizations compete for relative military and economic power, strive for the control of international institutions and third parties, and competitively promote their particular religions, cultural and political values.

Groups or states belonging to one civilization that become involved in war with people from a different civilization naturally try to rally support from other members of their own civilization. With the transformation of the post Cold-War world, the *kin-country* syndrome is replacing political ideology and traditional balance of power considerations as the principal basis for cooperation and coalitions. Its gradual emergence was observed during the three conflicts in the Arab Gulf (1980-88, 1990-91, 2003), in the Caucasus, and in Bosnia. None of these erupted to a full-scale war between civilizations, though each of them did involve certain elements of civilization rallying, which turned out to be more important as the conflict continued.

As present, the West seems to be in an extraordinary peak of power in relation to other civilizations, particularly after the disappearance of its superpower opponent. Military conflict among Western states is, as analyzed earlier, unthinkable–with Western military power still unrivaled. The West faces no direct or immediate economic challenge apart from Japan.[6] It dominates international

---

[6] In respect of Japan, three observations are recalled here. **First:** a set of history textbooks approved first in 2002 and then in 2005 for use by students aged 13-15 has sparked international controversy and eventually strained diplomatic ties with Japan's neighbors. The textbooks seek to justify Japan's Asian conquests, assert that Japan had a military outpost in Korea in the 5th century, challenge description of the cause of the 1904-1905 Russo-Japanese War, and condemn omission of any mention of the Japanese military's system of forcing Korean women into sexual slavery in World War II. South Korea is upset by phrasing in the textbooks that suggest Korea benefited from the colonization because of the development of railways and manufacturing industries. One of the books states 'South Korea is illegally occupying' the islands, known as Dokdo in South Korea, and as Takeshima in Japan. North Korea harshly condemned the textbooks. China reacted and presented its own list of demanded changes in the textbooks. For instance, one of the texts refers to the Japanese slaughter of some 300,000 civilians in the Chinese city of Nanjing as an 'accident,' rather than the 'massacre' it is known elsewhere. Protestation arouse, as well, from Indonesia, Malaysia, and Taiwan. The Japanese government, which stressed that it could only press textbooks to be amended if they contained factual errors, stated it was up to individual school districts to decide which books they use. (See: Doug Struck, "Koreans' Anger About Textbook Surprises Japan," *IHT*,

political and security organs, and with Japan international economic institutions. Global political and security issues are effectively settled by a 'directorate' of the United States, Britain and France, while economic issues by a directorate of the United States, Germany and Japan. Decisions made at the UN Security Council or at the IMF that reflect the interests of the West are presented to the world as reflecting the desires of the world community. The phrase "the world community" or "the international community" has become the euphemistic collective noun to give global legitimacy to actions reflecting the interest of the United States and other Western countries.[7] Through the IMF and other international economic institutions, the West promotes its economic interests and imposes on other nations the economic policies it deems appropriate.

At least, that is the way in which non-Westerners see the new world–with a significant element of truth in their views. Differences in power and struggles for military, economic and intuitional influence, therefore, become one source of conflict between the West and other civilizations. Cultural differences (i.e., basic values and beliefs) are a second source of conflict. At a superficial level, much of the Western culture has indeed infiltrated the rest of the world. At a more basic level, however, Western concepts differ fundamentally from those prevalent in other civilizations. Western ideas and understanding of individualism, liberalism, constitutionalism, human rights, equality, liberty, the rule of law, democracy, free markets, the separation of church and state, all often beam little resonance in Islamic, Confucian, Japanese, Hindu, Buddhist or Orthodox cultures. Western efforts to propagate such ideas instead produce a reaction and a reaffirmation of

May 19-20, 2001, 8; "Japan History Textbook Sells Briskly," *IHT*, June 7, 2001, 10; and also: "Japan history texts anger E Asia," BBC News, online edition, April 5, 2005).

Second: Japan's Prime Minister in mid August 2001 worshipped at the symbolic heart of right-wing militarism, a shrine that honors the hanged leaders of Japan's war machine, in a visit that quickly drew criticism abroad for re-opening the wounds of the past. Protestation over the visit, once again, ranged from China, South Korea, Hong Kong, Singapore and the Philippines. (See: Doug Struck, "Koizumi Visits Japan War Shine," *IHT*, August 14, 2001, 1).

Third: Japan has recently adopted a series of laws (in 1992, 1999 and 2001) to open gates for any eventual military engagement–under various covers, such as "cooperation for international peace," "in case the security of Japan in the region is in jeopardy," "within the frame of 'special' measures against terrorism," or "legitimate collective defense." (See: Thérèse Delpech, *Politique du chaos: l'autre face de la mondialisation*, 2002, p. 45)

[7] A series of articles on "What is the International Community?" are available in *Foreign Policy* magazine, September-October 2002 edition. In one article, former UN High Commissioner for Refugees, Sadako Ogata, writes (page 39): "As a concept...the international community comes to life more on account of the substance to which it aspires rather than the entity it represents."

indigenous values, as remarked in support for religious fundamentalism by the younger generations in non-Western cultures.

In the words of Kishore Mahbubani, the central axis of world politics is likely to be a sort of conflict between *the West and the Rest*–engaging the responses of non-Western civilizations to Western power and values.[8] As with restricting information flow and globalization, those responses generally take one or a combination of three forms. At one extreme, non-Western states can attempt to pursue a course of *isolation*, to insulate their societies from penetration or from 'corruption' from the West, and accordingly, to opt out of participation in the Western-dominated global community. With the costs of this course high, only a few states have pursued it exclusively.

A second alternative, the equivalent of 'band-wagoning' in international relations, is to attempt to join the West and accept its values and institutions. In other words, to 'go with the flow.' The third alternative is to attempt to *balance* the West by developing economic and military power and cooperating with other non-Western societies against the West, while preserving indigenous values and institutions. That is, to "modernize" but not to "Westernize."[9]

Nevertheless, differences do not necessarily mean conflict, and conflict does not necessarily mean violence. What needs to be developed is a deeper understanding of the religious and philosophical assumptions underlying other civilizations, and the way other nations see their nations, to identify points and views in common. The forces behind clashes between civilizations can be contained only if they are recognized. In a world of different civilizations where mere political ideology or economic interests are not the ultimate considerations, each side will have to learn to co-exist with the other.

If the challenge is great, so is the opportunity. A re-examination of the evolution of human conflict offers little cause for despair. For the great bulk of

---

[8] Kishore Mahbubani, "The West and the Rest," *The National Interest*, Summer 1992, 3-13.

[9] In this contemporary world, most modern societies are Western societies. However modernization does not equal Westernization. Japan, Singapore and Saudi Arabia are all modern, prosperous societies but they clearly are non-Western.

humanity, co-existence has been more the norm than coercion. Human beings are just as capable of living in peace as they are of living in war with one another. To conclude, getting along is perhaps ever more rooted in human nature than is fighting to the finish. A key dilemma remains how to resolve serious, profound differences without resorting to domination or force.

III.I.II. Mounting Concerns over Demographic Issues

III.I.II.I. An Increasing Aging and Low Fertility World

A study conducted by the International Institution for Applied Systems in Laxenburg (Austria) in mid 2001 estimated the world population currently at around 6.1 billion. The world's population is likely to peak at 9 billion in 70 years before beginning a decline into the 22nd century.[10] Based on historical demographic data, the statistical computer model predicted that the world population would drop to 8.4 billion by the year 2100. Figure 3.2. illustrates projections of the world populations in 2020, according to regions and based on a representative group of 100 people.

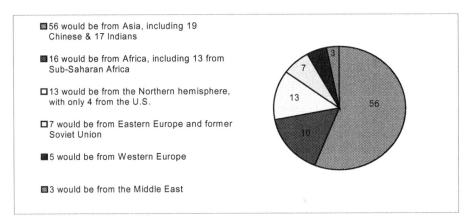

Figure 3. 2. Telescoping the Population of the World to 2020 (Source: *Long-Term Global Demographic Trends: Reshaping the Geopolitical Landscape*, CIA publication, July 2001: 5)

---

[10] Noting that some researchers have argued the predictions are misleading because there could be changes in everything from air quality to food supply, which cannot be foreseen. ("Researchers See 2070 Peak in Population at 9 Billion," *IHT,* August 2, 2001, 2.)

The world's population is also aging at an accelerated rate. Declining fertility rates combined with steady improvements in life expectancy over the latter half of the 20th century have produced dramatic growth in the elderly population. People aged 65 and over now compromise a greater share of the world's population than ever before, while this proportion will increase during the 21st century. This trend has immense implications for several countries around the globe because of its potential to overburden existing social institutions for the elderly.

Population aging refers to an increase in the percentage of elderly people (65 and older). According to a report prepared by a panel of experts, the number of elderly increased more than threefold since 1950 from approximately 130 million (about 4% of global population) to 419 million (6.9%) in 2000.[11] The number of elderly is at present increasing by 8 million per year; and by 2030, this increase is expected to reach 24 million per year. The most rapid acceleration in aging will occur after 2010, when the large post-World War II baby boom cohorts begin to reach age 65.

Moreover, the elderly population itself is growing older. The *oldest old* (80 and older) population is the fastest-growing group among the elderly. Levels of illness and disability among this group far exceed those for other age groups. And hence in the 21st century, the needs of this group are likely to increase substantially.

Italy, in 2000, was the world's 'oldest nation,' with more than 18% of its population aged 65 and over (compared with 8% in 1950). Other notably high levels (about 17%) included Sweden, Belgium, Greece, and Japan. According to regions, Europe has the highest proportion of population aged 65 and over, and is expected to remain the global leader in this category well into the 21st century. Other regions, however, will commence to age much more rapidly in coming decades. The percentage of those aged 65 and older in Asia, Latin America and the Caribbean, Near East / North Africa is estimated to more than triple by 2050. See Figure 3.3.

---

[11] *Preparing for an Aging World: The Case for Cross-National Research,* Washington, DC: National Academy Press, 2001.

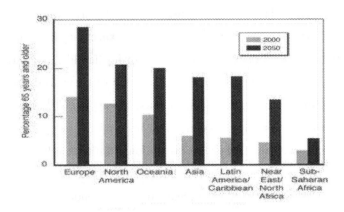

Figure 3. 3. Aging predictions up to 2050 (Source: U.S. Bureau of the Census, 2000)

These shifts in global age structure highlight several areas in which policymakers need a clearer understanding of the effect of aging and the impacts of alternative policies. Among others, such areas include: work, retirement and pension, private wealth and income security, health, and well-being. Though aging trends raise difficult issues, the report concludes there is no crisis. Aging is gradual and its consequences tend to appear gradually and predictably. Policymakers have time to deal with these issues before they turn into acute problems. Also, since aging is at different stages around the world, there are opportunities for countries to learn from each other's experiences.

Further noteworthy, the 20th century ushered in profound and continuing changes in childbearing driven by social and economic development. Central to these changes in childbearing are shifts in nuptiality and increase in the use of contraception. Contraceptive use related to reproductive health is an issue of high priority worldwide, whereas government views and policies in this domain are diverse and evolving.

The UN World Fertility Report 2003 presents a compilation of key estimates and indicators of fertility, nuptiality and contraceptive use for 192 countries whose population in 2000 was greater than 100,000, referring mostly to the 1970s and to the 1990s.[12] The set of data permit an assessment of the unprecedented changes in nuptiality, contraceptive use and fertility occurring since the 1970s. Among other points, the report documents the following key findings in particular.

- *A major worldwide shift in the timing of marriage to older ages has occurred.* The median value of the singulate mean age at marriage for the world rose from 25.4 to 27.2 years among men and from 21.5 to 23.2 years among women. For developed countries,[13] the increase has been even more striking, with the median rising from 25.2 to 28.8 years for men and 22.0 to 26.1 for women. Also, with some 2.8 billion people–two in five–still struggling to survive on less than $2 a day, poor women tend to give birth at earlier ages and have more children throughout their lives than wealthier women.[14]

- *Delayed marriage among young adults has not yet resulted in noticeable reductions in the percentage of persons marrying at least once over their lifetime.* Marriage or some form of consensual union continues to be nearly universal. In the 1970s, in three out of every four countries, around 89% or more of all men and all women aged 45-49 had been married at least once. By the 1990s, that figure was still close to 89%.

- *Divorce rates have increased in most countries with data available.* In developed countries, the median divorce rate rose from 13 divorces per 100 for men and women in 1970s to 24 divorces per 100 men and 27 per 100 women in the 1990s. In developing countries, the median divorce rate increased from 7 to 12 divorces per 100 men and from 5 to 15 divorces per 100 women. That is, not only has there been a tendency

---

[12] *World Fertility Report: 2003,* Population Division, Department of Economic and Social Affairs, the United Nations, New York, March 12, 2004.

[13] For statistical convenience, the report designates countries in terms of 'more developed', 'less developed', and 'least developed'.

[14] "State of world population 2004," United Nations Population Fund, Press Summary, New York, September 15, 2004.

for people to marry later, but also the instability of marital unions has been rising. Clearly, both trends have significant implications for reproductive behavior.

- *A tremendous increase has taken place in the use of family planning.* Between the 1970s and 1990s, the use of contraception among women currently married or in union increased in nine out of every ten countries with information available. The median level of contraceptive use at the world level increased from 38% of women currently married or in union in the 1970s to 52% in the 1990s. For developing countries, the median prevalence rose from 27% to 40% between those years. By the 1990s, contraceptive prevalence in a quarter of all developing countries was 62% or higher.

- *Between 1970 and 2000, the world population experienced a major and unprecedented reduction of fertility levels, driven mostly by fertility decline in developing countries.* Average fertility levels in the developing world dropped from over 5.9 children per woman in the 1970s to about 3.9 children per woman in the 1990s. The median fertility reduction in developing countries between the 1970s and 1990s was of 1.8 children per woman, noting that a quarter of all developing countries appear to have achieved reductions of 2.6 children per woman or more.

- *Childlessness levels vary considerably among major areas.* In the 1990s, the proportions of childless women among those aged 45-49 tended to be high in developed countries and in the Caribbean region. At least 7% of women aged 45-49 were childless in four of every five developed countries with data, and in nine developed countries the proportion childless surpassed 10%. Childlessness levels were relatively low in Africa and Asia in the 1990s, and moderate in Latin America. Between the 1970s and 1990s, childlessness levels declined in Africa, as sterility caused by sexually transmitted diseases decreased during the 1970s and 1980s (see Figure 3.4. below).

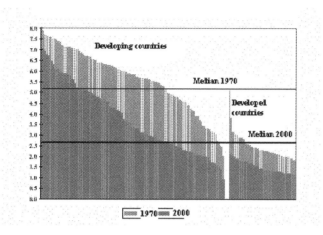

Figure 3. 4. Distribution of 160 countries by total fertility level around 1970 and 2000 (World Fertility Report, 2003)

- *The profound changes in fertility levels occurring since 1970 have been made possible by major behavioral transformations related to union formation, marriage and contraception use.* Government policies on contraceptives have played an important role in modifying reproductive behavior. In 1976, 52% of all governments reported they had no intervention to modify fertility levels, but by 2001 that percentage had dropped to 32%. Since the 1970s, government support for family planning has increased steadily. By 2001, 92% of all governments supported family planning programs and the distribution of contraceptives either directly (75%), through government facilities, or indirectly (17%), by supporting the activities of non-governmental organizations such as family planning associations.

Governments views on the adequacy of fertility levels have also changed considerably. In 1976, some 27% of all governments wanted to lower fertility, and by 2001, some 45% did so. There was also a percentage increase in the governments wishing to raise fertility: from 9% in the 1976 to 13% in 2001. In other words, today more governments wish to change the fertility levels of their populations and are prepared to devise adequate interventions to achieve such goals. Examine Figure 3.5.

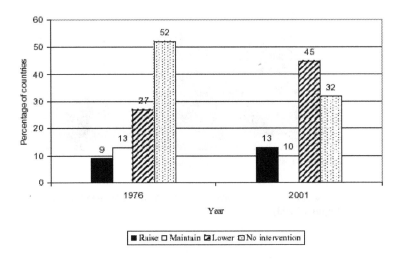

Figure 3. 5. Government policies on the level of fertility, 1976-2001 (World Fertility Report, 2003)

III.I.II.II. The Demographic Challenge Awaiting Europe

A study intended to improve the understanding of the interrelations between policy and demographic change examined the interactions between European government policies and demographic trends and behavior, and assessed which policies can prevent or mitigate the adverse consequences of current low fertility and population aging.

Almost all European nations are experiencing long-term downtrends in fertility, and consequently, aging of their populations. In nearly all countries, fertility rates are now below replacement level (2.1 children per couple).[15]

To take one example, France in 2004 has seen life expectancy pass the age of 80 for both sexes, in a constant evolution tracing back to the mid 18th century. Part

---

[15] Jonathan Grant et al., *Low Fertility and Population Ageing: Causes, Consequences, and Policy Options*, Summary, RAND (Europe), 2004, pp. xiii-xviii.

of the remarkable rise in life expectancy during the end of the 19th century is attributed to the progress in the fields of hygienics and medicine (with particular reference to the pasteurization revolution).[16] Children were the first to benefit from such achievements in health, noting that the first childcare and protection policies were also introduced during that period.

As for adults, life expectancy beyond 60 years of age for men has increased to 21.5 years in 2004 (6 years more than that of 1954). For women, it is 26.5 years in 2004 (7.7 years more than that of 1954). With cardiovascular diseases and cancer being the main causes of death at those ages, progresses in their treatment since the 1970s have contributed to higher life expectancy.

Eventually, natural population growth rates are entering periods of declining growth or outright decrease. Meanwhile, the proportion of elderly dependents continues to grow while the working-age population declines as a share of the overall population. Taken as a whole, these demographic trends could, according to the study (Grant et al., 2004), have potentially damaging consequences for European economies. Consider the following:

- as the working-age population decreases, countries experience declines in human capital–which eventually and potentially reduces productivity;

- pension and social insurance systems can become heavy burdens;

- the ability to care for the growing elderly population declines as household sizes decrease; and,

- the elderly face sharply increased health care needs and costs.

Such developments, in turn, are likely to pose significant barriers to achieving the goals of the European Union Social Agenda in respect of full employment, economic growth and social cohesion. Concern over these trends has sparked intense debate over the most effective policies to reverse them, or at least mitigate their consequences. However, any discussion on the issue needs to be seen in the

---

[16] «Population et sociétés, no. 410», March 2005, ('Population and Societies', a monthly information bulletin of the National Institute of Demographic Studies, INED), Paris.

context of the complex political debate associated with policies aiming to affect demographic behavior. Above all, it is a legitimate question to ask whether a given government has a right to intervene and influence the private discussion of individuals and their partners in making decisions about their own fertility and family formation.

Accordingly, the same study (Grant et al., 2004) outlines the five main conclusions below:

1. *Population aging cannot be remedied through replacement immigration.* The sheer numbers of immigrants required to offset population aging in the European Union would be unacceptable in Europe's current socio-political climate. Record numbers of annual immigrants would be needed to offset aging–at a time the European Union (and its member states) is actively trying to prevent immigration. The debate, thus, is more appropriately on whether immigration may be effectively used to *slow* as opposed to *prevent* population aging.

2. *Government policies can slow fertility decline rates.* Case studies showed instances where countries that experienced a relaxation of pronatalist policies, such as Poland and the German Democratic Republic (GDR), saw declines in fertility. Spain currently has the second lowest fertility rate of the EU member states (behind Italy). Yet, a generation ago (in 1971) Spain had the second highest European fertility rate. The dramatic fertility decline since then is associated with a shift from the Franco reign–prohibition, contraception, and honoring large families–to a democratic system with a passive population policy. France at present, in contrast with Spain, has the second highest fertility rate in Europe (behind Ireland) and enjoys one of the most interventionist set of policies aimed at encouraging families to have children. Polices that affect fertility may typically have other objectives. In Sweden, both family policy and employment policies are linked to the primary objective of allowing couples to combine family

formation with work. Last, fertility declines and subsequently reverses, in turn, may be attributable less to policy changes than to the social and economic environment. In Spain once again, low fertility rates have been explained by (among other matters) high unemployment rates for people under 30, high housing costs, and the tendency of young adults to live with their families for more years than in other European countries.

3. *No single policy works.* Historically, governments have had success in slowing fertility declines through a variety of interventions. France in recent decades has had success by focusing on the birth of the third or subsequent child. Sweden's policy of parental leave during the 1980s allowed many women to raise children and remain in the workforce. The *combination* of policies targeted at equal responsibilities for men and women in Sweden as wage earner and care provider, and at the children welfare were together essential for supporting family formation and for family life quality. The introduction of a family policy scheme in the former GDR in 1976, including prolonged maternity leave, paid educational leave, interest-free loans to newly-wed couples, substantially raised birth grants, increased monthly family allowances, and improved day care, altogether as a generous package had subsequent impacts on fertility. Obviously, what works in one country may not work in another.

4. *Political, economic, and social contexts influence policy impacts.* Different interventions have varying effects because of the complex and shifting political, economic, and social contexts within which they are implemented. This is best illustrated with the political transitions of countries. For instance, the fertility decline in the former GDR after unification cannot be attributed to a specific policy, but rather to changing social environment. Women who faced the unification with concerns about their personal economic situation were less likely to have children in the following months. Likewise, the transition to a free market economy in Poland changed the economic environment and

incentives for childbearing and also diffused Western ideas and values to broad segments of the public. In Spain, a dramatic fertility decline was associated with the demographic rule that emerged following the dissolution of Franco's regime.

5. *Population policies take effect slowly.* Government policies intended to reverse fertility declines, directly or indirectly, tend to have a long-term focus and require many years to implement. For that reason they tend to lack political appeal as well as political initiators (though some population policies may have an exceptional and immediate impact, such as abortion policy). The final stage in the cycle for population policies to affect fertility takes a generation before they affect the number of new entrants to the labor force. A number of implications lie here. One, there is a disconnection between electoral cycles (typically 4-5 years) and the longer cycle of population policy– meaning that politicians have limited incentive to advocate such policies. Two, politicians tend to focus on policies that have shorter time horizons including, for example, social security reforms that aim to reduce the economic burden facing states on the expense of the overall welfare systems. Three, a way to mitigate the adverse consequences of low fertility and population aging is to increase human capital by encouraging people to work longer. This can mean promoting a longer working life (as in France with regard to the recent retirement age reforms) and encouraging new entrants (such as women) into the workforce. Related to this is the need for new development *pro-elderly* policies that encourage elderly people to be active and productive members for the workforce. However, it must be added that employment policies that encourage women to enter the workforce can have a perverse effect on fertility–particularly if women choose a career over family.

In the coming years women are expected to gain more rights and freedoms, whether in education, political participation, or in work force equality. Despite the narrowing difference between women and men's earnings during the last decade, women are expected to continue to receive less pay than men (ranging from 20 to 50 percent less).

III.I.III. The Global Wave of Migrants in the Information Age

III.I.III.I. Tracing the Early Signs of Migrants

Immigration is among the inter-cultural issues that are increasingly replacing inter-superpower subjects as the top items on the international agenda. People on the move have always carried their wants and needs, their fears and their hopes along with them. Now more than ever they also carry their politics and their culture.

Some migrants are highly skilled cosmopolitans who travel the world easily in the comfortable balloon of the transnational network. Others are low skilled economic migrants, refugees or asylum seekers whose global journey is more in question since, when relocating out of political or economic necessity, they also place their social identity at risk. Francart and Patry draw attention, as well, to the various types of human masses with particular psychological characteristics. They are:

- *Fleeing masses:* which are constituted of flows of refuges or disbanded armies;
- *Masses of refusal:* which show a clear, collective resistance to the government;
- *Aroused masses:* which appear and disappear suddenly and are featured to be extremely brutal; and,
- *Masses of upheaval:* which are uncontrollable movements aimed at overthrowing the power in place.[17]

---

[17] Loup Francart and Jean-Jacques Patry, *Mastering Violence: An Option for Operational Military Strategy,* 1998, p. 31.

Refugees have always been a part of Europe's landscape in particular, more in the previous century than ever so far. In 1919-1920, a million people fled the Bolshevik armies in European Russia, as the massive human floods continued throughout the decades: 320,000 Armenians scattered all around Europe a few years later, nearly two million Greeks and Turks transferred to friendly territory under a 1923 agreement between the two old enemies, hundreds of thousands of people uprooted during the Spanish Civil War in the late 1930s along with a quarter million people fleeing Germany in the same period.[18] By 1942, there were more than 21 million homeless and displaced people scattered all over Europe.

The Cold War era spawned new refugee movements. Displaced people became both political pawns and political capital in the struggle between East and West. Asylum took on an ideological basis that favored refugees from communism who found the doors open to them in a charged atmosphere. Their moral and legal rights were underpinned by the creation of the United Nations and the Council of Europe. The 1948 Universal Declaration of Human Rights assured people the right to seek and enjoy asylum, and the 1951 Convention relating to the status of refugees codified the principle that no one should be returned to a country where his life or freedom would be at risk.

Europe's doors to asylum seekers are today, at best, slightly open. In fact, the picture varies from country to country, often reflecting colonial links. Accordingly, asylum seekers from Guinea-Bissau often go to Portugal, those from the Congo (ex-Zaire) to Belgium, and those from Sri Lanka to the United Kingdom. Almost all countries, however, began tightening their asylum policies when numbers started to rise and the proportion of non-Europeans also increased.

Until the early 1980s, the number of asylum seekers arriving in Western Europe remained fairly stable at under 100,000 annually. Around 70% came from Eastern Europe, who were rapidly granted asylum and easily integrated. When individual countries were eventually unable to cope, as in 1956-1957 when some

---

[18] The following figures on migrants, unless stated, are taken from the official publication: *Refugees*, Vol. 2, no. 113, 1998, published by the Public Information Section of the UN High Commissioner for Refugees. Also see: *L'Atlas du monde diplomatique*, January 2003, 54-55, and 92-93.

200,000 Hungarians streamed into Austria and Yugoslavia, other European countries, the United States, Canada, Australia, South Africa and Argentina, all willingly offered permanent settlement to numbers of refugees–in what may be considered an early form of 'burden-sharing,' which four decades later became a contentious issue among European nations.

The continent's first large-scale experience with non-Europeans came with the resettlement starting in the late 1970s of Vietnamese boat people and other Indochinese refugees who were not allowed to stay in first asylum countries in Southeast Asia. That flow was controlled and manageable. By the mid-1980s, however, the picture began to change. With over 300,000 applications in 1989, more came from Africa, Asia and the Middle East.[19] At the time the number of asylum seekers in Europe reached an unprecedented peak of some 700,000 in 1992, governments were applying (or at least trying to) a sweeping *zero immigration policy*, as the emphasis shifted decisively from one of protecting refugees to exclusion and control.

The background to the dramatic increase in the number of asylum seekers is a largely European one. In 1992, one-third of asylum applicants in Western Europe were Romanians and Bulgarians who were allowed to travel abroad. As the freedom of movement increased, asylum applications from former East-bloc countries declined. That same year, one fourth of all applicants were citizens of the former Yugoslavia. The influx of people fleeing war and persecution in the Balkans continued throughout the 1990s. Germany took the pressure of that influx, sheltering 350,000 Bosnians and as many as 100,000 Croats. They were rapidly replaced by an increasing number of Kosovors, Albanians and Turkish Kurds, reflecting two of Europe's most intractable problems.

---

[19] A poll conducted by the Arab Human Development Report team in 2001 showed more than half of the young Arab people surveyed wanted to immigrate to other countries, mostly to industrialized countries outside the region. Jobs and education topped the list of concerns amongst the 13-20 year-olds polled, with some differences amongst older and younger groups. "These findings clearly indicate the dissatisfaction of Arab youth with current conditions and future prospects in their home countries. If these issues are not addressed, more young and qualified Arabs will join the million Arab experts who have migrated to other parts of the world." See: Arab Human Development Report 2002, UNDP, Press Kit, "The Arab World: Let the Numbers Speak!" p. 3.

Consequently, current refugee policy in both European and non-European countries is framed mainly as an issue of immigration control and national security. The fruits of that policy are evident by the number of asylum seekers arriving in industrialized countries, a figure that fell sharply for the third year in a row in 2004–reaching its lowest level for 16 years.[20] In the 38 industrialized countries for which comparable historical statistics are available, the total of asylum applicants arriving in 2004 was the lowest since 1988, at 368,000. Examine Figure 3.6.

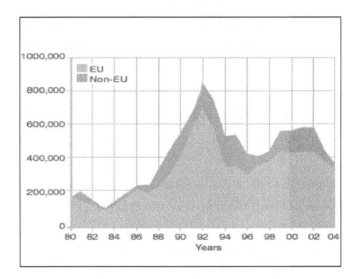

Figure 3. 6. Overall asylum applications in 38 industrialized countries (UNHCR, March 2005)

Marking a similarly steep decline to that in 2003, the number of asylum claims in industrialized countries fell by 22% in 2004. In the European Union, the number fell by 19%, in North America by 26%, and in Australia and New Zealand by 28%. The year 2004 total was the lowest for many years in most individual asylum countries. For example, the number is the lowest in Germany since 1984. In the United States and Switzerland, it is the lowest since 1987; and it is also the lowest in the Netherlands since 1988.

---

[20] "Asylum Levels and Trends in Industrialized Countries, 2004," United Nations High Commissioner for Refugees (UNHCR), Geneva, March 1, 2005.

France was the top receiving country in 2004, with an estimated 61,600 asylum seekers. The United States, being the top receiving country in 2003, came second with 52,400. The United Kingdom was third with 40,200. Germany, the top asylum country in 13 of the past 20 years, was fourth, with 35,600. In fifth position came Canada with 25,500.

Based on a per capita formula over the past five years, Cyprus, Austria, Sweden, Luxemburg and Ireland are ranked the top receiving countries in the European Union (25 members). Meanwhile, the United Kingdom, France and Germany all appear in mid-table (see Figure 3.7.). Interesting to observe is the fact that the 10 new EU members witnessed their combined total of asylum applications increasing by 4% in 2004.

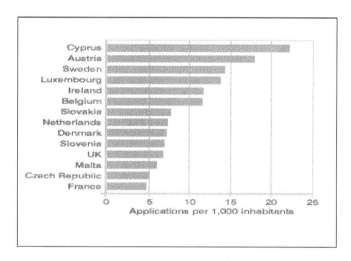

Figure 3. 7. Asylum applications per capita in Europe (UNHCR, March 2005)

Last to note, in 2004 the largest group of asylum seekers was from the Russian Federation (with 30,100, the majority of whom are Chechens). That is followed by asylum seekers from Serbia and Montenegro (with 22,300, mainly from Kosovo), China (with 19,700), Turkey (with 16,200), and India (with 11,900). In the past three years, the number of Afghans (the top group in 2001 with more than 50,000 asylum seekers) has seen a sharp fall by 83%, standing in 2004 in 13th place with

8,800. On the other hand, the number of Iraqis claiming asylum half way through 2004 started to rise again. Review Figure 3.8.

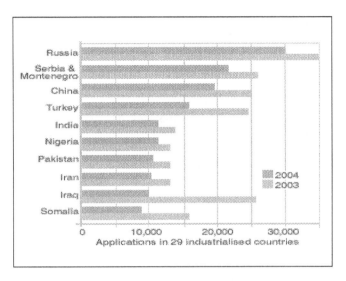

Figure 3. 8. Main origin countries of asylum seekers (UNHCR, March 2005)

III.I.III.II. The Cultural and Social Integration of Migrants in Recipient Societies

UN recent figures indicate that the number of international migrants in the world increased from an estimated 75 million in 1960 to almost 175 million in 2000. In 1991, the break-up of the former Union of Soviet Socialist Republics (USSR) gave rise to a discontinuity in the growth of the migrant stock, where individuals living in the newly independent successor countries but born in another one of these countries became international migrants at the time of independence without having actually migrated then. This change resulted to the addition of some 27 million persons to the international migrant stock.[21]

Estimates available show that the number of international migrants constituted 2.5% of the world's population in 1960, 2.2% in 1970, 2.3% in 1980, and 2.9% in

---

[21] Refer to: *Trends in Total Migrant Stock: The 2003 Revision,* Population Division, Department of Economic and Social Affairs, the United Nations, New York, 2003.

both 1990 and 2000.[22] In recent decades, developed countries have absorbed the vast majority of the growth in the number of international migrants. Between 1960 and 2000, the number of international migrants in Australia, New Zealand, Japan, Europe, Northern America and the successor countries of the former USSR increased by 78 million persons, whereas the number in less developed regions rose by 27 million. The United States is the largest recipient of international migrants, with 35 million migrants in 2000. It was followed by the Russia Federation (13 million), Germany (7 million), Ukraine, France, and India.

With global migrations now near historic peak once again, the difference between past movements and migrants today is that at present the cultural and political roots people carry are not planted in the new *terra firma* while adjusting to conditions there; Rather they are nourished in a hydroponic fashion from selected streams of cultural and political ideas flowing constantly around the globe. For the ex-territorial cosmopolitans who see national boundaries and nation-states as increasingly irrelevant to life in the 21st century and whom are connected by e-mail and mobile phones to the business at hand, they are deliberately detached from any roots that bind to a community of place.

Low skilled economic migrants, refugees or asylum seekers, on the other hand, are disconnected from the territory in which they work or seek refuge precisely because they are still attached to a community of place elsewhere. In diasporas, people identify even more intensely with a homeland. They carry their belongings with them, and, when they migrate in large numbers together, their communal culture travels too. Communication media that liberate communities from territory intensifies political and cultural identity on the part of billions of individuals colliding and converging as the result of extensive physical movement. At times before where the dominance of print media both created and bound cultures in an expanded but still physical space, today's electronic media erase–all at once–geographic boundaries altogether.

---

[22] The 27 million persons figure mentioned above was backdated to 1990 so as to make the 1990 figures comparable with those for 2000 in terms of the number of countries covered.

In the place of common mediated images of the *other world* brought by national broadcast media and general interest newspapers and magazines, the Information Age in its current phase has made it even more possible for people to exercise their psychological inclination to filter what they choose to hear, see and read. Personalized electronic editions of the daily news–from where individuals can pre-select precisely what interests them and avoid inconvenient information that might challenge their worldviews–already exist. By communicating only with those who already share their perspective, people are likely to move toward a more extreme point in the direction to which their group's members were already inclined. Oglesby emphasizes:

> the group polarization that results is potentially dangerous for democracy and social peace because such in-group communication intensifies rather than bridges gaps with groups holding other views. 21st century information technology rather than creating a digital global forum, in which ideas are debated cross-culturally, enables greater cultural apartheid with consequent conflict.[23]

When citizens do not share common experiences, dreams and memories as a result of their gradual and separate worlds of emotions and significance while sharing the same physical space, the national community dissolves into fragments. People, in the current de-centralized era, are no longer as easily gathered into patriotic prides by governmental powers standing on guard. The concepts of nation and state become loose as individuals living within these sovereign spaces are *free* to identify with communities of fate elsewhere and pursue survival. *Global Trends 2015* (p. 41) concludes likewise:

> Using opportunities afforded by globalization and the opening of civil society, communal groups will be better positioned to mobilize their co-religionists to assert their interests or defend against perceived economies or political discrimination.

---

[23] Donna Oglesby, "diplomacy.cultural 2015@state.gov," *iMP Magazine*, July 23, 2001.

In the United States, fears over immigration effects on natural values and on a coherent sense of American identity have prevailed since the early years of the nation, and they have been accentuated by the September 11 attacks. Both the numbers and the origins of the new immigrants have raised concerns about immigration effects on American culture. Data from the 2000 census alerted a rising Hispanic population driven largely by waves of new immigrants, legal and illegal, with Hispanics about to replace blacks as the nation's largest minority.[24] Demographic projections portray a country in 2050 where non-Hispanic states will only constitute a slim majority. There and then, Hispanics will reach 25%, blacks 14%, and Asians 8%.[25]

The United States spends as much as $2 billion a year to build walls, post 24-hour patrols and crack down on illegal immigrants streaming across its 2000 mile border with Mexico. Once inside the border after evading the Border Patrol and surviving scorching deserts and treacherous mountains, however, illegal immigrants find a country increasingly willing to ignore laws that forbid hiring them. They also find a nation willing to embrace them in homes and workplaces more as *de facto* immunity members than as 'outlawers.'

But even so, twice as many Americans are skeptical about immigration as are sympathetic to it. Various polls show a plurality or majority wanting fewer immigrants to come into the country. They fear the effects on wages and the costs to taxpayers, and above all, they worry that the culture cannot assimilate large numbers of new immigrants.[26] In the past, the United States successfully absorbed millions of immigrants from scores of countries because they adapted to the prevailing European culture and enthusiastically embraced the American understanding of liberty, equality, individualism, and democracy. As 50% of the population becomes Hispanic or non-white, the question now is whether or not this

---

[24] Eric Schmitt, "New Census Shows Hispanics Are Even With Blacks in U.S.," *The New York Times*, March 8, 2001, 1.

[25] Steven Holmes, "Census Sees a Profound Ethnic Shift in U.S.," *The New York Times*, March 14, 1996, 16.

[26] Alan Wolfe, *One Nation, After All: What Americans Really Think About God, Country, Family, Racism, Welfare, Immigration, Homosexuality, Work, the Right, the Left and Each Other*, New York: Viking, 1998, p. 138.

pattern will continue to prevail. Will the de-Westernization of the United States, if it does occur, also imply its de-Americanization?

In Europe, spurred by anti-immigrant talk from ring-wing parties that are both provoking and capitalizing on fears of immigrants, many countries are under immense political pressure from voters to prove their policies are as tough as those of their neighbors–if not tougher. At a Summit Meeting in Tamper (Finland) in 1999, the European Union countries pledged to work toward a common asylum policy that would put an end to so-called *asylum shopping*, in which would-be refugees try to settle in the country with the most liberal policies. Denmark, for example, grants asylum to 43% of applicants, a far higher percentage than in most European countries. Britain, by contrast, grants asylum to 26% of those who apply, while Austria to 4%.[27]

Many proposals put forward since that Summit in 1999, on issues like the right of immigrants to work while their asylum applications are being processed, and the reunification of immigrants' families in Europe, have been delayed and hindered by bureaucratic debates. With an estimated 300,000 to 500,000 people arriving illegally in Western Europe each year, Europe has not even been able to agree on a definition of what constitutes a refugee under the 1951 United Nations Convention Relating to the Status of Refugees.

The European Union's demand that countries wishing to join the Union should comply with basic standards on asylum issues without doubt lead to a degree of "harmonization." Yet, a problem persists in the major difficulties the small number of recognized refugees have in genuinely integrating in the new asylum countries of Central and Eastern Europe. This serves as a "push factor" encouraging asylum seekers and refugees to continue their east-west trek through countries such as Poland, the Czech Republic and Hungary.

Governments have introduced restrictions to try to reduce what they perceived to be an excessive number of people seeking protection, including reducing social

---

[27] Sarah Lyall, "When Asylum Seekers Knock, Europe Is Deaf," *The New York Times*, online edition, June 20, 2002.

benefits, detaining asylum seekers and applying a narrow legal interpretation of who can qualify as a refugee.

As asylum applications in Britain soared in 2002 (with 19,520 applications in the first quarter of the year), the country announced tightening its immigrations laws by ordering failed asylum seekers to leave the country within days and to file any appeals from their home country or whatever country they had last been in before arriving there. The statistics pointed to a situation that has aroused anger among many British who argue that the country's immigration policies are too tolerant and have made Britain a *soft touch* for asylum seekers.[28]

In Germany, although there is no official immigration policy, there are already around 7.3 million *legal* foreign residents (accounting for some 9% of the population). Most of them or their parents arrived as temporary guest workers or refugees benefiting from the country's generous asylum laws. Its conservative Christian Democratic Union stresses Germany had a *leitkultur* (prevailing culture) that both citizens and new immigrants had an obligation to accept.

The Party supports immigration, since German industry needs tens of thousands of new migrants every year to supplement its aging, shrinking population. However and in return, newcomers are expected to show more cultural integration by learning the German language and respecting German traditions and law, including equality for women (Germans are becoming more and more uncomfortable at the sight of Muslim women wearing scarves in Turkish neighborhoods). Failing to attend German-language courses for long-term immigrants could count against a foreigner's application for an extension to his stay.[29] Bonn already gives applicants assistance in kind rather than in cash and at 80% of the level a need citizen receives. And it further reduced benefits to asylum seekers entering the country illegally or whose applications had been rejected.

---

[28] Warren Hoge, "New Immigration Plan in Britain Would Restrict Asylum Seekers," *The New York Times,* online edition, May 31, 2002.

[29] "New Immigration Law Proposed in Germany," *IHT,* August 4-5, 2001, 4, and also: "German Party Sets Immigration Policy," *IHT,* November 7, 2000, 7.

The Netherlands introduced, as early as 1998, a system in which new arrivals are housed in tents and put on a 'waiting list' for proper accommodation. The threat of detention is also applied as a deterrent. Those arriving at Frankfurt airport are held in a closed facility until their claims have been decided, in a practice the government has refused to label detention, arguing that the people are free to leave at any time, back to the country they came from.

France is another European country that has decided to take action in view of its mounting political refugee applications in 2004. Government authorities announced a list of countries of which applicants will be treated on a 'priority basis' not to exceed 15 days. Deemed as respectful of human rights, the countries concerned (for the moment) are Benin, Cap-Vert, Ghana, Mali, Mauritius, Senegal, and Mongolia. The list and measures were reported to be a first step, noting that the refugee demands from those seven countries in 2004 only represented 6% (1500 demands) of the more than 60,000 figure. However, setting and reviewing a list of the countries concerned is not an easy task for the French authorities. For example, Britain would have preferred to add the Maghreb countries to the list, at a time Mali was added despite the will of Germany.[30]

Implementing a narrow interpretation of who can qualify as a *bona fide* refugee is, whatsoever, probably the most worrying aspect of asylum trends in Europe. Even as an increasing number of people flee from countries wracked by civil wars such as Angola, or where state authority had totally collapsed as in Somalia, the idea of excluding people who have been persecuted by so-called "non-state agents" (like rebels or religious extremists) has grown.

Germany's Federal Administrative Court, for instance, ruled that individuals who fled Afghanistan's Taliban could not qualify for refugee status because the Taliban do not represent a recognized government. Bosnian Muslims, Somalis and moderate Algerians have also run against this interpretation. Sweden, however, amended its law in order to explicitly recognize there is nothing in the 1951 Convention that would exclude refugee status for persons prosecuted by non-state

---

[30] Refer to Marie-Christine Tabet, «Droit d'asile: la France plus stricte pour sept pays», ('Asylum rights: France becomes stricter for seven countries'), *Le Figaro*, April 13, 2005, 8.

agents. Important court rulings in the United Kingdom and in the Netherlands confirmed the Convention's interpretation, long advocated by the United Nation's High Commissioner for Refugees.

III.II. The Evolution of Languages in the Information Age

Thanks to the advances in the field of sociolinguistics, and the availability of detailed surveys and studies on world language use, it is now much easier to gain information (and eventually draw analyses) on the social and cultural circumstances that govern language status and change. This section of the dissertation attempts to underline the importance of multilingualism in the Information Age; and also seeks to contribute to the politically controversial debate of the role of the English language in today's world.

III.II.I. The Rise of a Global Language

A language may achieve a genuinely global status when it develops a special role that is recognized in every country.[31] Such a status can be realized only after other countries around the world have adopted that language. There are two essential ways in which this can be assured. First, a language can be made the official language of a country, where it is to be used as a medium of communication in the government, the law courts, the media, and in the educational system. To adapt in these societies, it is essential to master the official language in life as early as possible. Such a language is usually described as a *second language*, since it is seen as a complement to a person's *mother tongue*, or *first language*.

Second, a language can be made a priority in a country's foreign-language teaching, although that language may have no official status. It becomes the language children are most likely to be taught when they begin school, and the one most available to adults who–for one reason or another–never learned it, or rather learned it badly, in their early educational years.

In reflecting on these observations, it is important to note to the several ways in which a language can be official. It may be the sole official language of a country, or it may share this status with other languages. It may also have a *semi-*

---

[31] The following presentation on the evolution of languages is based on the work of David Crystal, *English as a Global Language*, Cambridge: Cambridge University Press, 1997.

official status, used only in certain domains, or take second place to other languages while still performing certain official roles. Many countries formally acknowledge a language's status in their constitution (as in India);[32] some make no special mention of it (as in Britain, where no mention is made of English in any of the documents that are significant for the history of Britain, nor as in the United States where English was not signaled out for reference when its constitution was being drafted).[33] In some countries, the question of whether the special status should be legally recognized is a source of considerable controversy (as in Iraq, after April 2003 with its initial draft constitution).[34] In other words, rulings are needed to regulate conflict. If there is no conflict, there is no need for rulings.

In addition, there is variation in the reason for choosing a particular language as a favored foreign language. That may include historical tradition, political expediency, and perhaps the desire for commercial, cultural or technological contact. Even when chosen, the presence of the language can vary greatly, depending on the extent to which a government or foreign-aid agency is prepared to give adequate financial support to a language-teaching policy.

Why a particular language becomes a global language has little to do with the number of people who speak it, explains world authority on the English language,

---

[32] The constitution of France underlines French as the language of the Republic despite the fact seven regional tongues exist (Alsacian, Basque, Breton, Catalan, Corsican, Flemish and Provençal).

[33] Concerning the United States, language controversies have recently been raised on two key issues. First, to what extent should the U.S. government promote the knowledge and use of languages other than English and also restrict the ability of governments, businesses and institutions to require the use of English? And second, should the country become a bilingual society, with Spanish enjoying equal status? This aspect, along with its implying jurisdiction cases in the past few decades, is well examined by Samuel P. Huntington, *Who Are We? America's Great Debate*, London: Simon & Schuster UK Ltd, 2004, pp. 158-70.

[34] Article 9 of the Law of Administration for the State of Iraq for the Transitional Period, issued on March 8, 2004 states:

"The Arabic language and the Kurdish language are the two official languages in Iraq. The right of Iraqis to educate their children in their mother tongue, such as Turcoman, Syriac, Armenian, in government educational institutions in accordance with educational guidelines, or in any other language in private educational institutions, shall be guaranteed."

The full text of the Law is available at: http://www.cpa-iraq.org/government/TAL.html. Another example to consider is the wide-ranging negotiation designed to lead to a comprehensive political settlement in Macedonia, which stalled out on a single issue, namely the recognition of Albanian as a second official language. See: Peter Finn, "Driving the Macedonian Conflict: A Language Argument," *IHT*, July 21-22, 2001, 2.

David Crystal.[35] It is much more to do with who those speakers are. Latin, for example, became an international language throughout the Roman Empire, but this was not because the Romans were more numerous than the peoples they ruled. They were simply more powerful. When the Roman military power declined, later on, Latin remained for a millennium as the international language of education, as a result of another sort of power–the ecclesiastical power of Roman Catholicism.

Here lies the association between language dominance and cultural power. Without a strong power-base, whether political, military or economic, no language can make progress as an international medium of communication. Language exists only in the brains, mouths, ears, hands and eyes of its users. When they succeed on the international stage, their language succeeds; when they fail, their language fails as well.

Obvious as it may seem, this point demands attention since many popular and misleading beliefs have grown over the years on why a language should become internationally successful. It is common to hear people claim a language is a paragon, on account of its perceived aesthetic qualities, clarity of expression, literary power, or mere religious standing. Arabic, English, French, Greek and Latin are among those languages that at various times have been lauded in such terms. It is often suggested, for instance, that there must be something inherently beautiful or logical about the structure of English, so as to explain why it is now so widely used. Some may note that English 'has less grammar than other language.' Others may note to the absence of endings on its words, or to the need to remember the differences between genders, and so it must be easier to master.[36]

Yet, such arguments are misconceived. Latin was once a major international language, despite its many inflectional endings and gender differences. French, as well, has been such a language, despite its nouns being masculine or feminine; and so, at different times and places, have the heavily inflected Greek, Arabic, Spanish and Russian. That is, ease of learning has nothing to do with it. This is not to deny that a language may enjoy certain properties making it appealing internationally.

---

[35] David Crystal, *English as a Global Language*, 1997, p. 5.

[36] These differences in gender were the most problematic while learning French.

The inherent structural properties, the volume of vocabulary, its great literature record in the past, or its association with a culture or religion all are factors that can motivate someone to learn a language. But, of course, none of them alone, or in combination, can ensure world spread of a particular language.

A language becomes international for one chief reason: the political power of its people–especially their military power. Consider examples throughout history. Over 2000 years ago, Greek became a language of international communication in the Middle East not because of the intellects of Plato and Aristotle, but through the swords and spears wielded by the armies of Alexander the Great. The legions of the Roman Empire well set Latin all over Europe. The spread of Islam led Arabic widely across northern Africa and the Middle East. The colonial policies of the Renaissance kings and queens paved way for Spanish, Portuguese and French into the Americas, Africa and the Far East.

However, international language dominance is not solely the result of military might. It may take a military powerful nation to establish a language, but it takes an economically powerful one to maintain and expand it. In the 20th century, this became an even more particular critical factor with economic developments beginning to operate on a global scale, backed by the new communication technologies (the telegraph, telephone, and the radio), and fostering the emergence of massive multinational organizations. The growth of competitive industry and business brought an explosion of international marketing and publicity. Reaching unprecedented levels, the power of the press was soon surpassed by the broadcasting media–thanks to their ability to cross national frontiers with electromagnetic ease. In the form of movies and records, technology generated new mass entertainment industries with a worldwide impact. Also, the drive for progress in science and technology gave birth to an international intellectual and research environment that rendered scholarship and further education a high profile.

Any language at the center of such a burst of international activity would suddenly have found itself with a global status. By the beginning of the 19th century, Britain, with its English language, had become the world's leading industrial and trading country. By the end of the century, the population of the

United States (then approaching 100 million) was larger than of any of the countries of Western Europe, with its economy being the most productive and the fastest growing in the world. During the 19th century, British imperialism sent English around the globe. And during the 20th century, that world presence was maintained and promoted significantly through the economic supremacy of the new American superpower. As we all know, the language behind the U.S. dollar was English.

For thousands of years, interpreters would be present whenever monarchs and ambassadors met on the international stage.[37] However, there are limits to what can be done in this way. The more a community is linguistically mixed, the less it can rely on individuals to ensure communication between different groups. The problem was solved by finding a language to act as a *lingua franca* or 'common language'.

The geographical extent to which a lingua franca can be used is governed by political considerations. The prospect that a lingua franca might be needed for the whole world, states Crystal (1997, p. 8), is something which emerged strongly only in the 20th century, and since the 1950s in particular. The principal international forum for political communications, the United Nations, dates only from 1945. Since then, other major international bodies were established: the World Bank (in 1945), UNESCO and UNICEF (1946), the World Health Organization (1948), and the International Atomic Energy Agency (1957). The pressure to adopt a single lingua franca to facilitate communication in such contexts is considerable, with the alternative being expensive and impracticable multi-way translation facilities.

A certain number of languages are usually designated official languages for the activities of an organization. The League of Nations, founded in 1921, adopted English and French as its two official and working languages. The United Nations was later founded with five official languages: Chinese, English, French, Spanish and Russian, before including Arabic afterwards (in comparison to the European Union with eleven languages before its enlargement in 2004). The working

---

[37] For information, it is recalled that until the 17th century most treaties were written in Latin, thereafter in French, and in the 20th century chiefly in English. However, since the end of the World War II, it has become much more common for copies of agreements to be translated into the language of each party. See: J.A.S. Grenville and B. Wasserstein, *The Major International Treaties since 1945: A History and Guide With Texts*, London: Methuen, 1987, p. 10.

languages of the General Assembly, however, are limited to English, French and Spanish, while those of the Security Council are English and French. There is now a widespread view on the necessity of reducing the numbers of languages involved in world bodies as a major step towards cutting down on the enormous amount of translation and clerical work required. Trimming a translation budget, whatsoever, is never easy, since clearly no country would appreciate the thought of its language being given a reduced international standing.

The urge for a global language is appreciated in particular by the international academic and business communities. In lecture rooms and board rooms, as well as in thousands of individual physical and virtual contacts on a daily basis all over the globe, lies most evidence of the adoption of a single lingua franca. In such circumstances of rapid change, there has never been a time before when so many nations were in need to talk to each other so much. There has never been a time when so many people wished and were able to travel to so many destinations, nor has there ever been such a strain placed on the conventional resources of translating and interpreting. Crystal asserts (1997, p.12) that need for more widespread bilingualism has never been greater to ease the burden placed on the professional few; and never has there been in human history a more urgent need for a global language.

III.II.II. <u>The Risks of an Emerging Global Language</u>

While the benefits that would come from the existence of a global language are numerous, there are also several possible threats. A global language may cultivate an elite monolingual linguistic class, more complacent and dismissive in their attitudes towards other languages. Those who are entitled to such a language–especially those who enjoy it as a mother tongue–may be more able to think and work quickly in it, and to manipulate it to their own advantage at the expense of those who do not have it. Perhaps the presence of a global language will make people lazy about learning other languages or reduce their opportunities to do so. May a global language hasten the disappearance of minority languages or, even more, make all other languages unnecessary? Linked with all this, of course, is the revolting nature of linguistic triumphalism–the danger that some people may celebrate one language's success at the expense of others.

While it is eminent to face up to these widely held fears, it is also difficult to deal with anxieties that are so speculative, or, in the absence of evidence, to determine anything can be done to reduce or eliminate them. The following arguments underlined by Crystal (1997, pp. 13-20) are each illustrated with reference to English (noting that the same arguments would apply to whatever language was a candidate for global status).

III.II.II.I. Linguistic power

The assumption that those who speak a global language as a mother tongue are automatically in a position of power compared with those who have to learn it as an official or foreign language is real. Scientists who do not have English as a mother tongue, for instance, take longer to assimilate reports in English compared with their mother-tongue colleagues, and will as a consequence have less time to carry out their own creative work. Also possible, people who write up their research in languages other than English may have their work ignored by the international community.

Once proper attention is paid to the question of language learning, however, the problem of disadvantage dramatically diminishes. If a global language is taught early enough for children from the early years of full-time education, and if it is maintained continuously and resourced well, the sort of linguistic competence that emerges in due course is a real and powerful bilingualism, quite indistinguishable from that found in any speaker who has encountered the language since birth.

In this respect, it is worth emphasizing that children are in fact born ready for bilingualism. Some two-thirds of the children on earth grow up in a bilingual environment, and develop competence in it. There is a naturalness with which they assimilate another language, once they are regularly exposed to it. Yet, it is an ability that seems to fade away as children reach their teens, where these 'critical periods' are subject to debate. Simply put, widespread agreement prevails that if we intend to take the task of foreign language learning seriously, the principle has to be *the earlier the better*.[38] And when that task is taken appropriately with reference to the acquisition of a global language, the elitism argument evaporates.

III.II.II.II. Linguistic complacency

The concern that a global language may eliminate the motivation for adults to learn other languages already prevails. Common observations point to clear signs of linguistic complacency among British or American tourists who travel the world assuming that everyone speaks English, and that it is somehow *the fault* of the local people if they do not. There already seems to be a genuine, widespread lack of motivation to learn languages, fuelled partly by lack of money and opportunity, but also by lack of interest, probably fostered by the increasing presence of English as a global language. Consider a few examples in this regard. Given that everyone else is learning English, it is perhaps unsurprising that the British are the worst at learning other European languages. Some 66% of them, judging by a survey, speak no foreign language at all compared to the EU's average of 47%.[39] Also, the UK-based Centre for Information on Language Teaching found that a third of British exporters miss opportunities because of poor language skills.[40]

In another example, U.S. intelligence and law enforcement officials have described an increasingly lack of foreign language expertise that is undermining American national security. In the post-Soviet world, some 80 federal agencies were reported to be in need of proficiency in nearly 100 foreign languages to deal with threats from terrorism, narco-trafficking and communicable diseases, and to

---

[38] In the Netherlands, for instance, English starts in first grade and it prominent on TV and radio. Movies are not dubbed. In Germany, depending on the state, English begins between ages 5 to 10. In the past decade, Eastern Germany, formerly focused on Russian, put emphasis on English. In France, children start at 10, but the format is often criticized as *too bookish*. In Italy, high school students average only one to three hours of English a week. In Spain, it is three hours a week starting at age 8. The Spanish government wants to lower it to kindergarten, yet faces a lack of teachers. With that said, the English-speaking children of Spaniards and Italians traveling around appear to be in charge, as they order food in English for their parents and arrange early-morning taxis to the airport.

[39] "English is still on the march," *The Economist*, online edition, February 22, 2001.

[40] David Crystal, *English as a Global Language*, 1997, pp. 16-17.

advance commercial and economic interests.[41] Furthermore, and according to testimony in September 2000 before a Senate subcommittee, around half of the State Department's diplomatic postings are filled by people lacking necessary foreign language skills.[42]

In education, government figures for 2000 show that American colleges and universities graduated only 9 students majoring in Arabic. There, the Arabic taught in classrooms is formal Arabic, the shared language used in newspapers and books–reminding that many varieties of colloquial Arabic are spoken). Only about 140 students graduated with degrees in Chinese, and only a handful in Korean. Just 8.2% of American college and university students enroll in foreign language courses–nearly all in Spanish, French and German, a figure that has remained essentially unchanged since 1976.

Here, we are dealing with questions of attitude or state of mind rather than questions of ability, although it is the latter that is often cited as the explanation. 'I'm no good at languages,' or 'I never got on with my French teacher at school,' or 'the British / Americans are not very good at learning languages' are all common, widely heard excuses for not making any effort at all to acquire even a basic knowledge of a new language. This self-denigration may also derive from an unsatisfactory language learning experience in school, with the speaker remembering a weak result in school tests (perhaps as a consequence of an unsuccessful teaching approach or a usual breakdown in teacher-adolescent relationship).

Nevertheless, there are clear signs of growing awareness within English-speaking communities of the need to break away from the traditional monolingual bias. As at the levels of business and industry, there are signs of a growing respect for other cultures at grass-roots tourist level, with fresh efforts and a greater

---

[41] Paul Simon (Chairman of the Board of the National Foreign Language Center at the University of Maryland), "Beef Up the Country's Foreign Language Skills," *The Washington Post*, October 23, 2001, A23.

[42] Diana Jean Schemo, "Use of English as Global Tongue: In U.S., a Lack of Linguists Weakens Security," *IHT*, April 17, 2001, 1. Also see: Dennis Baron, "America Doesn't Know What the World Is Saying," *The New York Times*, online edition, October 17, 2001.

readiness to engage in language learning. For instance, Australian schools now teach Japanese as the first foreign language, and both the United States and the United Kingdom are devoting more attention to Spanish (a language, which in terms of mother-tongue use, is growing more rapidly than English).

III.II.II.III. Linguistic death

To what extent can the emergence of a global language hasten the disappearance of minority languages and cause widespread language death? As a general perspective, the processes of language domination and loss have been known throughout linguistic history, and exist independently of the emergence of a global language. Countless languages have died since humans became able to speak. And in many of those cases, the death has been caused by an ethnic group coming to be assimilated within a more dominant society, and adopting its language.

That situation continues today, as the matter is being debated with increasing urgency because of the unprecedented rate at which indigenous languages are being lost. Some recent victims from the rich world include Catawba (Massachusetts), Eyak (Alaska) and Livonia (Latvia). Most others are in the jungles of Papua New Guinea, Indonesia, or Nigeria (India, Mexico, Cameroon, Australia and Brazil follow).[43] According to estimates, some 80% of the world's 6000 or so living languages are perhaps expected to die out in the current century.[44]

Such losses, if they turn out to appear, do indeed represent an intellectual and social tragedy. Especially in languages that have never been written down or that have been written down only recently, so much is lost when the language dies since it is the repository of the history of a people. Similar to arguments that are used in

---

[43] "The triumph of English: A world empire by other means," *The Economist*, online edition, December 20, 2001.

[44] See: «Cause toujours! A la découverte des 6700 langues de la planète» (Still a cause ! Discovering the 6700 languages of the planet), *Courrier International*, (culture special edition), March-April-May, 2003.

relation to the conservation of species and the environment, once a language is lost it is even more difficult to recapture.[45]

The struggling movements in support of linguistic minorities, commonly associated with nationalism, illustrate an important truth about the nature and significance of language. The need for mutual intelligibility, part of the argument in favor of a global language, is only one side of the debate. The other side is the need for identity, where language is a principal means of pointing to where people belong and distinguish one social group from another. All over the world, there is more and more evidence of linguistic divergence rather than convergence.

For decades, people in the countries of the former Socialist Federal Republic of Yugoslavia made use of a common language, Serbo-Croatian. Since the civil wars of the early 1990s, however, the Serbs have begun to refer to their language as Serbian, the Bosnians to theirs as Bosnian, and the Croats to theirs as Croatian–with each side drawing attention to the linguistic features that are distinctive. The Serbians also write in the Cyrillic script of their Russian kinsmen, not in the Western script of their Catholic 'enemies.' In contrast, Azerbaijan, Turkmenistan, and Uzbekistan have shifted from the Cyrillic script of their Russian masters to the Western script of their Turkish kinsmen.

The situation exists likewise in Scandinavia, where Swedish, Norwegian and Danish are largely mutually intelligible, yet are considered to be different languages. That is, on the language front, *Babelization* prevails over *universalization* and furthers the evidence of the rise of civilization and cultural identity.[46]

Debates over the need for national or cultural identity are often seen as being opposed to those about the need for mutual intelligibility. This is, whatsoever,

---

[45] This is not to say that it is impossible to keep endangered languages in being. Mohawk, for instance, spoken by some indigenous people in Quebec, was in retreat until the 1970s, when efforts were made first to codify it and then to teach it to children at school. Welsh and Maori have both made a comeback thanks to television and government interference, and Navajo, Hawaiian and several languages spoken in Botswana have been reinvigorated artificially. (Source: "The triumph of English: A world empire by other means," *The Economist,* December 20, 2001)

[46] Samuel P. Huntington, *The Clash of Civilizations?: The Debate,* 1996, p. 60.

misleading, since it is absolutely possible to develop a situation in which intelligibility and identity "co-exist." The notion leads to the familiar one of bilingualism, where one of the languages within a speaker is the global language (providing access to the world community) and the other is a regional language (providing access to a local community). In this case, the two functions can be taken to be complementary, responding to different needs. Crystal (1997, p. 19) points "it is because the functions are so different that a world of linguistic diversity can in principle continue to exist in a world united by a common language."

Nevertheless, this is not to deny that the emergence of a global language can influence the structure of other languages–especially by providing a fresh source of loan words for adoption by other languages. Influences like these can be welcomed (in which cases, people talk about their language being *varied, enriched*) or opposed (and in which cases, the metaphors are those of *injury, invasion,* and *death*).

Several examples are noted in this respect. The French language, in recent years, *has tried* to protect itself *by law* against what is widely perceived to be the harmful influence of English. In official contexts, it is illegal (for the moment) to use an English word where a French word already exists, even though the usage may have widespread popular support (e.g., 'computer' for *ordinateur,* or 'e-mail' for *courriel*). Established in 1989, *Le Conseil superieur de l'audiovisuel* (CSA, France's broadcasting authority) is responsible among other things for protecting and regulating the use of French and foreign languages on television and radio. About 40% of the songs played on French radio must be in French, and a similar formula exists for television programming.[47]

In Poland, a law went into effect in 2000 obliging all companies selling or advertising foreign products to use Polish in their advertisements, labeling and instructions. Latvia tries to keep Russia at bay by insisting on the use of the Latvian language in business. In another example, the Iraqi government during its last few years before the invasion in March 2003 prohibited reference to the word "dollar," and instead referred to it as *foreign currency* or *hard currency* in official and public

---

[47] The CSA up-dates on a monthly basis a list of English words and their equivalents to be used in formal texts. The list may be consulted at: http://www.csa.fr/infos/langue/langue_listemots.php.

texts. Purist commentators from several other countries also express concern at the way in which English vocabulary–particularly that of American English–has come to penetrate their streets and TV programs.[48] And all these arguments are carried on with intense emotional, political and cultural force.

III.II.III. <u>The Status of English as a Global Language</u>

According to Crystal (2002), the present-day global status of English is primarily the result of two factors: one geographical-historical, the other socio-cultural.

The historical account traces the movement of English around the world, beginning with the pioneering voyages to the Americas, Asia and the Antipodes. In the 17th and 18th centuries, English was the language of the leading colonial nation, namely, Britain. In the 18th and 19th centuries, it was the language of the leader of the Industrial Revolution–also Britain. With the start of the 19th century, Britain had become the world's leading industrial and trading nation. Among the innovations of the Industrial Revolution that were of British origin are: the harnessing of coal, water and steam to drive heavy machinery; the development of new materials, techniques and equipment in a wide range of manufacturing industries; and the emergence of new means of transportation. By the year 1800, the principal growth areas, in textiles and mining, were producing a range of manufactured goods for export. All that entitled Britain, stresses Crystal (1997, p.71), to be named the "workshop of the world."

This expansion continued even further with the 19th century-colonial developments in Africa and the South Pacific. In the late 19th century and early 20th century, English was the language of the leading economic power, namely, the United States of America. As a result, when new technologies brought new linguistic opportunities, English emerged as a first-rank language in industries that affected all aspects of society: the press, advertising, broadcasting, motion pictures,

---

[48] Also, CNN International broadcasts in Germany in German language for half an hour daily in the evening.

sound recordings, transport and communications.[49] During that period, the world was forging fresh networks of international alliances–a matter calling for an unprecedented need for a lingua franca.

The pre-eminence of the language was established by the 1960s, while two events ensured its global status. The first was the worldwide movement towards political independence, out of which English emerged as an official or semi-official language in many newly independent countries. English is now represented in every continent and in islands of the three major oceans: the Atlantic (Saint Helena, the Indian (the Seychelles), and the Pacific (Fiji and Hawaii). There are some 75 territories in which English has held or continues to hold a special place, and each year brings new political decisions on the matter.

Rwanda, for instance gave English official status in 1996, and in the same year, English replaced French as the main foreign language in schools in Algeria (a former French colony). English is now the language most widely taught as a foreign language in over 100 countries, such as China, Russia, Germany, Spain, Egypt and Brazil. All this is in fact far more than the status achieved by any other language– although French, German, Spanish, Russian and Arabic are among those which have also developed a considerable official use. The other event which enforced the global status of English was the electronic revolution, where here too English was in the right place (in the United States) at the right time (in the 1970s).

The socio-cultural explanation examines the way people all over the world, in many aspects of life, have come to depend on English for their well-being. The language has penetrated deeply into the international domains of political life, business, safety, communications, entertainment, the media, and education. The convenience of having a lingua franca available to serve global human relations and needs in international political, academic and community gatherings has come to be appreciated and valued by millions.

---

[49] Crystal, in *English as a Global Language* (1997, p. 74), notes that the only country to have developed comparable financial and industrial strengths, during the last quarter of the 19th century, was Germany. Yet, these were to disappear following defeat in 1918, leaving the ground clear for American economic domination. Also, the German language remained relatively influential only within the regional scope. Signs of its revival are currently obvious particularly after the unification of the two Germans, and with the European Central Bank based in the country.

A number of illustrations are worth mentioning. To start with business and technology, Alcatel and Finland's Nokia embraced English in the early 1990s as the corporate language. And where the Germans and French have long battled for supremacy, English found its way as the closest thing to linguistic neutral territory. In the late 1980s, when France's Rhône Poulenc and German's Hoechst joined to found Aventis, they set up headquarters in the border city of Strasbourg, as they further defused cultural tensions by adopting English as the company language.

At the new Toyota and Peugeot plant in the Czech Republic, English is the working language of the Japanese, French and Czech staff. In China, the Beijing Organizing Committee for the 2008 Olympics is pushing English among staff, guides, taxi drivers and ordinary citizens.[50]

In international travel, a particular aspect of safety is the way language has come to be used as a means of controlling international transport operations, especially on water and in the air. With world travel reaching peak records, more people and goods are being transported more quickly and simultaneously to more places than ever before. Given the variety of language backgrounds involved, the communication demands placed on air and sea personnel have thus grown correspondingly. And in such circumstance, the use of lingua franca has proved to be a great value.

A project was set up in 1980 to produce Essential English for International Maritime, often referred to as *Seaspeak*. With radio and satellite systems greatly extending a ship's communication range, mariners need to assure clear and unambiguous speech to reduce the possibility of confusion in sending and receiving messages. Likewise, progress has also been made in recent years in devising systems of unambiguous communication between organizations involved in handling emergencies on the ground (notably, the fire service, ambulance and police). When the Channel Tunnel between Britain and France came into operation in 1994, for instance, new possibilities for international confusion emerged. Research is thus underway to initiate a way of standardizing communication

---

[50] Carla Power, "Not the Queen's English," *Newsweek*, international edition, March 7, 2005, 50.

between the United Kingdom and the rest of the European continent in what is referred to as *Emergencyspeak* (Crystal, 1997, p.98).

In respect of international aircraft control, English did not emerge as the official language until after World War II. Allied leaders organized a conference in Chicago in 1944 where they laid the foundations for the post-war global civil aviation system, bringing birth to the International Civil Aviation Organization. Seven years later, they agreed English should be the common language of aviation when pilots and controllers speak different languages. However, and even within a single language, terminology and phrasing need to be standardized to avoid ambiguity.

Here, great efforts have been made to develop such a system for English, widely called *Airspeak*. Consider the mid-air collision over Lake Constance on July 1, 2002 between a Russian passenger jet and a DHL cargo aircraft. In German's worst post-war disaster, Russian officials denied suggestions that their pilot failed to understand instructions because of inadequate grasp of English.[51] An accident prevention study carried out by Boeing found that in the decade 1982-1991, pilot-controller miscommunication contributed to at least 11% of fatal crashes worldwide (Crystal, 1997, p. 101).

In education, not everyone has viewed the triumph of English in such a positive light, although the dominant view is certainly that a person is more likely to be in touch with the latest thinking and research in a subject by learning English than by learning any other language.[52] A study in 1981 on the use of English in scientific periodicals showed that 85% of papers in biology and physics were being written in English at that time, whereas medical papers were some way behind with 73%, and papers in mathematics and chemistry further behind with still 69% and

---

[51] See: Mark Odell et al., "Air crash over Germany sparks safety fears," *Financial Times*, July 3, 2002, 1; and Owen Bowcolt et al., "Russia rejects sole blame for accident", *The Guardian*, July 3, 2002, 4. Another aircraft incident also caused by language miscommunication, by a Colombian airline on January 25, 1990, is cited in: Jean-Paul Nerrière, *Don't Speak English: Parlez globish*, Paris: Eyrolles, 2004, pp. 49-50.

[52] A key observation drawn from several years of teaching English at CFILC is that the learners (from various nationalities) sought to learn, speak, and use English without any real interest in the British or American civilizations and cultures, in what may as well constitute a weakness of the English language.

67%, respectively. Yet, all these areas had shown a significant increase in their use of English during the preceding fifteen years–with over 30% in the case of chemistry, and over 40% in the case of medicine–as the figures fifteen years further on would certainly be much higher. This trend can even be observed in a language-sensitive subject such as linguistics, where in 1995 nearly 90% of the 1500 papers listed in the journal *Linguistics Abstract* were in English. In computer science, the proportion mounts even higher.[53]

In terms of Internet content, the latest statistics available on the distribution of languages also reveal the overwhelming majority of sites and content in English. The second language in content, German, is far distanced from English; and no predictions seem foreseeable for any narrowing in the huge gap. The following chart in Figure 3.9. illustrates the overdominance of English on the Internet.

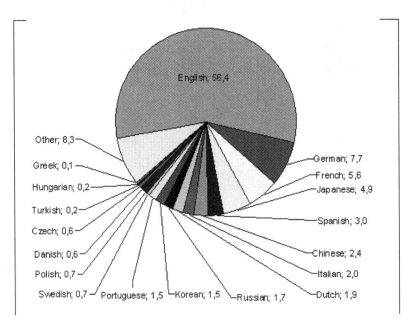

Figure 3. 9. Language distribution of Web content in 2002, in percentage (Source: http://www.netz-tipp.de/languages.html)

---

[53] These figures are quoted from David Crystal, *English as a Global Language*, 1997, p. 102.

Since the 1960s, English has become for many countries the normal medium of instruction in education, particularly in higher education. This includes several countries where the language has no official status. In Quebec, the only predominately French-speaking jurisdiction in all of North America, there is a growing movement of French-speaking parents who encourage their children to speak English as well. These educated, middle-class Montrealers see bilingualism not only as a cultural treasure, but also as a practical tool for the workplace. For them, the survival of French is as important as learning English.[54]

In Switzerland, the history of conflict between French and German speakers is long and varied, but it is probably safe to say that the battle lines have never before been drawn in a third-grade classroom. In September 2000, the German-speaking canton of Zurich announced its plans to introduce English for all third-graders and push back French instruction to fifth grade. According to the traditional practice aimed at fostering national cohesion, German speakers have learned French as their first foreign language, and French and Italian speakers have learned German.[55] English always came second or third. Here, too, the reaction in many quarters was swift. Educators and traditionalists, especially in French-speaking cantons, complained "the cohesion of the country was being sold out for crass commercial goals."[56]

In Chile, the government introduced a national program to teach English in all elementary and high schools. The goal is to make the nation of around 15 million people bilingual within a generation or so. And in a country thousands of miles from the nearest English-speaking country, Mongolian Prime Minister announced developing a national curriculum devised to make English replace Russian (in September 2005) as the primary foreign language taught there. Within a decade,

[54] Susan Semenak, "An English Comeback: Quebec French Speakers Want More Bilingualism," *IHT*, February 12, 2001, 19.

[55] The fourth official language in Switzerland is a linguistic fossil of Latin called Romansch that is still spoken in a few remote Alpine valleys.

[56] Rick Smith, "Swiss Squabble Over What 2d Language to Teach," *IHT*, February 12, 2001, 19.

Mongolia is expected to convert its written language from Cyrillic characters to the Roman alphabet.[57]

In South Korea, thanks to simple procedure: just a snip in a membrane and the tongue is supposedly longer, more flexible, some South Koreans believe to be able to pronounce such notorious English tongue-teasers as *rice* without sounding like *lice*. The procedure, though a controversial aspect, is known as "frenectomy," and has been used for years to correct a condition popularly known as "tongue-tie," in which the thin band of tissue under the tongue, the frenulum, extends to its tip. If the tongue cannot easily touch the roof of the mouth, it is difficult for a person to pronounce certain sounds (noting that for South Koreans, as for the Japanese, their languages make no distinction between *L*s and *R*s). The operation, done mostly on children younger than 5, takes as little as ten minutes and can be done in outpatient surgery with local anesthetic (costing only between $230 to $400). In another display of linguistic zeal, the Seoul city government set up a hotline for citizens to call if they see spelling or grammar mistakes on public signs in English.[58]

In the Netherlands, advanced courses are widely taught in English. If most students are going to encounter English routinely in their monographs and periodicals, it is suggested that it makes sense to teach advance course in that language–to better prepare them for such an encounter. Likewise, French universities now accept post-graduate theses and dissertations presented in English. Elsewhere, the pressure to use English has grown as universities and colleges increasingly welcome foreign students, and lecturers find themselves faced with mixed-language audiences. And for his part, Saudi Arabian Minister of Islamic Affairs called upon the necessity of mastering a language (other than Arabic) such as English to avoid any loss or effect of translation. He stated such competence would also enable people to follow publications all over the world.[59]

---

[57] James Brooke, "For Mongolians, E Is for English, F Is for Future," *The New York Times*, online edition, February 15, 2005.

[58] Barbara Demick, "A snip of the tongue and English is yours!" *IHT*, online edition, April 8, 2002.

[59] Among the other languages called to be learnt are French, Indonesian, Malaysian, Russian and German. "Saudi Arabia calls for learning foreign languages," *AlQuds*, online edition at: www.alquds.co.uk, October 26, 2004.

In line with the above examples, it is not surprising to observe that in the past thirty years the English Language Teaching (ELT) business has become one of the major growth industries around the world. With thousands of schools and centers worldwide now devoted to English-language teaching, other than the hundred or more office networks of the British Council, the Council had estimated over 1 billion people learning English by the year 2000 (roughly 1 person out of 7 on the globe).[60]

To end up with the press, the English language has been an important medium in this domain for nearly 400 years. In the early 17th century, several European countries were publishing rudimentary newspapers, yet censorship, taxation, wars and other constraints allowed little growth. Progress was much greater in Britain, despite periods of censorship that greatly limited newspaper content until towards the end of the century.

The 19th century was the period of greatest progress, thanks to the introduction of new printing technology along with new methods of mass production and transportation. It also saw the evolution of an independent press, chiefly fostered in the United States, with some 400 daily newspapers operating by 1850 and nearly 2000 by the turn of the century. Censorship and other restrictions continued in Europe during the early decades, and so, the provision of popular news in languages other than English developed much more slowly.

In one estimate of the influence of individual newspapers on a world scale in 1977, the top five papers were all in English. Top was *The New York Times*, followed by *The Washington Post, The Wall Street Journal,* and two British, The *Times* and *The Sunday Times* (Crystal, 1997, p. 84). Of particular importance are those English-language newspapers, intended for a global readership, such as the *International Herald Tribune, US Weekly,* and *International Guardian.*

As from April 6, 2002, a 12-page English-language supplement of *The New York Times* accompanies *Le Monde*, France's biggest intellectual daily newspaper,

---

[60] David Crystal, *English as a Global Language*, 1997, p. 103.

in what has now become a weekly feature. Meanwhile, three other European distinguished dailies, Spain's *El Pais*, Italy's *Repubblica*, and Germany's *Suddeutsche Zeitung*, *Die Welt*, and *Frankfurter Allgemeine Zeitung* considered following suit.[61] Also, German *Der Spiegel* magazine issued a 240-page special edition in English (in April 2005) dedicated to introducing modern German to the rest of the world. Coinciding with the 60th anniversary of the end of World War II, the first English edition featured articles ranging from the changing German-American relationship to the problems with the country's aging population to the revival in the German rock music scene.[62]

To conclude, while there are ample data to track the cross-border movement of people, merchandise, and money, it is much more difficult to measure the global spread of ideas and trends. Nevertheless, it is quite possible to get a hint of a country's level of cultural integration by identifying "cultural proxies"–the conduits by which ideas, beliefs, and values are transmitted. One approach to measure the globalization of culture is to chart the movement of popular media, which have more impact on our thinking than some of the other more frequently cited symbols of cultural globalization.

Foreign Policy magazine initiated a ranking of the 20 most cultural globalized countries by measuring each nation's export and imports of books, periodicals, and newspapers.[63] These total exports and imports would then be divided by the nation's population size. The higher a country is on this index, the more likely an individual in that country is to receive foreign cultural products. The leading countries in the Index were as following: Singapore, Switzerland, Ireland, Canada, United Kingdom, Denmark, Finland, Norway, Sweden, Netherlands, France, Australia, Germany, Portugal, Italy, United States, Czech Republic, Israel, Chile, and Greece.

Interestingly, one clear pattern that emerges from this ranking is that cultural globalization may have a significant linguistic component. Three of the top five

---

[61] Christina White, "A French Beau for the New York Times," *Business Week,* online edition, April 12, 2002.

[62] Andreas Tzortzis, "Der Spiegel flirts with the Anglophone world," *IHT*, April 18, 2005, 10.

[63] Randolph Kluver and Wayne Fu, "The Cultural Globalization Index," *Foreign Policy,* online edition, posted February 2004.

nations (Singapore, Switzerland, and Canada) have official bilingual policies. English-language permeation also ties into a country's capacity to absorb international cultural products. Seven of the top 20 nations in the Cultural Globalization Index (the United States, the United Kingdom, Canada, Australia, Ireland, Singapore, and Israel) are among the top 10 English-speaking countries of the world.

Yet, when considering the bottom 10 countries (Peru, Romania, Morocco, Thailand, Turkey, the Philippines, Egypt, Indonesia, China, and Pakistan), one realizes that multilingual nations are not guaranteed a high degree of cultural globalization. The Philippines and Pakistan, two countries where English is widespread, still rank near the bottom.

The principal barrier to cultural globalization seems to be poverty, as all of these countries have a per capita gross domestic product of under $8,000 and 4 of the 10 have a literacy rate of less than 60%. Furthermore, some countries, notably China and Indonesia, have government policies that restrict the import of foreign books and journals. In brief, poverty, illiteracy, and lack of social openness are all associated with a lack of cultural globalization.

Among the several key indicators of cultural globalization available to consider are cinematic films. Although it is true that many nations are overwhelmingly influenced by Hollywood, and most nations tend to demonstrate cultural dependence more than globalization, it is still a valuable indicator.[64] With both Hollywood and Bollywood having significant media industries, and with India producing seven times more movies than the United States, it is Hollywood that has the greatest global impact. UNESCO estimates that 85% of movie screenings worldwide are of Hollywood productions (Kluver and Fu). To note, China's reluctance to have more than a handful of American produced films clearly illustrates a conviction that this particular media form can have significant cultural

---

[64] A distinction is made between "globalization," taken to be openness to a variety of international sources for media content, and between "cultural dependence," in which a nation, because it has no significant cultural industry within itself," relies primarily, or even solely, on one other source.

impact. In highly globalized nations, such as Singapore, films from literally all around the world play consistently throughout the nation.

Television programming, another useful indicator of cultural globalization, is less prone to demonstrate cultural dependence. This stems from the fact that television production is less costly than feature film production, and thus, many nations do have a local industry. In many cases, such programs can become regionally important among, for instance, Spanish, Chinese or Arabic-speaking nations. Eventually, many more nations have become capable of producing and exporting this media form, making the source pool much larger for other nations.

The last indicator of cultural influence to be considered here is the volume of imported print publications, including books, newspapers, magazines and other periodicals. It is through the transmission and circulation of international newspapers and news magazines that one is able to access to political and economic opinions around the world. In addition, popular interest magazines, including home decorating magazines, celebrity magazines and sports magazines have a 'reciprocal' effect. When they are introduced to a nation (or penetrate), they often prompt similar local titles, which most typically attempt to emulate the "style" or formula of the foreign versions.

The two magazine covers in Illustration 3.1. demonstrate the point. The French *Le Monde* idea of the May 2002 presidential-elections suspense seems to be based on that of the American *Newsweek* (international edition) design of the much-debated U.S. elections in November 2000. This may reveal the way in which such media types help create a way of looking at the world that is not bound by cultural tradition.

Illustration 3. 1. The influence of cultural penetration on local media

III.II.IV. <u>Possible Scenarios on the Future of English</u>
      <u>in View of Its Global Status</u>

An obvious, inevitable consequence of the growing use and development of English is that the language will become subject to linguistic changes. This has already been demonstrated with the emergence, since the 1960s, of new varieties of English in the areas where the language has taken root. The change has become a major talking point only recently, and hence comes the term by which these varieties are often known as *new Englishes*.

The most familiar examples are the different dialects of British and American English, where these two varieties diverged almost as soon as the first settlers arrived in America. In a deeper insight, one finds many distinctive forms that also identify the Englishes of other countries: Australian English, New Zealand English, Canadian English, South African English, Caribbean English, and even within Britain, Irish, Scottish, and Welsh Englishes.

Furthermore, the emergence of these new Englishes expands the scope of fragmentation as English eventually dissolves into a range of mutually unintelligible languages (consider, for instance, what happened to Latin as it gave rise to the Various Romance languages of French, Spanish, and Italian over a thousand years ago). Even if the new Englishes (such as *Euro-English* now used by French, Greek and other diplomats in the corridors of power in the European Union) become increasingly different as years pass, the consequences for world English may not necessarily be fatal. A likely scenario, as viewed by Crystal (1997, pp. 136-37), is that the current ability to use more than one dialect would simply extend to meet the fresh demands of the international situation. Referring to this new form of English as the *World Standard Spoken English* (WSSE), he notes the foundation for such a development is already being laid down.

Already multidialectal to a greater or lesser extent, most people use one spoken dialect at home–where they are with their family or talking to other members of their local community. This dialect tends to be an informal variety, full of casual pronunciation, colloquial grammar, and local expressions. Just to name a few, we now hear of *Singlish* (in reference to Singapore English), *Swinglish* (Swiss English), *Denglisch* (German English), and *Franglais* (in reference to French English).

Those same people use another spoken dialect when they are away from home, traveling to different parts of their country or interacting with others at work. This dialect, on the other hand, tends to be a formal variety–full of careful pronunciation, conventional grammar structures, and standard vocabulary. We now also hear reference to *Globish* (Global English). Those who are literate have grasped a third variety, as well, that of written Standard English that currently unites the English-speaking world (apart from a few slight differences, notably in British vs. American spelling).

In a future with so many national Englishes, therefore, little would change. People would still guard their dialects for use within their own country, but would shift to WSSE when they communicate with people from elsewhere. Although it has hardly yet been born, the most influential variety of English in the development of WSSE seems likely to be that of American English. The direction of influence, comparing with British English, has for sometime been remarkably one-way. Several grammatical aspects in contemporary British usage show the influence of American forms.

Some British may regret, for example, the passing of the *bullet-proof waist coat* (in favor of the *bullet-proof vest)*, the arrival of *hopefully* at the start of every sentence, and the partial disappearance of the present perfect tense. American spellings are increasingly widespread, particularly in computer contexts; and there is a greater passive awareness of distinctively American lexicon in the United Kingdom than vice versa. Few British mind or even notice that their old *railway station* has become a *train station*, the *car park* is turning into *parking lot*, and that people now live *on*, not *in*, a street.

To end, the concept of WSSE does not intend to replace a national dialect, rather it supplements it. In 500 years' time, Crystal (1997, pp. 138-40) questions whether or not it may be the case that everyone be automatically introduced to English as soon as they are born? This can only be a good thing if it is part of a rich multilingual experience. But, if it is by then the only language left to be learned, "it will have been the greatest intellectual disaster that the planet has ever known."

Two more scenarios remain relevant on the global status of English. If language dominance is a matter of political power, as illustrated earlier, then "a revolution" in the balance of global power could have consequences for the choice of a global language. Some may foresee a future in which, following some 'tragic' scenario, the universal language is Chinese, Arabic, or even a certain 'alien' tongue. To come up with such a scenario however, that revolution would indeed have to be devastating. That is, smaller-scale revolutions in the world order would unlikely have much effect–given the fact English is currently widely established and it is no longer owned nor practiced by a sole nation.

A more convincing scenario is that an alternative communication method/means could emerge, which would gradually eliminate the need for a global language (in the present situation, English). Here, the chief candidate is "machine translation" (automatic translation). As progress continues in this domain, there is a distinct possibility that, within a generation or two, it will be common for people to communicate with each other directly in their first languages, with a computer assuming the burden between them. This feature is already in practice. On the Internet, some firms offer a basic translation services between certain language pairs, although the need for post-editing is still considerable.[65] And with translation software currently very limited in its ability to handle idiomatic, stylistic, and several other linguistic features, the machines are therefore nowhere near replacing their human counterparts.

Thanks to round-the-clock developments in technology, the accuracy and speed of real-time automatic translation is undoubtedly expected to improve in the coming twenty-five to fifty years.[66] Even so, it will take much longer before the medium becomes *globally widespread,* and *economically accessible* to all, that it poses a threat to the current availability and appeal of a lingua franca. All along that timeframe, evidence points to that the position of English as a global language is going to become even more enforced. In the words of Crystal (1997, p. 22):

> It will be very interesting to see what happens then–whether the presence of a global language will eliminate the demand for world translation services, or whether the economics of automatic translation will so undercut the cost of global language learning that the latter will become otiose. It will be an interesting battle for 100 years from now.

---

[65] Some experts doubt computers will ever be able to translate as accurately and artfully as people do. See: "Web translation services not always accurate," *USA Today*, online edition, June 21, 2002.

[66] One translation device, known as *infoscope*, is equipped with a digital camera that can take snapshots of a text in English, French, German, Spanish, Italian and Chinese and then translate the image to another language in a matter of seconds. The device displays characteristics of augmented reality, by presenting the real world in the form of a captured image, such as a restaurant sign or menu, and emerging it with virtual data. With its GPS, wireless communications and digital camera, Infoscope is intended for speedy translation hits of three or four text lines. See for more information: http://almaden.ibm.com/software/user/infoScope/index.shtml.

Post September 11, 2001 Observations

The attacks perpetrated on September 11, 2001 constituted a significant strategic surprise for the United States, and to varying extents to the entire world. Despite the prevailing recognition that the attacks were both dramatic and disastrous in volume, the events are here to be considered as only one incident along the course of the Information Age (consider as well, for example, the attacks in Madrid on March 11, 2004). What was perhaps more shocking to the Americans was the fact they were subject to a strike on their own 'protected' homeland, rather than the mere collapse of the World Trade Center (the Twin Towers) in New York, or the strike on the Pentagon.

Within the framework and contents covered in this dissertation, and in line with its inherent findings, a number of developments have been observed after those attacks. Presented in the form of an alphabetical list (from A to Z), the points cover certain evolving aspects around the globe–linked in one manner or another to the political environment arising from the events. Some of the points are directly linked to the events. Some relate to the aftermath American policy, while certain points address particular implications pertaining to other world countries.

A. The attacks on New York and Washington clearly demonstrated the vulnerability of the United States, as of any modern society, to an intelligently prepared and determined strike. Military officials, together with the uniformed and civilian analytic agencies involved in the U.S. defense establishments, have for decades formulated speculative scenarios of attacks on the country; yet their work has all but invariably been dominated by the high-technology mindset of the Pentagon and by the engineering ethos of the American society. The planning has always suffered from the planners' assumption that their opponent would attack them in a manner symmetrical to the defense they already had or what they planned to have.

That is, they concentrated speculation and planning on the dangers of an attack with mass destruction weapons–probably with more or less high-tech methods. This discussion had overwhelmingly concerned missile attacks, rogue nuclear weapons, and chemical and biological agents. Rogue commercial aircraft were not in the mind of defense planners. "The real lesson, which was not learnt, was provided nearly 60 years ago, shortly before the end of the Second World War, when an American medium bomber, lost in the fog, crashed into the Empire State Building in New York City–then the country's highest building."[67]

B. The sheer crash of three old-fashioned airplanes into vulnerable targets set the United States in mass panic. The attacks slowed down travel, commerce, government functions, and led to increased security worldwide. For the first time in American history, the Federal Aviation Administration shut down air traffic nationwide (while incoming trans-Atlantic flights were diverted to Canada). All major U.S. stock exchanges were closed. All federal offices in Washington closed. The United Nations in New York was evacuated as a precaution. The evacuation also covered the centers of Washington and New York, along with other major cities such as Chicago, Seattle, San Francisco, Boston, Cleveland and Minneapolis. U.S. military installations all over the world were placed on high alert. Furthermore, many sports, entertainment and tourist attractions were put to a halt.[68]

C. Words can be weapons, and the word "terrorist" is indeed a heavy loaded weapon. It is used (more and more) to convey the impression that anyone labeled so is a villain who operates outside the standards of morality and civilization, someone who merits universal condemnation and must be stopped.

Interestingly to recall, the word "terrorism" was first popularized during the French Revolution of 1789. In contrast to its contemporary usage, Hoffman notes

---

[67] William Pfaff, "Attacks Show that Political Courage is the only real defense," *IHT,* September 12, 2001, 10.

[68] Details of the halt listed in "Attacks slow nation to a halt," *CNN,* online edition, September 12, 2001, at: http://www.cnn.com/SPECIALS/2001/trade.center/closing.roundup.html.

that terrorism at that time had a 'positive' connotation.[69] The concept or *régime de la terreur* (of 1793-1794), from which the English word emerged, was adopted as a means to establish order during the transient anarchical period of turmoil and upheaval that followed the uprisings of 1789.

Thus, unlike terrorism as it is commonly understood nowadays (to mean a revolutionary or anti-government activity undertaken by non-state or subnational entities), the *régime de la terreur* was an instrument of governance wielded by the recently established revolutionary state. That is, it was designed to enforce the new government's power by menacing counter-revolutionaries, subversives and all other dissidents whom the new regime regarded as 'enemies of the people.' The Committee of General Security and the Revolutionary Tribunal were, explains Hoffman (1988, p. 15), accordingly accorded wide powers of arrest and judgment, publicly executing persons convicted of treasonous, reactionary crimes. That was how "a powerful lesson was conveyed to any and all who might oppose the revolution or grow nostalgic for the *ancien régime*."

The on going U.S.-led "War on Terror" provides numerous examples of how the label of "terrorist" is today applied to enemies. Governments, in some cases, have even re-labeled their foes to enlist international support.

Russia has consistently identified the Chechen problem as a case of fundamentalist terrorism; Ariel Sharon of Israel described Yasser Arafat as a second "Osama Bin Laden," whom America and Israel should cooperate in crushing. China sees that its troublesome minorities and dissident provinces as in Taiwan, Tibet and Xinjiang are terrorists and separatists. China demanded that they should be condemned by the United States in exchange for Beijing's support for Washington's anti-terrorism campaign.[70] India claims that separatists in Kashmir are terrorists. And Sri Lanka says the same thing about its Tamil insurrection. Turkey identifies

---

[69] Bruce Hoffman, *Inside Terrorism*, Great Britain: Victor Gollancz, 1988, 15. Also see: Charles Townshend, *Terrorism: A Very Short Introduction*, New York: Oxford University Press, 2002, Chapter 3.

[70] John Pomfret, "China Puts A Price on Its Support for Any U.S. War," *IHT*, September 19, 2001, 7.

Kurd national resistance as terrorism. Serbia signals that Al Qaida has branches in Bosnia-Herzegovina, Kosovo and in Albania.

However, the very same people and actions can quickly shift from "terrorists" to "freedom fighters" and back again. Noam Chomsky, in *9-11* (2001, pp. 90-91), illustrates this with the KLA-UCK who were officially condemned by the United States as "terrorists" in 1998 because of their attacks on Serb police and civilians in an effort to elicit a disproportionate and brutal Serbian response, as they openly declared. Yet policies did change when the United States and the United Kingdom decided to launch an attack on Serbia in late March 1999, and the "terrorists" instantly became "freedom fighters." After the war, those "freedom fighters" and their close associates become *once again* "terrorists", "thugs" and "murderers" as they carried out what from their point of view are similar actions for similar reasons in Macedonia, a U.S. ally. Interestingly, the same analogy applies to leaders who turn, at occasions, from the rank of "friendly ally" to "dictator" (and back forth).

Historically, comments terrorism expert Brian Jenkins, "terror" was sometimes a component of enforcing colonial rule, with terrorism being a component of the armed struggles against it.[71] Anti-colonial wars provided examples of both, leaving a generation of leaders in the newly independent states of Africa and Asia deeply suspicious of any efforts to brand as "terrorism" tactics that had won them freedom. Thus, it is not surprising that international consensus has been hard to reach in terms of defining terrorism.

Scholars and jurists, in an attempt to get around the political difference, have tried to define terrorism according to the quality of the act itself, rather than the identity of the perpetrators or the nature of their cause.[72] A consensus has developed that all terrorist acts must involve violence or the threat of violence. Also, a terrorist act ordinarily would be considered a crime–such as murder, kidnapping or arson. In

---

[71] Brian Michael Jenkins, Commentary: "Semantics are Strategic in the War on Terror," *The Globe and Mail*, at: www.globeandmail.com, September 30, 2004, A23.

[72] A draft EU common definition of terrorism described it as criminal acts committed with the intent to seriously intimidate the public; to force an authority, state or international organization to act; or to destroy structures of a state, society or international organization. See: "EU to Speed Up Terror Extraditions," *IHT*, November 17-18, 2001, 3.

addition, most terrorist acts also violate the rules of war, as in attacks against innocents. Ordinary criminals may terrify but they are not terrorists. A single perpetrator pursuing his own cause may be a terrorist; nevertheless, *"lone wolves"* often turn out to be lonely crackpots. That is, not every act of even the most extreme violence is terrorism.

Political differences did not prevent international cooperation against terrorism. By stating conventions that outlaw specific tactics and targets (i.e., airline hijackings and sabotage, attacks on diplomats, taking hostages, and bombings) the international community chipped away at terrorism without attempting an all-encompassing definition. Wherever terrorist attacks occurred on a smaller scale, governments sought to apprehend the perpetrators and bring them to trail. Only on occasion was military force used to retaliate.

Remarkably, the September 11 attacks changed perceptions. Few nations accept American use of the phrase "War on Terror," still preferring to instead deal with terrorism as an intelligence and law enforcement problem.[73] Yet, on November 26, 2001 the U.S. President broadened *his* definition of terrorism, by declaring:

> If anybody harbors a terrorist, they're a terrorist. If they fund a terrorist, they're a terrorist. If they house terrorists, they're terrorists. I mean, I can't make it any more clearly to other nations around the world. If they develop weapons of mass destruction that will be used to terrorize nations, they will be held accountable.[74]

With many nations now recognizing that prevention of September 11-scale events is paramount, it is now no longer necessary to define a terrorist act. Since those attacks, Canada, Australia, the United States, European Union members, and other countries have cooperated in officially listing terrorist organizations along

---

[73] On the use of the world "war" to describe the anti-terrorist efforts in the wake of the September 11 attacks and its far-reaching implications for international law, refer to: Frédéric Mégret, "War? Legal Semantics and the Move to Violence," *European Journal of International Law,* Vol. 13, (2002), no. 2, Italy: European University Institute.

[74] Elizabeth Bumiller, "Readmit Inspectors, President Tells Iraq; 'Or Else' Is Unstated," *The New York Times,* online edition, November 27, 2001.

with the *charities* that finance them–although disagreement on some of the listings prevail.

D. Stating the United States is "reaping the thorns planted by its rulers," Saddam Hussein of Iraq was the only Arab leader who did not condemn the attacks, and called upon the United States not to use retaliatory force. His vice-president said the events forecast the downfall of the United States.[75]

Meanwhile, Iran, although deemed by the U.S. State Department to be a sponsor state of terrorism, flirted with the United States by issuing a strong statement of condemnation following the attacks, sending a condolence message to New York City in the name of mayors of Tehran and Isfahan, and by observing a moment of silence with 60,000 fans at an Iranian football game.[76]

Regardless of that, George W. Bush described North Korea, Iran and Iraq as constituting an "axis of evil, arming to threaten the peace of the world."[77] Iran dismissed the accusations as evidence that President Bush is, in the words or Iran's spiritual leader Ayatollah Khamenei, "thirsty for human blood."[78]

E. The U.S. government campaign to build an international anti-terrorism coalition turned into a heyday for American arms makers as the Bush administration quickly turned to arms transfers as the easiest way to make and keep friends. Following are some of the anti-terrorism rewards:

---

[75] "Confronting the Terrorist Threat," *IHT,* September 17, 2001, 6.

[76] Alan Sipress and Steven Mufson, "U.S. Explores Recruiting Iran Into New Coalition," *The Washington Post,* September 25, 2001, A01.

[77] "President Delivers State of the Union Address," The White House, Washington, DC, January 29, 2002.

[78] "Great Satan v axis of evil," *The Economist*, online edition, February 5, 2002.

Armenia: $4.3 million in military aid and training

Azerbaijan: Arms sanctions lifted; border control aid given

Colombia: More aid planned to flight "narco-terrorists"

India: Nuclear test-related sanctions lifted

Kenya: Weapons and combat training planned

Pakistan: Nuclear-test and military coup related sanctions lifted; $73 million worth of military aid and $600 million in economic support funds approved

Philippines: $92.3 million of excess weapons promised

Tajikistan: Military aid and weapons sanctions dropped; border control aid planned

Turkey: Excess weapons and training pledged; military debt forgiveness negotiated

Uzbekistan: Equipment and training.[79]

F. Attempts to shield Americans from terrorism have spawned fears that civil liberties are in danger of irreversible erosion. Law-enforcement and intelligence agencies at all government levels enjoy wider power than before the attacks to collect information on private citizens. Employers and universities are also more emboldened to investigate who is working for them or studying with them.

The U.S.A. Patriot Act, passed in October 2001, entitled the government to sweeping authority to subpoena data on both immigrants and American citizens under the rubric of investigating terrorism or clandestine intelligence activities. In the past, the Federal Bureau of Investigation (FBI) could obtain the credit card or library-borrowing records of 'anyone suspected of terrorism.' Today, the Patriot Act allows the FBI to go into public library and ask for the records on everybody who ever used the library, or who used it on a certain day, or who checked out certain kinds of books.[80]

The government defends such data mining as a vital tool to spot terrorists-in-waiting, or *sleepers*. In March 2002, the Justice Department unveiled $1.9 million in additional funding for the community-lookout program known as National

---

[79] "Arms Sales Monitor: Highlighting U.S. Government Policies on Arms Exports and Conventional Weapons Proliferation," *Federation of American Scientist,* no. 47 (January 2002), Washington, DC, p. 2.

[80] "How Sept. 11 changed America," *www.msnbc.com*, March 8, 2002.

Neighborhood Watch, in an aim to expand the program's mission from deterring burglars to stopping terrorists within, according to former attorney general John Ashcroft, *the great tradition of American volunteerism.*[81]

Furthermore, with the help of consumer-data banks, companies can run computer checks on employees for such red tags as a brief residence in the United States, gaps between jobs, and addresses shared with several unrelated people. Companies also dig for clues from in-house travel agencies about employees' personal trips, and can also look at whether, for instance, they visit bomb-making sites on the Internet. From their point of view, legal experts stress that profiling a work force for such behavioral characteristics, rather than religious or ethnic traits, is legal as long as employees have signed routine consent forms allowing personal information verifications.

G. In a proclaimed effort to prevent terrorist attacks, the U.S. State Department announced on November 9, 2001 slowing the process for granting visas to young men from Arab and Muslim nations. Visa applications from 26 nations for any man between 16 to 45 years old would be checked against databases maintained by the FBI.[82] In a security procedure taking up to 20 days, the applicants would also be required to complete a detailed questionnaire on their backgrounds, including questions about any military service or weapons training, previous travel, and whether they had ever lost a passport.

In the past, anyone with a college admission letter and the right INS form was almost assured of getting a visa. No longer now. Under new rules, if a consular officer has reason to suspect anything about the applicant's past, character or political affiliations, the student's visa request will be denied. Schools are also

---

[81] "How Sept. 11 changed America," *www.msnbc.com*, March 8, 2002.

[82] Countries affected by the new visa restrictions are: Afghanistan, Algeria, Bahrain, Djibouti, Egypt, Eritrea, Indonesia, Iran, Iraq, Jordan, Kuwait, Lebanon, Libya, Malaysia, Morocco, Oman, Pakistan, Qatar, Saudi Arabia, Somalia, Sudan, Syria, Tunisia, Turkey, the United Arab Emirates, and Yemen. See: Neil A. Lewis and Christopher Marquis, "Longer Visa Waits for Arabs; Stir Over U.S. Eavesdropping," *The New York Times,* online edition, November 10, 2001.

required to notify the government when foreign students fail to show up, change their addresses, take reduced course loads or drop out of school.

Months later (June 2002), John Ashcroft signaled that as many as 100,000 visitors a year would be fingerprinted, photographed and registered. These measures would mostly affect students, workers, researchers and tourists from Muslim and Middle Eastern countries–those who do not hold green cards. "On September 11, the American definition of national security changed and changed forever," he stressed.[83]

The move on visas drew immediate criticism in the United States, where pro-immigration groups and organizations representing Americans Muslims said the new requirements amounted to profiling by religion or nationality, a shift to methods they consider antithetical to American values.

H. The growing technological capacity of small groups and individuals to destroy things and people, along with increasing vulnerability of economic and technological systems to carefully aimed attacks, have together led to a new and sinister kind of mass violence–a *complex terrorism*.[84] It is this evolution of terrorism that threatens modern high-tech societies in the world's most developed nations.

Al Qaida's manual, for instance, outlines three stages of any operation: *research, planning and execution.* One U.S. senior government official described the September 11 attacks as being "well organized, far from a half-baked operation. They had good coordination, excellent communication that is hard to track, and a good, simple plan. Somebody did their homework."[85] Consider Illustration 3.2.

---

[83] "New rules for foreign visitors," at: www.msnbc.com/news/762432.asp, June 5, 2002. And also: Eric Schmitt, "U.S. Will Seek to Fingerprint Visa's Holders," *The New York Times,* online edition, June 5, 2002; and Richard Ernsberger Jr., "Fortress America," *Newsweek,* international edition, November 12, 2001, 50-56.

[84] Thomas Homer-Dixon, "The Rise of Complex Terrorism," *Foreign Policy,* online edition, January-February 2002.

[85] Don Van Natta Jr. and Kate Zernike, "Hijackers' Meticulous Strategy of Brains, Muscle and Practice," *The New York Times,* online edition, November 4, 2001.

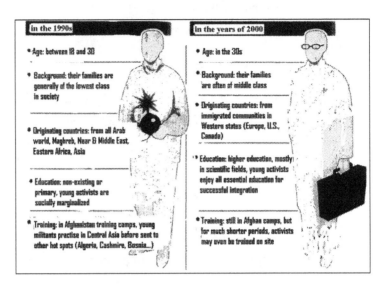

Illustration 3. 2. A look at old and new 'terrorist' activists (Source: « Les anciens et les nouveaux terroristes », 'Ancient and new terrorists', *Le Figaro*, September 20, 2001: 6)

I. Information-processing technologies enable activists to hide or encrypt their messages, where anyone can make use of this power to run widely available state-of-the-art encryption software. Sometimes even less advanced computer technologies are just as effective. For example, individuals can employ steganography ("hidden writing") to embed messages into digital photographs or music clips. Posted on publicly available Web sites, the photos or clips are downloaded by collaborators as necessary. Many other off-the-shelf technologies, such as "spread-spectrum" radios that randomly switch their broadcasting and receiving signals, allow individuals to obscure their messages and make themselves invisible.

J. The World Wide Web, as well, provides access to critical information, where details and information about the floor plans and design characteristics of the World Trade Center were easily obtained, and about how demolition experts may use progressive collapse to destroy large buildings. Yet, in the aftermath of the attacks much *sensitive* posted information was removed from the Web. For example (among many others):

- The U.S. Department of Transportation limited access to the National Pipeline Mapping System, which lays out the network of high-pressure natural gas pipelines throughout the country;

- The Centers for Disease Control and Prevention pulled a report about lack of preparedness against an attack using poison gas or other chemical agents;

- The Agency for Toxic Substances and Disease Registry dropped a report critical of chemical plant security;

- The Federal Aviation Administration pulled data from a Web site listing enforcement violations–such as weaknesses in airport security;

- Geographical Information Services, which provides highly detailed maps of roads and utilities, limited access to federal, state, and local government officials;

- The Nuclear Regulatory Commission shut down its Web site; and;

- The National Imagery and Mapping Agency stopped selling large-scale digital maps to the public through its Web site.[86]

K. Years after the September events, the United States still foresees a more pervasive sense of insecurity, which may be partly based on physical threats. "Mapping the Global Future" states that coming attacks may be "most original not in the technologies or weapons they employ but rather in the operational concepts– i.e., the scope, design, or support arrangements for attacks."[87]

---

[86] For more details, see: Sabin Russell, "Web sites pull information in interest of national security fear of giving useful data to terrorists," *San Francisco Chronicle*, October 5, 2001, A-13; and also: "The Post-September 11 Environment: Access to Government Information," *Federation of American Scientists*, at: www.fas.org, October 2001.

[87] "Mapping the Global Future," Report of the National Intelligence Council's 2020 Project, U.S. National Intelligence Council, Washington, DC, December 2004, p. 95.

In terms of cyber warfare, it predicts:

> Over the next 15 years, a growing range of actors, including terrorists, may acquire and develop capabilities to conduct both physical and cyber attacks against nodes of the world's information infrastructure, including the Internet, telecommunications networks, and computer systems that control critical industrial processes such as electricity grids, refineries, and flood control mechanisms. Terrorists already have specified the US information infrastructure as a target and currently are capable of physical attacks that would cause at least brief, isolated disruptions....
>
> A key cyber battlefield of the future will be the information on computer systems themselves, which is far more valuable and vulnerable than physical systems. New technologies on the horizon provide capabilities for accessing data, either through wireless intercept, intrusion into Internet-connected systems, or through direct access by insiders.[88]

L. In a drive to improve its image among Americans, the Saudi government was reported to have spent more than $5 million on well-connected lobbyists and national television advertisements during the first year following the September 11 attacks. Hiring several public relations firms within an American political campaign to overhaul its image in the country, Saudi officials stated the publicity was intended to counter intensified anger or skepticism among Americans toward their country, which was home to 15 of the 19 hijackers.[89]

From the inside, Saudi life has begun to be being re-examined in the following sectors:

- Education: Saudi intellectuals say a narrow, religious-oriented educational curriculum that employs a degree of brainwashing helped shaped the mentality of the Saudis who hijacked four U.S. jetliners on September 11. The educational system teaches an Arab-centric view of the world, in which Israel is not a legitimate state and people who do not practice the Saudi state religion are considered infidels.

---

[88] "Mapping the Global Future," 2004, p. 97.

[89] Details of the publicity campaign in: Christopher Marquis, "Worried Saudis Try to Improve Image in the U.S.," *The New York Times,* online edition, August 29, 2002.

- Religion: No Saudi disputes the primacy of Islam in the country where it arose in the 7th century. Yet, there are rising complaints about the government's promotion of only one interpretation of Islam. It is known as Salafism there, but in the rest of the world, it is called Wahhabism, after 18th century-religious reformer Mohammed Abdul Wahhab.

- Government: Saudis defend the royal family, Al Saud, who unified the country 70 years ago, and only few seek a Western-style democracy. But there are rising complaints about corruption and a bureaucracy made up of officials appointed more for connections to the monarchy than on merit.

- Diplomacy: Saudi Arabia has always been a key player in its region's diplomacy, and has been increasingly concerned about the plight of Palestinians under Israeli occupation. Analysts, however, say the shock of September 11 was an added motivation for King Abdullah (then Crown Prince) to launch a new peace proposal in the hopes of cooling a conflict that has inflamed anti-American sentiment throughout the Muslim world, and which could eventually destabilize moderate Arab governments.

- The Media: Satellite television is giving Saudis increased exposure to the outside world. They are inundated by sensual images of foreigners in contrast to the black-shrouded women there who, in the words of 19th century French author Guy De Maupassaut, resemble "death out for a walk."[90]

M. The U.S.-Saudi relationship is based on common interests that are fundamental and critical to both countries. Since September 11, however, several factions from both sides are calling for a divorce. Yet, anyone advocating for a

---

[90] Refer to: Barbara Slavin, "Shaken Saudis take hard look at Society," *USA Today,* online edition, April 24, 2004.

divorce would need to take into account the powerful influence a strong U.S.-Saudi relationship has on American strategic interests and regional stability.

After the end of the Iraq-Kuwait conflict in the Gulf region (in 1991), the relations between the two have been largely neglected. There is no broad engagement of intellectuals, media, foreign affairs experts, and religious figures about the importance or benefits of the relationship. The cultures remain distant and the potential for misunderstanding and misreading remain wide. Symbols of common purpose have faded with time. September 11 did indeed reveal the degree to which the gap has grown.

In mutual dialog, for instance, "the superficiality of contact between American intellectuals and media and those in the Arab world is serving the interests of neither; the lack of depth and variety of contact is reflected in U.S. policies."[91] This trend will be difficult to reverse because dialogue will immediately focus on *hot button* issues and not proceed to deeper discussion. Therefore, American foundations and institutions have sought to engage in long-term consultations with Saudis who have studied at American schools and universities and with "next-generation" leaders, reminding that the grand majority of Saudi elites are American graduates.

In military, the relationship between the two is long-standing and a centerpiece of the U.S.-Saudi political relationship. Despite that, the American military presence in Saudi Arabia is not secure, since the absence of serious dialog and communication has resulted in mutual misunderstanding of goals and purposes of the military relationship at the highest levels of both governments. Both see their defense relationship differently. Both agree the U.S. military is present in Saudi Arabia in the event that the Kingdom and the Gulf region are invaded. The agreement stops here. Also, while Saudi cooperation has helped defer the cost of American operations in their country, Saudi Arabia sees it as a political and fiscal burden given their current economy.

---

[91] "Strengthening the U.S.-Saudi Relationship," A Paper Prepared for the Independent Task Force on America's Response to Terrorism, New York: Council on Foreign Relations, May 2002.

In oil security, both have had a long, successful petroleum relationship, although the United States has already envisioned lessening and diversifying reliance on imported oil. Domestic instability out of a domestic fiscal crisis and a malfunctioning labor market can constitute a potential threat to Saudi oil supply and world oil security.

In economic interdependence, Saudi Arabians have what is estimated to be around $700 billion assets invested in the United States. Maintaining these financial flows is important to the stability of American financial markets–rendering it essential and vital to monitor financial flows post-September 11.[92] To note, out of the nearly $60 billion trade business with the Arab countries in 2004, Saudi Arabia had a share of about 43%.[93]

N. A study titled "Civil Democratic Islam: Partners, Resources, and Strategies" calls for a strategy that can distinguish between Muslims with whom peaceful relationships and dialog are possible, and extremist Muslims whose values are fundamentally incompatible with 'democracy' and the contemporary

---

[92] Louis XI (1423-1483), the great Spider King of France, had a weakness for astrology. He kept a court astrologer whom he admired, until one day the man predicted that a lady of the court would die within eight days. When the prophecy came true, Louis was terrified, thinking that either the man had murdered the woman to prove his accuracy or that he was so versed in his science that his powers threatened Louis himself. In either case he had to be killed.

One evening Louis summoned the astrologer to his room, high in the castle. Before the man arrived, the king told his servants that when he gave the signal they were to pick the astrologer up, carry him to the window, and hurl him to the ground, hundreds of feet below.

The astrologer soon arrived, but before giving the signal, Louis decided to ask him one last question: "You claim to understand astrology and to know the fate of others, so tell me what your fate will be and how long you have to live."

"I shall die just three days before Your Majesty," the astrologer replied. The king's signal was never given. The man's life was spared. The Spider King not only protected his astrologer for as long as he was alive, he lavished him with gifts and had him tended by the finest court doctors.

The astrologer survived Louis by several years, disproving his power of prophecy but proving his mastery of power. (Quoted from: Greene & Elffers, *The 48 Laws of Power*, "Law II: Learn to keep people dependent on you," 1998, pp. 85-86.)

On strategic interdependence family reunions between Al Qaida and Taliban leaders in Afghanistan, see: Alexandrine Bouilhet, «L'état major d' Al Qaida», *Le Figaro*, October 10, 2001, 6.

[93] "Arab trade with America totals to 60 billion dollars," *www.aljazeera.net*, February 7, 2005.

international order.[94] It describes a number of key topics or *marker issues*–like democracy, human rights, Islamic criminal penalties, polygamy, women's role in society, Jihad, the status of minorities, and the principles of an Islamic state–all of which reveal a group's underlying ideology.

The study assigns groups and individuals a position along a spectrum based on their values, with radical fundamentalism at one end and radical secularism at the other. Most groups fall somewhere in between, and may be classified as *fundamentalists, traditionalists, modernists,* or *secularists.* A key characteristic of radical fundamentalists, according to the study, is their open and aggressive hostility toward the United States, coupled with a goal of damaging and destroying democratic society. They seek to impose and expand the strict observance of Islam. Traditionalists tend to concentrate on keeping their community and families within a virtuous Islamic framework. They tend not to challenge the state, and to oppose violence. However, they are often uncomfortable with modernity.

On the other end, modernists and secularists are more closely aligned with the West in their values and policies, although the more extreme secularists may hold radical views that place them beyond the bounds of democracy. Modernists support reform in the hope that the Islamic world becomes part of contemporary global society. Secularists go even further, urging Muslims to accept the Western idea of a state, relegating religion to a private matter.

The study concludes that the most effective approach to engage the Islamic world might include a strategic combination of the following set of elements: support the modernists first, support the traditionalists against the fundamentalists, confront and oppose the fundamentalists, and selectively support secularists.

---

[94] Cheryl Benard, *Civil Democratic Islam: Partners, Resources, and Strategies,* RAND Corporation, Santa Monica, CA, 2003.

O. In an emerging phenomenon among teenagers in the United States, the vocabulary and expressions in Table 3.1., referred to as "terror humor," have become a sort of comic relief:[95]

Expression	Translation
• Their bedrooms are *ground zero*	A total mess
• That teacher is such a *terrorist*	He's mean
• It was total *Jihad*	A student after being disciplined
• Is that a *burqa?*	Out-of-style clothes
• Are you a *Taliban?*	Are you weird?
• Do you have *anthrax?*	Are you weird?
• He's as hard to find as *Bin Laden?*	Can't reach/find him
• You're *emo*	Very emotional about September 11
• He's firefighter cute	Instead of "hottie"

Table 3. 1. Terror humor (Source: Wax, 2002)

P. Immediately after the September 11 attacks, the challenge to U.S. public diplomacy in the Arab and Muslim world has been to make clear that:

- the United States was a victim of an unjustifiable terrorist act;
- the United States in neither anti-Islam nor engaged in a war against Muslims; and;
- the United States will bring to justice the terrorist networks that planned and carried out the attacks, and will eliminate terrorism in the world.[96]

---

[95] Emily Wax, "Teens Talk the Talk Boys Are 'Firefighter cute,' Messy Room is 'Ground Zero,' in Sept. 11 Slang," *The Washington Post,* March 19, 2002, A01.

[96] Some practices of public diplomacy included hosting traditional *Iftar* (breaking of the fast) dinners during Ramadan in Saudi Arabia, instituting a mobile message system for U.S. information in Egypt, assisting a Pakistan Television and Radio team to visit the United States to film interviews with senior administration officials, and sponsoring series of lectures on the relationship between Islam and the West in Syria. See: "Creativity and Patience: Public Diplomacy

As George W. Bush began his second term of office in January 2005, two noteworthy appointments–directly linked to American public diplomacy–were made. First, former White House counselor Karen P. Hughes was named State Department Under Secretary for Public Diplomacy, with the rank of ambassador. And second, Egyptian-born Dina Habib Powell (former White House personnel director, a Christian born in 1973) was nominated Deputy Under Secretary of State for Public Diplomacy and Assistant Secretary of State for Educational and Cultural Affairs.

Both of them take over the Bush administration's troubled public diplomacy efforts intended to polish the American image abroad, particularly in Arab and Muslim countries. In 2004, the U.S. State Department spent $685 million on public diplomacy, yet critics complained it had not been increased enough since the September 11 attacks, and most of it has not targeted the Muslim world.[97]

Q. The newly formed U.S. Office of Homeland Security outlines five levels of terrorism alerts:

- Green: Low risk of terrorist attacks
- Blue: Guarded condition. General risk of terrorist attack
- Yellow: Elevated condition. Significant risk
- Orange: High risk of terrorist attacks
- Red: Severe risk of terrorist attacks.[98]

Post-Sept. 11," Matt Lussenhop, *American Diplomacy*, at: www.unc.edu/depts/diplomat, April 2002.

[97] See: Peter Baker, "Karen Hughes To Work on The World's View of U.S.," *The Washington Post*, March 12, 2005, A03; and also: Elisabeth Bumiller, "A Mideast Strategy That Includes a Mideast Card," *The New York Times*, online edition, March 21, 2005.

[98] For recommended actions for citizens, visit: www.ready.gov, "Citizen Guidance on the Homeland Security Advisory System," U.S. Department of Homeland Security.

With the French also being familiar with acts of terrors and with seeing the military on duty abroad, the new government "Vigipirate" plan enforced on March 26, 2003 includes four alerts levels:

- Jaune : accentuer la vigilance   (Yellow : Intensify vigilance)
- Orange: prévenir une action terroriste   (Orange: Warning of terrorist action)
- Rouge: prévenir des attentats graves   (Red: Warning of serious attacks)
- Ecarlate : prévenir des attentas majeurs.[99] (Scarlet: Warning of major attacks)

However, questions are being raised on the regular 'exaggerated' alerts, which tend to be timed for certain political and economic objectives. Former U.S. Homeland Security chief Tom Ridge clearly stated (after resigning) that he often disagreed with administration officials who wanted to elevate the threat level to 'orange,' but was often overruled.

> More often than not we were the least inclined to raise it. Sometimes we disagreed with the intelligence assessment. Sometimes we thought even if the intelligence was good, you don't necessarily put the country on [alert]....There were times when some people were really aggressive about raising it, and we said, 'For that?'.[100]

Tom Ridge also added Homeland Security officials did not want to raise the alert level because they knew local governments and businesses would have to spend money putting temporary security upgrades in place (*Ibid.*).

Concluding likewise, former U.S. National Security Advisor Zbigniew Brzezinski states:

---

[99] «Présentation du nouveau plan gouvernemental de vigilance, de prévention et de protection face aux menaces d'actions terroristes : Vigipirate», ('Presentation of the New Governmental Plan for Vigilance, Prevention and Protection Against Terrorist Action Threats'), March 26, 2003, at: http: //www.premier-ministre.gouv.fr/ressources/fichiers/vigipirate_dp270303.pdf.

[100] Mimi Hall, "Ridge reveals clashes on alerts," *USA Today*, online edition, May 10, 2005.

Yet a paradox haunts America: it is more powerful by far than any other state in the world, but its official rhetoric since 9/11 is that of a fear-driven nation. Though other states have also been victimized, none have politically elevated occasional terrorism into a national obsession.[101]

R. Despite the precautions and awareness of citizens and security agents all over the world over potential attacks or threats, serious goofs have been noticed. Among them are:

A German truck-driver was detained for more than 10 hours last weekend after Italian authorities searching the truck found the word "Laden" scribbled on his documents. Sniffer dogs and explosives experts were called in, the area was sealed off and the police even consulted with the anti-mafia squad before they realized their mistake. "Laden" means "load" in German.[102]

And also:

Two men, constantly ducking into the bathroom together–they must be terrorists! At least, so assumed the crew of a recent flight from London to New York. Within minutes, two Air Force jets scrambled to escort the plane home. As it turns out, the men weren't terrorists–just a lascivious gay couple.[103]

S. In Respect of Iraq, a blue print for the creation of a global *Pax Americana* was drawn up in "Rebuilding America's Defenses: Strategy, Forces and Resources For a New Century," written in September 2000 by the neo-conservative think tank, Project for the New American Century (PNAC).[104]

The plan shows the intention of the Bush administration cabinet (namely, Vice President Dick Cheney, Defense Secretary Donald Rumsfeld and former defense

---

[101] Zbigniew Brzezinski, "A Grand Alliance," *Newsweek*, international special edition, December 2004-February 2005, 96.

[102] "Time for a dictionary," *Newsweek,* international edition, November 19, 2001, 5.

[103] This, with a few other goofs, is quoted in: "Oops...They Did It Again," *Newsweek*, international edition, March 18, 2002, 5.

[104] "Rebuilding America's Defenses: Strategy, Forces and Resources For a New Century," A Report of The Project for the New American Century, New York, September 2000. Also see: Michael Meacher (former British environment minister), "This war on terrorism is bogus," *The Guardian*, online edition, September 6, 2003.

undersecretary Paul Wolfowitz) to take military control of the Gulf region whether or not Saddam Hussein was in power. It states (p. 14):

> Indeed, the United States has for decades sought to play a more permanent role in Gulf regional security. While the unresolved conflict with Iraq provides the immediate justification, the need for a substantial American force presence in the Gulf transcends the issue of the regime of Saddam Hussein.

Furthermore, it adds (p. 17):

> After eights years of no-fly-zone, there is little reason to anticipate that the U.S. air presence in the region should diminish significantly as long as Saddam Hussein remains in power. Although Saudi domestic sensibilities demand that the forces based in the Kingdom nominally remain rotational forces, it has become apparent that this now a semi-permanent mission. From an American perspective, the value of such bases would endure even should Saddam pass from the scene. Over the long term, Iran may well prove as large a threat to U.S. interests in the Gulf as Iraq has. And even should U.S.–Iranian relations improve, retaining forward-based forces in the region would still be an essential element in U.S. security strategy given the longstanding American interests in the region.

Last, it notes (p. 11):

> ...constabulary missions are far more complex and likely to generate violence than traditional "peacekeeping" missions. For one, they demand American political leadership rather than that of the UN.... Nor can the United States assume a UN-like stance of neutrality; the preponderance of American power is so great and its global interests so wide that it cannot pretend to be indifferent to the political outcome in the Balkans, the Persian Gulf or even when it deploys forces in Africa.

T. Where the United States may have achieved varying successes elsewhere, U.S. nation-building efforts in Iraq after March 2003 have certainly signaled several characteristic weaknesses.[105]

The United States has been sharply criticized for the following deficiencies in the case of Iraq:[106]

- planning for stabilization and reconstruction was based on unrealistic, best-case assumptions;

- the original stabilization force was too small;

- the United States was too slow to deploy civil administrators and police in adequate numbers; and;

- when deployed, those individuals proved of variable quality.

Furthermore, the United States failed to anticipate that:

- the fall of Saddam Hussein would be accompanied by the collapse of the Iraqi state;

- a power vacuum would open;

- this vacuum would be immediately filled by a combination of criminals and outside extremist elements;

- the Iraqi security apparatus would be unavailable to challenge these elements; and;

- criminals and extremists would become extremely difficult to displace if they were allowed to move into the power vacuum, organize and consolidate, intimidate the populace, and cow what was left of the police.

The United States seemed to have decided to model the Iraqi operation on its post-World War II occupations of Germany and Japan. In brief, if the United States learned from the Germany case that 'democracy' may be "transferred," and from the

---

[105] For a review of previous U.S. efforts in nation-building up to Afghanistan, refer to: James Dobbins et al., *America's Role in Nation-Building: From Germany to Iraq*, RAND Corporation, Santa Monica, CA, 2003.

[106] James Dobbins et al., *The UN's Role in Nation-Building: From the Congo to Iraq*, RAND Corporation, Santa Monica, CA, 2005, pp. 209-10.

Japan case that it may be "exported" to non Western societies, it has well learned from the Iraq case that democracy may not be "imposed" according to its style.

Consequently, and in a sense of admission that the Bush administration did not do enough before the invasion in Iraq to assure worldwide support, or even later to sustain contributions of allies in stability and reconstruction efforts, the Pentagon for the first time invited foreign allies into classified discussions that intend to shape America's missions and combat forces for years to come. The discussions aim to outline tasks that would become the responsibility of other nations and no longer the burden of the United States.

Expected to be completed in early 2006, the Quadrennial Defense Review (a document required by the U.S. Congress every four years) is framed in such an initial phase by guidelines set out in a secret document, known as 'Terms of Reference' (and which was approved by Secretary of Defense Donald Rumsfeld). The classified planning document states:[107]

> Although the United States has historically preferred to act in concert with other states, it has also maintained the ability to act unilaterally if necessary.

It stresses:

> Today's problems, however, are such that the United States cannot succeed by addressing them alone. The Terms of Reference, therefore, propose that the United States develop new partnerships to address nontraditional challenges.

In a significant departure from how America decides the size, shape and missions of its armed forces, these decisions could more closely bind the United States and its military allies in peacetime, and eventually allow them to operate together with more efficiency in disaster relief, peacekeeping, stabilization, and in full-scale combat operations.

---

[107] Thom Shanker, "Pentagon Invites Allies for First Time to Secret Talks Aimed at Sharing Burdens," *The New York Times*, online edition, March 18, 2005.

U. A noteworthy report by the Center for Strategic and International Studies (CSIS) set a model as a baseline to describe the status of Iraq's reconstruction in five vital areas, and to assess whether Iraq is progressing, regressing, or remaining static in those areas after the U.S. invasion in March 2003.[108] The model also provides an index for future measurement of progress. CSIS cross-referenced data against a series of simple statements that serve as a barometer of progress in following areas of Iraq's reconstruction: *security, governance and participation, economic opportunity, services,* and *social well-being.* The statements are:

Security: I feel secure in my home and in my daily activities

Governance and Participation: I have a say in how Iraq is run

Economic Opportunity: I have a means of income

Services: I have access to basic services, such as power, water and sanitation

Social well-being: My family and I have access to health care and education

In a cumulative view from June 2003 to July 2004, the report concluded Iraq had not reached by then the realistic goals described as the "tipping points" in any of the five sectors of reconstruction.

V. In its Third Annual Worldwide Index of Press Freedom issued in late 2004, *Reporters sans frontières* (Reporters Without Borders) ranked Iraq in the 148th position (out of 167 countries). It considered it as:

> one of the most dangerous places in the world, both for Iraqi journalists and foreign reporters. All are in danger of being targeted in the course of combat or by armed groups... Furthermore, the new Iraqi authorities have not yet established a framework guaranteeing press freedom and have reacted in an

---

[108] *Progress or Peril? Measuring Iraq's Reconstruction*, Center for Strategic and International Studies, The Post-Conflict Reconstruction Project, Washington, DC, September 2004. Also refer to the series of three articles by Rajir Chandrasekaran, in *The Washington Post,* titled "Mistakes Loom Large as Handover Nears," (June 20, 2004, A01); " An Educator Learns the Hard War" (June 21, 2004, A01); and "Death Stalks An Experiment In Democracy," (June 22, 2004, A01).

authoritarian manner towards the pan-Arab satellite TV news stations whose coverage they view as pro-terrorist.[109]

With 56 journalists and media assistants killed, and another 29 kidnapped in Iraq since March 22, 2003, Reporters Without Borders stressed in May 2005 that "the Iraq Conflict is the deadliest inter-state war for journalists since the one in Vietnam," when over a period of 20 years (1955-75), 63 journalists were killed, compared to 49 journalists killed during the fighting in the former Yugoslavia (1991-1995) while reporting.[110]

In addition, Transparency International in Global Corruption Report 2005 stressed the existence of "high levels" of corruption in Iraq after March 2003. Since then, bribery has taken place at all levels of government while officials within the Coalition Provisional Authority, contractors and ministry staff have admitted to corruption. Transparency International warned:

> If urgent steps are not taken, Iraq will not become the shining beacon of democracy envisioned by the Bush administration, it will become the biggest corruption scandal in history.[111]

W. The on-going invasion in Iraq signals a contrast of paradoxical proportions, as the U.S. and British occupiers–along with its selected interim government and recruited agents–prepared for elections in January 2005. Yet, a fierce resistance successfully destabilized such arrangements to a certain extent, striking soft targets, coalition troops and foreigners on a daily basis.

---

[109] Based solely on events between September 1, 2003 and September 1, 2004, the index measures the state of press freedom in the world. It reflects the degree of freedom journalists and news organizations enjoy in each country, and the efforts made by the state to respect and ensure respect for this freedom. The Reporters Without Borders' Index is available online at: www.rsf.org, Third Annual Worldwide Press Freedom Index, October 26, 2004.

[110] "The war in Iraq: the most deadly one for the media since Vietnam," *Reporters Without Borders*, May 3, 2005.

[111] "Global Corruption Report 2005," Transparency International, London, March 16, 2005.

While the occupying forces and their media are concerned only in counting 'their' deaths, *The Lancet* published the first scientific study of the effects of the invasion on Iraqi civilians. The study reported substantially more deaths in Iraq since the beginning of the invasion than during the period immediately before its outbreak. Much of that increased mortality is a consequence of the prevailing climate of violence in the country, and many of the civilian casualties described have been attributed to the actions of coalition forces. The study concludes:

> Making conservative assumptions, we think that about 100000 excess deaths, or more have happened since the 2003 invasion of Iraq. Violence accounted for most of the excess deaths and air strikes from coalition forces accounted for most violent deaths.[112]

Noting that the U.S. Pentagon does not give numbers for civilian deaths, the Iraqi Minister of Interior stated in an interview with CNN that violence in the country over the first 6 months of 2005 led to the death of 8,175 people, and wounding another 12,000.[113] Obviously, these findings–and the tentative countrywide mortality projections they support–have immediate translatable policy implications for those charged with managing the aftermath of invasion.

X. Within a given conflict theater itself, Psychological Operations (PSYOPS) may prepare the region for the introduction of foreign military or peacekeeping forces. They can assist in securing non-interference, if not cooperation, and contribute to the safety of forces engaged and even of regional factions and populations. Also, they can counter divisive or hostile propaganda and mold realistic, obtainable, local expectations, including preparing the local population for the eventual withdrawal of those forces. They can, furthermore, create a climate of opinion for the international media to report on events in a manner beneficial to the entire exercise.

---

[112] Les Roberts et al., "Mortality before and after the 2003 invasion of Iraq: cluster sample survey," published online on October 29, 2004, at: http://image.thelancet.com/extras/04art10342web.pdf.

[113] "Iraq: 8,000 killed in 6 months," *CNN News*, online edition, June 30, 2005.

Internationally, they can provide insight into the cultural, historical, political, religious and other psychological factors contributing to the conflict, advertise success and frame international expectations. PSYOPS, in humanitarian and disaster relief operations, can help reduce despair and build hope, defeat rumors and forestall panic, overcome shock and motivate local populations to self-help.

Consider, for example, the mere naming of U.S. and U.N. operations that aim to serve to this end: Operation *Just Cause* (in Panama), Operation *Provide Comfort* (in Kurdistan Iraq), Operation *Restore Hope* (in Somalia), Operation *Provide Refuge* (in Marshall Islands), Operation *Uphold Democracy* (in Haiti), Operation *Enduring Freedom* (in Afghanistan), *Operation Iraqi Freedom* (in Iraq), and among others, the *War on Terror*.

However, Taylor (1997, p. 200-01) cautions, if it is to achieve all of this, it must be considered as an integral part of the overall planning from the earliest possible stage. Whether or not it works depends upon how effectively it is planned. By not preparing the psychological environment, the entry of foreign forces could be jeopardized by factions uncertain of the identity or motives of the arriving forces, or those who have something to lose as a result of the deployment of forces. Accordingly, the ground is laid open for hostile propaganda portraying forces–regardless of their nature–as opportunistic aggressors, interfering and patronizing colonizers who wish to exploit natural resources. The lack of cultural respect and sensitivity from the part of American forces as they entered and continue to stay in Iraq is a point of concern in this respect.

Y. As the United States continues to conduct its "War on Terror" (with Afghanistan and Iraq still unsettled), reference is pointed here to a number of propaganda phrasings and speech campaigns addressed to the public at large.

- Nous ne voulons pas la guerre. (We do not want war.)
- Le camp adverse est seul responsable de la guerre. (The other side is the sole party responsible for war.)

- Le chef du camp adverse a le visage du diable. (The opponent's chief is a demon.)

- C'est une cause noble que nous défendons et non des intérêts particuliers. (We are defending a noble cause, and not particular interests.)

- L'ennemi provoque sciemment des atrocités ; si nous commettons des bavures, c'est involontairement. (The enemy deliberately provokes atrocities; yet blunders committed by us are accidental.)

- L'ennemi utilise des armes non autorisées. (The enemy is employing prohibited weapons.)

- Non subissons très peu de pertes, les pertes de l'ennemi sont énormes. (Our losses are few, yet the enemy is suffering enormously.)

- Les artistes et intellectuels soutiennent notre cause. (Artists and intellectuals are supporting our cause.)

- Notre cause a un caractère sacre. (Our cause is sacred in nature.)

- Ceux qui mettent en doute notre propagande sont des traîtres. (Those who doubt our media campaign are traitors.) [114]

It is worth observing that after the U.S. invasion in Iraq in March 2003, for instance, *resistance-fighters* and *Mujahideens* have been depicted and perceived by American (and some Western) press as *insurgents, terror groups, extremists, former Baathist elements* and *former Saddam supporters.*[115]

Z. The U.S. air campaign in Afghanistan, based on a high-tech-out-of-harm's way strategy, has produced a pattern of mistakes that have killed hundreds of Afghan civilians. As local politics tend to get in the way of American intelligence

---

[114] Examples for each case in Anne MORELLI, *«Principes élémentaires de propagande de guerre: Utilisables en case de guerre froide, chaude ou tiède»*, ('Elementary Principles of War Propaganda: Used in Cold, Hot or Mild War Cases'), Brussels: Labor, 2001. On media lies and misinformation, also see : Michel Collon, *«Attention médias ! Les média mensonges du Golfe, Manuel anti-manipulation»*, ('Attention Media ! The Media Lies of the Gulf, An Anti-Manipulation Guide'), EPO editions, 4th edition, 2000.

[115] It is hence not surprising that the word "insurgent" was one of the top ten words (in 4th place) most looked up by users on the Merriam-Webster Online Dictionary in 2004. Among the other ten of political or electoral nature are: "blog" (1st place); "incumbent" (2nd); "electoral" (3rd); "partisan" (8th); and "sovereignty" (9th). Source: "Merriam-Webster's Words of the Year 2004," retrieved on December 1, 2004, at: http://www.merriam-webster.com/info/04words.htm.

gathering, U.S. forces have made extensive use of untrustworthy Afghan informants who trick the Americans into sending lethal air strikes on their tribal rivals.[116]

The issue of relying on dishonest informants resurfaced once again during the U.S. invasion in Iraq. First, American officials have acknowledge publicly of the unreliable information provided to them by Iraqi defectors concerning the country's possession of weapons of mass destruction. Those same sources were also behind the dissolution of the Iraqi army, and behind the so-called "de-Baathification" immediately after the vacuum of power in the country. U.S. officials, on several occasions, later admitted these two strategic mistakes. Second, American forces, counting this time on local agents and recruits, have routinely bombed Iraqi cities (namely Falluja, Samarra and Mosul) under the pretext of running after *terror cells*. This has resulted, up to the date of this writing, to the death of several thousands of innocent civilians.

---

[116] See: Tim McGirk, "When Bad Information Kills People," *Time*, online edition, March 3, 2002; Charles Clover, "Afghans paying the price for US failures of intelligence," *Financial Times, July* 13-14, 2002, 24; and Dexter Filkins, "Flaws in U.S. Air War Left Hundreds of Civilians Dead," *The New York Times*, online edition, July 21, 2002.

CONCLUSION

"Information," since ever, has been both of intellectual value to the individual and of strategic importance to the state. Notably during the past few decades, information and knowledge have gained increasing significance, as they continue to guide global transformations in many aspects of our daily life.

Among the factors and developments behind such an evolution are the rapid, remarkable advances in information and communication technologies that have led to a vast, infinite growth of a modern information infrastructure. This has accordingly shifted the traditional means of communicating from one-to-many (e.g., the radio and television) to an interlinked, open-end many-to-many (e.g., the Internet). In the political, business and social realms, new actors are being empowered in the information era, as technological innovation renders interaction possible at all levels. Simultaneously, there are increases in the speed, capacity and flexibility in the collection, production and dissemination of information. And as decentralized network-based structures emerge, the state's traditional authority and monopoly on information fragments.

It is, thus, common sense to recognize the growing interlink between "information" and "power." In terms of labor, for instance, workers are expected to maintain their skills through lifetime training. With the rise of "knowledge workers," those with fewer skills command much lower salaries and even risk job loss to their better-trained counterparts. Employees are becoming more mobile and work in more decentralized firms, with less formal and more individualized employer-employee relations. To keep up with the pace and developments of the information age, technology-mediated learning offers promise for further training and retraining throughout the career.

Considering its immense volume, information may be viewed in three realms defined in respect of their technological, organizational and ideational developments.[117] The Cyberspace realm covers the global system of interconnected computers, communications infrastructures, on-line conferencing entities, databases, and information tools generally referred to as the 'the Net.' Although essentially used to refer to the Internet, cyberspace may also imply the electronic environments and critical infrastructures of a corporation, military, government, or other organization.

The second realm, the Infosphere, is far larger than the cyberspace, as it embodies both the latter and information systems that may not be part of the Net. This often covers broadcast, print and other media (also referred to as 'mediasphere'), in addition to libraries and other intellectual resource institutions (of which are not yet necessarily electronic-based). In the military domain, infosphere may refer to command, control, computer, communications, intelligence, surveillance, and reconnaissance (C4ISR) systems, which constitute the military information environment.

The last realm of information, the Noosphere, is the most abstract and the largest (*noos* from Greek means 'the mind'). Described as the 'thinking generator,' this realm encompasses both the cyberspace and the infosphere. Figure 4.1. below illustrates the three realms.

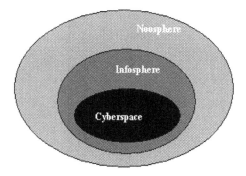

Figure 4. 1. Three Realms of Information (Source: Ronfeldt & Arquilla, 1999)

---

[117] David Ronfeldt and John Arquilla, *What if there is a Revolution in Diplomatic Affairs?*, United States Institute of Peace Virtual Diplomacy Report, Washington, DC, February 25, 1999, at: http://www.usip.org/vdi/vdr/ronarqISA99.html.

Many calls have emerged for creating a global noosphere based on freedom of information not only from individuals but also from non-state activists and civil-society institutes (such as churches, research centers, schools). After the September 11, 2001 attacks on the United States, there has been a remarkable diversity of new restrictions on access to information (with particular reference to the United States), leading to the removal of thousands of pages from government Web sites and also the withdrawal of thousands of technical reports from public access. Where the meaning of "unclassified" may be clear, the crucial term of "sensitive" information still remains undefined when dealing with national security.

Accordingly, the power and importance of information in the current era has led to advances in the practice of "noopolotik." Here, diplomacy and strategy focus on the shaping and sharing of ideas, values, norms, laws, and ethics through the concept of the soft power. The underlining conviction in noopolotik becomes that right makes for might (and not the reverse). And while realpolitik seeks to empower states, noopolotik empowers networks of state and non-state actors. This notion has direct implications for diplomats, who need to understand "power" mainly in terms of "knowledge," as they focus on the "balance of knowledge" as distinct from the "balance of power."

In terms of intelligence activity and information gathering, intelligence needs to be thought of as information, instead of secrets. Many state intelligence organs are undergoing reform in respect of information collection and analysis. Individuals responsible for leading intelligence communities are being empowered with more authority to commensurate with assigned responsibilities. Intelligence products should remain independent from policymakers, and thus not become an instrument of diplomacy or policy formulation.

Furthermore, improving the quality of analysis that policymakers rely on may result from a competitive environment where different prospectives are welcomed and alternative hypotheses are encouraged. Once again, analysts must be preserved from policy and political pressure. Many calls have also been made within the intelligence communities to share information with each other, whether between state agencies or among the organs of the same state. Finally, much debate is voiced on the inherently intrusive nature of intellectual and information gathering when it comes to protecting civil liberties. In this concern, the cultural environment of each society has its word.

In respect of the rising flow of globalization, indications show that the process is largely irreversible, and becoming less and less Westernized. In the next two to three decades, globalization will continue to benefit countries and groups that best access to, apply and integrate new technologies. Also, the already-widening gap between the "haves" and the "have-nots" is likely to increase even more unless the "have-not" countries support the application of those technologies into their systems and structures.

Nevertheless, globalization may be substantially slowed down or perhaps even stopped temporarily. A slow-down may result from "a pervasive sense of economic and physical insecurity,"[118] which would lead governments to set controls on the flows of capital, goods, and people. Wide-scale attacks on Western states or widespread cyber attacks on information technology may lead governments to react in such a certain manner. In addition, border controls and restrictions on technology exchanges would certainly cause an increase in economic transaction costs, and eventually hinder innovation and economic growth.

Furthermore, globalization may be endangered if a new pandemic appears in megacities, where the spread of the disease could put a halt to global travel and trade throughout an extended period. Growing threats, in this case, include infectious diseases that spread globally and quickly, increasing drug-resistant microbes, the lag of development of new antibiotics, poor patterns of land and water use, shifts in climate, and the rise of megacities with severe health care deficiencies.

But even so, new technology applications are fostering dramatic improvements in human knowledge and individual well-being. In addition to more adept international surveillance and control mechanisms, such benefits include medical

---

[118] "Mapping the Global Future," Report of the National Intelligence Council's 2020 Project, Washington, DC: U.S. National Intelligence Council, December 2004, p. 30.

breakthroughs to start to cure or alleviate particular common diseases and even stretch lifespan.

In the military field, the United States of America will continue to enjoy overwhelming advantage as a striking force up to at least around the years 2015-2020. Currently positioned in various locations around the globe, no assurances may however be given that those certain spots are the ones where war or conflict is most probably to erupt. Therefore, as priorities in national security and interests shift constantly, a mobile force is in the process of development that 'can go anywhere' and address a 'full spectrum of operations'. State militaries are also being trained to encounter and conduct non-traditional operations–ranging from relief operations, to police and security patrolling, to post-conflict stabilizing forces.

Yet, the competence of the United States to shape the course of the 21st century will depend on the quality of its leaders, of which it lacks when it comes to those who are able to combine substantive depth with international experience and vision. In other words, the current and coming global role of the United States demands "a deep understanding of particular languages and cultures...as well as broad, strategic perspectives on the economic and political forces that will shape the world."[119]

Risks of war among developed countries, in the next 10-20 years, are foreseen as low. In contrast, conflicts varying from relatively frequent small-scale internal upheavals to less frequent religious interstate wars may avail. With religious, ethnic and cultural identity becoming an increasingly important element in how people define and distinguish themselves, conflicts between civilizations (and clashes between opposing groups of the same civilization) are expected to supplant ideological and other sorts of dispute as the dominant form of conflict.

Whether or not Europe can become an influential superpower depends on its future international role. In addition to reinforcing a common political and

---

[119] Gregory F. Treverton and Tora K. Bikson, *New Challenges for International Leadership: Positioning the United States for the 21st Century*, RAND Corporation, Santa Monica, CA, 2003, p. 1.

economic policy, part of the European Union's role will rely on major structural economic and social reforms to deal with demographic concerns.

Widely perceived as a language of opportunity, the English language is by far a dominating *lingua franca* for a wide stream of communication. More than ever before, governments that intend to have an effective role in the world's linguistic future need to consider fundamental decisions, as they make political decisions and allocate resources for language planning. Long-term views are to be adopted, whether in terms of promoting English or the use other languages in their community, or simply both.

Finally, after the September 11, 2001 attacks the United States put together a historic, worldwide coalition in an aim to overthrow the Taliban in Afghanistan, and eventually destroy Al Qaida organization. The result was the subsequent scattering of the Organization–rather than eliminating it.

Some eighteen months later, the Bush administration invaded Iraq, this time to overthrow President Saddam Hussein of Iraq under the pretext of possessing weapons of mass destruction. Yet, most of the countries that backed the United States in Afghanistan bluntly opposed the campaign, as did most of the international community. Washington's failure to assure international support on Iraq was a diplomatic defeat in all implications–a failure that has damaged U.S. foreign policy for years to come. That is, the United States has yet to develop a clear strategic policy to guide the day-to-day conduct of its declared global "war on terrorism."

The American invasion in Iraq has been, and is likely to remain, one of the most controversial conflicts of modern times. The unilateral decision by the world's only superpower to invade Iraq without explicit authorization from the United Nations provoked deep divisions among the international community, and between states. Controversy prevailed the declared justification for the invasion, and whether or not the use of force was the most appropriate approach to deal with the cause. In brief, if the United States was able to destroy its enemy, it certainly was not able to compel its friends and the world community.

The invasion is also controversial because it raises deeper issues of principle and precedent. Among the issues are: whether or not, and under what circumstances, may the resort of force be a legitimate and effective response to certain threats; whether or not, and again under what circumstances, may the removal by force of governments or leaders ('regime change') be a legitimate and wise policy; the role of the U.N. Security Council in such matters in view of its inherent limitations; and last but not least, the role of the United States in world affairs given its current dominant military power.

Nevertheless, the problems facing the United States following the invasion have well proved that post-conflict stabilization may be of greater concern than mere military operations. The United States has also learned that the long-term costs (in human, financial and material considerations) of any similar action are indeed enormous. In any case, whatsoever, the United States will need to exert tremendous efforts to re-establish its credibility before it considers any other military action(s) in the years to come.

Further fields of research and study in the scope of the Information Age and Diplomacy may examine the extent to which people are increasingly becoming more familiar with digital forms of information sources rather than traditional paper prints. How are diplomats coping so that they still remain vital sources of information gathering and analysis to their respective countries? With constant evolutions in cyberspace technology, can we expect an alternative to the Internet? As the number of state-to-state conflicts decline year after year, what effect does economic interdependence have in this respect? And last but not least, is the United States of America already in the initial phases of its decline as the hegemony power in today's world?

APPENDICES

389

Kilobyte (KB)	$1,000$ bytes OR 10^3 bytes 2 Kilobytes: A Typewritten page. 100 Kilobytes: A low-resolution photograph.
Megabyte (MB)	$1,000,000$ bytes OR 10^6 bytes 1 Megabyte: A small novel OR a 3.5 inch floppy disk. 2 Megabytes: A high-resolution photograph. 5 Megabytes: The complete works of Shakespeare. 10 Megabytes: A minute of high-fidelity sound. 100 Megabytes: 1 meter of shelved books. 500 Megabytes: A CD-ROM.
Gigabyte (GB)	$1,000,000,000$ bytes OR 10^9 bytes 1 Gigabyte: a pickup truck filled with books. 20 Gigabytes: A good collection of the works of Beethoven. 100 Gigabytes: A library floor of academic journals.
Terabyte (TB)	$1,000,000,000,000$ bytes OR 10^{12} bytes 1 Terabyte: 50000 trees made into paper and printed. 2 Terabytes: An academic research library. 10 Terabytes: The print collections of the U.S. Library of Congress. 400 Terabytes: National Climactic Data Center (NOAA) database.
Petabyte (PB)	$1,000,000,000,000,000$ bytes OR 10^{15} bytes 1 Petabyte: 3 years of EOS data (2001). 2 Petabytes: All U.S. academic research libraries. 20 Petabytes: Production of hard-disk drives in 1995. 200 Petabytes: All printed material.
Exabyte (EB)	$1,000,000,000,000,000,000$ bytes OR 10^{18} bytes 2 Exabytes: Total volume of information generated in 1999. 5 Exabytes: All words ever spoken by human beings.

Appendix I: How big is an Exabyte?

(Source: "How Much Information? 2003," at: http://www.sims.berkeley.edu/research/projects/how-much-info-2003)

Bin Ladin Determined To Strike in US

Clandestine, foreign government, and media reports indicate Bin Ladin since 1997 has wanted to conduct terrorist attacks in the US. Bin Ladin implied in US television interviews in 1997 and 1998 that his followers would follow the example of World Trade Center bomber Ramzi Yousef and "bring the fighting to America."

> After US missile strikes on his base in Afghanistan in 1998, Bin Ladin told followers he wanted to retaliate in Washington, according to a ███████████ service.

> An Egyptian Islamic Jihad (EIJ) operative told an ███████ service at the same time that Bin Ladin was planning to exploit the operative's access to the US to mount a terrorist strike.

The millennium plotting in Canada in 1999 may have been part of Bin Ladin's first serious attempt to implement a terrorist strike in the US. Convicted plotter Ahmed Ressam has told the FBI that he conceived the idea to attack Los Angeles International Airport himself, but that Bin Ladin lieutenant Abu Zubaydah encouraged him and helped facilitate the operation. Ressam also said that in 1998 Abu Zubaydah was planning his own US attack.

> Ressam says Bin Ladin was aware of the Los Angeles operation.

Although Bin Ladin has not succeeded, his attacks against the US Embassies in Kenya and Tanzania in 1998 demonstrate that he prepares operations years in advance and is not deterred by setbacks. Bin Ladin associates surveilled our Embassies in Nairobi and Dar es Salaam as early as 1993, and some members of the Nairobi cell planning the bombings were arrested and deported in 1997.

Al-Qa'ida members—including some who are US citizens—have resided in or traveled to the US for years, and the group apparently maintains a support structure that could aid attacks. Two al-Qa'ida members found guilty in the conspiracy to bomb our Embassies in East Africa were US citizens, and a senior EIJ member lived in California in the mid-1990s.

> A clandestine source said in 1998 that a Bin Ladin cell in New York was recruiting Muslim-American youth for attacks.

We have not been able to corroborate some of the more sensational threat reporting, such as that from a ████████████ service in 1998 saying that Bin Ladin wanted to hijack a US aircraft to gain the release of "Blind Shaykh" 'Umar 'Abd al-Rahman and other US-held extremists.

continued

For the President Only

Appendix II: Text of a U.S. Presidential Daily Briefing (PDB)

(The text above, which is continued on the following page, is one of the few declassified, yet much-debated PDBs released in the aftermath of the September 11, 2001 attacks on the United States)

— Nevertheless, FBI information since that time indicates patterns of suspicious activity in this country consistent with preparations for hijackings or other types of attacks, including recent surveillance of federal buildings in New York.

The FBI is conducting approximately 70 full field investigations throughout the US that it considers Bin Ladin–related. CIA and the FBI are investigating a call to our Embassy in the UAE in May saying that a group of Bin Ladin supporters was in the US planning attacks with explosives.

Appendix II (continued): Text of a U.S. Presidential Daily Briefing (PDB)

His Excellency Tang Jiaxuan,
Minister of Foreign Affairs,
Beijing,
People's Republic of China.

Dear Mr. Minister:

On behalf of the United States Government, I now outline steps to resolve this issue.

Both President Bush and Secretary of State Powell have expressed their sincere regret over your missing pilot and aircraft. Please convey to the Chinese people and to the family of pilot Wang Wei that we are very sorry for their loss.

Although the full picture of what transpired is still unclear, according to our information, our severely crippled aircraft made an emergency landing after following international emergency procedures. We are very sorry the entering of China's airspace and the landing did not have verbal clearance, but very pleased the crew landed safely. We appreciate China's efforts to see to the well-being of our crew.

In view of the tragic incident and based on my discussions with your representative, we have agreed to the following actions:

Both sides agree to hold a meeting to discuss the incident. My government understands and expects that our aircrew will be permitted to depart China as soon as possible.

The meeting would start April 18, 2001.

The meeting agenda would include discussion of the causes of the incident, possible recommendations whereby such collisions could be avoided in the future, development of a plan for prompt return of the EP-3 aircraft, and other related issues. We acknowledge your government's intention to raise U.S. reconnaissance missions near China in the meeting.

Sincerely,
Joseph W. Prueher

Appendix III: Letter of U.S. Ambassador Joseph W. Prueher addressed to
Foreign Minister Tang Jiaxuan of China
Beijing, April 11, 2001

BIBLIOGRAPHY

Books

* Anderson, M.S., *The Rise of Modern Diplomacy*, London: Longman, 1993.

* Anton, Philip S., Richard Silberglitt and James Schneider, *The Global Technology Revolution: Bio/Nano/Materials Trends and Their Synergies with Information Technology by 2015,* RAND Corporation, Santa Monica, CA, 2001.

* Arquilla, John and David Ronfeldt, *Networks and Netwars: The Future of Terror, Crime and Militancy,* RAND Corporation, Santa Monica, CA, 2001.

    ---- *The Advert of Netwar*, RAND Corporation, Santa Monica, CA, 1996.

* Balta, Paul, *Idées reçues: L'Islam*, ('Ideas Perceived: Islam'), Paris: Le Cavalier Bleu, November 2001.

* Benard, Cheryl, *Civil Democratic Islam: Partners, Resources, and Strategies,* RAND Corporation, Santa Monica, CA, 2003.

* Bensahel, Nora and Daniel L. Byman, *The Future Security Environment in the Middle East: Conflict, Stability, and Political Change,* RAND Corporation, Santa Monica, CA, 2004.

* Berridge, G.R., *Diplomacy: Theory and Practice,* New York: Palgrave, 2002.

* Brass, Daniel and Marlene Burckhardt, "Centrality and Power in Organizations" in Nitin Nohria and Robert Eccles, eds., *Networks and Organizations,* Boston: Harvard Business School Press, 1992.

* Browning, Graeme, *Electronic Democracy: Using the Internet to Influence American Politics*, Wilton, CT: Pemberton Press, 1996.

* Buchan, Glenn C. et al., *Future Roles of U.S. Nuclear Forces: Implications for U.S. Strategy*, RAND Corporation, Santa Monica, CA, MR-1231-AF, 2003.

* Burkhart, Grey E. and Susan Older, *The Information Revolution in the Middle East and North Africa*, RAND Corporation, Santa Monica, CA, 2003.

* Burt, Ronald, *Structural Holes: The Social Structure of Competition*, Cambridge, MA: Harvard University Press, 1992.

* Byman, Daniel L. et al., *Iran's Security Policy in the Post-Revolution Era*, RAND Corporation, Santa Monica, CA, 2001.

* Callières, F. de, *The Art of Diplomacy*, ed. by H.M.A. Keens-Soper and K. Schweizer, New York: University Press of America, 1994.

* Carruthers, Susan L., *The Media At War*, London: Macmillan Press Ltd., 2000.

*   Carter, Ashton B. and William. J. Perry, *Preventive Defense: A New Security Strategy for America,* Washington, DC: Brookings Institution Press, 1999.

*   Carter, J., *Keeping Faith: Memoirs of a President,* New York: Bantam, 1982.

*   Chaigneau, Pascal, «Le nouveau profil du risque international», dans *Gestion des risques internationaux* ('The New Profile of International Risk', published in *Management of International Risks*), sous la direction de Pascal Chaigneau (Administrateur Général du Centre d'Etudes Diplomatiques et Stratégiques), Paris: Economica, 2001.

     ----   *Dictionnaire des relations internationales,* ('Dictionary of International Relations'), sous la direction de Pascal Chaigneau, Paris: Economica, 1998.

*   Chalk, Peter and William Rosenau, *Confronting the "Enemy Within": Security Intelligence, the Police, and Counterterrorism in Four Democracies,* RAND Corporation, Santa Monica, CA, 2004.

*   Chatwin, Bruce, *The Songlines,* New York: Penguin Books, 1988.

*   Chomsky, Noam, *9-11*, New York: Seven Stories Press, 2001.

*   Chua, Beng Huat, *Communitarian Ideology and Democracy in Singapore*, London: Routledge, 1995.

*   *CIA World Factbook 2000*, at: http://www.cia.gov/cia/publications/factbook.

*   Collon, Michel, *Attention médias ! Les média mensonges du Golfe, Manuel anti-manipulation,* ('Attention Media ! The Media Lies of the Gulf, An Anti-Manipulation Guide'), Anvers (Belgium): EPO editions, 4th edition, 2000.

*   Commynes, Philippe de, "The Memoirs of Philippe de Commynes," Vol. One, ed. Samuel Kisner, trsl. Isabelle Cazeau (Columbia, South Carolina: University of South Carolina Press, 1969).

*   Cragin, Kim and Sara A. Daly, *The Dynamic Terrorist Threat: An Assessment of Group Motivations and Capabilities in a Changing World,* RAND Corporation, Santa Monica, CA, 2004.

*   Crosby, Alfred, *The Columbian Exchange: Biological and Cultural Consequences of 1492,* Westport, CT: Greenwood Press, 1972.

*   Crystal, David, *English as a Global Language*, Cambridge: Cambridge University Press, 1997.

*   Danitz, Tiffany and Warren P. Strobel, "Networking Dissent: Cyber Activists Use the Internet to Promote Democracy in Burma," in John Arquilla and David Ronfeldt, *Networks and Netwars: The Future of Terror, Crime, and Militancy,* RAND Corporation, Santa Monica, CA, 2001.

*   Delpech, Thérèse, *Politique du chaos: l'autre face de la mondialisation*, ('The Politics of Chaos: The Other Side of Globalization'), Paris: édition du Seuil, 2002.

*   Dhia, Amir, "A Linguistic Analysis of Editorials Written by Arabs in English," unpublished Master of Arts thesis, University of Baghdad, College of Arts, Baghdad, September 1997.

*   Diamond, Jared, *Guns, Germs and Steel: The Fates of Human Societies,* New York: W.W. Norton, 1998.

*   Dobbins, James, et al., *The UN's Role in Nation-Building: From the Congo to Iraq,* RAND Corporation, Santa Monica, CA, 2005.

       ----   *America's Role in Nation-Building: From Germany to Iraq,* RAND Corporation, Santa Monica, CA, 2003.

*   Dufour, Jean-Louis Dufour and Maurice Vaisse, *La guerre au XXe siecle,* ('War in the 20th century'), Paris: Hachette, 1993.

*   Evan, William M. "An Organization-Set Model of Interorganizational Relations," in Matthew Tuite, Roger Chisholm, and Michael Radnor (eds.), *Interorganizational Decision Making,* Chicago: Aldine Publishing Company, 1972.

*   Garcin, Thierry, *Les enjeux stratégiques de l'espace*, ('The Strategic Stakes of Space'), Brussels: Bruylant, 2001.

       ----   "Les risques liés à la globalisation de l'information", in *Gestion des risques internationaux,* ('The Risks Linked to the Globalization of Information', in *Management of International Risks*), sous la direction de Pascal Chaigneau (Administrateur Général du Centre d'Etudes Diplomatiques et Stratégiques), Paris: Economica, 2001.

*   Giddens, Anthony, *Runaway World: How Globalization Is Reshaping Our Lives*, New York: Routledge, 2000.

*   Goldstein, E., "The Origins of Summit Diplomacy," in David H. Dunn (ed.), *Diplomacy at the Highest Level: The Evolution of International Summitry,* Basingstoke: Macmillan, 1996.

*   Grant, Jonathan et al., *Low Fertility and Population Ageing: Causes, Consequences, and Policy Options,* RAND Corporation, Europe Center, 2004.

*   Greene, Robert and Joost Elffers, *The 48 Laws of Power,* New York: Viking, 1998.

*   Grenville, J.A.S. and B. Wasserstein, *The Major International Treaties since 1945: A History and Guide With Texts*, London: Methuen, 1987.

*   Haas, Michael, ed., *The Singapore Puzzle*, Westport, CT: Praeger Press, 1999.

*   Hachigian, Nina and Lily Wu, *The Information Revolution in Asia*, RAND Corporation, Santa Monica, CA, 2003.

*   Hall, Edward T. and Mildred Reed Hall, *Understanding Cultural Differences: Germans, French and Americans,* Maine: Intercultural Press, Inc., 1990.

*   Hamilton, Keith and Richard Langhorne, *The Practice of Diplomacy: its evolution, theory and administration*, London: Routledge, 1995.

*   Held, David et al., *Global Transformations: Politics, Economics and Culture,* Stanford: Stanford University Press, 1999.

*   Hill, Kevin and John E. Hughes, *Cyberpolitics: Citizens Activism in the Age of the Internet*, Lanham, MD: Roman and Littlefield, 1998.

*   Himmelfarb, Gertrude, *One Nation, Two Cultures,* New York: Knopf, 1999.

*   Hoffman, Bruce, *Inside Terrorism*, Great Britain: Victor Gollancz, 1988.

*   *Hoover's Handbook of World Business 2001*, Austin: Reference Press, 2001.

*   Horn, D.B., *The British Diplomatic Service 1689-1789*, Oxford: Clarendon Press, 1961.

*   Hosmer, Stephen T., *Operations Against Enemy Leaders,* RAND Corporation, Santa Monica, CA, 2001.

*   Hundley, Richard O. et al., *The Global Course of the Information Revolution: Recurring Themes and Regional Variations*, RAND Corporation, Santa Monica, CA, 2003.

*   Huntington, Samuel P., *Who Are We? America's Great Debate*, London: Simon & Schuster UK Ltd, 2004.

       ---- "The Clash of Civilizations?" in *The Clash of Civilizations? The Debate*, New York: Council on Foreign Relations, 1996.

*   Karoly, Lynn A. and Constantijn W.A. Panis, *The 21st Century at Work: Forces Shaping the Future Workforce and Workplace in the United States*, RAND Corporation, Santa Monica, CA, 2004.

*   Kent, Sherman, *Strategic Intelligence for American World Policy,* Princeton, NJ: Princeton University Press, 1949 (reprint 1966).

*   Kissinger, Henry, *Does America Need a Foreign Policy? Towards a Diplomacy for the 21st Century,* New York: Simon Schuster, 2001.

*   Langhorne, Richard, *The Coming of Globalization: Its Evolution and Contemporary Consequences*, New York: Palgrave, 2001.

*   Lasswell, Harold, "Political and Psychological Warfare," in W. Daugherty and M. Janowitz (eds.), *A Psychological Warfare Casebook,* Baltimore: John Hopkins Press, 1958.

*   Lecherbonnier, Marie-France, *Le Protocole: Histoire et coulisses*, ('Protocol: History and Secrets'), Paris: Perrin editions, 2001.

*   Matsumara, John et al., *Preparing for Future Warfare with Advanced Technologies: Prioritizing the Next Generation of Capabilities*, RAND Corporation, Santa Monica, CA, 2002.

*   Meyer, Cord, *Facing Reality: From World Federalism to the CIA,* New York: Harper and Row, 1980.

*   Morelli, Anne, *Principes élémentaires de propagande de guerre: Utilisables en case de guerre froide, chaude ou tiède,* ('Elementary Principles of War Propaganda: Used in Cold, Hot or Mild War Cases'), Brussels: Labor, 2001.

*   Nerrière, Jean-Paul, *Don't Speak English: Parlez globish*, Paris: Eyrolles, 2004.

*   Nicolson, H., *Diplomacy,* 3rd ed., London: Oxford University Press, 1963.

*   Norris, Pippa, *The Digital Divide: Civic Engagement, Information Poverty, and the Internet Worldwide*, New York: Cambridge University Press, 2001.

*   Nye, Joseph S. Jr., *The Paradox of American Power: Why the World's Only Superpower Can't Go It Alone*, New York: Oxford University Press, Inc., 2002.

*   Olshansky, Barbara, *Secret Trials and Executions: Military Tribunals and the Threat to Democracy,* New York: Seven Stories Press, 2002.

*   Pace, Scott, Kevin M. O'Connell and Beth E. Lachman, *Using Intelligence Data for Environmental Needs: Balancing National Interests,* MR-799-CMS, RAND Corporation, Santa Monica, CA, 1997.

*   Preston, Bob et al., *Space Weapons Earth Wars*, RAND Corporation, Santa Monica, CA, 2002.

*   Queller, D.E., *The Office of Ambassador in the Middle Ages*, New Jersey: Princeton University Press, 1967.

*   Rawnsley, G.D., "Monitored Broadcasts and Diplomacy," in J. Melissen (ed.), *Innovation in Diplomatic Practice,* Basingstoke: Macmillan, 1999.

*   Saxenian, AnnaLee, *Silicon Valley's New Immigrant Entrepreneurs*, San Francisco: Public Policy Institute of California, 1999.

*   Sen, Krishna and David Hill, *Media, Culture and Politics in Indonesia*, Melbourne, Australia: Oxford University Press, 2000.

*   Shulsky, Abram N. and Gary J. Schmitt, *Silence Warfare: Understanding the World of Intelligence*, Virginia: Brassey's, Inc., 2002.

*   Sivard, Ruth Leger, *World Military and Social Expenditures 1996,* Washington, DC: World Priorities, 1996.

*   Sterns, M., *Talking to Strangers: Improving American Diplomacy at Home and Abroad,* Princeton: Princeton University Press, 1996.

*   Taylor, A.J., *The Struggle for Mastery in Europe, 1848-1918*, Oxford: Oxford University Press, 1954.

*   Taylor, Philip M., *Global Communications, International Relations and the Media since 1945,* London: Routledge: 1997.

*   Townshend, Charles, *Terrorism: A Very Short Introduction*, New York: Oxford University Press, 2002.

*   Turner, Stansfield, *Secrecy and Democracy: The CIA in Transition,* New York: Harper and Row, 1986.

*   Tzu, Sun, *The Art of War*, trans. by Samuel B. Griffith, Oxford: Oxford University Press, 1963.

*   Ury, William, *Getting to Peace: Transforming Conflict at Home, at Work, and in the World*, New York: Viking, 1999.

*   Védrine, Hubert with Dominique Moisi, *France in an Age of Globalization*, Washington, DC: Brookings Institution Press, 2001.

*   Volkoff, Vladimir, *Petite histoire de la désinformation: Du cheval de Troie à l'Internet*, Monaco: éditions du Rocher, 1999.

*   Wolfe, Alan, *One Nation, After All: What Americans Really Think About God, Country, Family, Racism, Welfare, Immigration, Homosexuality, Work, the Right, the Left and Each Other*, New York: Viking, 1998.

*   Woodward, John D., Jr., *Privacy vs. Security: Electronic Surveillance in the Nation's Capital*, RAND Corporation, Santa Monica, CA, March 2002.

     ----   *Super Bowl Surveillance: Facing Up to Biometrics*, RAND Corporation, Santa Monica, CA, May 2001.

Journals, Documents, Reports and Articles

*   "Addressing the Challenges of International Bribery and Fair Competition 2001: The Third Annual Report Under Section Six of the International Anti-Bribery and Fair Competition Act of 1998," U.S. Department of Commerce: International Trade Administration, July 2001, at: http://www.mac.doc.gov/tcc.

*   "Amnesty International Report 2005: the state of the world's human rights," Amnesty International, London, May 25, 2005

*   "Arab Economies Need Rapid Growth–From a Strategy Knowledge Base," *Arab Human Development Report 2002: Creating Opportunities for Future Generations,* United Nations Development Programme (UNDP).

*   "Arab World: Let the Numbers Speak! (the)," Arab Human Development Report 2002, UNDP.

*   "Armed Conflicts Report 2004 (the)," Project Ploughshares, Institute of Peace and Conflict Studies, Conrad Grebel College, Waterloo, Ontario, Canada, 2004.

*   "Arms Sales Monitor: Highlighting U.S. Government Policies on Arms Exports and Conventional Weapons Proliferation," Federation of American Scientists (FAS), Washington, DC, no. 47, January 2002.

*   Arquilla, John and David Ronfeldt, "What if there is a Revolution in Diplomatic Affairs?" *Virtual Diplomacy Series,* February 25, 1999, at: http://www.usip.org/oc/vd/vdr/ronaryISA99.html.

*   Arquilla, John and Theodore Karasik, "Chechnya: A Glimpse of Future Conflict?" *Studies in Conflict and Terrorism,* Vol. 22, no.3, July–September 1999.

*   "Asylum Levels and Trends in Industrialized Countries: 2004," United Nations High Commissioner for Refugees (UNHCR), Geneva, March 1, 2005.

*   «Atlas 2001 des Conflits», ('Atlas of Conflicts 2001'), *Manière de voir,* 55, January-February 2001, Paris, le Monde Diplomatique.

*   Bidwai, Praful, "Talking Peace and Kashmir–Warily, Under a Nuclear Shadow," Washington, DC: Foreign Policy In Focus, July 6, 2004, at: http://www.fpif.org/commentary/2004/0407kashmir.html.

*   "Border Security: Improvements Needed to Reduce Time Taken to Adjudicate Visas for Science Students and Scholars," United States General Accounting Office (GAO), Report to the Chairman and Ranking Minority Member, Committee on Science, House of Representatives, February 2004.

*   Bournois, Frank, «La Stratégie de formation des élites: Comparaisons internationales», ('The strategy of training elites: international comparisons'), Lecture presented for the Cycle d'enseignement diplomatique supérieur, C.E.D.S., Paris, March 27, 2002.

*   Bowden, Mark, "Blackhawk Down: A Story of Modern War," New York Atlantic Monthly Press, 1999.

*   Brett, Jeanne M., Zoe. I. Barsness, and Stephen B. Goldberg, "The Effectiveness of Mediation: An Independent Analysis of Cases Handled by Four Major Service Providers," *Negotiation Journal,* 12:3, July 1996, Blackwell Publishing, 259-70.

*   Britt, Robert Roy, "Satellites Play Crucial Roles in Aid and Ground Battles," *www.space.com,* October 9, 2001.

*   Brown, J., "Diplomatic Immunity–state practice under the Vienna Convention," *International and Comparative Law Quarterly,* Vol. 37, 1988.

*   Brown, Sheryl J. and Margarita S. Studemeister, "Virtual Diplomacy: Rethinking Foreign Policy Practice in the Information Age," *Information and Security: An International Journal,* Sofia: ProCon, Ltd., Vol. 7, 2001.

*   Burt, Richard and Olin Robinson, *Reinventing Diplomacy in the Information Age,* The Center for Strategic and International Studies, Washington, DC, October 1998, at: http://www.csis.org/ics/dia/final.html.

*   Carlucci, Frank et al., "Equipped for the Future: Managing U.S. Foreign Affairs in the 21st Century," The Henry L. Stimson Center, October 1998, at: http://www.stimson.org/pubs/ausia/#final.

*   «Cause toujours! A la découverte des 6700 langues de la planète», ('Still a cause ! Discovering the 6700 languages of the planet'), *Courrier International,* (special culture edition), March-April-May, 2003.

*   "Charting the Global Course of the Information Revolution," RAND's National Defense Research Institute (NDRI), sponsored by the National Intelligence Council (NIC), Points of an International Conference held in Pittsburgh, PA, May 2000.

*   *China News Digest,* Global News, no. GL99-063, May 12, 1999, at: http://services.cnd.org/CND-Global.99.2nd/CND-Global.99-05-11.html.

*   Cincotta, Howard, "Post-Modern Diplomacy and the New Media," *iMP: The Magazine on Information Impacts,* McLean, Virginia: Center for Information Strategy and Policy, July 23, 2001.

*   Colby, William E., "Intelligence in the 1980s," *The Information Society,* no. 1, 1981, 54, New York: Taylor & Francis, Inc.

*   "Commission on the Intelligence Capabilities of the United States Regarding Weapons of Mass Destruction," Report to the President of the United States, Washington, DC, March 31, 2005.

*   Cornell, Eric A., "Stopping Light in its Tracks," *Nature,* London: Nature Publishing Group, Vol. 409, Issue no. 6819, January 25, 2001, 461-62.

*   "Counterterrorism Intelligence Capabilities and Performance Prior to 9-11," Report of the Subcommittee on Terrorism and Homeland Security, the U.S. House Permanent Select Committee on Intelligence, Washington, DC, July 17, 2002.

*   Courau, Christophe, «De Babylone à Bagdad: L'Irak terre de conflits», ('From Babylon to Baghdad: Iraq the land of conflicts'), *Historia,* no. 670, October 2002, 14.

* Denza, E., "Diplomatic Law: Commentary on the Vienna Convention on Diplomatic Relations," London: British Institute of International and Comparative Law, 1976.

* Dizard, Wilson, Jr., "Digital Diplomats," *iMP: The Magazine on Information Impacts,* McLean, Virginia: Center for Information Strategy and Policy, July 23, 2001.

* "Equipped for the Future: Managing US Foreign Affairs in the 21st Century," Stimson Center Project on the Advocacy of U.S. Interests Abroad, Stimson Center, October 1998, at: www.stimson.org/pubs/ausia/ausr1.pdf.

* Francart, Loup et Jean-Jacques Patry, *Mastering Violence: An Option for Operational Military Strategy,* Commandement de la doctrine et de l'enseignement militaire supérieur de l'armée de terre, Centre de recherche, Paris, November 24, 1998.

* *Future Strategic Context for Defense (the),* United Kingdom Ministry of Defense, London, 2001.

* Gabriel, Richard A. and Karen S. Metz, *A Short History of War: The Evolution of Warfare and Weapons*, Professional Readings in Military Strategy, No. 5, June 30, 1992, U.S. Army War College: Strategic Studies Institute, Carlisle Barracks, Pennsylvania.

* Gates, Robert, "An Opportunity Unfulfilled: The Use and Perceptions of Intelligence at the White House," *The Washington Quarterly*, 12, no. 1, winter 1989, 37.

* "Global Corruption Report 2005," Transparency International, London, March 16, 2005.

* "Global Trends 2015: A Dialogue About the Future With Nongovernment Experts," Washington, DC: National Intelligence Council (NIC), December 2000.

* Hachigian, Nina, "The Internet and Power in One-Party East Asian States," *The Washington Quarterly 25*, no. 3, Summer 2002.

  ---- "The Political Implications of the Internet in China," RAND Seminar, Center for Asia-Pacific Policy (CAPP), Santa Monica, CA, September 15, 2000.

* Hemery, John, "Training Diplomats for 2015," *iMP: The Magazine on Information Impacts,* McLean, Virginia: Center for Information Strategy and Policy, July 23, 2001.

* Henry, Clement M., "Challenge of Global Capital Markets to Information-Shy Regimes: The Case of Tunisia," UAE: The Emirates Center for Strategic Studies and Research, Occasional Papers no. 19, 1998.

* Hinrichs, Randy, "A Vision for Life Long Learning – Year 2020," (Introduction by Bill Gates), p. 2, in *Vision 2020: Transforming Education and Training Through Advanced Technologies*, U.S. Department of Commerce, September 2002.

* « Histoire de l'informatique: Traitement de l'information et automatisation », ('History of Computer Science: Treatment of information and automation'), at: http://www.histoire-informatique.org/grandes_dates/1_2.html.

*   "How Much Information? 2003," Regents of the University of California, October 27, 2003, at:
http://www.sims.berkeley.edu/research/projects/how-much-info-2003.

*   Huff, Toby E., "Globalization and the Internet: Comparing the Middle Eastern and Malaysian Experiences," in *The Middle East Journal*, Summer 2001, Vol. 55, no. 3, Washington, DC: Middle East Institute.

*   Huntington, Samuel P., "The U.S.–Decline or Renewal?," *Foreign Affairs*, Winter 1988-1989.

*   «Impact du cinéma français à l'étranger», Rapport de synthèse, ('Impact of French cinema abroad', Synthesis report), Association des Exportateurs de Films (ADEF), no. 33949, Paris, September 2004.

*   "Introduction: The Limitations of Literacy Statistics," International Literacy Explorer, Statistics, University of Pennsylvania, Graduate School of Education,
at: http://literacy.org/explorer/stats_critical.html, retrieved January 6, 2005.

*   "ITU Digital Access Index: World's First Global ICT Ranking," International Telecommunications Union, November 19, 2003,
at: http://www.itu.int/newsarchive/press_releases/2003/30.html.

*   Kaden, Lewis B., "America's Overseas Presence in the 21st Century," Overseas Presence Advisory Panel (Chairman), U.S. Department of State, November 1999.

*   Kalathil, Shanthi and Taylor C. Boas, "The Internet and State Control in Authoritarian Regimes: China, Cuba, and the Counterrevolution," Carnegie Endowment Working Papers, Carnegie Endowment for International Peace, Washington, DC, July 2001.

*   Kerley, E.L., "Some Aspects of the Vienna Conference on Diplomatic Intercourse and Immunities," *American Journal of International Law*, Vol. 56, 1962, 128.

*   Kinney, Stephanie Smith, "Developing Diplomats for 2010: If not now, when? The Challenges, Risks, Relevance, Resources and Renewals," *American Diplomacy*, Vol. V, no. 3, Summer 2000, Durham: American Diplomacy Publishers.

*   Klare, Michael T., "The New Geography of Conflict," *Foreign Affairs*, May/June 2001, Vol. 80, no. 3, New York: Council on Foreign Affairs.

*   Kluver, Randolph and Wayne Fu, "The Cultural Globalization Index," *Foreign Policy*, online edition, posted February 2004.

*   Langhorne, Richard, "The Regulation of Diplomatic Practice: The Beginnings to the Vienna Convention of Diplomatic Relations, 1961," *Review of International Studies*, Vol. 18, no. 1, 1992.

*   *L'Atlas du monde diplomatique*, ('The World Diplomatic Atlas'), Paris: le Monde Diplomatique, January 2003.

*   "Law of Administration for the State of Iraq for the Transitional Period," March 8, 2004, at: http://www.cpa-iraq.org/government/TAL.html.

*   Leonard, Mark and Liz Noble, "Being Public: How diplomacy will need to change to cope with the information society," *iMP: The Magazine on Information Impacts*, McLean, Virginia: Center for Information Strategy and Policy, July 23, 2001, at: http://www.cisp.org/imp/july_2001/07_01leonard.htm.

*   Liang, Qiao and Wang Xiangsui, "Unrestricted Warfare," stated in James Adams, "Virtual Defense," *Foreign Affairs*, Vol. 80, no. 3, May/June 2001, New York: Council on Foreign Relations.

*   Lindsay, James M., "The New Apathy: How an Uninterested Public Is Reshaping Foreign Policy," *Foreign Affairs*, Vol. 79, no. 5, September-October 2000, New York: Council on Foreign Relations.

*   "Literacy Overview: Using Literacy Statistics," International Literacy Explorer, at: http://literacy.org/explorer/overview.html, retrieved January 6, 2005.

*   "Long-Term Global Demographic Trends: Reshaping the Geopolitical Landscape," CIA publication, July 2001.

*   Lussenhop, Matt, "Creativity and Patience: Public Diplomacy Post-Sept. 11," *American Diplomacy*, April 2002, at: www.unc.edu/depts/diplomat.

*   Mahbubani, Kishore, "The West and the Rest," *The National Interest*, Summer 1992, 3-13.

*   Mak, Dayton S., "The Nature of French Diplomacy: Reflections of American Diplomats," *www.americandiplomacy.org,* September 22, 2003.

*   "Mapping the Global Future," Report of the National Intelligence Council's 2020 Project, Washington, DC: U.S. National Intelligence Council, December 2004.

*   Matic, Veran, "Between an Electronic Gulag and the Global Village," presentation at 'The Information Revolution and its Impact on the Foundations of National Power' conference, September 23-25, 1997, at: http://wwwz.opennet.org/b92/radio/info/people/veran_matic/vmatic-tx2.html.

*   McCarthy, John, "What is Artificial Intelligence?" Computer Science Department, Stanford University, Stanford, CA, September 28, 2001, at: http://www-formal.stamford.edu/jmc/whatisai/whatisai.html.

*   Mégret, Frédéric, "War? Legal Semantics and the Move to Violence," *European Journal of International Law,* Vol. 13, no. 2, 2002, Italy: European University Institute.

*   "Merriam-Webster's Words of the Year 2004," retrieved on December 1, 2004, at: http://www.merriam-webster.com/info/04words.htm.

*   Metzl, Jamie F. "The Perils of Secrecy in an Information Age," *iMP: The Magazine on Information Impacts,* McLean, Virginia: Center for Information Strategy and Policy, July 23, 2001.

*   Miles, D., "Diplomatic Couriers: On the Road, from Rangoon to Russia and Back!" *State Magazine*, February-March 2000, at: www.state.gov/www/publications/statemag/statemag_feb2000/feature1.html.

*   "Military Order: Detention, Treatment, and Trial of Certain Non-Citizens in the War Against Terrorism," the White House, Office of the Press Secretary, November 13, 2001.

* "MIT Technology Review," at: *www.technologyreview.com*, January/February 2001.

* Morse, Edward L. and James Richard, "The Battle for Energy Dominance," *Foreign Affairs,* March/April 2002, New York: Council on Foreign Affairs.

* Naim, Moisés, "Anti-Americanism: A Guide to hating Uncle Sam," *Foreign Policy*, online edition, January-February 2002.

* "Nation's Prison and Jail Population Grew by 932 Inmates per Week," U.S. Department of Justice, Office of Justice Programs, Bureau of Justice Statistics, Washington, DC, April 24, 2005.

* "Nearly 1,000 new individuals incarcerated each week in US," Justice Policy Institute, Washington, DC, April 25, 2005 (at: www.justicepolicy.org).

* Nye, Joseph S., "Ignoring Soft Power Carries a High Cost," May 16, 2004, at: http://www.ksg.harvard.edu/news/opeds/2004/nye_softpower_chitrib_051604.htm, reprinted from *The Chicago Tribune.*

  ---- "Europe's Soft Power," May 3, 2004, at: http://www.globalpolicy.org/empire/analysis/2004/0503softpower.htm.

* Oglesby, Donna, "diplomacy.cultural2015@state.gov," *iMP: The Magazine on Information Impacts,* McLean, Virginia: Center for Information Strategy and Policy, July 23, 2001.

* Olsen, Jody K. and Norman J. Peterson, "International Education Exchange in the Information Age," *iMP: The Magazine on Information Impacts*, McLean, Virginia: Center for Information Strategy and Policy, July 23, 2001.

* "Open Doors 2004: International Students in the U.S.," Institute of International Education (IIE), Washington, DC, November 10, 2004.

* "Open Doors 2003: International Students in the U.S.," Institute of International Education, Washington, DC, November 3, 2003.

* "Peace between the State of Israel and the Hashemite Kingdom of Jordan," Ministry of Foreign Affairs, Information Center, Jerusalem, October 26, 1994.

* Poole, Patrick S., "ECHELON: America's Secret Global Surveillance Network," Washington, DC: Free Congress Research and Education Foundation, undated document retrieved on March 22, 2005, at: http://www.shire.net/big.brother/echelon.htm.

* «Population et sociétés, no. 410», March 2005, bulletin mensuel d'information de l'Institut national d'études démographiques (INED), ('Population and societies', no. 410, monthly information bulletin of the National Institute of Demographic Studies), Paris.

* Powell, Adam Clayton, III, "New Media: How They Are Changing Diplomacy," *iMP Magazine,* McLean, Virginia: Center for Information Strategy and Policy, July 23, 2001.

* "Preparing for an Aging World: The Case for Cross-National Research," Washington, DC: National Academy Press, 2001.

* «Présentation du nouveau plan gouvernemental de vigilance, de prévention et de protection face aux menaces d'actions terroristes : Vigipirate», ('Presentation of the New Governmental Plan for Vigilance, Prevention and Protection Against Terrorist Action Threats'), Office of the Prime Minister, Paris, March 26, 2003, at: http: //www.premier-ministre.gouv.fr/ressources/fichiers/vigipirate_dp270303.pdf.

* "Progress or Peril? Measuring Iraq's Reconstruction," Center for Strategic and International Studies, The Post-Conflict Reconstruction Project, Washington, DC, September 2004.

* "Rebuilding America's Defenses: Strategy, Forces and Resources For a New Century," A Report of The Project for the New American Century, New York, September 2000.

* "Recent Espionage Cases, 1975-1999: Summaries and Sources," U.S. Defense Security Service, Security Research Center, September 1999, at: www.dss.mil/training/pub.htm.

* *Refugees*, Vol. 2, no. 113, 1998, published by the Public Information Section of the UN High Commissioner for Refugees.

* "Reinvention Diplomacy: A Virtual Necessity," *Virtual Diplomacy Series*, February 25, 1999, at: http://www.usip.org/oc/vd/vdr/gsmithISA99.html.

* «Repères et références statistiques sur les enseignements, la formation et la recherche», Ministre de l'éducation nationale, ('Statistical Indicators and References on Education, Training and Research', Ministry of National Education), Paris, edition 2004.

* "Report on the Existence of a Global System for the Interception of Private and Commercial Communications (ECHELON interception system)," Temporary Committee on the ECHELON Interception System, European Parliament, July 11, 2001.

* "Review of FBI Security Programs," Commission for Review of FBI Security Programs, U.S. Department of Justice, March 31, 2002.

* Roberts, Les et al., "Mortality before and after the 2003 invasion of Iraq: cluster sample survey," published online on October 29, 2004, at: http://image.thelancet.com/extras/04art10342web.pdf.

* Roberts, Walter R., "Government Broadcasting," *iMP: The Magazine on Information Impacts*, McLean, Virginia: Center for Information Strategy and Policy, July 23, 2001.

* Rosenau, James N., "States, Sovereignty, and Diplomacy in the Information Age," *Virtual Diplomacy Series,* February 25, 1999, at: http://www.usip.org/oc/vd/vdr/jrosenauISA99html.

* Schmitz, Charles A., "A Vision of an American Embassy in 2015: A Disquisition in Three Acts and Six and a Half Premises," *iMP: The Magazine on Information Impacts,* McLean, Virginia: Center for Information Strategy and Policy, July 23, 2001.

* Shariffadeen, Tengku Mohd. Azzman, "Moving Toward a More Intelligent Use of Human Intelligence," presented at INFOTECH 95 Malaysia, Kuala Lumpur, November 1-5, 1999.

*   "SIPRI Yearbook 2005: Armaments, Disarmament and International Security," Stockholm International Peace Research Institute (SIPRA), Solna, Sweden, June 2005.

*   "SIPRI Yearbook 2004: Armaments, Disarmament and International Security," Stockholm International Peace Research Institute (SIPRA), Solna, Sweden, June 2004.

*   "Soviets Launch Computers Literacy Drive," *Science*, January 10, 1986, 109-10.

*   "State of world population 2004," United Nations Population Fund, New York, September 15, 2004.

*   Steele, David, "The New Craft of Intelligence: Making the Most of Open Private Sector Knowledge," *Time,* online edition, March 3, 2002.

*   "Strengthening the U.S.-Saudi Relationship," A Paper Prepared for the Independent Task Force on America's Response to Terrorism, New York: Council on Foreign Relations, May 2002.

*   "Swords and Ploughshares 2003," Project Ploughshares, Institute of Peace and Conflict Studies, Conrad Grebel College, Waterloo, Ontario, Canada, at: www.ploughshares.ca.

*   "Trends in Total Migrant Stock: The 2003 Revision," Population Division, Department of Economic and Social Affairs, United Nations, New York, 2003.

*   "Tsunami Disaster's Diplomatic Implications," South East Monitor, no. 79, published by the South Asia Program, Center for Strategic and International Studies (CSIS), Washington, DC, February 1, 2005.

*   Wenger, Andreas, "The Internet and the Changing Face of International Relations and Security," in *Information Security: An International Journal*, Vol. 7, 2001, Sofia: ProCon Ltd.

*   "World Bank Supports the Knowledge and Learning Needs of the Middle East and North Africa Region," The World Bank, News Release no. 2004/262/WBI, March 15, 2004.

*   "World Fertility Report: 2003," Population Division, Department of Economic and Social Affairs, United Nations, New York, March 12, 2004.

*   Young, E., "The Development of the Law of Diplomatic Relations,*" British Yearbook of International Law 1964,* Vol. 40, 1966, London: Oxford University Press.

Information and news Web sites consulted regularly

* http://iraq4allnews.dk	Iraqi news Web site (Arabic version)
* www.afp.com	Agence France Presse (AFP)
* www.aljazeera.net	Al Jazeera News Channel
* www.alquds.co.uk	Al Quds daily newspaper (in Arabic)
* www.archive.org	The Wayback Machine (Internet archive Web site)
* www.bbc.co.uk	British Broadcasting Corporation news
* www.businessweek.com	Businessweek weekly magazine
* www.cnn.com	Cable News Network
* www.cyveillance.com	Cyveillance: Online risk monitoring and management
* www.economist.com	The Economist weekly news magazine
* www.elaph.com	Elaph news Web site (in Arabic)
* www.fas.org	Federation of American Scientists
* www.foreignpolicy.com	Foreign Policy magazine
* www.ft.com	Financial Times daily newspaper
* www.guardian.co.uk	The Guardian daily newspaper
* www.internetworldstats.com	World Internet Users and Population Statistics
* www.jpost.com	The Jerusalem Post daily newspaper
* www.latimes.com	The Los Angeles Times daily newspaper
* www.lefigaro.fr	Le Figaro daily newspaper (in French)
* www.lemonde.fr	Le Monde daily newspaper (in French)
* www.mouwatana-iraqiya.com	Al Mouwatana ('The Iraqi Citizenship') news Web site
* www.msnb.com	MSNBC news Web site
* www.newsweek.com	Newsweek weekly magazine
* www.nytimes.com	The New York Times daily newspaper
* www.reuters.com	Reuters news agency
* www.rsf.org	Reporters sans frontières (Reporters Without Borders)
* www.stratfor.com	Stratfor intelligence forecasting
* www.time.com	Time weekly magazine
* www.transparency.org	Transparency International
* www.usatoday.com	USA Today daily newspaper
* www.washingtonpost.com	The Washington Post daily newspaper

www.ingramcontent.com/pod-product-compliance
Lightning Source LLC
Chambersburg PA
CBHW081502050326
40690CB00015B/2886